with me must have felt help...
out bound up with the last som...
...ry Brother gentle & loving conte...
outside the ordinary sphere of a woman's ...
standard of excellence which should discourage any new
attempt to leave the beaten track of a woman's duty.
And I having secretly revelled in feeling, having yielded
up my soul, believing that I was indeed freed satisfaction
in this. She made me ready to overcome my own arms
& acknowledge the sway of the new feeling. Besides that
... Those three days at Southsea seemed designed to
increase the sensitiveness ... to the blow.
And when it came, when I realised by the tone & the
expression that all was over, my whole return gave
way before it. Both ideals had fallen. Life alone,
life together; remaining me the seemingly dreary round
of common-place duties. And the blankness,
& weariness within my soul brought strikingly into
relief by the ... & cheerfulness of my surroundings
The whole seemed a nightmare. There is glitter all
around me & darkness within; the darkness of
blind desire yearning for the light of love. All sympathy
is shut from me. I stand alone with my own nature
now too strong for me. I clutch desperately at my duty
& those around me, that last hope for the soul despairing
of its own happiness; my head whirls, my courage fails
me & yet I am goaded on by the misery of guilt brought
into one activity which disgusts me. Still there rise
up before me the ... forms of three maidens: Humility,
Tenderness, Discretion, & they beckon me with loving
... & I follow them.

July 9th Amen.

# The Diary
## of
## BEATRICE WEBB

### *Volume One*
#### 1873–1892

Glitter Around and Darkness Within

BOOKS BY BEATRICE WEBB

*The Co-operative Movement in Great Britain* (London, 1891)
*My Apprenticeship* (London, 1926)
*Our Partnership* (London, 1948)


BOOKS BY SIDNEY AND BEATRICE WEBB

*The History of Trade Unionism* (London, 1894)
*Industrial Democracy* (London, 1897)
*English Local Government* (London, 1906–29)
*A Constitution for the Socialist Commonwealth of Great Britain* (London, 1920)
*The Consumers Co-operative Movement* (London, 1920)
*The Decay of Capitalist Civilization* (London, 1923)
*Methods of Social Study* (London, 1932)
*Soviet Communism: A New Civilization?* (London, 1935)

# The Diary
## of
# BEATRICE WEBB

### *Volume One*

## 1873–1892

## Glitter Around and Darkness Within

*Edited by*
*Norman and Jeanne MacKenzie*

Virago

published in association with
THE LONDON SCHOOL OF ECONOMICS
AND POLITICAL SCIENCE

Published by Virago Press Limited 1982
Ely House, 37 Dover Street, London W1X 4HS
in association with
The London School of Economics and Political Science

Typeset by King's English, Cambridge
Printed in Great Britain by
The Anchor Press, Tiptree, Essex

Designed by Adrienne Gear

*British Library Cataloguing in Publication Data*

Webb, Beatrice
    The diary of Beatrice Webb.
    1 : 1873–1892
    1. Webb, Beatrice
    I. Title     II. MacKenzie, Norman, *1921–*
    III. MacKenzie, Jeanne
    335'.14'0924     HX243

ISBN 0–86068–209–9

# Contents

*List of Illustrations*

(Acknowledgements and thanks are due to the individuals and
institutions listed in brackets below)

*Between Pages 106 and 107*

Beatrice with her parents 1865 (Lord Parmoor)
Lawrencina Potter c. 1860 (Kitty Muggeridge)
Richard Potter c. 1860 (Kitty Muggeridge)
Martha Jackson date unknown (Lord Parmoor)
Herbert Spencer c. 1875 (Passfield Papers, London School of
    Economics and Political Science)
Beatrice in Germany c. 1881 (Lord Parmoor)
Beatrice 1883 (Passfield Papers)
Lawrencina and Catherine c. 1862 (Lord Parmoor)
Mary date unknown (Lord Parmoor)
Georgina date unknown (Daniel Meinertzhagen)
Blanche 1865 (Lord Parmoor)
Theresa 1875 (Lord Parmoor)
Margaret 1880 (Lord Parmoor)
Rosalind c. 1883 (Kitty Muggeridge)
Standish House, Vale of Severn, Gloucester (Passfield Papers)
Rusland Hall, Cumberland (Passfield Papers)
York House, Kensington Palace Gardens, London (Royal Borough of
    Kensington and Chelsea Libraries and Arts Service)
Dried Flowers in Beatrice's Diary (Passfield Papers)
Family group 1865 (Passfield Papers)

# LIST OF ILLUSTRATIONS

# POTTER*

John   William   George   Jane   Ann   Elizabeth

Richard — Lawrencina
1817–1892 | Heyworth
1821–1882

—Lawrencina 1845–1906 — Robert Durning Holt 1832–1908
5 sons 3 daughters

—Catherine 1847–1929 — Leonard Henry Courtney 1832–1918
No children

—Mary 1849–1923 — Arthur T. Playne d. 1923
1 son

—Georgina 1850–1914 — Daniel Meinertzhagen 1842–1910
4 sons 6 daughters

—Blanche 1851–1905 — William Harrison Cripps 1850–1923
4 sons 2 daughters

—Theresa 1852–93 — Charles Alfred Cripps 1852–1941
4 sons 1 daughter

—Margaret 1854–1921 — Henry Hobhouse 1854–1937
4 sons 3 daughters

—Beatrice 1858–1943 — Sidney James Webb 1859–1947
No children

—Richard 1862–4

—Rosalind 1865–1949 — Arthur Dyson Williams 1859–1896
1 son
— George Cumberland Dobbs 1869–1946
4 sons 1 daughter

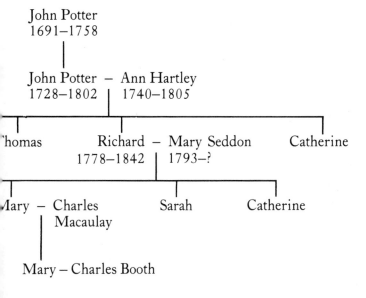

John Potter
1691–1758

John Potter — Ann Hartley
1728–1802 | 1740–1805

Thomas     Richard — Mary Seddon     Catherine
        1778–1842 | 1793–?

Mary — Charles     Sarah     Catherine
     Macaulay

Mary – Charles Booth

*WEBB*

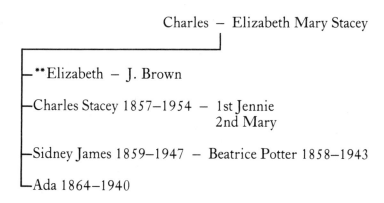

Charles — Elizabeth Mary Stacey

**Elizabeth — J. Brown

Charles Stacey 1857–1954 — 1st Jennie
                          2nd Mary

Sidney James 1859–1947 — Beatrice Potter 1858–1943

Ada 1864–1940

---

*This simplified family tree has been based, by permission of Lord Methuen, on a most extensive genealogy of the Potter family prepared for private circulation.

**Birth date unknown and family order uncertain. Not mentioned by Sidney or Beatrice, or in family papers.

## Acknowledgements

WE ARE PARTICULARLY GRATEFUL to the London School of Economics and Political Science, as the copyright holder of Beatrice Webb's diary, for permission to abbreviate and reproduce it; and to the Leverhulme Trust for its generous help with the costs of the project. We are also indebted to Professor Ralf Dahrendorf, Director of the London School of Economics, for his encouragement of this project from its inception; to Professor Matthew Anderson, and to Patrick Davis, Publications Officer of the L.S.E., who ensured that the initial discussions came to a successful conclusion. The staff of the British Library of Political and Economic Science, moreover, have been invariably helpful, and we very much appreciate the unflagging interest of Angela Raspin. We are obliged to Lord Methuen for permission to use a privately circulated list of Potter descendants.

There are many individuals and organizations who have contributed substantially to the preparation of this version of Beatrice Webb's diary by the help they gave to the companion edition of *The Letters of Sidney and Beatrice Webb*, and we would like to repeat the thanks to those named in the first of those volumes. We must also thank those who have particularly assisted with factual information and advice for the present project, especially Margaret Anderson, Dr Joyce Bellamy, Betty Drewitt, Carol Dyhouse, Beata Kaspar, Lord Methuen, Kitty and Malcolm Muggeridge, Lord Parmoor, Professor John Saville and the Rector of Sternfield. We would wish to thank the staff of the British Library, the Library of the University of Sussex, the London Library, the Mitchell Library, Sydney, the Alexander Turnbull Library, Auckland, the Bacup Public Library, and the Rawtenstall District Library; and we are also most grateful to the Cornwall, Dorset, Gloucester and Greater London record offices. The illustrations are separately acknowledged. Margaret Ralph and Brenda Mauthner helped greatly to produce a readable manuscript from a mass of not always legible matter; and the whole project was made possible by the unremitting enthusiasm of Carmen Callil.

# The Long Record of a Life

MARTHA BEATRICE POTTER was born on 22 January 1858 at Standish House, on the edge of the Cotswolds, where she spent much of her childhood and youth. She began life with many advantages. Her father, Richard Potter, was a wealthy railway promoter with cultivated habits, who filled his house with books and intelligent friends; and her mother, Lawrencina Potter, also valued things of the mind. They were both of liberal provincial background, and their nine daughters, almost all of whom married able and eminent men, were permitted to read widely and to discuss candidly, and their father's encouragement gave them a sense that all things were possible. 'He admired and loved his daughters,' Beatrice recalled many years after his death: 'He was the only man I ever knew who genuinely believed that women were superior to men, and acted as if he did.'

In such a home Beatrice was free to let her natural talent roam far beyond the subjects and accomplishments considered suitable for girls of her class in mid-Victorian society. In *My Apprenticeship*, the only volume of her planned autobiographical trilogy which she completed, and also in the pages of this diary, she describes an eclectic education in which speculation about religion and philosophy played as large a part as the study of literature and the classics, modern languages, history, mathematics and science. Yet she was not merely the earnest bluestocking that such high-mindedness suggests. She was strikingly handsome, unconventional, and sociable. After her mother's death in 1882, indeed, she became her father's close companion, running his households in London and in the country, and delighting to share in the stimulating conversation round his dinner-table.

Well-to-do, intelligent and attractive, Beatrice was apparently set for a conventionally successful marriage. But appearances were deceptive. Her odd upbringing, she said, left her with 'a tireless curiosity together with a double dose of will-power'. It also left her with a profound inner conflict between emotion and intellect, between her feminine instincts and her desire to be independent and successful in a man's world; and that ambivalence led to the first great crisis of her life, when she conceived an obsessive passion for the Radical politician Joseph Chamberlain.

It came to nothing, but it left an enduring mark upon her. All through the 1880s she sought relief from that self-tormenting attachment in the anodyne of work in the East End of London. In its poverty-ravaged slums Beatrice discovered a craft and a creed. As a rent-collector for a philanthropic housing association, a researcher for the great survey of London poverty launched by her cousin-in-law Charles Booth, and then as the author of a book on the Co-operative movement, she painstakingly taught herself to be a social investigator; and, though she had abandoned formal Christianity when she was still an adolescent, she was sustained by a vague deism and she found spiritual comfort in prayer and in a vocation for public service. She had the makings of a great *religieuse*, but the circumstances of her life made her a great social scientist instead.

She had already settled on her career when she met Sidney Webb, the fast-rising civil servant and Fabian ideologist; and, with no idea in her mind beyond a professional collaboration based upon common interests and complementary abilities, she struck up a friendship that was to end in marriage two years later, on 23 July 1892. It was a troubled courtship, in which Sidney had both to win her reluctant affection and to satisfy her that marriage would not be 'an act of *felo de se*', as she put it, but, rather, a working partnership which would enhance their usefulness to society quite as much as their personal happiness – the only line of argument, as their fretful correspondence shows, which had any prospect of success. 'One and one, placed in a sufficiently integrated relationship', Sidney said repeatedly in his letters, 'make not two, but eleven.'

So it proved, despite the superficial incongruity of a match between the beautiful heiress, seemingly headed for spinsterhood at the age of thirty-four, and the dumpy, dowdy and infatuated son of a Soho shopkeeper. 'The world will wonder,' Beatrice understandably wrote in her diary when they became engaged, and Sidney felt much the same. 'I can't help it being "Beauty and the Beast",' he told her, 'if only it is not a case of Titania and Bottom.' Within seven years the Webbs had published *The History of Trade Unionism*, which was their first joint work, and two other books on industrial problems. They had become, with George Bernard Shaw, the dominant personalities in the Fabian Society, and Sidney was its most prolific pamphleteer. They had founded the London School of Economics, which was to become their most enduring legacy to the social sciences. Through Sidney's membership of the London County Council they had made themselves into experts on educational and municipal reform, and they had committed themselves to a series of monographs on English local government which took them thirty years to complete.

As Beatrice remarked, they were 'curiously well combined' in so many ways. Her flair as an investigator was matched by his extraordinary capacity for work; her private income supported them, modestly but in quite sufficient comfort for their austere tastes, so that Sidney was able to leave the Civil Service and devote his days to research, writing and politics and they were able to dine and be dined by prominent politicians, administrators, academics and writers; her febrile vitality was sustained by his unremitting affection; and while she beguiled he persuaded. Long before they decided to take a working holiday in 1898, and set off across the United States on their way to New Zealand and Australia, their partnership had become a marvel to everyone who knew them and a professional phenomenon that had already made them famous.

During the next phase of the Webb partnership, which coincided with the Edwardian decade, Beatrice was in her prime, and full of energy and ideas. She was a striking, if austere, hostess, who used her *salon* so effectively to promote Webbian policies that she deservedly earned a reputation for political intrigue; she was a forceful and uncompromising member of the Royal Commission on the outmoded Poor Law; and it was she, rather than Sidney, who controlled the national campaign which the Webbs subsequently launched to promote their own proposals for the break-up of the Poor Law and the creation of a welfare state.

The Webbs, in this period, were in an ambiguous position. They were among the best-known socialists in the country, but they were at odds with many of their fellow-Fabians; they disliked the new Independent Labour Party led by Keir Hardie, and they were opposed to the formation of a national Labour Party as an alliance of individual socialists and affiliated trade unionists. They also fell out with the anti-imperialists in the Liberal Party over the Boer War, with the Nonconformists over their support for the Conservative government's education policies, and with Lloyd George and Winston Churchill over the Liberal plans for reforming the Poor Law. While those differences kept them out of the mainstream of progressive politics, and certainly reduced their direct influence on events, they also made for a varied and lively public life, as the voluminous entries in Beatrice's diary reveal.

In the summer of 1911, when the Webbs found themselves without significant allies in any of the parties, and without any notion what they should do next, they set off on another journey across the world, starting in Canada and going on through Japan, China, Burma and India; they were therefore abroad when the Liberal struggle to reduce the power of the House of Lords was at its height, when the suffragette movement was gathering momentum, and when a great wave of industrial unrest swept across the country. On their return to London in 1912 they immediately began to plan two new ventures. The first was designed to restore their political base in the Fabian Society, which had fallen away into squabbling factions: the remedy, Beatrice decided, was to enlist the younger and more able members into a Research Department, and to produce a new set of policies for social reconstruction to replace those devised by the founding Fabians thirty years before. The second venture was intended to give them their own means of publicizing their ideas, and creating a cross-party current of collectivist opinion. In 1913, with the help of Bernard Shaw, they founded the weekly *New Statesman* as an independent radical journal.

Both these schemes were scarcely launched when the First World War begun, and the Webbs were at a loss what to do with their talents. There was a moratorium on political activity and, though the Webbs were invited to serve on a number of committees, they both felt frustrated; the only serious piece of work that Beatrice produced in these four years was a minority report to one of these committees arguing the case for equal pay, and for much of the war she was ill and depressed – feelings that were intensified by the collapse of her working partnership with Sidney. They continued with their research into the history of local government, and soon after the war they produced two theoretical books, *A Constitution for the Socialist Commonwealth of Great Britain* and *The Decay of Capitalist Civilization*; but after 1916, when the Webbs were at last converted to the idea of a Labour Party, Sidney was increasingly drawn into its affairs, working with Arthur Henderson and Ramsay MacDonald to reorganize it and drafting the manifesto, *Labour and the New Social Order*, which marked its emergence as the main opposition party in post-war years.

For the next ten years, indeed, Beatrice had to subordinate her own interests to the claims of Sidney's career as a Labour politician. In 1922 he was elected to Parliament, and in 1924 he became a cabinet minister in the first Labour government. Beatrice again became a political hostess, though much more reluctantly, for she now preferred to spend her time at Passfield Corner, the country home in Hampshire which the Webbs acquired in 1923; and her main concern was the revision of her diaries, with the aim of publishing one or more volumes of autobiography. In 1926 she published *My Apprenticeship*, but the advent of another Labour government in 1929, in which Sidney once more sat as a member of the Cabinet, was a fresh distraction.

So, too, was the fascination of the Soviet Union, which dominated the last years of the Webb partnership. Beatrice had already begun to draft the second volume of her autobiography, which was to describe the busy years between her marriage and the First World War, but after the collapse of the Labour government in 1931 she became disillusioned with the gradualist socialism that had been so distinctively Fabian. Turning towards Moscow, and what she saw as a new creed that reminded her of Auguste Comte's Religion of Humanity, she carried Sidney along with her enthusiasm; and in 1932 they set off to the Soviet Union to collect the material on which they based *Soviet Communism: A New Civilization*. The book was a last and immense effort, for both the Webbs were over seventy-five when it appeared in 1935, and its optimism about the Soviet regime, though qualified by Sidney's natural caution, was the one gleam in the growing darkness which Beatrice saw descending on the world.

Their last years were indeed a time of sadness. After Sidney's stroke in 1938, from which he never really recovered though he lived until 1947, the Webbs were housebound in the country, and they became even more cut off when the outbreak of war a year later made it difficult for their friends to visit them. Beatrice tried to keep in touch with events, and especially with those that affected the Soviet Union, to care for Sidney, to run a house under wartime conditions, to maintain her diary, and to go on with the book she proposed to call *Our Partnership*. But her own health was failing. On 19 April 1943 she wrote a last entry in her diary: eleven days later she was dead.

\*

Beatrice Webb's long life thus spanned a whole epoch. Born just before Darwin published the *Origin of Species*, and dying two years before the atom bomb was dropped on Hiroshima, she saw the transition from mid-Victorian individualism to the modern collectivist state, from a society in which people grew up with the certainty of a revealed religion to one in which they sought for secular creeds to replace it.

Although the Webbs knew more about poverty, trade unionism and public administration than anyone else in England, imperial and foreign policy meant very little to them; they were not greatly interested in cultural pursuits; and they preferred work to social intercourse, unless there was some useful point to it. Yet they lived close to great people and great events, and in the confidence of her diary Beatrice displayed her 'tireless curiosity' about them. They knew nine prime ministers – Lord Rosebery, Arthur Balfour, Sir Henry Campbell Bannerman, Herbert Asquith, David Lloyd George, Bonar Law, Ramsay MacDonald, Winston Churchill and Clement Attlee, – as well as members of all their Cabinets. Beatrice had learnt much from her father's friend, the individualist philosopher Herbert Spencer. She had known the great housing reformer Octavia Hill, worked with Charles Booth, and been deeply attached to Joseph Chamberlain, the most controversial politician of his day. The Webbs knew the early trade union leaders, such as Henry Broadhurst, Tom Mann and John Burns, as well as all their successors in the first half of the twentieth century; they had close academic and literary friends, including Bernard Shaw, H. G. Wells, Graham Wallas, Bertrand Russell and Harold Laski; they were professionally involved with some outstanding public servants, of whom Robert Morant and William Beveridge are the best known; and on their travels they met Woodrow Wilson, Theodore Roosevelt, Maxim Litvinov, Grigori Zinoviev and Lazar Kaganovitch.

Their travels were just as varied. They were in Washington when the United States declared war on Spain in 1898; they arrived in Hawaii on the day the island was annexed; they visited New Zealand and Australia when these two distant countries were the first to experiment with democratic socialist governments. They travelled through Japan when few intellectuals from the West had ever been there; they reached Peking at the height of the revolution which overthrew the Manchu dynasty in 1911, and they were in the Soviet Union on the eve of Stalin's great purges.

It is thus scarcely surprising that Beatrice's diary names over four thousand persons, a thousand places and more than six hundred institutions and organizations. It is an extraordinary compendium, running to close on three million words of scrawled and notoriously illegible handwriting, and though it is not a daily record – for Beatrice often let a week and sometimes a month or more go past without an entry – it is continuous and very comprehensive. The more one reads it, the more this long record of a life begins to assume a life of its own, as if a second self were writing with perfect freedom and extraordinary verve.

*My Apprenticeship* in fact shows what a stylist was submerged by the pedestrian prose in which Sidney wrote their books, and the pages of this diary repeatedly mention Beatrice's belief that she was a talent lost to literature. 'This last month or so', she wrote on 30 September 1889, 'I have been haunted by a longing to create characters and to move them to and fro among fictitious circumstances: to put the matter plainly, by the vulgar wish to write a novel.' At one point she proposed writing a utopian novel in collaboration with her literary friend, Auberon Herbert, and three years after she married, when she and Sidney were just completing their first book together, she came back to the idea. 'For the last three months', she noted on 1 February 1895, 'an idea has haunted me that after we have finished our stiff work on trade unions I would try my hand at pure "Fiction" in the form of a novel dated *60 Years Hence*. . . . The truth is, I want to have my "fling". I want to imagine anything I damn please without regard to facts as they are. I want to give full play to whatever faculty I have for descriptive and dramatic work. . . . I am sick to death of trying to put hideous facts, multitudinous details, exasperating qualifications, into a readable form.'

It was only in her diary, however, that she could release that impulse; and even there, when she reflects on the contrast between fiction and fact she dismisses fiction as 'vulgar' because it does nothing for 'the advancement of society', and persuades herself that the craving for 'a day's fame' was merely vanity and an unworthy aspiration for one who might otherwise be discovering 'the truths about social organization'. Leonard Woolf remarked in his autobiography that Beatrice had the soul of an artist but suppressed her passion and her imagination.

Beatrice had all the talents a great diarist needs. She was a well-informed, well-connected and reflective person, and she lived an active life; she had a sharp eye, a turn of mordant wit, and a knack for catching a character in a telling phrase; and all through these thousands of pages of self-analysis and self-explanation she was as critical of herself as she was of others — the gift a diarist needs above all, for a diary ultimately depends upon its truth to art, its autonomy. There are many passages where she explicitly recognizes that the denial of instinct emotionally impoverished her and cramped her sensibilities, especially when she describes how she recoiled from the prospect of marriage to Joseph Chamberlain: a woman's choice between suffocating domesticity and independence has seldom been more insightfully expressed, or recounted with such vigorous honesty. She was as frank about the willpower and sense of duty which she saw as the strengths of her character as she was about the vanity and self-indulgence for which she repeatedly chastised herself. And even in small things she did not deceive herself or those who now read what she wrote. She knew that she had only received opinions about the visual arts, and that music meant very little to her until, late in life and living in the country, the B.B.C. programmes helped her to discover it. She usually judged books by a utilitarian rule of thumb. She disliked Viriginia Woolf's novels, for instance, because the characters had 'no predominant aims, no powerful reactions from the mental environment', and because 'one state of mind follows another without any particular reason'. Beatrice always wanted reasons for things; and whenever she found herself preferring enjoyment to usefulness a twinge of guilt would quickly remind her of her lapse from grace.

Such double-mindedness, in which feeling struggles in vain against duty, was Beatrice's tragedy, and she knew it. She even began *My Apprenticeship* with a memorable sentence that expresses it precisely. 'Beneath the surface of our daily life, in the personal history of many of us, there runs a continuous controversy between an Ego that affirms and an Ego that denies.' That inner dialogue points the contrast between her physically attractive, light-hearted and worldly father and her frustrated, intellectually ambitious and puritanical mother, and the diary is full of paradoxes that echo two very different parental voices, setting self-indulgence against self-sacrifice, impulse against self-control, affection against the urge to dominate. These paradoxes, moreover, are not merely the dialectic of Beatrice's private life. The same moral calculus controlled her attitude to public affairs. If one believes that spontaneity is wrong, then regulation must be right; if individualism is a social evil, collectivism must be a social good.

As Beatrice said many times, the diary personifies the Other Self. Like the 'secret sharer' in Conrad's story of that name, it is always at hand, expressing the ideas that have been suppressed in consciousness and giving haunting reminders of an alternative life which can be glimpsed but never grasped. She began it as so many young girls begin a diary, treating it as a secure place for the confidence of an unhappy child, and it always served as a confidante of last resort for a woman who found it difficult to talk openly about her feelings. In adolescence she began to make notes on her foreign holidays, to record impressions of relatives and friends, and to summarize books that interested her; and by the time she was twenty she was beginning the experiments with structure and style which give the mature diary its extraordinary texture. It was already more than a habit: Beatrice was becoming dependent upon it, as if the Other Self compensated for some deficiency in her personality, just as the Other One (as she came to call Sidney) later supplied what she needed to sustain her everyday life.

There were, in effect, two partnerships. One was the lifelong colloquy with the diary, which kept her sane and helped her to cope with the self-destructive impulses that punctuated her career: the laudanum bottle was never far away, she said more than once in her youthful years, and she was subject to bouts of depression whenever she had finished a book or some other substantial piece of work. The other was with Sidney, who kept her effective, and steadied the erratic rhythms of her work.

This personal ambivalence was to some extent related to the ambivalent position of women in late-Victorian society, which still elevated the domestic virtues and deprecated attempts by women to copy or compete with men, in the professions and in public life. Beatrice was actually in revolt against the feminine ideal of her day, and breaking new paths for women who wanted satisfying and useful careers, but she did not see her own struggle for independence in that light. She was in no sense a conventional feminist. She was long opposed to women's suffrage; she always saw women as the weaker sex; she favoured special legislation to protect them against exploitation and to improve their working conditions; and she never made an issue of legal, political and educational discrimination on grounds of sex. On the contrary, finding little or no difficulty in doing what she wanted to do, she failed to appreciate that she had exceptional advantages and that most women were not so fortunate. She had money, she was charming, intelligent and good-looking, and she was well connected. Whether she was visiting slums in the East End, or sitting smoking in a hotel lounge with delegates to a trades union congress, travelling without a chaperone, or sitting on a committee, she had the style of effortless superiority which enabled energetic women from the upper classes to get their way. Lady Bountiful and Lady Researcher were not so different when it came to dealing with the cap-in-hand masses of the late-Victorian age.

It was not that Beatrice was insensitive to the constraints and disqualifications which made it difficult for other women to follow her emancipated example. She wrote sympathetically about women who chose or were obliged to choose a career rather than marriage; she saw spinsters forming a 'working sisterhood'; she took it for granted that men should treat women as equals; and she noted the rare occasions when a man was rude or deliberately unhelpful to her. But she never addressed her mind to the differences between the sexes in the same way that she thought about the differences between the classes; and she had very little influence on the women's movement in her own lifetime. It is only as one reads on through her diary that one sees how much her struggle to find herself was, in some measure, a woman's struggle in a man's world, and that a diary which begins as an intensely personal document can become a testament for a whole generation of women.

There are three different versions of the diary. The first is the original manuscript which is written in Beatrice's slapdash and scarcely legible hand in fifty-seven exercise-books. In addition to the text it contains two wills, letters, newspaper clippings, fragments of poetry, and even pressed flowers. The divisions between these volumes, which do not always coincide with calendar years, are indicated in the printed text. The other two versions are typescripts, typed partly by Beatrice herself, partly by her secretaries and partly in the British Library of Political and Economic Science when it was found that there were no transcripts of Volume 5 and Volumes 7 to 14 in the Passfield Papers which were handed over after Sidney Webb's death.

The typed versions differ from the original, and from each other, though only in minor respects. The variations are either simply errors of transcription, because Beatrice as well as her typists found it hard to read what she had written many years before, or her corrections when she was going through the manuscript to prepare extracts for her volumes of autobiography – corrections which occasionally introduced misdating as well as grammatical improvements. Though she sometimes added a later note where she thought she had been harsh or inaccurate, she was scrupulously honest and generally resisted the temptation to censor the text with hindsight. There are a few pages torn out, and these may once have contained entries she found too painful to keep, but in later years she inserted confidential material which she had withheld from earlier typists. Most of the corrections, in fact, are simply stylistic.

This edition is based on the first typescript which Beatrice used as a working text, with reference back to the original manuscript in cases where the meaning is uncertain, and with slips of the pen, careless punctuation, ampersands and abbreviations silently converted as Beatrice herself converted them in the extracts she reprinted. Square brackets show additional interpolations, and the addition of a query indicates doubt about a date, place or word.

The diary has also been cut substantially. There are long passages, especially in the first ten years, which are somewhat banal travelogues, copyings from books Beatrice was reading, or working notes. There are the diaries of the Webb visits to the United States, New Zealand and Australia in 1898 which have been published separately, and were partly written by Sidney. These again, have been reduced to specimen extracts. There is a vast manuscript, much of that also written by Sidney, which describes the Webb journey round the world in 1911. Since Beatrice herself considered it the most dispensable part of her diary, and even omitted a long summary of it from her first draft for *Our Partnership*, this has also been cut. And there are many places where Beatrice let herself run on with a personal description or a reflection, or where her entries digressed into trivia and ephemera. Brief omissions have been indicated by ellipses, and longer cuts have been mentioned in the prefatory notes. Even so, it has not been easy to bring the whole text down to publishable length, and in the end the excisions become a matter of personal judgement. But the aim throughout has been to preserve the spirit, the spontaneity and the substance of the diary.

The whole typescript and the manuscript have been made available in micro-fiche (Chadwyck-Healey, Cambridge, 1978) and scholars can thus secure access to these versions or to the originals in the British Library of Political and Economic Science. All the same, there has been no overall or systematic edition of the diary until now and a large part of it is thus published in book form for the first time. In 1926, when Beatrice Webb drew on her diaries to write *My Apprenticeship*, she omitted all intimate entries, including those which referred to her relationship with Joseph Chamberlain. The second, *Our Partnership*, posthumously completed by Barbara Drake and Margaret Cole, was more thematic than chronological, and the entries were divided into roughly assembled chapters with some linking narrative. After Beatrice Webb's death, Margaret Cole prepared two more volumes of extracts, which carried the story forward to 1932, though with much personal material omitted, and unlike *My Apprenticeship* and *Our Partnership* – recently reprinted – these two volumes have long been unobtainable. No selection has ever been made from the last ten years of the diary. In this new edition, therefore, the general reader can for the first time see the whole shape of Beatrice's life as she herself saw it.

PART I

The Search for a Creed

*September 1873–December 1882*

## Introduction to Part I

STANDISH was a substantial but plain four-square Georgian mansion, situated in its own grounds where the Cotswold escarpment plunges steeply to the Vale of Severn. It was close to the Stonehouse station of the Great Western Railway, on whose board Richard Potter served for many years, and to Gloucester, where he was a partner in a timber business which was the foundation of his fortune.

For Beatrice, Standish seemed a world in itself, always full of people, for the Potters were a big family; they entertained a good deal, and they naturally employed the usual flock of retainers that was needed to keep such large Victorian households going. She recalled that Standish felt more like an institution than a home, and so it seems today, when it has become the nurses' home of a large hospital; but she was more attached to it than to any of the other Potter homes. The Argoed, an extended Jacobean farmhouse in the Wye Valley, was acquired as a holiday retreat, and when Beatrice inherited it she continued to go down to Monmouthshire for vacations until some years after her marriage. Rusland Hall, in Cumberland, was also taken for a time as a holiday home, convenient to Barrow-in-Furness, where there was a branch of Richard Potter's timber firm; and in Beatrice's youth the family regularly took a town house, first in Prince's Gate and then in Kensington Palace Gardens, for the London Season.

Her parents thus lived in some style. They both were the children of self-made men, and both still had humble relations. Richard Potter's father began life as a small farmer and shopkeeper in Tadcaster, not far from York, made his money in a Manchester wholesale house which became a rendezvous for the political and philanthropic reformers of the fast-growing cotton metropolis, was elected as Radical M.P. for Wigan after the Reform Act of 1832, and

3

was one of the founders of the *Manchester Guardian*. His mother, whom Beatrice later described as a 'tall dark woman of Jewish type who read Hebrew', suffered from the delusion that it was her mission to lead the Jews back to Jerusalem, and for much of her life she was confined to an asylum. Richard Potter himself had a comfortable start in life. He was educated at the newly founded and strongly utilitarian University College in Gower Street, London, and at Queen's College, Cambridge, where he was elected to a fellowship before going on to become a barrister. He lost his inherited wealth in a financial collapse in 1848, started afresh in the timber firm of Price & Co. in Gloucester, which did very well by supplying wooden huts to the French army in the Crimea, and then became caught up in the railway boom. He was a director of the Great Western Railway for many years, and became its chairman in 1863. He was a director of the Grand Trunk Railway of Canada from 1862, and its president from 1869–76. He was also on the board of the Hudson's Bay Company, and a number of lesser enterprises. He had the temperament of a speculator, investing heavily in Canada, Holland and Turkey, and even toying with the notion of building a rival to the Suez Canal. He was equally volatile in his opinions. He was born into a Dissenting family, and grew up in an atmosphere of religious Nonconformity and Liberal politics, but by middle life he had become an easy-going Anglican Tory, who had narrowly missed election as the Conservative candidate in Gloucester in 1862, and got on as well with his neighbouring squires as with the eminent and stimulating friends who shared his intellectual interests.

Lawrencina Potter came from much the same background as her husband, though she was very different in temperament. Her father, Lawrence Heyworth, was the youngest son of a prosperous millowner in Bacup, Lancashire, and when he was still a youth, during the Napoleonic wars, he had gone to Portugal and then to Brazil to sell his family's woollen goods; he became a railway director and Liberal M.P. for Derby. He was a strict utilitarian, a Free Trader, a temperance reformer and a strong supporter of popular education, who founded a Mechanics' Institution in Bacup and presided over it until his death in 1872. He was the author of an earnest tract entitled *The Origin, Mission and Destiny of Man*. In 1820 he married Elizabeth Aked, a second cousin and one of many poorer relations in Rossendale who worked as handloom weavers and were active Co-operators and chapel-goers. He had several sons, and when his daughter was born he christened her Lawrencina and brought her up much as if she were yet another boy – an education which brought out her talents at the price of lifelong frustration.

After Lawrencina Heyworth married Richard Potter, whom she met in Rome when he was making the Grand Tour, she was caught in an unending cycle of child-bearing and child-raising which she heartily resented. 'She had visualized a home life of close intellectual comradeship with my father, possibly of intellectual achievement, surrounded by distinguished friends,' Beatrice wrote, but marriage actually brought her 'a nursery full of children, and a husband who was preoccupied and often away'. And there was a final disillusionment. 'She had been reared by and with men, and disliked women,' Beatrice added. 'She was destined to have nine daughters and to lose her only son.'

The account Beatrice gave of her mother in *My Apprenticeship* shows what a formative influence Lawrencina had on her talented daughter. She had, Beatrice said, 'a divided personality' which manifested itself in a never-ending controversy about the right conduct of life, and she longed for the moral discipline of religious orthodoxy. She was schooled in the strictest kind of utilitarian economics, to an extent that made her daughters notoriously parsimonious, and she found it much easier to urge them to avoid self-indulgence than to express warm and motherly feelings towards them. Self-improvement was, she believed, the only means by which the human race could evolve towards a more civilized life, and her restless mind made her languish for an intellectually satisfying career. She did write a novel, *Laura Gay*, which was published but was not well thought of. She also kept a diary for a short time during Beatrice's childhood. Eventually she settled on the study of foreign grammars as her main interest. To pursue that study, which took the increasingly eccentric form of, say, studying a Greek grammar in French, or a Spanish grammar in some Scandinavian tongue, she increasingly withdrew from normal social activities, leaving her daughters to make their own way in life. Even then, Beatrice sadly remarked, 'she was not at peace with herself'. Lawrencina Potter never suffered anyone gladly, let alone her daughters, and they were all affected by her self-obsessed and depressive personality.

The eldest daughter was Lawrencina ('Lallie'), born in 1845, who married Robert Durning Holt, a cotton merchant in Liverpool whose brothers ran a well-known shipping line. Catherine ('Kate') was born in 1847; she married Leonard Henry Courtney, a Liberal politician who became Deputy Speaker of the House of Commons. The third sister was Mary, born in 1849, who was the wife of a millowner in the Stroud Valley named Arthur Playne, and lived all her life at Longfords, not far from Standish. Georgina ('Georgie') was born in 1850 and she married the banker Daniel Meinertzhagen. Blanche, born in 1851, had an unhappy marriage to a well-known surgeon named William Harrison Cripps. Theresa, born in 1852, married his brother, Charles Alfred Cripps, later Lord Parmoor, a barrister who became a Conservative attorney-general, a pacifist and then a member of the first Labour government. Margaret ('Maggie'), born in 1854, was the wife of Henry Hobhouse, a barrister, Liberal Unionist politician and country gentleman. Beatrice was the eighth daughter. The next child was Richard ('Dickie'), who was born in 1862 and died two years later. Rosalind ('Rosy') was the youngest of the Potter sisters, born in 1865 and married twice, first to Arthur Dyson Williams, another barrister, and then to a travel courier named George Dobbs. There were twenty-seven sons and sixteen daughters born of these marriages, and the family, which had many dis-tinguished connections in literary and public life, grew so steadily that over a hundred Potter descendants attended a garden party held in 1937 to mark the retirement of Beatrice and Sidney Webb, and more than four hundred and fifty are listed in a family tree completed in 1980.

As one of the younger children Beatrice felt neglected, both by her parents and by her sisters, who were naturally involved in their courtships and marriages; and this feeling was intensified by her mother's attachment to little Dickie. When she was small, 'creeping up in the shadow of my baby brother's birth and death', Beatrice suffered from a profound sense of rejection; she was morbidly unhappy, and afflicted by chronic psychosomatic illness. She had persistent neuralgia, attacks of bronchitis, bouts of insomnia and indigestion – all conditions which recurred later in life when she was overworked or emotionally upset. She was apparently so sickly that she was thought incapable of sustained intellectual effort, and she was left so much to her own devices that her only formal education was a few uncomfortable months at a small 'finishing' academy for girls in Bournemouth.

All through childhood, indeed, Beatrice preferred the rambling backstairs of Standish to the public front of the house; she was comfortable with the servants, and she was particularly attached to Martha Jackson, called 'Dada' by the whole family. 'Dada' had been Lawrencina Heyworth's personal maid. She had been with her mistress in Rome when she met Richard Potter, followed her into married life, and became the nurse to all the Potter children. She was a warm-hearted woman – 'the one and only saint I ever knew', Beatrice said – and she gave the girls the loving care that was lacking in their mother. She seems to have been the pivot of all domestic relations, able to speak freely to master and mistress, to chide as well as to cherish the children, and, illuminated by a religious faith, she gave 'an overpowering consciousness of love'.

What Beatrice did not know until she was grown up was that 'Dada' was a blood relation, and came from her mother's connections among the Lancashire weavers. But through 'Dada' and the families in Bacup whom they later visited together, and through a childhood ease with the servants, running freely through the kitchens, playing in stables, haylofts and vegetable gardens, Beatrice discovered a sympathy with the self-respecting poor that persisted throughout her life; and yet, as a daughter of the house, she was brought up to take 'the possession of power over other people' for granted, and to assume that the lower classes laboured to sustain the rich and clever in comfort.

As Beatrice grew older, and the other Potter sisters married, she began to benefit from her father's friendships – in particular, from the friendship and intellectual encouragement of Herbert Spencer (1820–1903). As a youth Spencer was sent to live with an uncle who was strong for temperance and other social movements, and an early interest in science led him to begin a career as a railway engineer. He soon changed his occupation, becoming a Nonconformist publicist who combined extreme individualism with support of anti-slavery, anti-religious, anti-Corn Law and suffrage agitation. He was employed for some years as an editor on *The Economist*, and it was during this period of his life that he came to know the Potters, recently married, and also George Eliot, whom he described as 'the most admirable woman, mentally, I ever met'. His *Social Statics*, which began to appear in 1851, argued for minimal state provision and regulation in matters of social policy. When he was working on *The Principles of Psychology*, which appeared in 1855, he suffered a nervous breakdown, from which he never fully recovered, but he continued to write assiduously. From 1857 he was at work on a systematic exposition of an evolutionary philosophy, of which the *First*

*Principles* appeared in 1862. The first volume of *Principles of Biology* was published in 1864, the second in 1867. One volume of the *Principles of Sociology* was produced in 1876, the second in 1882, and the third in 1896. By this time he had become one of the most influential and respected thinkers of the Victorian age. His influence on Beatrice was most important. Spencer was a shy man, self-obsessed, hypochondriacal and subject to such morbid irritability that he was an eccentric and difficult companion. Yet he was much attached to Beatrice, and a natural teacher who believed that children should be encouraged to develop freely, without parental constraints and penalties; his treatise on *Education* in 1861 became a leading textbook. On his frequent visits to the Potter home he became something like a personal tutor to Beatrice, guiding her reading and prompting her to speculate about the place of human beings in society and in the universe. She affectionately called him 'the old philosopher'. He considered her 'a born metaphysician', and said that she was the only woman of his acquaintance who could be compared to George Eliot. Beatrice made several moving tributes to his influence in her autobiography and her diary. She said that she took over Spencer's faith 'in the application of scientific method to human nature', and she declared that it was his 'heroic disregard to material prosperity and physical comfort' in his efforts to advance human knowledge that served her as a model when she turned to social investigation and reform — even though she rejected his obdurate individualism in favour of an equally dogmatic collectivism. He was always her touchstone of intellectual honesty.

Herbert Spencer was only one of many able men who came to the Potter house. There was John Tyndall (1820–93), who was a geologist, a physicist and a great popularizer of the new scientific ideas. Thomas Henry Huxley (1825–95) was the pugnacious advocate of Darwin's evolutionary theories; Sir William Hooker (1785–1865) was a great botanist; and Sir Francis Galton (1822–1911) was a man of many talents whose work had a significant influence on Beatrice in mid-career. He was a good friend of Beatrice's sister, Georgina, and her husband, and it was at their house that she met him. Galton came from a prosperous and educated Quaker family, had sufficient means to abandon his training as a doctor and, after a period of extensive foreign travel, could devote himself to geographical studies and research into the laws of heredity. He helped to establish fingerprinting as a means of distinguishing one person from another, and he

8

sought to apply measurement to other human characteristics. He made many psychological experiments, mostly concerned with perception, and after his cousin Charles Darwin had published the *Origin of Species* in 1859 he began to consider the effect of heredity on human evolution. Noting that distinction seemed to run in families, over the next forty years he made a number of statistical inquiries – which helped to lay the foundation of modern statistics – to demonstrate the heritability of genius. His work led him to the conclusion that the human race could be improved by breeding from the best stocks and by restricting the progeny of the worst. This doctrine of 'eugenics' had a considerable impact on English social thought in the first years of the twentieth century, when the problem of the fecund poor was much under discussion and the development of imperialism had raised questions about the capacity of 'inferior' or 'subject' races. While Galton did not subscribe to the extreme and racialist views of some French and German writers on inherited traits, there is no doubt that his theories had an influence on the élitist doctrines of social reform to which Beatrice and Sidney Webb, as well as George Bernard Shaw, were inclined at this time.

All these men of science, indeed, greatly contributed to the current of thought which was eroding the foundations of revealed religion, and causing much mental turmoil for intellectuals growing up in the second half of Victoria's reign. 'There are many about us,' W. H. Mallock said of such persons in the *Nineteenth Century* in the autumn of 1878, 'though they never confess their pain, and perhaps themselves hardly like to dwell on it, whose hearts are aching for the God they no longer believe in.'

That crisis of faith was strongest among young men, for few young women were sufficiently exposed to the new theories of science and society to shake their received opinions. But Beatrice was a different case. Growing up in a family so much affected by the climate of Dissent and utilitarian liberalism, in a house where such men as Spencer, Tyndall and Huxley were welcome visitors, and their writings were freely available, she was naturally much affected, and her father did nothing to inhibit her mental development or to influence her towards the more orthodox views he had himself come to favour as he grew older. Beatrice had considerable trouble about her confirmation in the Church of England, and especially about the doctrine of the Atonement, and while she was little more than a schoolgirl she had passed from conventional Christianity to an interest

9

in occultist and oriental creeds. Then, as she tried to reconcile what her father's intellectual friends taught with her innate sense of mystery, with her feelings of moral obligation and her desire for social purpose, she passed through a phase in which she questioned the Religion of Science she took from Spencer and came to something very like Comte's Religion of Humanity.

A generalized form of Comte's Positivism continued to influence her all her life, and in marrying Sidney Webb she chose a man who had been equally influenced by Positivist thinking. Auguste Comte (1798–1857), the French social philosopher, had coined the word 'Positivism' for a system of belief designed to replace the Catholicism he abandoned at the age of thirteen. He saw human history divided into three epochs – the religious, the metaphysical and the scientific; like Spencer and Huxley after him, he sought to reconstitute the law, morality, politics and religion of the modern world on a rational and scientific basis. Much affected by the French Revolution, and seeking a means to reconcile the ensuing antagonism between the protagonists of order and the apostles of progress, he developed a social theory which sought consensus within a hierarchical society by the assertion of moral principle. As Beatrice put it, he hoped, in effect, to retain the spiritual energy of religion while secularizing its motive force from the service of God to the self-subordinating service of Man; society, he believed, would be run for the good of all by a disinterested – indeed, a moralized – élite of unselfish businessmen and high-minded administrators whom he called the Priests of Humanity.

Stripped of its more fanciful aspects, Positivism fitted well into the need for a creed which could divert evangelical fervour to social ends, and for this reason it was peculiarly attractive to young persons who had lost their formal religious faith but required some kind of philosophical frame within which they could organize their impulse to altruism and reform. It is the search for some such creed which dominates the first part of this volume, and almost all the passages in which Beatrice discusses her religious problems have been retained. The only substantial omissions are long accounts of her holidays in the United States in 1873, central Europe in 1878 and Germany in 1882, and of her 'finishing tour' of the art treasures of Italy in 1880 – all entries that are conventionally dull, and in marked contrast to the vigour with which she discusses her secret hopes and fears. The first surviving fragment was probably written in 1868. In both style and content it remarkably foreshadows the adult diary entries.

I am quite confident that the education of girls is very much neglected in the way of their private reading. Take, for instance, a girl of nine or ten years old, she is either forbidden to read any but child's books, or she is let loose on a good library; Sir Walter Scott's novels recommended to her as charming and interesting stories – 'books that cannot do any possible harm', her adviser declares. But the object in reading is to gain knowledge. A novel now and then is a wise recreation to be offered to a growing mind; it cultivates the imagination, but taken as the continual nourishment, it destroys many a young mind. The whole of their thought (for a child of nine or ten spends little or no thought on her lessons) is wasted on making up love scenes, or building castles in the air, where she is always the charming heroine without a fault. I have found it a serious stumbling-block to myself; whenever I get alone I always find myself building castles in the air of some kind; it is a habit that is so thoroughly immured in me that I cannot make a good resolution without making a castle in air about it.

Another fragment, also undated but from the same period, contains a most competent summary of a sermon Beatrice had heard on the consolations of religion and the bleak outlook for Deists who believed in God but not in the immortality of the soul. 'Perhaps ambition, patriotism or vanity will stand instead of religion during their life,' Beatrice wrote in a question which also foreshadowed an adult concern, 'but on their deathbed, there is the dreadful blank, what hope and comfort have they got?'

The third fragment, written on 23 December 1872, is so much more substantial that it appears to be part of a more regular diary of which nothing else remains.

This autumn unsatisfactory to me in many ways, I have hardly learned anything in the way of lessons; honestly speaking, I have been extremely idle, especially during and after the company. But one thing I have learnt is that I am exceedingly vain, to say the truth I am very disgusted with myself; whenever I am in the company of any gentleman, I cannot help wishing and doing all I possibly can to attract his attention and admiration; the whole time I am thinking how I look, which attitude becomes me, and contriving every possible [way] to make myself more liked and admired than [my] sisters. The question is, how can I conquer it, for it forwards every bad passion and suppresses every good one in my heart; the only thing I can think of is to avoid gentlemen's society altogether. I feel I am not good enough to fight any temptation at present. I have not enough faith.

Talking about faith, I don't know what to think about myself. I believe and yet I am always acting contrary to my belief. When I am doing any silly action, when I am indulging my vanity, I hear a kind of voice saying within me, 'It doesn't matter at present what you say and do, if there is a God, which I very much doubt, it will be time to think of that when you are married or an old maid,' and what is worse still, I am constantly acting on that idea. Meanwhile I feel my faith slipping from me. Christ seems to have been separated from me by [a] huge mass of worldliness and vanity. I can no more pray to Him with the same earnest faith as I used to do; my prayers seem mockeries. I pray against temptations, which I run into of my own accord, and then I complain secretly that my prayers are not answered, and intellectual difficulties of faith make it impossible to believe. I am *very very* wicked; I feel [as] if Christ can never listen to me again. Vanity, all is vanity. I feel that I have transgressed deeply, that I have trifled with the Lord. I feel that if I continue thus I shall become a frivolous, silly, unbelieving woman, and yet every morning when I wake I have the same giddy confident feeling, and every night I am miserable. The only thing is to give up any pleasure, rather [than] go into society. It may be hard, in fact I know it will, but it must be done, else I shall lose all the remaining sparks of faith and with those all the chances of my becoming a good and useful woman in this world, and a companion of our Lord in the next.

May God help me to keep my resolution.

The diary proper begins in September 1873, when Beatrice was fifteen. It was her father's custom, whenever he went to inspect his railway interests in Canada and the United States, to take some of the family with him. On this occasion he took Beatrice, her sister Kate, and Arthur Playne, who was married to her sister Mary. From New York the party went on to Albany, Niagara Falls and Chicago. Here Richard Potter stayed to do business while the others travelled on, in the comfort of a private coach, to San Francisco, the Yosemite Valley and Salt Lake City. Beatrice enjoyed visiting the Californian goldfields, was immensely impressed by the grandeur of Yosemite, and was fascinated by Salt Lake City and its Mormon inhabitants.

## VOLUME 1
## ∽ 1873 ∾

We left England on the 13 September, two days after Georgina's marriage. I only enjoyed our passage pretty well, the people not being anything particular. . . .

*25 September*
We landed at New York. . . . I was delighted with New York, there is such a cleanliness and elegance about the town, with trees all down its streets and no smoke, and then Central Park is so lovely, beats all our town parks to pieces. . . .

*1 November*
Salt Lake City is not to be compared with any town in England or America; it is so utterly different from anything I have ever seen. The streets are very wide, and on both sides of them flow beautiful streams of crystal water brought from the mountains ten to twenty miles off. It is through this water that Brigham Young and his few followers transformed this sandy desert into a fertile farm. . . . The houses are for the most part low, built rather in the French style, and of wood whitewashed over, with green shutters and doors. This gives the city a fresh innocent appearance, especially as . . . each house has its garden and orchard.

The Tabernacle is by far the most important building in Salt Lake City; then come Brigham's two houses, 'The Lion' and 'The Beehive', and a very pretty villa he is building for Mrs Amelia Young, his last and most beloved wife. Most of his other wives either live in one of his two houses, or else have small houses round them in his garden. The only one of his wives we saw was Mrs Eliza Young, No. 17, who separated from him, and is now lecturing on Mormonism all over America. She was staying at Walker's Hotel; she was rather a pretty woman at a distance, but decidedly coarse when you examined her near.

In the afternoon we went to hear Anson Pratt, an Apostle, and one of the original founders of the Mormon creed. During the summer the service is held in the Tabernacle, but as it is built of wood they are afraid of heating it, which of course makes it impossible to use it in winter. So each ward has its own meeting-house where they assemble on Sundays during the winter months. We went to the 13th ward. The congregation was mostly of the working men's class. They seemed to be very attentive and earnest in their devotions. I noticed here particularly the dejected look of the women, as if they had continually on their mind their inferiority to their lords and masters. The service was begun by a hymn. Then a decidedly clever-looking man (a bishop) stood up and recited a prayer, in itself very good, but said more in a tone of 'we only demand what we have a right to' than of humble supplication. Then the sacrament was handed round and another hymn sung, after which Anson Pratt got up and began his discourse. . . .

*Chicago. Arrived 6 November, left 3 December*
Four weeks spent in getting through scarlet fever and measles, accompanied by a severe attack of rheumatism . . . nursed by Kate, spoilt by Papa, feared by everybody except a stranger.

Tuesday – the day before we leave New York! . . . It seems a long time since I passed through the hall at Standish, feverish with excitement and longing to see the world, with sisters kissing us, and giving us a tearful goodbye, and with a file of wedding guests on each side. . . . I wonder if I have altered? And if altered, whether for the better or the worse. I shall find my own level when I get home, that is one good thing in a large family.

One thing I want to do, when I get home, that is to make more a friend of Maggie. Hitherto I have lived a great deal too much apart

14

from my sisters, partly from indolence and partly from my unfrank disposition. Dear Kitty, I have got quite fond of her, she has been such a dear, kind devoted sister. I can't imagine why she does not get on better at home. Though we lived on the most intimate relationship for the last three months or more, I really have not found out one serious fault.

End of my diary in America, which I wrote principally in the train between Ogden and Omaha, and at Chicago during my illness.

## ∽ 1874 ∾

Ludwig Tieck (1773–1853) was a German romantic novelist and poet. Torquato Tasso (1544–95) was an Italian poet, whose main work was *Jerusalem Delivered*. Miss Mitchell was one of the governesses in the Potter household.

### 18 January. Standish

I am now busily engaged in studying. I am translating *Faust* and reading a novel of Tieck's. [Goethe's] *Faust* is wonderfully clever and often very beautiful. Putting the introductory piece out of the question, which is fearfully blasphemous, it might almost have been written by a good man, as a satire of the philosophers of the present day. . . . As far as I have gone I think it is far more powerful than Tasso, which I must say I neither admired nor liked. I have left off music almost entirely. I practise exercises and scales for half an hour, half because Mother wishes it, and half because I do not want to leave it off entirely. Drawing is what I should like to excel in, and now in the evenings before I go and read Shakespeare to Miss Mitchell, I make a point of copying one of the patterns in the School of Art book, and correcting it with compass and ruler.

Maggie and Blanche are very much improved the last four months. Maggie has become much softer and much more charitable towards the world. Blanche is now a practical, kind, cheerful girl, working hard at German and becoming quite useful in household matters. Theresa is as dear a girl as ever; of course this autumn she has been very much disturbed by the affair with Mr Trench. I believe she has acted in the most unselfish and best way, and has been guided by higher principles than most of us are capable of. To think that this time last year we did not even know Townsend Trench, and that since

15

then he has been on the point of carrying away our dearest sister, and certainly did captivate her heart for a time. Not that he has not behaved in the most honourable and chivalrous way all through. He is one of those men, who, if he had paid me the attentions that he paid Theresa, and done me the honour to fall so desperately in love with me, I should have been too weak to refuse. I do not think he would be a safe man to marry; he has too much Irish rashness and self-confidence. . . . He is personally the most attractive man I know, with wonderful fluency of speech and great originality of thought. Poor fellow, I believe he has been very ill and sad since he heard Theresa's final refusal. He attempted gallantly to gain a great jewel: who can blame him for failing?

*25 January.* [Standish]
I am not thoroughly contented with the way that I have passed this week. I have been extremely irregular in all my duties. I have not worked as much as I ought to have done, I have been lazy about my religious duties, I have been lazy in getting up; altogether I have been totally devoid of any method. Now I must really try and be more regular, go to bed early, get up early, practise and not be lazy about my drawing, else I shall never get on. I don't think it hurts at all, now and then to read some of St Paul's life, instead of studying German, say twice a week. . . . I am in a complete muddle about politics. I think they are one of those things of which you cannot see the 'right' or the 'wrong'. I can't help having a sort of sympathy with the Radicals, they are so enthusiastic, but I don't think that their time is come yet. They require a much more perfect state of society than that at present. But it is ridiculous for me to waste my time in scribbling about politics, when I am so ignorant on all those questions.

Joaquin Miller (1837–1913), American poet of frontier life, had a great success in England with his *Songs of the Sierras* (1871).

*6 March.* [Standish]
Sometimes I feel as if I must write, as if I must pour my poor crooked thoughts into somebody's heart, even if it be into my own. I am fascinated with that book of Joaquin Miller's, a lover of the wild half-savage state and a hater, because a stranger, of the civilized world. It's queer after reading of nothing but the influence of civilization on this or that nation, of progress, to hear a man boldly stand up and declare that civilization often is degradation, that the savage is often better,

16

wiser and 'nearer God' than the civilized man; and that too from an American.

Dear me! my trip to America seems to have opened a new world to me, and into which I seemed to have had a glimpse, a glimpse long enough to make one wish for another.

*9 March.* [Standish]
Why am I such a coward! If I was going to have a leg cut off it could not be worse. Instead of which I am going to have a tooth stopped. Gracious goodness! where's the world going to next! Coward, coward, coward, that's what I am, morally and physically.

*13 March.* [Standish]
On the eve of my departure for London. I intend to enjoy it very much, and now funnily I don't dread the dentist half so much. It's sometimes so odd how different things look when one is ill to when one is well. When I went to Mary's [Playne] it seemed like a fearful bugbear but now I look at it as a little disagreeable job which must be got through. I am not exactly in what one calls a settled happy state; I am altogether unsettled and discontented. What if my trip to America has made me so? I think that the spoiling I received from Kate and Father has had something to do with it. Then I was *the* important person but now I am the least important of six or seven others, and naturally my interests and my health cannot be considered first, and I am a great fool to think so. I have got into a silly self-conscious way of always taking the least word or action as an offence to me, as if anybody wanted to hurt me, morally or physically!

Now if I am a wise girl I shall go away at Easter, especially if F.G. [F. Galton?] comes – ten to one if I see him again I shan't be able to resist making a lot of silly castles in the air about him; and that is what I want to avoid. And now, my dear friend, I want to tell you something seriously, because nobody else will have the chance of telling it you. You are really getting into a nasty and what I should call an indecent way of thinking of men, and love, and unless you take care you will lose all your purity of thought, and become a silly vain self-conscious little goose. Do try and build no more castles in the air; do try to think purely and seriously about Love. I often think you are something like Rosamund in *Middlemarch*. . . . Oh that I had thorough command over you.

17

*24 March.* [Standish]

What is this feeling between Mother and me? It is a kind of feeling of dislike and distrust which I believe is mutual. And yet it ought not to be! She has always been the kindest and best of mothers, though in her manners she is not over-affectionate. She is such a curious character I can't make her out. She is sometimes such a kind, good affectionate mother, full of wise judgement and affectionate advice, and at other times the spoilt child comes out so strong in her. But whatever she is, that ought not to make the slightest difference to my feeling and behaviour towards her. Honour thy Father and Mother was one of the greatest of Christ's commandments. . . .

*4 April.* [Standish]

I am really trying to gain a firm belief for myself. I think it is no good going to others to have your belief cut out for you; you must examine, study, both the Bible and the lives of those who follow the Bible and those who don't. It is no sin to doubt, but it is a sin, after you have doubted, not to find out to the best of your capability why you doubt, and whether you have reasons to doubt. It was because no one doubted, and because everyone was too idle to examine and to probe, that Christianity became so corrupted in the Middle Ages. I must make a faith for myself, and I must work, work, until I have.

*3 August.* [Standish]

It is a long time since I last wrote in my diary. April 4th is the last date. It was just then that the whirl of the London Season was beginning, which included me, though a schoolroom girl, in its rush. I enjoyed it immensely. It is seldom I have had so much pleasure in so small a space of time. And yet at times one was hardly happy. One looked from day to day for some new excitement, and in the intervals between these excitements one hardly knew what to do with oneself. The theatricals were the climax of all the pleasure and excitement. The getting up of them was in itself great fun, though I was only a looker on. And then that tremendous excitement the week before them, the thought of my having to act Kate Hardcastle [in Goldsmith's *She Stoops to Conquer*] before two audiences of two hundred people! But, however, that never came to pass, Maggie got well in time and carried off the laurels. The Dance, oh how I did enjoy that! It was the first dance I had ever been at as a grown-up lady, and I felt considerably satisfied with myself, as I had two or three partners for each dance. Ah vanity! vanity! unfortunately for me my ruling passion. . . .

### 23 September. [Standish]

There must be a change! I am getting decidedly self-satisfied, conceited and selfish. I have not enough of that Christian humility which is at the root of all virtues. I think too much of myself and not enough of other people. And then when I am thinking of myself I do not think of myself in the right way. Half the time I spend in building castles in the air, instead of examining myself.

### 27 September. [Standish]

Here we are alone, Mother, Blanche and myself. Poor Mother, she has two rather broken crutches to lean upon. Blanche is a dear good girl, but she is unpractical and rather inclined to bore you; and as for me, I am, as Mother says, too young, too uneducated and, worst of all, too frivolous to be a companion to her. But, however, I must take courage, and try to change, and above all I must guard against that self-satisfaction which I consider is one of my worst faults. If I give into it, it will prevent my ever improving myself. And the only way to cure myself of it is to go heart and soul into religion. It is a pity I ever went off the path of orthodox religion, it was a misfortune that I was not brought up to believe that to doubt was a crime. But since I cannot accept the belief of my Church without inward questioning let me try and find a firm belief of my own, and let me act up to it. That is the most important thing. God help me to do it!

### 11 December. [Standish]

I think that the great benefit one receives from keeping a diary is that it often leads one to examine oneself and that it is a vent for one's feelings, for those feelings in particular that one cannot communicate to other people. Since I have been poorly this autumn I have been thinking of nothing but myself, and I am sure that it is the most unhealthy state of mind. . . . I have never felt so low spirited as I have this autumn. I have felt for the first time in my life how much unhappiness there is in life. But one has not been given the choice of existing or not existing, and all one has to think of is how to live the best, the most useful and the happiest life. I have come to the conclusion that the only real happiness is devoting oneself to making other people happy. I feel that it is very discouraging to lose so much valuable time when I might be studying, but I believe that if I take this ill-health in a proper way and bear it bravely and cheerfully I shall improve my character more than I should have improved my mind in the same time. And character weighs more than intellect in the scales of life.

Beatrice was now sent for a short time to Stirling House, a fashionable school for girls run by a Miss Tapp in Christchurch Road in Bournemouth, where she spent much of her time 'in lonely study and religious meditation'. It was here that she briefly found 'mental security in traditional Christianity' and decided to be confirmed. When the Potter family was in London for the Season it was Richard Potter's habit to take his daughters to hear the most interesting speakers on a Sunday, whether they were to be found in a Catholic church, a Nonconformist chapel or a Positivist meeting-room. 'Except for this eclectic enjoyment of varieties of metaphysical experience', Beatrice wrote many years later, 'the atmosphere of the home was peculiarly free-thinking'. At Bournemouth she found Mr Eliot, a Low Church evangelical, a preferable spiritual guide to the High Church cleric favoured by the school.

## ∾ 1875 ∾

*27 March. Easter Eve.* [Stirling House]
The day before I receive for the first time the holy sacrament. The last month or two has been a very solemn epoch in my life, and may God grant that I may never cease remembering the vows which I have made before God and man, that I intend to become a true Christian, that is, a true disciple and follower of Jesus Christ, making Him my sole aim in life. And now I am going to receive the great sacrament, which He Himself instituted as a perpetual means of remembering His visit on earth. God grant that it may really strengthen me. There are many things which remain still mysteries to me, like the doctrine of the Atonement. The idea that God demanded that some innocent person should die for the sins of men, and that by the voluntary death of that just man, wicked and damned men who would not otherwise have been saved, are saved, is repugnant to me. I firmly believe that Jesus Christ has and will save the world, but not so particularly by His death, as by His Word, which He came down to preach. His whole preaching seems to me to indicate that He never says that we shall be saved by His death but by belief in Him and in the Word which He has preached. . . . And yet it is evident that every one of

His disciples believed in the Atonement as a saving doctrine, and Christ Himself seems to set it forth once as a great truth in the institution of the Lord's Supper.

*11 July. Stirling House*
I always think it is profitable just before one leaves a place, where one has been residing for a considerable time, to think over one's life and see what new lessons one has learnt, and what books one has been reading and what friends made. The first weeks here were not very happy ones, though I think I might have been more contented. But now that I have a room to myself I do not think there could be a happier and more peaceful life. I have enjoyed the little reading I have been able to do immensely; and I am looking forward to studying at Standish more methodically than I have been able to do here. . . . Though I have hardly read *Jane Eyre* carefully enough to be able to judge of it fairly, I must say it impresses me disagreeably. I do not think it a pure book. The author's conception of love is a feverish, almost lustful passion. Her hero is frankly speaking a bad and immoral man, whom she endeavours to render attractive by giving him a certain force of character and much physical and intellectual power.

*19 September.* [Standish]
I must confess I am much more sorry to leave Standish than I expected. The last fortnight I have enjoyed very much and have been blessed with good health. But I hope at Bournemouth to grow much stronger, and I must be resolved to allow no pleasure or interesting study to interfere with care of health; and I must be particularly careful of my diet. The two studies I have taken up, Jewish history and English law, are both very interesting. I have chosen the latter because it is so thoroughly different from the former and employs a different set of muscles. I must try and not become egotistical in my thoughts, for that is a great danger when one leads a solitary life, for my life with regard to thought is completely solitary at Stirling House. . . . I must also above everything endeavour not to think myself superior to the other inmates of Stirling House, because I have been brought out more by circumstances and encouraged to reason on subjects which other girls have mostly been told to take on faith. Both systems have their advantages and disadvantages. But perhaps the mistake I felt most was joining gossiping conversations. And [to

21

correct] this is certainly most difficult because it in a great way necessitates keeping myself aloof from the girls' society.

*21 September*. [Stirling House]
The first day at Stirling House. I must confess I feel rather wretched. I feel wrenched from a home which for the first time this year agreed with me and where I have been thoroughly happy, and a family who I was beginning to appreciate and love. Today also and probably for the next week I shall have no very settled occupation, and it will require a little time to make me forget the superior comforts of home. The continual din of the pianos, the want of interesting conversation, the absence of small comforts, and the little restraints on one's actions are all circumstances which require to be got accustomed to. On the other hand I have a greater certainty of health and have perfect peace and very little responsibility. These advantages I hardly appreciate, because my family knowing that I should soon leave them made rather a pet of me.

But if I compare my life here for the next thirteen weeks with my life last autumn at Standish I shall see how much happier I am. Then I was alone with Mother and Blanche and Rosy; and had all the responsibility of Mother's happiness on my shoulders, at the same time continuing lessons with Mademoiselle with whom I did not agree. I shall never forget the agony I suffered; the dreadful feeling of unfitness and incompetency for the work which was forced upon me, and at the same time feeling my health diminishing every day. After that, that period between Father's return and going to Bournemouth was a black blank. No health, no God, no love, nothing but moping, wounded vanity, desperation. . . . That was indeed a wretched time, much more wretched than the preceding autumn, when at least, though I might not have been happy, I felt that I was doing my best to fulfil difficult duties. God grant that this thirteen weeks of peace and study be a blessing to me and a preparation for the perplexing duties of a come-out girl.

There are, in fact, no 'lie' crosses in the succeeding entries.

*4 October*. [Stirling House?]
Lied again today. I will make a practice of noting these lies, by putting a cross for every one to the day of the month. I am quite convinced that it is a most disagreeable habit.

*10 October.* [Stirling House]
Another week passed. I have read only pretty well. I suppose I cannot expect to do much in the way of quiet study. But let me devote my energy to becoming truthful, and to guarding against that feeling of satisfaction and vanity, and to speaking not for effect but from conviction. Oh! that by the next time I take the sacrament I may be more truthful and less vain.

*9 December.* [Stirling House]
The reason why I tell so many stories is pride and vanity. It is very often from the wish that people may think me or my people better in one way or another that I exaggerate so fearfully. I see clearly that if one wishes really to become truthful one must seek to be so in one's smallest actions and words. . . .

All through the autumn Beatrice was troubled by the doctrine of the Atonement, which she found both irrational and immoral, and on 17 December she had a long religious discussion with Mr Eliot in which she felt 'at a decided disadvantage' though she stuck to her point. The matter continued to trouble her after her return to Standish.

*17 December.* [Stirling House]
I hope when I return home I shall not lose the little earnestness I have gained; that I shall be diligent in the study of religion. I do not want to 'come out', and I hope I shall have enough determination and firmness to carry my point. The family does not really want another come-out member; they are almost too many as it is. I wish my aim in life to be the understanding and acting up to religion. Before I can enter society with advantage I must conquer two great faults, love of admiration and untruth, and I must become a little more settled in my religious belief.

∽ 1876 ∾

Beatrice made a few diary entries in 1876. She decided, after all, to 'come out' that summer. 'I joined my sisters in the customary pursuits of girls of our class,' she wrote in her autobiographical *My Apprenticeship* fifty years afterwards, 'riding, dancing, flirting and dressing-up, an existence without settled occupation or personal responsibility, having for its end nothing more remote than elaborately expensive opportunities for getting married.'

With this round of 'restless and futile activities', she said, she lost her feeble hold on orthodox Christianity: 'the inevitable reaction in self-disgust and corresponding depreciation of other people's motives did not constitute a fruitful soil for religious experience'. Her intellectual curiosity led her to study the religions of the Far East and the 'religion of science'.

*16 August.* [Standish?]
I have indeed altered my religious belief this last six months to an extent I should never have thought possible a year ago. I see now that the year I spent at Bournemouth I was vainly trying to smother my instinct of truth in clinging to the old faith. And now that I have shaken off the chains of the beautiful old faith, shall I rise to something higher or shall I stare about me like a newly liberated slave, unable to decide which way to go, and perhaps the worse for being freed from the service of a kind of master? Do I look on death and trouble with less calmness than I used?

## ∽ 1877 ∾

There were also few entries for 1877, apart from many pages of notes on Buddhism and the ideas of Herbert Spencer. Beatrice was influenced at this time by Brian Houghton Hodgson (1800–94), an Oriental scholar who had served in India and retired to Gloucestershire; and at this time Spencer was the dominant intellectual influence in the Potter household.

*19 March.* [Standish]
As for my religious opinions they are as Mr Spencer's *Social Statics* left them. I am afraid I may say that I have no religion whatever, for I have not yet grasped the religion of science. Of one thing I am quite certain, that no character is perfect without religion.

Harriet Martineau (1802–76) was a well-known novelist, moralist and traveller whose autobiography was published posthumously in 1877. She had a strict Unitarian upbringing, was strongly evangelical in outlook, and translated Comte's *Philosophical Positivism* in 1853, thus introducing his ideas into English liberal circles. Her exemplary stories illustrating the principles of political economy did something to popularize the 'gloomy science'. Beatrice saw Harriet Martineau as a necessitarian, a person who believes that all events, including human actions, are predetermined, whether by God, history, social or psychological circumstances; but as her *Biographical Sketches* (1876) make clear, she sought to tell what a man did and to describe the factors which shaped his personality while leaving room for moral judgements on his 'faults and foibles'.

*31 March.* [Standish?]

I have just finished Miss Martineau's autobiography. I do not agree with the very severe criticism passed on her by reviews. That she was self-centred, egotistical, I quite see, without much love in her character; that she looked at people through unloving spectacles, that she perceived their faults if anything sooner than their virtues, it is impossible to help remarking. But I believe notwithstanding she was a high-minded honourable woman with on the whole a just appreciation of men and ideas. I was struck particularly with what remarkable candour she describes her faults and her disagreeable and unlovable nature when a child – her nervous irritability when a woman. I believe her autobiography to give a faithful picture of her character with no false modesty about her talents and her achievement, and no false shame about her faults and weaknesses, which she, as a necessarian, considered inevitable. She seems to have left her mind and character to be dissected as she did her brain, for the good of science and truth. . . . The picture of her old age and waiting for death is full of hope and true religion. Her life, unlike most lives, begins with piteous whining at the unhappiness and wickedness of the world and intense egotism, and ends in a song of praise and an ignoring of self in the wider interests of humanity. Altogether, even keeping in view her many faults, her life was a noble one, devoted to what she believed her duty; the search for truth, and the unfearful propagation of it. Miss Martineau's *Autobiography* has given me a higher idea of the religion of science. . . .

Is it any good registering good intentions? Perhaps as a wholesome warning when one finds them unfulfilled.

I do intend trying to lead a more serious life, so that when I have to give up my existence I may feel that I have done my little towards fulfilling the law of progress. I do not wish either to be quite idle. I wish to work at and to get on with logic. Knowledge gives happiness and I believe power to render other lives happier. I only wish I had more sympathy with other people, more energy and more love. One hardly feels that one has a right to live if one is not fulfilling some duty towards humanity. As it may be interesting in future years to know what my religious convictions were at nineteen, I might as well state roughly what are my vague beliefs. I do not see that there is sufficient

25

evidence either for believing in a future life or in a personal Creator of the universe. I at present believe (by no means without inward fear at my audacity) that Christianity is in no way superior in kind, though in degree, to the other great religions, and that it was a natural product of the human mind, that Christianity is not the highest religion conceivable. That the idea of working out your own salvation, of doing good and believing blindly in order to arrive at eternal bliss is, through its intense selfishness, an immoral doctrine. I believe also that, as soon as our religion becomes truly unselfish, enormous interest in speculations as to the future existence of the individual will die out. But what seems to me clear is that we are at a very early period of man's existence and that we have only just arrived at the true basis of knowledge: and that bright and glorious days are in store for our successors on this earth.

*13 September. Moorcroft* [near The Argoed]
This book, begun as a diary, ends in extracts and abstracts of books. One's interest in one's own character ceases to be so absorbing as one grows in knowledge. Christianity certainly made one more egotistical, more desirous to secure one's own salvation. Whatever may be the faults or rather the shortcomings of the new religion it accomplishes one thing; it removes the thoughts from that wee bit of the world called Self to the great whole. The individual has no part in it; it is more than silent as to his future existence. Man sinks down to comparative insignificance. He is removed in degree but not in kind from the mere animal and vegetable. In truth it requires a noble nature to profess with cheerfulness this religion, and the ideal it presents to us is far higher than any presented by the great religions of the world. . . .

## VOLUME 2

Towards the end of the century there was a vogue for surrogate religions, quasi-religious sects and secular organizations which retained vestigial religious rituals, such as sermonizing and hymn-singing. There was also a growing interest in exotic and esoteric faiths, in which Beatrice shared, and she began her second volume with some thoughts on Indian philosophy and religion. She also showed a passing interest in Spiritualism – there were table-rapping sessions with Theresa, Maggie and her mother. 'We quite came to the conclusion that as far as our experience went Spiritualism was nothing more than some kind of semi-conscious action of the brain,' she concluded on 15 November. She also made notes on Herbert Spencer's *First Principles* (1862) and George Sand's *Histoire de ma Vie* (1854).

*15 December.* [Standish]

Mr Spencer's *First Principles* has had certainly a very great influence on my feelings and thoughts. It has made me feel so happy and contented. . . . I do admire that still reverent consciousness of the great mystery, that fearless conviction that no advance in science can take away the beautiful and elevating consciousness of something greater than humanity. One has always feared that when the orthodox religion vanished, no beauty, no mystery would be left, nothing but what could and would be explained and become commonplace, but instead of that each new discovery of science will increase our wonder at the Great Unknown and our appreciation of the Great Truth.

## ∽ 1878 ∾

*8 March.* [Standish]

The religion of science has its dark side. It is bleak and dreary in sorrow and ill-health. And to those whose lives are one continual suffering it has but one word to say – suicide. If you cannot bear it any longer, and if no ties of duty turn you from extinguishing that little flame of your existence, depart in peace, cease to exist. It is a dreadful thought. It can never be the religion of a 'suffering humanity'. The time may come, and I believe will come, when human life will be sufficiently happy and full to be unselfish. But there are long ages yet to be passed, and generations of men will still cry in their misery for another life to compensate for their life-long sorrow and suffering.

In June, Beatrice went with Mary and Arthur Playne and their adopted daughter Polly on an extended tour of Germany and Hungary. They were away from England for five months.

*4 June.* [Ems?]

After 24 hours' tedious whirling over sea and land we arrived at Ems, a pretty bright little town of hotels and boarding houses, surrounded by wooded mountains very similar to the Wye hills on a larger scale.

After three days' experience of the life, I decide in my own mind that it is very dull, and I am a wee bit sorry that I have left London town, but I console myself with the reflection that it is better for my bodily health and perhaps for my morale. The life is wanting in aim, and I feel a long way on the road to absolute boredom. Perhaps the German lessons will become an aim, and I may find some congenial spirit to help me out of my boredom. . . . Mary is not an interesting companion; she has really thought little, and felt little. Polly is an attractive child but very uninteresting, perhaps from extreme shyness and reserve, or from genuine dullness, I cannot at present judge. And of course Arthur is out of the question.

*15 June.* [Ems?]
Our life here is a modest one, but with the German lessons as a *raison d'être* pleasant, if one only had tolerable health. The people we know at present are decidedly dull; I don't know how the Americans will turn out. Mr Barclay has brought a certain amount of fun into the *ménage*. Yesterday evening we spent at Dr Geiser's drinking and smoking and talking and laughing in a very rowdy way. I had got up a mock flirtation with Mr Barclay, which Mary thought proper to reprove, in not the gentlest of language. However, she was right; one can't be too careful in this comical existence where half of one's time must be spent in considering and working for the good opinion of the little world mannikins that surround us. Thank Heavens one has books – a society whose good opinion you need never consult, and which is always there and infinitely varied. *Les Misérables* is a glorious drama. The description of the Bishop and of the criminal is simply splendid. . . . And then he is such a *pure* writer – there is no hidden sensuality. He describes vice not as a cool and somewhat enjoying observer like George Sand, but as a great pitying moralist. . . .

*3 July. Marienburg* [North Holland]
A diary is a blessing when one has no companion; I mean no one with whom one is intimate. I feel more and more the impossibility of making a real friend of Mary. Even with Polly, who is not interesting and whom one feels obliged to be careful with, I feel more at home and more inclined to be communicative. We arrived here on Tuesday. It has poured ever since. The house is delightful, especially for hot weather, but the inhabitants are certainly a rum lot. They consist of a few nondescript ladies apparently unattached and from thirty to fifty

years, four or five elderly Dutch and German commercial travellers, rather dirty, a weak young man, a gay young man of the behind-the-counter style, an unfortunate creature (has been a drunkard (?) and I should think will be a madman) who, by the by, we met literally howling, rushing along a dark and lonely path in our first evening walk; and a couple of married people. . . .

I think on the whole at present I have settled that I am sorry to miss the Season. That the pleasure of seeing new countries does not compensate for the intimate companionship of one's family and the society of London. On the other hand, one must remember that, though I feel inclined for gaiety now and sorry on the whole to have missed it, yet it would most probably have knocked me up. If I choose to be self-denying I can make it well worth my while to have missed one short Season. And what with the German and sketching I can employ my time very advantageously. But health, and goodness, must be my aim.

*15 July.* [Boppard, on the Rhine]
The last two or three days have been very amusing. We have made friends with all the inhabitants. It has been an odd experience, chumming with a set of people from all nations and classes. They certainly have very much better manners and understand sociability much better than the English. There is a nice feeling of unexclusive-ness and general goodwill. . . . The 'howling man' has turned out to be a Baron who has spent the last year or two in water-cure establishments with an English friend, evidently a sort of keeper. I made his acquaintance yesterday. He is a perfect gentleman with a certain amount of cultivation, but I should think has led a fast life and brought on his complaint by drink. . . .

Mary and I are very good friends now that I let her lead the conversation and follow. In order to get on with her you must be content to talk of nothing but personalities, particularly about those individuals who are nearest to her. We have really led such different lives, have lived in such a completely different atmosphere, that it is impossible for us to talk on any serious subject. When I attempted to do it, we disagreed, and disagreed without understanding each other. Mary's great fault is jealousy and vanity. She has a grudge against 'intellectual people' and 'learning' because she feels that she is 'inferior' or, rather, that they think her inferior. She has the same grudge against the family, particularly Mother. In spite of that, she is a

29

charming woman, and most kind and considerate. She is also a clever, shrewd woman. Had she been led by a fine strong character and brain instead of leading a weak one, she would probably have lost that self-complacent jealousy which prevents her from taking a true and just view of the people surrounding her.

It was a long and leisurely tour, taking in Wiesbaden, Nuremberg, Vienna, Budapest, Prague, Dresden and Berlin, which Beatrice chronicled in a conventional travel-diary. Carrie Darling was the governess for the Playne children. It was with this 'intensely lovable' and well-educated woman, Beatrice recalled, that she formed her first friendship outside her family. See the diary entry for 30 September 1889.

*9 November.* [Wiesbaden]
Our party is broken up. Arthur and Mary left this morning and, as is usual where the feeling has not been quite what it should be, when one has parted one begins to regret not having made more of the opportunities for friendship. I got on admirably the last three months with Arthur and Mary, but I suppose it was impossible that I should become really intimate with the latter. I suppose I had nothing to offer her and she nothing to give. On the whole, this trip to Germany was a mistake, that is to say from a worldly point of view – but still the last two months I have enjoyed, and I was wise to stay once I had missed the London Season. At any rate I can read German quite easily.

Poor Arthur has been miserable and Mary has not enjoyed herself nearly as much as she expected. How she can be happy with such an inferior man I cannot understand. Still, he is a most affectionate devoted husband and I suppose love covers a multitude of sins.

I wonder what sort of woman Polly will turn out – she has a small nature, but what is there is good. She is so honest and straightforward and there is a good deal of affectionate faithfulness behind her still awkward manner. It will be the making of her having a strong vigorous nature like Miss Darling's as a companion.

Miss Darling is a dear little woman, a person it is impossible not to be intimate with. She is so thoroughly frank about herself, and is quite destitute of touchiness, or she manages to hide it completely. Dear Mary, she is a sweet unselfish woman, and has wonderful pluck. I am afraid I did not appreciate her sufficiently but I suppose it could not be helped and that it came from some unalterable fault in my character.

## ∽ 1879 ∾

After Beatrice returned, she went up to stay at Rusland Hall, to the west of Lake Windermere, and spent much of the time reading Hesiod and other Greek authors, as well as Goethe and Ruskin.

### 30 March. Rusland Hall

Another three months have passed, and on the whole not very happily for me. The first two months after my return I was altogether wrong – and the quiet and perfectly lonely life here was not calculated to shake me right again. The old story of anaemia; want of employment, which makes life almost torture, a silent misery, all the more painful because apparently causeless. But the last month has been spent very happily with my dear Goethe and my dearest old Father in quiet reading and long rambling walks in this lovely country. I feel I am not appreciating this time of perfect freedom and without care. I am longing for something else, which when it comes will bring with it real troubles and perhaps real misery, and then I shall look back on these days, in a happy home, with envy and regret that I had not been more content to enjoy the simple pleasures of living.

The one thought that I have been pondering over is: does my want of happiness come from my want of belief in the old faith which has helped so many thousands along this weary way? Or is it simply physical melancholy which attaches itself to my pet grievance, and which, if I had been without education and culture, would have attached itself to some passing trifle? And when one looks around and sees some good Christians fussing and fretting about little holes in their purses, little disappointments to their vanity and their greed, one begins to think that each human being has his share of 'distemper', but perhaps the patient is on the whole happier who has it out in surface irritations, than he who believes it to be a sign of an inward and incurable complaint, peculiar not only to himself alone but to the whole human race.

I cannot help having a half-conscious conviction that, if the human race is mortal, if its existence is without aim, if that existence is to end, at however remote a period, in a complete dissolution, like that which overcomes the individual, then life indeed is not worth living. . . .

Thomas de Quincey (1785–1859), author of *Confessions of an Opium Eater* (1821), and Hartley Coleridge (1796–1849), the poet and eldest son of Samuel Taylor Coleridge, both stayed at Knab's Cottage, close to William Wordsworth's home at Rydal Mount, in the Lake District.

*8 September.* [Grasmere]
It was last autumn when I was in Germany that Maggie first proposed that we should spend a week or so together at a little cottage on Grasmere and the fourth of this month found us comfortably settled in Knab's Cottage, Rydal, the former abode of de Quincey and Hartley Coleridge. We came armed with books, sketching materials, but we have not had much inclination to improve our minds, and we are hardly advanced enough in art to do much at the very quick sketching required in touring about. The 7th was a glorious day. . . . Today was not so bright though Maggie and I enjoyed it sitting on a wall on the hill dividing Rydal from Grasmere, attempting to draw in the magnificent outlines of the hills at the head of Grasmere.

## VOLUME 3

*30 October.* [Rusland]
'Man goes through his short life with no more knowledge than is comprised in his own slender fraction of observation and experience. He struggles in vain to find out and explain the totality but neither eye, nor ear, nor reason, can assist him.' Fragment of Empedocles.

Beatrice started this volume of her diary with twenty pages of notes on Greek history taken mainly from the great work by George Grote (1794–1871). Grote was a banker, Radical politician, rationalist and classical scholar, who was one of the committee of eminent utilitarians who founded University College, London, in 1828. Elected for the City of London after the Reform Act of 1832, his multi-volume history of Greece was published in the ten years following 1846.

She then included an essay on 'The Character of Richard II as developed by Shakespeare' which was 'written in competition with Maggie for a prize of six pairs of gloves'. In the event, 'Father professed himself so delighted with both our essays that he presented each of us with £1.' Maggie left on a trip to Egypt with Kate and Herbert Spencer.

*8 November. Rusland*
Maggie left this morning. I feel her loss terribly. We are so perfectly

intimate and at one with each other, and when I am with her I want no other society. We have had a very happy time here together – have read, talked, walked and slept together, and now she is gone it is a dreary blank. I do hope the dear girl will enjoy herself and come back much happier and more contented with life as she is likely to get it. I must go on plodding towards some goal that may never be reached. Ah me! Courage, mon ami, courage. . . .

The Athenian History is so full of interest that it is impossible to know where to pause and mark, learn and digest – and yet one feels obliged to hurry on. Life is short and art is long (as Goethe says) yet I know no more painful feeling than this striving after all the knowledge that is essential to the comprehension of some particular subject, combined with a desire to shut one's eyes and ears to the non-essential, or, rather, the non-characteristic, for as [John] Stuart Mill says, we only conceive a thing by its difference from other things. And this of course is all the more difficult studying Grecian history when, like me, one has no other historical pictures stored away in one's brain with which to compare it.

Beatrice was much affected by reading Goethe's autobiographical *Wilhelm Meister*. It was her interest in drawing and watercolour that led her to a study of John Ruskin.

### 14 December. Rusland

This autumn has been a very happy one for me. And the secret of my happiness has been plenty of occupation of a varied description. Perhaps before my health disabled me from much exertion, and I look forward with a sort of dread to the effect the Standish climate and water may have; but I do believe, independently of being in better health, I have started on a brighter path of existence; that I have gained immensely by taking up drawing and music with a spirit of love instead of with a spirit of jealous ambition; and this I owe to Ruskin and to Goethe. . . .

Some parts of this autumn have been very sweet. We three sisters have seen much of each other, and Maggie and I particularly have had a perfect communion of pursuits and ideas. We had a delightful little trip among our sublime little hills, and read through the first two volumes of *Modern Painters* together, and this little experience has inspired us with a wish to go sketching and reading tours together, should we remain lonely spinsters. . . .

One thing is clear. Goethe wishes to impress on his reader the

33

advantage of liberty, of unrestrained liberty in thought and deed. I do not mean licentiousness, i.e. giving free scope to your passions: this involves an enslavement of the intellect or, rather, the cessation of its rightful activity. But Goethe would go on the principle – both in the education of children and in life – that it is better to develop the whole of your nature, looking upwards to a noble ideal, and allowing perhaps some ugly weeds to grow, than to repress the good with the bad. . . . In life you should seek a really congenial career, as a life occupation, and then you should keep your heart and mind open to the outer world. . . . Until you have found this career you should wander up and down regarding no place as too low and dirty, no society too licentious or too frivolous – perhaps in the lowest society you may light on some human soul who will impart to you some vital truth. . . .

I have enjoyed the country immensely. I shall never forget the lovely walks on those moors, with the beautiful effects of cloud, mist, rainbow and sunshine on the distant hills, lakes and valleys, and the cold and drear-looking foregrounds so rich and stern in their colouring. It is past ten – the owl is hooting, the fire is dying and a comfortable bed awaits me. I cannot close this without a feeling of gratitude for all the blessings of health and strength, intellectual and artistic enjoyments, I have received these last months. I can only feel gratitude and reverence, I know not to whom.

## VOLUME 4
### ∽ 1880 ∾

Beatrice wrote 'Book of Thoughts and Days' on the first page of her diary for 1880, and many of the entries were simply notes on her readings in Greek history and philosophy, or comments on the six-month visit to Italy which she began in October of that year after the marriage of her sister Margaret to Henry Hobhouse. The trip to Italy re-inforced the ambivalence of her feelings about religious mysticism. An elderly couple, Mr and Mrs Cobb, and a Mr Watson were travelling companions for the first part of the trip. She then met Theresa and the Hobhouses, who were spending their honeymoon in Italy. During the winter of 1880–1 she was ill in Rome with congestion of the lungs. She joined her parents on the Riviera in the spring.

*20 September.* [Standish?]
The London Season passed with a happy result, and Theresa and I are

left to divide the honours of the Potter sisterhood! I, with my little plan of Italy, or the less brilliant alternative of German literature and philosophy.

### 23 October. The Italian Trip

The first day of our travel has not been over-pleasant – a heavy sea out, a long day spent at the Lord Warden [hotel] watching it from a smelly coffee-room. At present I get on well with the party, though the only one I am really attracted to in the least is Mrs Cobb, who is a really genuine motherly woman, with an honest straight-forward mind and a warm heart. Mr Cobb, I am uncertain whether I shall get to like. There is something mediocre about him, though he is accomplished and above the average in cultivation. But his cultivation seems to me to consist in the knowledge of facts, and not in the appreciation of the spirit. . . . However, they are taking me to Rome so I must not be over-critical.

### 24 October. [Florence?]

A glimpse of Paris – a perfect modern city. . . . The morning we spent in Notre-Dame. It a little disappointed me. The building is beautiful, but after the romantic vision I had formed of it, from Victor Hugo's description, it seemed more like other cathedrals, and not so devotional in its feeling as some. The aisles are beautiful, and the apse – in fact the construction seemed to me perfect. . . . I was struck very much by Paris itself with its peculiar and unique charm. So much that one had felt about the French character was here pictured. . . . Our journey in the *wagon lit* was not over-comfortable, and the Alps did not quite come up to my expectations, or perhaps I was hardly in the right humour to enjoy them. . . .

I can't help smiling at finding myself settled down with this very elderly trio, with none of whom have I had the slightest previous connection. They are none of them persons to whom I should naturally have taken. They are exceedingly kind, and I think they like me, which is pleasant, but I do not feel as if I were one of them.

That feeling has disappeared. One cannot be in the constant companionship of kindly people, with sincere and warm-hearted natures, without a tie springing up between you and them. . . . We were only one evening at Bologna, spent in walking about the streets. It was the first Italian town in which one felt the Italian mediaevalism, as one feels the German mediaevalism at Nuremberg – arcaded houses and palaces lighted dimly with every now and then a dark courtyard or alley with one red light, shining out mysteriously.

The journey to Florence would have been delightful had not I been troubled with a hard boil at the back of my head and a good deal of vanity in my heart! The view from San Miniato was too glorious for expression, and as I shall return to Florence I shall leave it. Perugia was intoxicating, another glorious view over the Apennines far away to their snowy summits. . . . The town itself is perfect as a specimen of a mediaeval fortified town. . . .

*7 November.* [Rome]
The journey to Rome was not pleasant for me nor the first few days there, but the idea of being actually in the Eternal City sustained me through the worst of it. On Sunday we had a delicious drive out on the Campagna. The view looking towards the Alban Hills, with the broken line of aqueduct arches and stone pines, was very lovely. There was a sweet, soft feeling in the air, the birds were singing, butterflies flying, and flowers blooming. Yet we were surrounded by the tombs of Roman, Jew and Christian. In their great city, crowded with the memories and memorials of bygone worlds, the great mystery of the why and the wherefore seems ever more pressing. . . .

*8 November.* [Rome]
A long morning in the Vatican gallery of sculptures. Much time of course was spent in finding out what was what! . . . Returning from the Vatican, Mr Cobb and I ran into St Peter's and had just one glimpse of the interior. There is a solemnity in its gorgeousness, but surely it is not Christian? . . .

*9 November.* [Rome]
This morning we spent on the Palatine. It is difficult for an ignoramus to make much of this mass of the ruins. . . . From the Palatine hill I realized for the first time the position of ancient Rome and its seven hills. . . . The most striking features in the Roman architecture are those wonderful arches, so imposing in their simplicity. The Coliseum is grand as a mass of curves, but the proportion of the upper part to the lower seems to me heavy. There seems to me in all the ruins a great want of artistic imagination. . . .

The Barberini and Borghese palaces have some beautiful pictures, but one has to seek for them among many utterly inferior works. . . .

In the Barberini there are two world-famed pictures neither of which should I care to possess. Raphael's Fornarina and Guido Reni's Beatrice Cenci. The Fornarina is a brazen faced woman – one does not know how far it may have been ruined by restoration. The Beatrice Cenci is very disappointing. . . . In the Borghese, the *one* picture is Titian's so-called Divine and Human Love. There is nothing beautiful in the spirit, or much in its motive, but it is simply divine in its colouring. . . .

*13 November.* [Rome]
A glorious day on the Campagna among the ruins of the aqueduct. I spent most of the day sketching, and am not certain whether I should not have done better to have simply 'absorbed', but so much of my life is devoted to that pursuit that one likes to take an opportunity for 'doing'.

*Sunday. 14 November* [Rome]
I cannot write down what I felt on this Sunday morning watching the silent mass in St Peter's. Perhaps there was a good deal of mere emotion in it but it made me look back with regret on those days when I could pray in all sincerity of spirit to my Father in Heaven. I tried afterwards to work out in my mind the theory of the Roman Catholic faith as it might be accepted by the agnostic. Human nature is a circumstance with which we have to deal. It seems to be divided into two parts, the emotional and the intellectual.

My intellectual or logical faculty drives me to the conclusion that, outside the knowledges of the relative or phenomenal, I know nothing except perhaps that there must be an absolute, a something which is unknowable. But whether the very fact that it is unknowable does not prevent me from considering it, or thinking about it, or contemplating it, is a question which Mr Spencer's logic has not set at rest. My reason forces me to a purely negative conclusion, but I see very darkly before me and feel that my logical faculty is very insufficient to the task I set it. Nor do I feel that its present decision is a final one. But I possess another faculty, the emotional, which is the dominant spirit in all my better and nobler moments. This spirit unceasingly insists that there is something above and around us which is worthy of absolute devotion and devout worship. Sometimes it presents this something in the formula of 'the great mystery' and here it has attempted to join hands with my logical faculty, but this last persists that the unknowable has no qualities and cannot be an object for feeling. Then it points to a great ideal; Plato's idea of the Beautiful or Perfect, but this idea, though it may be a subject for contemplation, cannot be an object of worship. Lastly there is the great Father, and Creator, the perfect object for devotion. He is the God of Christianity, not a far-off personality, but united to man through His incarnation. This God is worshipped by Protestant and Catholic alike.

The Protestant, however, declares virtually the supremacy of his own reason. . . . But the Catholic Church deals differently with the question. . . . The Church declares herself to be the supreme reason. She does not ask you to interpret her, she provides her own interpreter in the priest, and suits her doctrine to the individual and the time. . . . Could not the agnostic, if he felt that his nature was not sufficiently developed to live without an emotional religion, could he not renounce his freedom to reason on that one subject, and submit to the authority of the great religious body on the subject of religion, as he would accept that of the great scientific body on the subject of science, even if in the latter case his own reason should lead him to different conclusions, on any phenomena of nature, to those arrived at by scientific men?

Add to this the beautiful Catholic ritual, and the temptation to commit this intellectual (and perhaps moral) suicide is strong, to one whose life without a religious faith is unbearable. How long this peace would last, how soon you would wake up to the mass of falsehood and corruption around you, belongs to another chapter, which we will hope is not the record of the experiences of the majority of those human souls caught in the net of the immortal Peter.

*21 November.* [Rome?]
Our party has broken up and the first chapter of my Italian trip is finished! It seems but yesterday since we four were feeling miserable together in that very stuffy hotel at Dover. Then I thought – I shall never become quite intimate with the Cobbs. . . . But when I got to really know them I felt my own inferiority to them in genuineness and simple-mindedness. . . . With Mr Cobb I soon became fast friends. It is always so much easier to get on with men; they seldom criticize a girl who is willing to make herself pleasant to them. And then their wider knowledge of human nature makes them more interesting as companions, and enables one to be freer in one's conversation with them. With a highly respectable matron I always feel rather concili-

atory and frightened lest I should let loose any of my bohemian sentiments. That feeling of constraint on my part soon passed away with Mrs Cobb when I felt that she was certain that I was not insincere. . . .

I feel, on this eve of separation, that they will be friends for life – at least it shall not be my fault if we lose sight of each other. One can never have too many true friends in one's own class, even if they are not so attractive or as well bred, as bohemian friends.

*28 November.* [Florence]
Settled with Theresa in this very airy house, looking over the golden and brown-tiled roofs of Florence. . . . Henry and Margaret are here, silently happy. One would hardly know her to be the same woman as the discontented, original, interesting young person who used to be so fascinating to me. As these books are more or less an autobiography I ought to have mentioned the great influence she has had on my life, for good chiefly, but also for evil. With a powerful nature like hers, her influence on a weaker one was complete, even when one secretly knew that she was mistaken. But on the whole, her principles of life were strong and wise, and she had a vigorous and straight intellect. Now she has found in Henry Hobhouse just the man to complete her, a man utterly without worldliness or power to compromise with evil. . . .

While I am in Florence I shall try as far as I am able to make a systematic study of the great painters; taking notes on each picture as I see it, and when I know it sufficiently to have digested it, I shall just put down what I feel and think about the author. . . .

Beatrice made notes on the works of Giotto, Botticelli, Mantegna, Leonardo da Vinci and Raphael.

*19 December.* [Florence]
The time has flown while we have been at Florence. I have hardly enjoyed it as much as I ought to have done; my health has been bad, and I have not been able to give the enthusiasm and time to the glorious works of art that I should if I had been quite up to the mark. . . . This is the close of the second chapter of my Italian trip. There have been a few tedious hours of absolute incapability, but it has been on the whole a happy life. . . . Rome again is before me, with its entangled net of interests and associations.

## ᔕ 1881 ᔐ

Margaret Hobhouse was already pregnant. Her son Stephen was born on 5 August.

*22 January.* [Rome]
Our stay in Rome up to now has hardly been very pleasant. There have been days of great enjoyment and a great freedom from any unhappiness during the whole time, but the Roman climate is detestable, varying daily, almost hourly, between depressing heat and intense cold. Xmas week, with all the museums closed and those dismal farces of church services, does not leave a happy impression, especially as Maggie was seedy and miserable, the natural result of the conditions of married existence. It was painful to see her so poorly, and now since her marriage, since the necessary break in our absolute intimacy it is rather painful to me to be with her. She was such a complete companion to me, and as such she is not to be replaced. It is rather bitter at first, however glad one may be for her sake, and one does not care to have the remembrance of an irretrievably past friendship forced upon one by her presence.

It is difficult to remember what one *has* done, one has seen so little for the last months. A whole fortnight in bed, and a not sufficiently complete recovery to promise much for the next fortnight!

Alice Ottley (1840–1912) was the devout headmistress of the Worcester High School for Girls for almost thirty years, and an opponent of ungentlewomanly innovations in education.

*2 February.* [Rome]
Alas, we must away. This wretched climate has undone me, and the only thing is flight. Poor Theresa who has been a most devoted nurse is torn away from unfinished sightseeing. She is a dear, sweet, unselfish creature, and I feel quite remorseful for being such an unlucky travelling companion. The time for me, chiefly spent in the queer-shaped room, has been by no means without its charm. There have been hours of depression and many of physical discomfort, but I have never had that utter, hopeless melancholy, which has come upon me when ill at home. Whether this is due to the difference of lung and liver complaints, or whether the happy change comes from a new faith

that has crept into my heart I cannot tell. Certain it is, that life seems nobler and more worth living, even if one rests incapable of much action. It is impossible for a woman to live in agnosticism. That is a creed which is only the product of one side of our nature, the purely rational, and ought we persistently to refuse authority to that other faculty which George Eliot calls the emotive thought? . . .

The *pension* life has been irksome, in its constant presentation of different types of inferior English people, but even in this it has been rather an amusing experience. Then the Ottleys were different from any people one has yet come across. Miss Ottley was an almost complete realization of the Christian ideal. Her life had been a constant self-sacrifice to others. From her childhood she had worked in order that her brothers should have a fair start, and now she is going to give herself entirely to a 'religious life' in its most beautiful sense – a life of continual communion with a spiritual ideal, and of continual work for others. She is one of those rare women, who seem to be perfect human beings; a possibility denied to the masculine nature? She was a revelation to me of the vitality still to be found in Catholic Christianity, and her companionship and the insight I had into her past and present life quite compensated for the disappointment of being incapacitated for sightseeing.

There was another mind that I really became better acquainted with through this illness – George Eliot's. Perhaps it was her noble influence which made me feel happier and more contented. In her stories of life, she always takes the deep earnest view, untouched by cynicism. I know no author who is so sad and so uncynical – consequently her sadness is ennobling and not discouraging. It is the pettiness and smallnesses, the little lyings and deceptions, which create the most real tragedies around us, but then there is much that is great and beautiful in human nature. She believes in man, but not in his happiness? All the nobler natures are struggling both within and without – it is only the baser ones that are continually placid. She is always in her works provoking the question – why this noble suffering, for what end if it does not result in happiness? And to this question she gives no answer but an assertion that it is right.

*Daniel Deronda* interested me deeply, because in it she seems to express her last thoughts, the conclusions of her experience of life. One sees from it the preference she gives to emotive over purely rational thought, and also her conception of the ideal human being. . . . Daniel Deronda has no real existence but in her attempt

41

she gives us elements of real human greatness, elements of the really perfect character which are ignored by the ordinary Englishman. Then in this book George Eliot shows almost a naïve belief in human nature which most English readers would call morbid idealism. All Daniel Deronda's relationships are ideal and involve a simplicity of heart which few believe in as existing in the intelligent human creature, certainly not in the male! . . .

Now before I finish this third chapter of Experiences in Italy, one word about that Rome, so fascinating and so depressing. It is impossible to describe —!

*20 March.* [Rome]
Leave Rome in peace. It is too painful to think of all those delights, half seen and not appreciated. Since that, Theresa and I have had a black time. Poor girl, how irritating to have her whole year spoilt by an incapable sister, but it will soon be over, this long stay in this most *ennuyant* of places.

I have given myself up to Balzac for the last five weeks, which has perhaps not contributed to my happiness. . . . He is an utter cynic and complete disbeliever in the progress of human nature. . . . I have never read such disgustingly true analysis of mean, base thought and feeling. Perhaps his most revolting type is the *célibataire*, . . . . especially women. Her only nobility is in self-immolation to her lover and child – if these two feelings are undeveloped there is no chance for her. And in his analysis of these two feelings, it is purely the instinctive and not the spiritual love that he describes. . . . French society, if Balzac is as true a portrait painter as one would judge from the manner of the pictures, must be a sink of impurity and dirt. . . .

*28 April.* [San Remo]
Father arrived at San Remo and found us in not a very happy condition. The incapability produced by the relaxing climate, the deadly *ennui* from the absence of any occupation and of sympathetic companionship had forced me into an abnormal condition of body and soul out of which I have not yet emerged, nor shall emerge till I recover my moral balance by being forced out of myself.

It has been sadly disappointing, this finale of 'our trip in Italy', begun with so much enthusiasm and promise of interest and pleasure, and ending in ill-health and self-disgust, with increased estrangement between me and Mother. Too utterly discouraged to think with any hopefulness of the future – too pluckless to take up any pursuit – and yet suffering acutely from absence of any occupation and from irritating restlessness. However, all things must end, and misery after a certain time consumes itself or its subject.

Theresa is a sweet girl, full of bright sympathy, but lacking in judgement. For Rosy, in spite (perhaps because) of her nobility of character, I see rocks ahead if she does not quickly leave her state of spinsterhood on emerging from the schoolroom. Dearest old Father – it adds to one's self-disgust, the thought that some day one will regret bitterly having added to his worries. I write this, Friday evening, our last day in Italy after a fortnight spent at this most enchantingly lovely place – Ah me! . . .

### 14 May. Standish

The English country looks perfectly enchanting clothed in its spring loveliness. No foreign land, however exquisite it may be, can have the same power of calling out the sympathy and affection of the beholder as the native country with its manifold associations of happiness and struggles which sum up one's past existence. So entirely are we creatures of ideas and not of the senses.

All those miserable egotistical feelings are for the time fled, and, though from lack of health a not altogether pleasant prospect is before me, still I am determined to set again cheerfully to work and try to appreciate all the loveliness and beauty around me, hoping all the while to add to it instead of lessening it. With this immense amount of leisure, with this perfect comfort, one ought to add to one's power of usefulness when that usefulness comes to be tested. One has such a short term of life, it is hardly worthy to moan over the little imperfections of our lot when suffering and misery surround us.

The course of reading I propose for myself this autumn is English history and literature, with Shakespeare as the aim and centre. . . . Not a moment of my time, except what is required for positive rest, shall be unemployed – that is the true secret of happiness and freedom from egotistical broodings. No more foolish trifling with health, but a steady perseverance in the path of duty – alas! the only straight way left to us poor children of the nineteenth century.

### 12 June. [Standish?]

Quite recovered from the extraordinary state of mind into which I had fallen. A really pleasant four weeks at Standish and a complete re-establishment of pleasant relationship to Mother.

Theresa Potter was married to Alfred Cripps in the summer of 1881. Beatrice was reading W. E. H. Lecky's *History of European Morals* (1869).

*8 September. Rusland*
The last of the sisterhood, at least of those of my generation, pledged herself!

Dear Theresa, with her sweet sunny nature, never meant to live alone, or without devotion and love given and returned. Still it is sad this last final break-up of the home life with all its ups and downs, through which we have been loving companions – though our intimacy has not been so direct and unclouded as between Maggie and me.

Now I am left alone, with this 'problematical' younger sister. Shall I rise equal to the occasion, and casting aside all self-consciousness and miserable morbidity, make the best of the materials at hand for the good of all? As Mary says, it is on these occasions that the true stuff of a character is tested, whether it is one which moulds or is moulded by circumstances.

*12 September.* [Rusland]
Mr Spencer's visits always interest me, and leave me with new ideas and the clearing up of old ones. He leaves me too with a due realization of the poverty of my intellect and its incapability of dealing with most of the problems which are continually cropping up; the comparative uselessness of all my miserable little studies; and with the feeling too that I should do better to sacrifice all other aims to that of health. . . . One thing seems clear to me both from my own experience and from Mr Spencer's theoretical demonstration, that there is a fatal mistake being made in the 'improved education of women', in that it is a purely intellectual one, and restricted even in its intellectuality in as much as it neglects one great faculty of the intellect, the observation.

Also there seems to me little doubt but that women should have a real knowledge of the different branches of household work, at least for them to understand the difference between bad and good work, that they should be taught to apply *method* to the practical duties of life and not allowed to be content with covering the very slight demands made by society on their usefulness. But then comes the personal question – how am I to remedy this in myself, I who fully recognize the evil? I dislike all mechanical work and have an instinctive feeling that it is a waste of time. . . .

There has been another great deficiency in one's education – which is now past remedy – and that is the deficiency in the love of games and sport. One was so early imbued with utilitarianism of the more short-sighted kind that one never had the heart to employ oneself in any way which did not seem productive of some immediate benefit either to oneself or to others. . . .

These twenty-four years of my life now are nearly past and gone. I know now pretty clearly what I ought to *do* (though less than ever what I ought to think) and yet I cannot maintain my reason as the ruler of my nature, but am still constantly enslaved by instinct and impulse. What extraordinary blindness it is, which leads one for one moment to congratulate oneself on one's own little group of qualities and attainments. And yet, on the other hand, however one may blame oneself, has one the energy to do better – might it not be that this small allotment of energy cannot be used in all directions? Perhaps the whole question lies in the right choice of the direction! . . .

## VOLUME 5
## ᦕ 1882 ᦔ

Mary Booth (1847–1939) was a first cousin. Her mother was a sister of Richard Potter, and her father was a younger brother of the historian, Thomas Babington Macaulay (1800–59). Her husband, Charles Booth (1840–1916) did well in the shipping business at Liverpool before a crisis in physical and mental health made him turn away from his business career and use his capital to underwrite a seventeen-volume study of *The Life and Labour of the People in London. John Inglesant* by J. H. Shorthouse (1834–1903), published in 1881, was a best-selling psychological novel set in England during the civil war. Beatrice spent much of the winter reading Plato and copying passages into her diary.

*9 February.* [London]
The last six weeks spent in London with friends and sisters. The Booths' house dark, dull and stuffy and somewhat smelly, but the inmates exceedingly charming and lovable. Mary really a remarkable woman, with an unusual power of expression, and a well-trained and

cultivated mind. She makes one feel, in spite of her appreciative and almost flattering attitude, a 'very ignoramus'. To me there is a slight harshness in her literary judgements; they are too correct, too resting on authority and not the result of original thought. Perhaps it is this very orderliness of mind and deference to authority which makes her so attractive as a woman; and to this culture and polish of intellect add a deep vein of emotion, of almost passionate feeling.

Charlie Booth has a stronger and clearer reason, with a singular absence of bias and prejudice. It is difficult to discover the presence of any vice or even weakness in him. Conscience, reason, and dutiful affection, are his great qualities; what other characteristics he has are not to be observed by the ordinary friend. But he interests me as a man who has his nature completely under control, who has passed through a period of terrible illness and weakness, and who has risen out of it, uncynical, vigorous and energetic in mind and without egotism. Many delightful conversations I had with these two charming cousins, generally acting as a listening third to their discussions.

At their house I read *John Inglesant*, a most originally conceived book, with scenes and passages of great power. Especially interesting to me as realizing 'sacramental' Christianity, the phase of Christianity for which I have the most sympathy, the author having evidently experienced that striving after inward purity of heart and mind, the continual cleansing and keeping pure of the whole man, as a temple 'built unto God' and suited to His reception in the symbolical form of the supreme and divine sacrifice. Surely there are two ways of viewing the sacrifice of the Mass, one as an atonement to an exacting deity, the other as a grand symbolical expression of the greatest of human characteristics, the power of self-sacrifice in the individual for the good of the community.

If it were only possible for the priesthood to be pure, what an immense power the Roman Catholic Church would become. What a curious psychological fact is that great and mysterious joy in the prostration of soul and body before the symbol of infinite goodness uniting all individuals in one aspiration.

Beatrice's second cousin, Margaret Harkness (b. 1854) was related to her through Richard Potter's mother. They were on close terms when Beatrice first went to London. She was earning a precarious living as a free-lance writer under the pseudonym of 'John Law'; and her knowledge of East End life influenced Beatrice. She was an active socialist and feminist, and her radical friends included Eleanor Marx and Friedrich Engels, who praised 'the realistic truth' of *A City Girl*, published in 1887, which was the first of several social novels of indifferent literary quality. She broke with the labour movement in 1889, when she wrote *Captain Lobe*, a novel which presaged her conversion to the Salvation Army. She went to Australia soon afterwards and on to India. She wrote two travel books and a novel on Indian themes. Her last published book was *A Curate's Promise*, which appeared in 1921 with a preface by General Booth of the Salvation Army. R. S. Poole (1832–95) was an archaeologist and orientalist who was keeper of the coins at the British Museum. He wrote an introduction to *Assyrian Life and History* which Margaret Harkness published over her own name in 1883.

*13 February.* [Standish]

My stay with the Hobhouses was not a very fortunate one. . . . The old intimacy with Maggie is quite broken, but the breach has not resulted in bitterness of feeling, and a faithful affection may rise up from the ashes of the old intimacy. I shall never be really friends with Henry. He has not the gift of drawing out what is best in you, nor does he understand anyone's thoughts but his own. And this deficiency in him is at present acting like a wet blanket on Maggie's intellect. His own inferiority makes him disapprovingly suspicious of her great freedom, originality and variety of thought. His mind is better trained and better stocked than hers; this superiority he is conscious of, and she assents to it, but her greater superiority is not yet acknowledged by either. Until it is so she will limit the working of her mind to his power of appreciation.

By the time I left London I was rather weary of conversation and had a distaste for second-rate 'interesting people'. . . . Heaven preserve me from living any but a quiet home life, filled with wholesome work and simple pleasures, and well regulated for health of body and mind.

The little glimpses into the British Museum life through Maggie Harkness and the Pooles interested me. There you get real intellectual drudgery, and though the various curators with their various hobbies sometimes verge on boring you, there is a strong and refreshing flavour of earnestness and thoroughness in their conversation.

They are like the worms, who prepare the soil. Without the labour of these myriad literary and scientific human insects, the grander creations of intellectual life could scarce exist; the individual efforts of genius would not be connected one with the other, or result in addition to the great sum of human knowledge. And now here I am settled down again, for two months' quiet reading and enjoyment of the country, to fortify body and mind for the campaign of the London Season.

Lawrencina Potter died unexpectedly on 13 April. Margaret Harkness, who had some training as a nurse, was called to help in her last illness, when she was brought back from the Argoed to die at Standish. She was suffering from pleurisy and kidney failure.

[Undated note.] *Mother's Last Illness*
On Thursday, 6 April, Kate received a telegram from Father asking her to meet them at Gloucester and if they were not there to go on to Monmouth. When she had left I had a glorious walk through the young larch and round by the park, standing for some time under those beeches with that magnificent stretch of sky, river, hill and valley. All seemed very bright and hopeful. I had been very happy at home these last weeks. Mother had been very affectionate and we had had much intimate conversation and we were both full of plans for the London Season. I felt we were on the verge of a true and complete intimacy – perhaps it would never have come – we were both proud.

Soon after I returned, the carriage drove up and Mother was helped out by Father, Kate and I. She looked in pain, but neither Kate nor I thought much of it. We got her to bed and that night I slept with her. She seemed to have a fairly good night, but in the morning the pain returned, Dr Walters was sent for, and I saw him with her. There was then no question of danger. He said it was a rheumatic affliction, sent her some mixture and promised to return in the evening. But by the afternoon Mother had become very anxious and restless and so sent for Dr Washbourne who arrived before Dr Walters. After their consultation they injected morphia to alleviate the pain, and decided that Dr Walters should give her an injection to relieve if possible the bowels, which were very much distended with wind and caused her what I fear now was great agony. Kate remained with her until five. The injection did not act. After I came to her she seemed quieter. That morning about 11 o'clock she told me she thought she was mortally ill, begged me to write down instructions about jewellery, hoped that we should all of us take care of Father and attend to all his little comforts, look after the interests of Blanche and Rosy and not entirely desert her relations. I was very much affected, but was too anxious not to appear so, and too certain that her fear was a delusion to encourage her to tell me more; perhaps now I regret it. One thing I proposed, as I lay by her side and petted her, that we should give Carrie some little thing;

she was pleased at that. A trained nurse had been recommended by Dr Washbourne and we decided that she should stay the night with her (Saturday). I slept in the dressing-room, getting up at intervals to see Dr Walters and hear his report. She did not like the nurse; she was a roughish woman. I regretted afterwards I allowed her to be with Mother, but I did it for the best. The whole of the next morning Kate stayed with her – in the afternoon we sent for Maggie Harkness. Theresa and Alfred had come on the Saturday and Mary drove over and stayed the night.

After that afternoon there seemed to be no division of day and night. It was one continual strain to think and act. I was continually with Mother until Wednesday at 3 o'clock in the morning, when I left her for good, and only returned twice again for two short moments to give her the last farewell kiss and to take poor little weeping Rosy to her deathbed. During the whole time I nursed her she was always tender and loving and grateful. It was Tuesday at two o'clock, when I returned to her after 24 hours' rest from nursing, that I first lost hope and began to realize that I was in the presence of coming death. All that afternoon I sat and watched her; she was lying in a half-conscious state, muttering and thinking (as she said) incoherently. She picked and clutched nervously at the bedclothes – she seemed in no pain, and was perfectly willing to take and do everything ordered by the doctors. I asked her, towards supper time, whether she would like anyone besides the new nurse from London to stay with her through the night. She asked me to stay with her. The last words she spoke to me, about 11 o'clock that Tuesday night, were to beg me to ask Dr Washbourne to see her first, before she saw Dr Walters – and to tell him that if she took more food she would die of inflammation of the bowels. I do not think that she despaired of her life. When I returned to her after Dr Washbourne had left she was under morphia and appeared to me quieter. The nurse from London was most successful with her and Mother took to her from the first. About 3.30 I went to bed; the next morning at seven I saw Dr Walters. She was worse; they had thought her dying in the early morning.

Wednesday was the blackest day. None of us went in to her. Maggie Harkness and the nurse stayed with her. There was really no hope, but it was thought wiser to avoid exciting her in any way. That afternoon and evening brought all the sisters. On Thursday morning about four o'clock we were called up and spent a miserable hour waiting for death. There was a slight improvement towards six; she

49

asked for food. She lasted until a quarter to twelve; her spirit passed away without struggle and without pain after half an hour of quiet sleep.

Maggie was with her for those last six hours and told me afterwards that Mother had asked after little Stephen [Maggie's son] and Hadspen [the Hobhouse estate] and old Mrs Hobhouse. Poor girl, she was terribly grieved and felt the awfulness of death tragically. Once again we were very perfectly intimate and in the middle of the night of Friday she told me much about her married life and all its troubles.

Sunday at Longfords was spent in sleep and walking in those lovely woods – body and soul were weary. The next day the house was full of half-intimate relations; there was little time for thought.

*Sunday, 23 April.* [Standish]
We all joined with Father in that beautiful communion service. Now that I have experienced what the death of a dear one is, and have watched it and waited for it, a deep yearning arises for some religion by which to console grief and stimulate action. I have, if anything, less faith in the possibility of another life. As I looked at our mother dying, I *felt* it was a final dissolution of body and soul, an end of that personality which we call the spirit. This was an instinctive conviction; on this great question we cannot reason. But though my disbelief in what we call immortality was strengthened, a new and wondrous faith has arisen within me – a faith in goodness, in God. I must pray, I do pray and I feel better for it, and more able to put aside all compromise with worldliness and to devote myself with single-heartedness to my duty.

Surely the sacrifice of the body and blood of Christ is the greatest symbol of the sacrifice we all ought to strive to make, by which we may gain a noble immortality. In this spirit I took the holy communion, for the first time for six years, years of more or less dreary materialism. Rationally I am still an agnostic, but I know not where my religious feeling will lead me, whether I may not be forced to acknowledge its supremacy over my whole nature. . . .

My duty now lies clearly before me – to Father and Rosy first, secondly to the home as a centre for the whole family.

Rosy has picked up wonderfully with complete rest to her intellect and yet with a fully occupied day and more responsibility and call on her affections. She has the making of a fine woman if we can add to her great nobility, joyousness of character and briskness of action and thought.

On 13 June, in a few hastily scribbled and roughly corrected lines, Beatrice wrote the first of two informal wills she included in her diary. 'In case of my death', she wrote, 'my little property' was to go to her nephew Alfred Standish Cripps, Blanche's son born in 1881. She wanted each of her sisters to have an item of jewellery; and she hoped that her father would make a small settlement 'on my only two great friends', Carrie Darling and Margaret Harkness. On 26 September she added a codicil, which began by asking her father to burn the diary-books when he had read them, and ended by asking him to send them to Carrie Darling. 'I don't want any of the *sisters* to see them.' Her distressed state of mind was epitomized in one sentence. 'If I do die I hope no one will regret it for me', she wrote, 'as I shall not regret it myself.'

Between these two despairing moments she had spent a long holiday in Germany and Switzerland with her father, Rosy and Herbert Spencer. Queenborough on the Isle of Sheppey was at that time the departure-point of the steamer for Flushing in Holland.

*27 June.* [The Hague]

A sad parting with Carrie Darling, probably for ever; a sorrowful scene with Father, the first ten minutes of our journey. 'Lost her for ever', a truth which he is beginning to realize. Then silence, as we whirled down to Queenborough. A little disagreement as to the advisability of remaining on deck during the first half of the night, producing in my throat a bone of irritation and gulp of determination. However, I had my way and considerably regretted it (though perhaps after all it was the wisest) as we stewed in a stuffy cabin with an odour of bad tobacco and the ceaseless tread of the heavy Dutchman overhead. As I lay awake with these far from pleasant sensations, with the immediate remembrance of perhaps a last parting, and the still sadder recollection of a first experience of death, with all the feeling of unreality which follows it, I was exceedingly sad and I meditated and prayed.

I thought anxiously as to the best means of educating Rosy, not controlling her; control which is not discipline and does not result in the development of more power of self-control in the subject is worse than useless.

Arrived at Flushing. Rosebud and I enjoyed sugary and indifferent tea, bread and butter and eggs for 9d each, stood for twenty minutes among staring and bad-tobacco-smoking foreigners and then with Father seated ourselves in a crimson, velveteen carriage and lived through (I with the help of the three times and four times of the multiplication table) a tedious dusty hot journey to La Hague. Happily Father's spirits improved every hour. The new sights and interests please him. He is full of loving affection to us – and enjoys his little joke against my despotism.

*29 June.* [Holland]
A pleasant afternoon at Scheveningen. . . . As we wait for our supper the philosopher arrives; some constraint on both sides all through that evening. Father likes his society and watches us with amused interest. . . .

*1 July*
We spent at Amsterdam, rattling over stone pavements and walking through some rooms of horrors. I can kindle no enthusiasm for the Dutch pictures, the philosopher and I agreeing in this. At Utrecht we lived through a banquet, on my part with mixed feelings of disgust and interest. The Dutchmen certainly are an unspiritual race. I sat between two Dutch youths, watched them gorging and drinking and listened to their harshly expressed self-satisfaction and self-complacent account of their do-nothing and luxurious lives. After dinner amid much chaff I and two other young women smoked a cigarette. . . .

*2 July.* [Cologne]
Cologne Cathedral. Even the philosopher does not criticize the interior, though he objects to the curved outline of the spires. 'In architecture what I require', spoke he, 'is that the lines should be defined, that either they should be continuous or definitely broken.' When we entered service was going on. Father, Rosy and I overpowered by the beauty of the building, sat and listened with solemn delight to the rhythmical chant of the vespers. 'This is excessively monotonous,' whispered the philosopher to me. 'I rather like it,' say I, venturing to disagree with him, though with a conciliatory smile. But feeling inwardly out of sympathy I move with Rosy to the seat lower down and join more completely in the service. This the philosopher observes, and when we meet again in the nave he remarks: 'The primitive man would here have a feeling of superstitious awe. It is only through the power of self-analysis and by tracing our feelings to their ultimate psychological cause that we are able to rid ourselves of it.' 'I confess to a certain amount of superstitious awe,' say

I defiantly. 'I should be sorry that these cathedrals should pass out of the hands of the Catholic Church with its beautiful ritual.' The philosopher simply cleared his throat of any disposition to dispute this last contemptible suggestion and continued: 'Awe is quite legitimate. It arises in our minds from a perception of power, but we must bear in mind when we give way to this feeling that these cathedrals were erected by the Princes of the Church, who were military chieftains and as bloodthirsty as their secular neighbours.' . . . This little tirade over, we passed out of the church.

Beatrice and her companions went on to spend two days on the Rhine, then to Lucerne, the steamer to Flülan, over the Brünig pass, and on to Murren in Switzerland. One of the guests at the hotel where they stayed was John Frederick Main, who taught at the South Kensington School of Science. See the entry for 11 March 1883. He was suffering from tuberculosis.

*15 July.* [Murren]
The first three days were hardly pleasantly employed in suffering a nervous bilious attack. . . . This air makes one feel rather lightheaded and excited. The inhabitants look wretchedly thin, pale and cadaverous and are mere beasts of burden, born to carry *Messieurs and Mesdames les voyageurs* and their requirements to this 'Pleasant Alpine Resort'. Father says, and I agree, that the Swiss do not seem endowed with a high moral nature. The wretched landlord, a most thriving one, actually refused to count our humble afternoon tea in with our *pension*. . . . However, we have done him, with the help of an Etna [patent stove], borrowed teapot and milk and bread and butter for one. . . .
As for the scenery it is simply glorious. . . .

*22 July.* [Murren]
The professor of mechanics [Main] and I had a long and serious talk last night, wandering round metaphysics. He is a clever, sensitive man, short in stature with a pleasant, open, sympathetic face. Was brought up by a spinster aunt, without games or companions, was sent to inferior school, went to Cambridge, took high honours both there and at London University, accepted professorship of mathematics and afterwards of mechanics at Bristol, lived there five years during which time he was seriously ill and had a tremendous struggle with his work, and now at the age of 28 has accepted a junior professorship of mechanics at South Kensington. He told me that he was brought up in

rigid orthodoxy, was suddenly thrown into a more or less freethinking set at Cambridge and was now reverting to the old thing. . . .

Father, I find, is still restless, and looks anxiously towards home. With all his activity of mind he has little resource, and, though he needs occupation, he would remain idle rather than make it or interest himself in that which has not some direct practical result. For a man of power and capability he has singularly little capacity for moulding his own life independently of circumstances, to some end. Happily for him, circumstances forced him into work early in life, but the groove he was then forced into — moneymaking — he has remained in and always will remain in, though his instincts and faculties would lead him elsewhere, but the will is wanting. . . .

*24 July.* [Murren]
A week spent with nature and alas! with the young professor. After four months of loneliness, it was delightful to have the companionship of a refined and sympathetic mind, deeply appreciative of nature and yet steadfast in devotion to work and duty. Many delightful walks we had with discussion and silence, according to our mood. But still in looking back there is bitterness in the consciousness of having given way to a pleasure, thoughtlessly ignoring what pain might come of it. . . . Altogether the last week has been spent unworthily. Father and Rosy neglected, no work done, every day a restless ambition grows, an ambition for a life with some result, vulgarly apparent to myself and others, and yet the necessary self-denial, even sufficient to accomplish well the duty nearest me, is not there. If a weakly mortal is to do anything in the world besides eat the bread thereof, there must be determined subordination of the whole nature to the one aim, no trifling with time which is passing, with strength which is only too limited. My short intimacy with Mr Main has at least given me an example in determined self-control; of a delicate constitution conquering ill-health and succeeding in the world's struggle. . . .

Though restless and anxious for change, yet there was sadness in leaving Murren, sadness in leaving those glorious Alps. . . .

Beatrice was staying with her sister Kate in her lodgings in London.

*3 August.* 26 Grosvenor Road
What I should like to do this autumn would be to get on with arithmetic, if possible going in for a little mild mathematics and

geometry, and to take up chemistry so as to have some sound practical knowledge of the elements of one science.

Herbert Spencer had left Beatrice a copy of a letter to the Rev. T. Mozley in which he outlined his doctrine of evolution. Mozley had 'insulted' Spencer by saying that in his boyhood he had derived similar ideas from Spencer's father. Herbert Spencer's *First Principles* was published in 1862. See also Spencer's article in the *Athaneum*, 22 July 1882.

*13 August.* [London]

Alfred [Cripps] and I had a long discussion over Mr Spencer's résumé of his philosophy, resulting in my taking it up to bed and spending a couple of hours over it, eventually rushing downstairs and plunging into *First Principles*, a plunge producing such agreeable sensations that I have since continued the practice every morning before breakfast.

So far I seem to be able to work my brain with greater ease than hitherto, and so long as I do not neglect the duties nearest to me, I think I may indulge in dreams of attainment, perhaps never realized or even approached, but still as an incentive to self-culture. Now I have within me a definite ambition, perhaps a foolish and vain one. Still, it has taken possession of me and filled a vacancy with – wind? Anyhow, I know more decidedly than ever what materials and what tools I want – the mastery of some sympathetic philosophy to bind together isolated groups of ideas and experiences, experiences of human nature by careful observation and experiment, and certain necessary tools such as a fair knowledge of numbers and their relation, and some power of correct expression. I feel sadly the lack of a good groundwork. I am simply ridiculously stupid with arithmetic – a sort of paralysis taking place in my brain when I look at numbers.

My diary, which began as a register of good intention, shall continue such. I do honestly and earnestly pray that no foolish vanity will lead me away from the *thorough* accomplishment of my real duties. It is so difficult with my very limited energy not to devote it to pleasant occupation, especially when that occupation advances self. One good thing about my present study is that it naturally inclines me to sympathy, to an interest in persons as the only means of collecting material. . . .

Theresa gave birth to a son, Alfred Henry Seddon, on 27 August 1882.

*27 August.* [London]

This time last year I had recognized the inevitable; and now poor Theresa is suffering the inevitable.

A woman gives much when she consents to become mother and wife. I put the mother first because it is *the* relationship which absorbs her life, for which she suffers and should be loved. Poor little Mother. Looking back I see how bitterly she must have felt our want of affection and sympathy and for that I feel remorse. Now I can do nothing but keep her memory holy and her influence living, and recognize regretfully the multitude of her gifts and the slightness of my gratitude. I never knew how much she had done for me, how many of my best habits I had taken from her, how strong would be the impress of her personality, when the pressure had gone, a pressure wholesome and in the right direction, but applied without tact. Tact, that quality which gains for people more affection and consideration than any other, and yet in itself not one necessarily belonging to the noblest groups of moral and intellectual qualities.

Poor little Mother! Her death was so sad – so inexpressively sad in its isolation. Is all death like that? Can we not in that supreme moment bind the past with the future and through our influence force one link in the chain of human development, and our last mortal act be one of prayer and blessing? And who knows that Mother did not bless us with her last breath and that we, that I, am not now feeling the working of that blessing within me. It is strange, how I now feel the presence of her influence and think of her as an absent friend who does sympathize with my new life, but cannot tell it me. I never asked for her sympathy when she lived, but now she, through the medium of my memory, gives it me. When I work, with many odds against me, for a far distant and perhaps unattainable end, I think of her and her intellectual strivings, which we were too ready to call useless, and yet will be the originating impulse of all my ambition, urging me onward towards something better in action or thought. When I feel discouraged and hopeless, when I feel that my feeble efforts to acquire are like a blind grasping in space for the stars, the vision of her will arise persistent always in action and in desire. Persevere.

And I *will persevere.* I may be baffled, my present aim may be withdrawn from sight, and new and lovelier ones rise up; still the struggle is for good (God help me) and for truth, and the direction right. Why I have written this I know not. This morning I took the sacrament, and again solemnly vowed 'to endeavour to lead a new life, following the commandment of God and walking henceforth in His holy ways'. I get so much comfort, help and peace from this service. How strange it is. . . .

*31 August.* [London?]
A day of terrible anxiety. Theresa lying between life and death. Poor Alfred bearing up with grand courage. How deeply illness and death impresses on one that life in itself is worthless; only what it achieves is enduring. All deep feeling does this, love as much as any, because it foresees parting and separation; it foresees the dissolution of all its elements but that of noble influence; influence has all eternity before it. God help me. . . .

*10 September.* [Standish]
That evening I walked through the fields, after a day spent with Arthur [Playne] at The Argoed. There was a glorious sunset. Masses of cloud, wonderful in colour and form, more solemn than lovely, swept across the sky, here towards the south, built up in ominous layers of dark blue and grey, tossing wildly waves of fiery gold to meet the glory of the west. . . . I paused, from above seemed to come some inspiration, I bowed my head. . . . Strange these feelings are, of an outward presence, this sense of downcoming help, this real answer to prayer. Where does this 'peace' come from, which was absent before, this rest in endeavour, this hope in despair?

I know not where my religious feeling, once awakened from the dreams of vague idealism, and acknowledged helpful in times of trial, sorrow and endeavour, where this religious feeling may lead me. And truly every day it takes me more wholly under its guidance. Sometimes I wonder whether it is a dream, a vanity which I am imagining, but then I see the outcome, in strength and peace, activity and health. How wonderful, that an 'idea' should so govern and an idea breathed in from without and yet not from man.

Thoughts seem to crowd, at present all undefined. Clear only is humility and intense desire. Every night I sigh at the little done, each morning I wake with fresh vigour and work. And when on the week's resting-place I rest, with prayer refreshed, 'though little be done, with faith persevere'. Test not by extent, but by the spirit impressed.

*14 September.* [Standish]
Quite clear in my mind that I am on the right way in reading Herbert

Spencer and in the study of mathematics and geometry, but not so clear as regards literary reading. Was tempted by foolish vanity and desire to accomplish, to read French literature with a view to an article on Balzac, whose extraordinary power of analysis always attracts me. Surely these great analytical students of human nature will be found of use in any future of the mental life of humanity, when psychology has advanced beyond the study of primitive man, and of human characteristics in so far as they distinguish man from other animals.

But my instinct tells me that I must work with order, that any attempt to escape from the direct line of historical study will only produce friction, contending purpose. Then I am anxious to be about English literature. As for the study of Christianity I dread it. Perhaps because I have allowed myself to accept as a working faith and to practise a system of devotion, the foundation of which I intellectually distrust. And yet it is impossible for me to live without it – to live the life which I know to be true and good. That thought which I remember so well flashing across my mind as a child, as I stood near those witch elms now clothed in the beauty of sunlit mist, that inward conviction that what led to goodness must be the work of truth, would still persuade me that in humble and trusting faith, in constant prayer and endeavour, in whatever forwards this, there must be an underlying truth, a truth more substantial than the unknowable. It is unworthy to shrink from examination, unworthy alike of the spirit of faith and of the spirit of inquiry. God help me.

*20 September*. [Hadspen]
Three or four days spent with Henry and Margaret. I was wrong in my estimate of Henry. He has a sweet and gentle nature, great refinement of feeling and great persistency in it. Lives in a world of ideas, chosen by his moral sense. Dislikes to study the imperfect or to watch disease either mental or physical. Is uninteresting from this narrowness, and lack of variety in the substance matter of his thought. Phraseology curiously pedantic. . . . Self-culture is a duty to him and has been all through his scholar's life. No desire to see things as they are, but a will to see them as he thinks they should be. Unconventional in small matters, dreading real scientific audacity, and incapable, from want of imagination (a deficiency arising from his powerlessness to realize evil), of foreseeing the probable action of social forces. Probably from all one hears he has good abilities and better industry but no original thought and great intellectual nervousness. Will never

attain to power and influence except to that blessed influence of pure motive and well-directed life.

Margaret is the same strong genuine woman. A fine intellect and robust imagination, warped by want of faith. As a girl this cynicism did not injure her intellectual development. Her ambition gave her a motive, and her bored existence impelled her to learn and to think. This cynicism arose partly from a breadth of intellectual vision, and partly from a narrowness of moral nature, an absence of benevolence or desire for disinterested action, and deep-rooted contempt for 'idea-inspired' action. All good impulses, apart from those generated by instinct, were to her mind foolish and unnecessary. She never made a *friend*, except within her own family. 'I do not care to give or to receive.' This was her feeling towards the world. A dutiful regard for the weal of the commonwealth and a strong disapproval of any principles which interfere with the absolute freedom of the individual to lead an egotistical life make her at once kindly and considerate in her own circle and strongly averse to the breaking down of the barrier of respectability between the endowed classes and the outer mob of the uneducated and unclothed. Any intimacy with these barbarians is dangerous except it be for the purpose of impressing upon them moral maxims which will lead them to a peaceful resignation, as they watch those who have, enjoying and wasting, while they are dying of hunger. . . .

And here we discover her 'first principle' – belief in instincts as the only permanent and reliable thing in human nature. There is no sacrifice Margaret would not make for her husband and children – no effort she would grudge for her family; their relative rights would be determined by the degree of blood relationship. 'The Family' is to her the only 'holy thing'; all individual and all social life should be based on it.

It is natural she should feel utterly uninterested in all which does not affect this 'Holy of Holies'. . . .

Francis, Lord Jeffrey (1773–1850), Scottish critic and judge, was founder and editor of the *Edinburgh Review*.

*22 September.* [Standish]
The individual here to be described [Alfred Cripps] is a short man with broad shoulders, clear-cut features and imposing chin. His first nickname in our family was 'Chin Chin', afterwards increased in

dignity and length to [Thomas] Carlyle's epithet for Jeffrey, 'The Little Jewel of an Advocate'.

You are struck at first sight by the self-complacency of his expression from which you would argue conceit; but with increasing intimacy the careful observer will trace it to the simple amiability of his disposition, to the absence of struggle in his nature and no doubt partly to a very justifiable satisfaction at his own success in life.

For success and approval have attended him from the time when as a schoolchild of eight he was invariably sent for as the model little boy to prove to the anxious-minded mother what her little boy with the same early training could do. Little Alfred was as independent as he was good. There is a story – I will not vouch for its truth, not knowing the manners of public schools – that this model little boy now developed into a Winchester scholar and, justly offended at the Head Master doubting his word, demanded and, with the help of his father, obtained an apology. However, I have carefully inquired from more reliable sources than the sweet imagination of a young wife, and find it to be a fact that he was universally treated as grown-up, that his father wrote to him at fourteen as he would write to another Q.C., consulted him on his business and legal affairs, and never offered him advice much less administered chastisement.

In later years this dependability of character and independence of disposition gave him a position in his family which the vulgar would deem unpleasant. His father, finding he could support himself, forgot the allowance, his brothers and sisters attracted loans and presents, gamekeepers looked for tobacco, servants for fees and old women for flannel.

But though the first effect of his kindliness was decrease in material substance, his goodness is of the sort that reaps its own reward. It is the virtue of perfect adaptability to social life as it now is in the endowed classes. His physique is under control, his affections are strong but well directed, so that hitherto he has gained nothing but satisfaction from them, his tastes are rational and lead him to appreciate most the life he must lead, and his ambition is proportionate to his faculties. In short he is a near approximation to that ideal, which Herbert Spencer says can only be reached in infinite time when man will be 'a combination of desires that correspond to all the different orders of activity which the circumstances of life call for – desires severally proportionate in strength to the needs for these orders of activity'.

Intellectually he is the genius of common sense. . . . He *is* in most things, and believes himself to be in all, reasonable. In the many talks I had with him I always stumbled on two persistent ideas – a practical belief in the wisdom of sincerity and an equally practical hatred of control. . . . This theory of individual freedom he carries into all his relationships and will, if he is consistent to his nature, work out in his political views. His principal intellectual interest is the constitution of society and his ambition the government of men. . . . One evening in the billiard room, while enjoying the delicious sensations of summer twilight and cigarettes, the talk turned on religion and the necessity of it for men and women. Theresa and I poured out our feelings. Alfred listened, his self-satisfied expression changing to one of earnestness and humility, and he said, 'Merely from a personal point of view, in time of trouble or sorrow, I should not rely on religion for support and comfort, but more on that firmness and dignity of character, which comes from a will to master circumstances, and a determination to bear what one can't avoid. . . .'

I should doubt whether he would make a great politician. There is a tameness in his phraseology which extends to his personality, reminding one of a perfectly flat well-cultivated country, over which the eye wanders with complacency. The details interest you, the general effect is satisfactory, but there is no one object of interest or attraction nor such a combination of colour and form which from its beauty or originality would strike your imagination and impress it permanently. . . . I can imagine Alfred, with all his charm and with all his power, becoming either a selfish and less worthy man or failing to gain much in life but money.

Alfred's philosophy, political and moral, is pretty well expressed by 'freedom for the individual'. Freedom from outside pressure will be best secured by a truly representative Government, representative of the various interests of the community, the self-government of a society being perfect so far as justice is concerned *when all interests are equally represented.* (I should humbly disagree. Equality of representation would be unjust. There is no quantitative or qualitative equality between the different interests.)

The great danger of democracy is that if unqualified it will tend to become a class tyranny and, what is worse, a tyranny by the most ignorant class; it will only be by measures securing to numerical minorities, representation, that you will avert this. . . .

He is an optimist and looks forward to the time when benevolence will be so developed that the gratification of it will become the only egotism.

Henry Fawcett (1833–84) was Professor of Political Economy at Cambridge, and from 1865 he was a Liberal M.P. on the Radical wing of the party and Postmaster General under Gladstone. He was a close friend and political associate of Leonard Courtney. Despite the handicap of many years of blindness – an affliction of which Courtney himself was much afraid – he and his wife Millicent Garrett Fawcett were active and influential reformers, and she became a leader of the female suffrage movement.

## 15 October. Rusland

Rather a weary fortnight spent in entertaining. . . . Hobhouses, Leonard and Kate, and large party of unattractive Americans. Leonard Courtney is no doubt an excellent and an able man, but not companionable to an ignorant young woman. His conversation bores me. It is made up of a certain measure of facts, given out in an assertive tone, and quotations from English poets, which from his ugly pronunciation are difficult to catch. He never argues (with his inferiors, i.e. with us) but denies and quotes. . . . As Father says, 'Politics are with him a trade secret'. On general subjects he is wonderfully well informed but surely neither original nor powerful. . . . He is a theorist without being a reasoner; his conversation and his speeches are coarse (not in the bad sense) in matter and manner, lacking in subtlety and depth of thought. It may be that we shall learn to appreciate him and that the fault lies with us and not with him. A man like Fawcett would hardly say that he was one of the ablest men in the Government unless he were really a man of mark, though I am inclined to doubt the pre-eminence of those whom circumstances have placed in the upper branches of the political tree; and my acquaintance with Leonard Courtney makes me doubt it still more. However, I will get to know him. His evident contempt for my 'scattered' ideas will be valuable – and who knows how much the evident contempt has to do with my dislike? Which of us is quite fair in our judgement of a person who *we* think under-rates us? If I ever am intimate with him, our intimacy will not be based on intellectual sympathy. That may come, but intimacy must spring from other sources. With Maggie I had many delightfully doleful talks, reminding me of old times (only three years ago) when we wandered over moor and moss, gossiped cynically and talked tragically, and enjoyed and suffered *Weltschmertz*. Henry was most amiable – is developing under Margaret's influence into a genial warm-hearted man, losing much of his narrowness.

*4 November*. [Rusland]

Two or three weeks passed in the mental contortions consequent on attempting mathematics, without possessing mathematical faculty. I naturally refuse to believe that it is the highest faculty of the brain, though perhaps a necessary tool in the application of the highest faculties to the most important subjects. Anyhow, without it one cannot get even a glimpse of the land of science. . . . I confess my attention has been mostly confined to getting over so much ground daily. The geometrical side is the most pleasing – it is always easier to prove the existence of something which you *see* exists. Numbers are to me only half-believed-in facts which my unimaginative mind persists in deeming fictions. . . .

How subjective women are. Does it belong to their education or their nature? Certainly if psychology is to be advanced by self-analysis, women will be the great psychologists of the future. A perfectly frank account of the inner workings of our brain would be interesting, a quantitive as well as a qualitative analysis of motive and thought. As it is there is much that goes on within one, which one, as a prudent mistress winks at and overlooks. To dwell on it even with disapproval might give it an ugly significance. It is not wise to stop the ruffianly-looking vagrant, and inquire from him whence he comes and whither he goeth. If thoughts and actions really run in the line of least resistance, we should be careful of enlarging with self-consciousness the channels in the wrong direction. . . .

*25 November*. [Rusland]

Making but small progress with mathematics and doing nothing else. Anyhow it is a healthful life – forcing one to own inferiority to the average man's mind, and a splendid corrective for the daydreams of last summer. Altogether the winter months with their short and often dreary days do not lend themselves to exaltation like the long sunlit hours of the summer months. . . . .

What a blessing I can write in this little book without fearing that anyone will ever read and ridicule the nonsense and half-sense I scribble. That has been the attraction of a 'diary-book' to me – one can talk one's little thinkings out to a highly appreciative audience, dumb but not deaf. And sometimes this is a necessary safety-valve to save one from that most painful operation, watching one's most cherished chicks hatched by unwearied perseverance coolly trodden underfoot. Now my honest desire is to appear commonplace and sensible, so that none of my dear kind family will think it necessary to remark to themselves or to me that I am otherwise than ordinary; to be on the right side of ordinary is the perfection of prudence in a young woman, and will save her from much heartburning and mortification of spirit.

There is a certain pleasure in following and noting the 'order of thought' uninfluenced by the outside world of things or ideas – letting oneself go and seeing where one will get to. It is a harmless amusement so long as there is no self-deception as to its value. . . .

*3 December.* [Rusland?]
Today is a day for self-examination and looking back on the past month I see much unwholesomeness. That bad old habit which as a child took such possession of me, building castles in the air, so nourishing to vanity, has again cropped up. It is a bad habit because it is at the time a false life and leads to a false self-estimate. And the wise ordering of one's life depends on self-knowledge. Also most of these castles are essentially vulgar in their nature and are based on what one acknowledges in one's better moments to be a false valuation of the different conditions of life and gradually they insinuate desire for what is worthless. Lastly they are the quintessence of egotism. No doubt their somewhat sudden reappearance is due to the sterility of my present intellectual life, fatiguing and straining as it is to the mind and yet absolutely barren of ideas.

Again I am not at rest with my own conscience. I know I might have done better by Rosy and made this autumn more healthful to her. My difficulty lies in her imitativeness. She will learn only by example, and yet it is well nigh impossible for me to live as she ought to live. I cannot order my diet either physical or mental to suit her constitution. I acknowledge that I am not equal to the position of mother to her, perhaps I confess, too, that my effort is rather a half-hearted one – that I am not willing to sacrifice my own interests to hers. . . . And alongside of this inner conflict is a recognition that (probably owing to this egotism) I am losing ground in the affections of my sisters. Of course there will be unavoidable criticism, and some of it will be unjustified. It is no use being over-sensitive, but if one wishes to feel philosophically towards it, one must be honestly convinced of the rightness and thoroughness of one's own intentions.

PART II

# A Multiple Personality
*January 1883–December 1885*

## Introduction to Part II

'THE DEATH of my mother revolutionized my life,' Beatrice wrote in *My Apprenticeship*. 'I became a principal, a person in authority, determining not only my own but other people's conduct; the head of a large household, perpetually on the move; the home, wherever located, serving as the meeting-place of seven married sisters and their growing families; a busy hostess in town and country . . . my father's counsellor and my younger sister's virtual guardian. . . . From being an anaemic girl, always paying for spells of dissipation or study by periods of nervous exhaustion, often of physical illness, I became an exceptionally energetic woman, carrying on, persistently and methodically, several separate, and, in some ways, conflicting, phases of life – undergoing, in fact, much of the strain and stress of a multiple personality.'

At the age of twenty-four Beatrice thus began to feel 'the rival pulls on time and energy', the pull of the family commitments implicit in the Victorian code of feminine domesticity and the pull of 'a domineering curiosity into the nature of things, reinforced by an awakening desire for creative thought and literary expression'. She was willing to play the part of a dutiful unmarried daughter, as her sisters expected of her, but she was not prepared to graduate from that domestic apprenticeship into 'a good marriage' merely to please her family. On the contrary, she said, 'I silently withdrew all my own aspirations and plans for self-culture from family discussion – a reserve which entailed isolation and loneliness'.

The only place where she did discuss those aspirations, apart from an occasional personal confidence to a friend, was in her diary, and for the first two years after her mother died there are many entries which relate to that process of self-education and growing self-awareness. 'Thrown back on books, books, and again books', she was reading a good deal of philosophy, especially the works of Herbert Spencer, studying mathematics, taking instruction in biology from her medical brother-in-law William Harrison Cripps (1850–1923), and cultivating the clever and coming men she met as she moved through smart society. But she was becoming increasingly bored with the fashionable world: though she enjoyed balls and dinner parties, and was much admired, she chided herself for succumbing to such temptations, complaining that this hectic life made serious thought impossible and contrasting it with the miserable condition of the people.

Beatrice was not alone in this feeling. In the last quarter of the nineteenth century Britain was still the dominant power, her far-flung colonial territories protected by the Royal Navy, her industry making her the largest workshop of the world, and her trade sustaining the financial empire which paid tribute to the City of London. The landed interest represented by the Conservative Party, which dominated the House of Lords, was being challenged by the Liberals, speaking for the increasingly powerful commercial interests and standing for *laissez-faire* economics and for political rather than social reform. The arrival of cheap wheat and refrigerated meat from America and the Antipodes began the long decline of British agriculture; by 1870 the balance within the country had tipped from the fields to the factories.

At the same time British manufacturers were beginning to feel the pinch of competition from Germany, France and the United States, and the 'invisible hand' of Providence which had seemingly guided the country through much of Victoria's reign now seemed less sure of its touch. The year 1880 was, indeed, a turning point. William Ewart Gladstone (1809–98), the Grand Old Man of the Liberal Party, led it to a sweeping victory and five ensuing years of frustration. He had promised peace abroad and prosperity at home; once in office, however, his government was plagued by a succession of foreign crises, colonial wars and domestic problems.

Everything seemed to go wrong at once. There was a slump of such severity that the word 'unemployment' was coined to describe its effects; it was matched by a deteriorating condition in the countryside, and by an appalling situation in Ireland, where the problem of the land flowed into the rising tide of nationalism. The country could only be kept manageably quiet by filling it with troops and police, and imposing a Coercion Act that put it in a state of siege. The demand for Home Rule became such an issue in Parliament that it split the

Liberal Party, and put the Conservatives back in office for another generation.

The whole country was moving into a new and more troubled age. In London the problems were accentuated by the peculiar circumstances of the East End, made worse by a series of bitter winters. For the area that ran east from Aldgate, and north from the docks and waterside slums of Wapping, was so cut off by railway lines and the walls of warehouses that it formed a social ghetto; and as thousands of Jewish immigrants poured into it from eastern Europe after 1880 parts of it became increasingly like a real ghetto. In 1880 conditions were generally no better than they had been fifty years before, when Dickens scathingly described them in *Oliver Twist*; in some respects the situation had become worse. The stock of houses had been reduced by decay, by the construction of new roads, railways, factories and storehouses, and by well-intentioned schemes for 'model' housing schemes (such as Katherine Buildings) in which the 'cleared' tenants could not afford to live. The overcrowding of slum properties pushed up rents; and such killer diseases as cholera, diphtheria, tuberculosis and typhoid were as rampant as crime, drink and immorality. There was no regular employment for most of the wretched population of the East End; silk-weaving had declined, ship-repairing had moved down the river to the newer and bigger docks. Most dock work relied, in any case, on low-paid casual labour, as did the other available trades from piece work in tailoring to employment as carters, porters and building labourers. All in all, as Beatrice later vividly described in *My Apprenticeship*, it was a blighted area, packed with demoralized people. Gradually the respectable classes began to take note of what was happening and to worry about its consequences.

'This flood of sin and misery is gaining on us,' declared the author of *The Bitter Cry of Outcast London*, a pamphlet published in 1883 which took the stench of the East End slums into the West End drawing-rooms and evoked what Beatrice called 'a new consciousness of sin among men of intellect and men of property'. She did not mean personal sin but 'a collective or class consciousness; a growing uneasiness, amounting to conviction, that the industrial organization, which had yielded rent, interest and profits on a stupendous scale, had failed to provide a decent livelihood and tolerable conditions for a majority of the inhabitants of Great Britain'.

That sense of social failure and of social responsibility for putting things to rights was what the late Victorians meant by the word 'compunction', and it was the spring of many reforming movements in the 1880s. London was full of them. The Democratic Federation, which later branched into the Social Democratic Federation and the Socialist League, was founded in 1881, and it was the first sign of the socialist upsurge which was to culminate twenty years later in the launching of the Parliamentary Labour Party. There were groups which thought nothing could be done until Ireland had Home Rule, and others, much influenced by Henry George's *Progress and Poverty* which was published in England in December 1881, who believed that the private landlord should be taxed out of existence or simply nationalized, or that municipal improvement was the best approach. There were spiritualist cliques and dress-reform coteries, occultists, vegetarians and a plethora of social missionaries from the Christian churches, or from such secular bodies as the Progressive Association, the Fellowship of the New Life and the Fabian Society, all of which offered combinations of moral and social regeneration. The first pamphlet published by the Fabian Society after it was founded by a dozen enthusiasts in January 1884 was called *Why Are The Many Poor?* and there were hundreds of troubled, conscience-stricken people from the comfortable classes who asked the same question and went 'East Ending' in search of an answer.

The most obvious response was private philanthropy. There were missions, orphanages and soup-kitchens scattered all through the East End, and in times of cold weather or near-riot there was a sharp rise in subscriptions to the Lord Mayor's Fund and a score of lesser charities. But there was also a doctrinaire reaction against indiscriminate alms-giving, exemplified by the Charity Organization Society, set up years before in an attempt to co-ordinate the hugger-mugger of London charities on strict utilitarian lines. Its members, Beatrice wrote in *My Apprenticeship*, were undoubtedly 'devoted men and women . . . yearning to spend their lives in the service of the poor', but they were also ideologues, convinced that a man who lacked work lacked character, that paupers were born, not made, and that doles corrupted the deserving poor and coddled the thriftless. The effort to distinguish between these categories, in which subjective moral judgements weighed as heavily as social circumstances, turned the C.O.S. case-workers into unpopular busybodies.

At first Beatrice found the harsh C.O.S. philosophy congenial. Still under the influence of Herbert Spencer when she joined its Soho Committee in April 1883, she liked the individual emphasis on saving

70

for a rainy day, self-help, and the kind of moralization of the propertied classes which she had learnt from her Positivist friends and from her reading of Auguste Comte. She also thought the C.O.S. was genuinely trying 'to apply the scientific method of observation and experiment, reasoning and verification, to the task of delivering the poor from their miseries'. But she soon saw that the C.O.S. neither sought for the real causes of poverty nor had any cure for them. The Society was not only calling for a limitation of personal charity at a time when tens of thousands were hopelessly destitute, but it was also putting up 'an equally determined resistance to the extension of state or municipal action, whether in the way of the physical care of children at school, housing, accommodation, medical attendance or old-age pensions'.

Beatrice's change of attitude was confirmed by her experience in the management of a tenement owned by a philanthropic housing trust, by her friendship with Samuel Augustus Barnett (1844–1913), the rector of St Jude's, Whitechapel, who was an increasingly critical leader of the C.O.S., and by her friendship with Mary and Charles Booth. Booth's desire to apply scientific methods to social problems coincided so exactly with Beatrice's views that, as she moved away from the teaching of Herbert Spencer, she found Booth an ideal mentor.

The Booths gave Beatrice emotional support as well as intellectual stimulus when she became infatuated by Joseph Chamberlain (1836–1914), the rising star of the Liberal Party. He was a handsome and vigorous man who had made a substantial fortune from the family engineering business in Birmingham. In 1873 he became Mayor of Birmingham and, as such, he was a notable civic reformer. Three years later he was elected to the House of Commons, and in 1880 Gladstone put him in the Cabinet as President of the Board of Trade. Chamberlain's rise to power marked a seminal change in Liberal politics. He played a decisive role in replacing the ideas of the party's traditional élite – 'whiggery' – by a programme of social and agrarian reform supported by new radical groups from the provinces. To this end he reorganized the Liberal Party – starting in Birmingham – by forming large local organizations on a representative basis and federating these into a central organization. 'Caucus' politics introduced the first permanent democratically based party machine for national and local elections, the purpose being to provide popular support to a progressive social élite and to strengthen the local parties against the leadership in Parliament.

'Radical Joe' was a powerful demagogue, but in private he was a reserved man, and domestic misfortune had saddened him. In October 1863, when his wife died in childbirth after two years of marriage, he was left to bring up his daughter, Beatrice, and his son, Austen (a future foreign secretary). Married again in 1868, he was widowed for the second time seven years later with four more motherless children – one of them being Neville, the future Conservative prime minister. 'This life is a d—d bad business for me,' he told Sir Charles Dilke, 'and I wish I were out of it'; and after his second wife's death he certainly displaced his emotional energy into politics. All the same, as success and public acclaim revived his spirits he began to go about in society and, as a very eligible widower, was said to be on the look-out for a wife.

From the beginning of this intermittent and fraught relationship, Beatrice was ambivalent. It was the source of exaltation and depression, of desire and self-denial in work. Chamberlain and Booth came to represent the poles of her life. On the one hand the 'great marriage' to please her family and to absorb her passion; on the other, the selfless dedication to a craft, to independence and to public service.

# ∽ 1883 ∾

J. A. Froude (1818–94) was a Oxford historian and Carlyle's literary
executor. He wrote a four-volume biography of Carlyle (1882–84).

## 2 January. Rusland Hall

After ten days of absolute idleness, I ought to have sufficient clearness
of mental vision to see the value, the worth of the past year's life. A
summary of it will not be useless. It opened with the implanting of a
vague literary ambition. Until last Christmas I had been a student, so
far as my unhealthiness allowed it, but my feeble study had been
directed to the gaining of principles whereby I could live wisely and
contribute to the commonweal, and to the development of faculties
which add variety and interest to my life. . . .

This little gem of ambition was soon buried beneath the unpleasant
sensations of *ennui* and ill-health. The first three months of the year
will always remain impressed on my memory. They were the last of
the inactive and irresponsible part of my youth, and as such are typical
of the many years I passed in self-contemplation and self-commisera-
tion. Whether this is a necessary phase in a woman's life (of the leisure
class) and whether there are advantages which counterbalance the
dreariness and apparent barrenness of the egotism, is a question
unsolved by me at present.

Mother's death opened a new world to me in thought and action. It
stamped, by a new experience, the conviction which had been slowly
growing from the first dawning of conscious thought within me, a
conviction that the world was either an infernal chaos or that all life
was a manifestation of goodness; and death, disease and misery,
horrible only to our imperfect vision. The death of one dear and near
to me did not strike me as sadder than the death of the thousands who
vanish unknown around us. Either 'the all' is so inexpressibly sad that
there is no room for an increase of sadness through personal affliction,
or else there is a mysterious meaning which, if we could divine it and
accept it, would hallow all things and give even to death and misery a
holiness which would be akin to happiness. And the result of this
ultimatum, presented by the thoughtful to the practical part of my
nature, was a powerful reversion to religion. I was satisfied that this
would be the last word of thought unaided by experience gathered in

action. The question remained, how am I to live and for what object? Physical annihilation would be preferable to this spiritual annihilation. But physical annihilation is impracticable. One's own life and one's own nature are facts which one must deal with, and with me they must be directed by some one consistent principle. . . .

A position of responsibility was forced upon me and I accepted it heartily and threw myself into active work. Two months at Standish were spent in clearing the ground and establishing myself as mistress. I thought of little but my duties and prayed earnestly that I might fulfil them. Sundays were a delightful rest – service in the morning and Froude's *Life of Carlyle* in the afternoon, intensely interesting as an analytical study. Driving through the streets of London on my way from Paddington I had that curious 'sensation' of power which I suppose comes to most people who have lived within themselves, who have seldom had their self-estimate righted by competition with others. Every face in the crowded streets seemed ready to tell me its secret history, if only I would watch closely enough. Again that vain hope for a 'bird's eye view' of mankind floated before my eyes; a grasping after some spectral idea which vanished as I tried to describe its outline. My energy and my power for work were suddenly increased. I remained in a state of exaltation all the summer possibly to some extent due to the physical effect of the high air at Murren. . . .

In most of us there is a desire to express our thought, feelings or impressions. Women generally choose music or drawing, but there is really no more pretension in writing, so long as one does not humbug oneself as to the value of the stuff written. . . . It is a difficult question whether the present 'intellectualism' is over-estimated in its good effect. Just at present I fancy there is a reaction against the idea that intellectual education is the cure for all evils. . . . Does culture increase power to act? I am inclined to think it increases the power but decreases the desire. . . . Probably the hankering after novel-writing in the literary amateur springs from somewhat the same causes as the preference given by the same individual to the metaphysical and moral sciences. The study of metaphysics and novel-writing can be attempted without the drudgery of mastering a difficult and tedious groundwork.

*1 February.* [Standish]
Again at this old (I cannot say dear old) place where I have droned out so many years of existence, twenty-five. Much the same surroundings

as last year, but one gone for ever and I in her place, at least not in the hearts of those who loved her – (I was not made to be loved, there must be something repulsive in my character) – but outwardly holding the same position. The family becoming middle-aged, all but the pet lamb, and the father becoming aged. The family is successful and the children thriving. A hateful feeling of unreality clouds all things. I can understand insanity. An experience of death undermines one's faith in the reality of life which after all is dependent on the persistence of individual life in one's consciousness.

Richard Potter rented 47 Prince's Gate, Kensington, for the Season. As a girl Beatrice had greatly enjoyed the summer whirl of smart entertainment. When she became her father's hostess, however, she saw a different side of things. 'I realized', she wrote in *My Apprenticeship*, 'that the pursuit of pleasure was not only an undertaking, but also an elaborate, and to me a tiresome undertaking, entailing extensive plans, a large number of employees and innumerable decisions on insignificant matters. There was the London house to be selected and occupied; there was the stable of horses and carriages to be transported; there was the elaborate stock of prescribed garments to be bought; there was all the commissariat and paraphernalia for dinners, dances, picnics and week-end parties to be provided.'

*14 February*. [Standish]
Tomorrow we take possession of our house in London. I go with a sincere intention of devoting myself to Society and the family, but that familiar 'daemon' desire for self-improvement threatens to overcome intention. Perhaps vanity will step in and help 'good' intention.

*22 February*. [Standish]
One word before leaving. . . . A conflict has been going on within me. Shall I give myself up to Society, and make it my aim to succeed therein, or shall I only do so as far as duty calls me, keeping my private life much as it has been for the last nine months? On the whole the balance is in favour of Society. It is going with the stream, and pleasing my people; it is doing a thing thoroughly that I must do partially; it is taking opportunities instead of making them; it is risking less and walking on a well-beaten track in pleasant company. . . . and lastly, and perhaps this is the reason which weighs most with me, there is less presumption in the choice.

Therefore, I solemnly dedicate my energies for the next five months to the cultivation of the social instincts, trusting that the good daemon within me will keep me from all vulgarity of mind, insincerity and falseness. I would like to go amongst men and women with a determination to know them, to humbly observe and consider their characteristics, always remembering how much there is in the most inferior individual which is outside and beyond one's understanding. Every fresh intimacy strengthens the conviction of one's own power-lessness to comprehend fully any other nature, even when one watches it with love. And without sympathy there is an impassable barrier to the real knowledge of the inner workings which guides the outer actions of human beings. Sympathy, or rather *accepted* sympathy, is the only instrument for the dissection of character. . . .

*26 February. Prince's Gate*
A pleasant bedroom in front of the house and looking towards the west. In the afternoon I can sit here and watch the sun slowly setting behind the Museum buildings and gardens. . . . undisturbed by the rushing life of the great city; only the brisk trottings and even rollings of the well-fed horses and well-cushioned carriages. Altogether we are in the land of luxury, we are living in an atmosphere of ease, satiety and boredom, with prospect and retrospect of gratified and mortified vanity. Father has found a little occupation in inquiring into, and to some extent organizing, a large railway amalgamation scheme. The promoters anxious to get his time, and still more his name. . . . Father really anxious for work. Still suffers silent agony and lonely grief for Mother. He is really a deep nature, but from his extraordinary unselfconsciousness his emotions seem transient. But this sorrow is permanent though intermittent. There is a deep sadness in decaying power, more terrible to me than death itself. And all who have passed the prime of life, who have lived those few golden years for work, must exhibit this decline in the power for *persistent* work.

Constantly, as I walk in one of the crowded streets of London, and watch the faces of the men and women who push past me, lined, furrowed, and sometimes contorted by work, struggle and passion, and think that all this desire and pain, this manifold feeling and thought is but a condition of force and matter, phantom-like forms built up to be destroyed, a hopelessness overtakes me, paralysing all power of wishing and doing. Then I sink into inertia, relieved only by a languid curiosity as to the variations in structure and function of those individuals who will let me observe them and inquire of them. Cold-blooded inquiry takes the place of heartfelt sympathy. But this one should shake off sternly.

*1 March.* [Prince's Gate]

Huge party at the Speaker's [House of Commons] – one or two of such would last one a life-time. Find it so difficult to be the 'universally pleasant'. Can't think what to say. Prefer on the whole the crowd in Oxford Street, certainly the feminine part of it. 'Ladies' are so expressionless. Should fancy mental superiority of men greatest in our class. Could it be otherwise with the daily life of ladies in society? What is there in the life which is so attractive? How can intelligent women wish to marry into the set where this is the social regime?

Catherine Potter married Leonard Henry Courtney, M.P., at St Jude's Church, Whitechapel, on 15 March 1883. She was then thirty-six and he was fifty-one. The son of a Cornish banker, Courtney had made his mark at Cambridge before becoming a barrister and journalist. In 1865 he became leader-writer on *The Times*, and between 1872 and 1875 he was Professor of Political Economy at University College, London. He was then elected as Liberal M.P. for the Cornish constituency of Liskeard. He supported the Radical wing of the party, becoming Secretary to the Treasury in 1882; but he developed a passionate belief in proportional representation and quixotically resigned his post on this issue in 1884. He was an opponent of Home Rule, and became a Liberal Unionist. He was Deputy Speaker of the House of Commons 1886–92, but was passed over as Speaker. Though previously a supporter of Chamberlain, he was a strong critic of imperial expansion and military adventures, and in 1901 he again sacrificed his career to his convictions, losing his seat in that year for his opposition to the Boer War. After the Liberal victory in 1906 he was elevated to the House of Lords. William Rathbone (1819–1902) was a Liverpool merchant of Dissenting convictions who was an uncompromising Free Trader, an active philanthropist and a Liberal M.P. for Liverpool after 1868.

*17 March.* [Prince's Gate]

Kate's wedding. The pleasantest wedding I have ever been at. Congregation of true well-wishers, and the breakfast thoroughly enjoyed. Leonard spoke with much genuine feeling in reply to good old Mr Rathbone's emotional meandering. He [Courtney] is a thoroughly true-hearted strong-minded man. Every day one respects him more. His eldest sister, though she has little pretension to refinement, has a genuine ring about her. The evening before the marriage Kate goes up to her and says, sentimentally, 'I am afraid Leonard has a cold on his chest'. 'Cold!' says Miss Courtney in a hearty emphatic tone. 'Cold! Rubbish! Stomach cough. Look after the champagne', and the advice is not altogether unneeded. Leonard was nervous that night and much excited. No wonder. Marriage at their ages is rather a leap in the dark – curious to see how it turns out. . . .

*20 March.* [Prince's Gate]

Thursday before Good Friday. London deserted and a bitter cold wind blowing. Father, Rosy, Polly and myself alone. Others of the family scattered. Father naturally depressed at this anniversary of Mother's death. Have much conversation with him now on social and economic subjects. He, a strong political economist, not from the theoretical point of view, but from a practical acquaintance with a great variety of commercial undertakings, and an experience of the inevitable action of certain economic laws. If he would apply his mind to the subject he could surely, with his wide experience, throw some light on the probable success of the many schemes being now suggested to ensure the control and the profit of industry to the workman. Seems to me great disadvantage of the plan of small capitalists lies in their incapability of supporting a concern in depressed state. Large capitalists [are] virtually insured [because they invest] in other industries probably not subject to coincident depression. Alfred [Cripps] suggests that most concerns in the worst times would yield a subsistence to the good labourer – and, if not, there would be the large profits of good times accumulated in *their hands*. Father's great objection is a doubt as to the co-operative economy of a large body of workmen-shareholders. If only 20 per cent of the labourers accumulated capital in good times, they would practically have to support the industry in bad times and would eventually take the place of capitalist to the 80 per cent without capital. This, however, is a moral and not an economic question. Another objection is the one raised against all joint stock companies versus private business, the inferiority of salaried officers as managers, to the actual owners.

So long as there is an unlimited supply of labourers, that is to say, so long as they increase up to their means of subsistence while the classes of bosses, men with brains and capital, from the very nature of their qualifications at present cannot increase, and so long as there is a real advantage in the management of a concern by the owner versus that of a salaried officer, co-operative schemes will not in the majority of cases succeed in the competition for business. . . .

All this is no doubt very crude. I have read nothing on Political Economy, but all these problems are beginning to fascinate me and I want to think them over before reading about them.

Beatrice was reading the work of the German philosopher Arthur

Schopenhauer (1788–1860) at this time and she filled her diary with summaries, extracts and her own observations on it. The reference is to St Giles rectory in Salisbury, where Margaret Harkness was living in the late 1870s; at this time she and Beatrice exchanged a number of letters on religion, the prospects of marriage and their future careers.

*24 March.* [Prince's Gate]

Reading Herbert Spencer's *Psychology* diligently every morning. Those quiet three hours of study are the happiest ones in the day. Only one trouble continually arises – the stimulus a congenial study gives to my ambition, which is continually mortified by a gleam of self-knowledge. Meeting with the most ordinarily clever person forces me to appreciate my own inferiority. And yet, fool that I am, I can't help feeling that could I only devote myself to one subject, I could do something. However, I suppose that the most commonplace of persons every now and again catches sight of possibilities in his nature which from lack of other qualities are doomed to remain undeveloped. . . . What distresses me about my own little work is the small amount of material I have to work upon, the trivial subjectiveness of my thought. That is what I am painfully conscious of when I meet really clever men. My work, if it can be dignified by that name, is so amateurish and yet I don't know that I have a right to pretend to anything better and more businesslike.

All my duties lie in the practical direction; why should I, wretched little frog, try and puff myself into a professional? If I could rid myself of that mischievous desire to achieve, I could defend the few hours I devote to study by the truly satisfactory effect it has on my physical nature. It does keep me in health, whether through its direct influence on my circulation or through the indirect effect of a certain self-satisfaction it induces. Dissipation doesn't suit me, morally or physically, and I don't see why I shouldn't be true to my own nature and resist it.

It's extraordinary the improvement in Margaret Harkness since she has given herself up to work. When I first remember her at St Giles she was an hysterical egotistical girl with wretched health and still worse spirits. Her clerical and conventional parents tried to repress her extraordinary activity of mind, causing a state of morbid sensibility and fermentation which gave almost a permanent twist to her nature. Now that she has broken loose from all ties, supporting herself by literary piecework, living in a queer unconventional family with whom she is by no means one, she is blossoming out into a clever, interested and amusing young woman with much charm of looks and manner. Whenever she visits me we have delightful talks. She attaches much more importance to individuals, resenting what she has nicknamed 'my phantom theory'. She won't admit that persons, past and present, are as it were groups of qualities, bound up for the time in one form – this form perishing, the qualities alone being persistent. . . . Her mind naturally seizes upon and magnifies the characteristics of persons and the peculiar nature of their surroundings. This gives a charm to her companionship, especially as she takes a half-humorous, half-compassionate view of human nature and has a quaint picturesque way of expressing herself. . . .

Beatrice went on to give a long summary of Herbert Spencer's metaphysical arguments.

Rosy Potter was sent to an advanced school at Fontainebleau in France. The school was run by Marie Souvestre (d.1905), who later opened a similar establishment at Wimbledon, which was noted for its intellectual standards and its remarkably advanced attitude to the education of girls. She moved freely in English intellectual company, especially among the Positivists, free thinkers and radicals. Beatrice admired this 'brilliant and irreligious Frenchwoman' who seemed in some ways to be a model for her own life.

*31 March*. [Prince's Gate]
Rosy left for school. She has a sweet touching character which already is the centre of much love and will be of more. By no means deficient in strength of a passive kind – a certain solidity and steadfastness of feeling. Intellectually she has been much damaged by overstraining. . . . No imagination, no spirit of adventure has been developed. . . . What is so very attractive about her is her humility and the refreshing absence (for our family) of a hard self-assertiveness, of a determination to make our view of things felt and if possible noted upon. . . . At present all her intellectual interests are false. She has none, but she knows it, and acknowledges to herself that she affects them in order to interest others. And with Father this desire is prompted by real love and wish to be some comfort to him. Her ideal, intellectually, is like that of many of us. Rather too high for her capacity. . . . The serious mind that seeks perpetually the 'why and the wherefore' of all things it comes across must be tedious and tiresome, unless it possesses a transcendent analytical ability and even then it is a straining companion, to be on the whole avoided by the real workers. That is the worst of having no real aim and occupation, one

loses the capacity for true recreation. One goes into society to learn and not to amuse and when one loses the charm of youth one becomes an unmitigated prig, a future which I myself firmly foresee and which is confidently prophesied for me by Mary. At present I feel like a caged animal, bound up by the luxury, comfort and respectability of my position. I can't get a training that I want without neglecting my duty. This volume has witnessed a decided advance in the knowledge of what I require – perhaps the next may tell of my little attempt to grasp after it. Let us hope so! Amen.

## VOLUME 6

*20 April.* [Prince's Gate]
Changed my room to one looking on the square garden behind. I found that with my very limited power of concentration the rattling down Exhibition Road disturbed my morning meditations on 'Divine Philosophy'! Now I look upon green turf and budding trees which to my cockney eyes form quite a charming scene. Nevertheless my brain this morning is as muddled as it was yesterday, the truth being that the power one has for real honest thought is much more limited than one's time. . . .

'The circumstances of my life did not permit me to seek out one of the few university institutions then open to women,' Beatrice remarked in *My Apprenticeship* and, though she met enlightened and stimulating men, she realized that their 'casual conversations at London dinner-parties' could not take the place of the disciplined training the same men might give in a laboratory or lecture-room. She was thus obliged to make what she called 'pitifully ineffectual attempts' to educate herself in algebra, geometry, and then physiology, the last of these by 'casual attendance' on her brother-in-law, William Harrison Cripps. Cripps was at that time studying cancerous cells in the hope of discovering a carcinogenic bacillus.

*24 April.* [Prince's Gate]
My heart is so troublesome (physically, mentally it does not trouble me much!) that I can't read much this morning. It is useless keeping a couple of manuscript-books going – one can't have two confidants. One becomes attached to one of them, an affection which grows with the more or less perfect reflection of one's own little Ego. After all, one of the chief attractions of a 'diary-book' is that it serves as a mental

looking-glass, wherein to look at oneself complacently, and one does not like always to be reflected in the unbecoming clothes of tiresome effort to understand what is just outside the grasp of one's little intellect. Sometimes a pleasant chit-chat with oneself is refreshing. The other book shall be kept exclusively for that lowest result of social intercourse, a collection of amusing stories about 'big' people, all of them 'warranted untrue', and for any superficial observation and reflection on the typical persons I meet with in society. This book shall be devoted to 'Truth' or rather it shall be dedicated to Truth, for devotion implies intimacy or at least acquaintanceship, and that is more than I can pretend to.

Now my life is divided sharply into the thoughtful part and the active part, completely unconnected one with the other. They are in fact an attempt to realize the different and almost conflicting ideals necessitating a compromise as to energy and time which has to be perpetually readjusted. My only hope is that the one ideal is hidden from the world, the truth being that in my heart of hearts I'm ashamed of it and yet it is actually the dominant internal power. Fortunately for me all external forces support the other motive, so perhaps the balance is a pretty just one. But it is a curious experience, moving about among men and women, talking much, as you are obliged to do, and never mentioning those thoughts and problems which are your *real life* and which absorb, in their pursuit and solution, all the earnestness of your nature. This doubleness of motive, still more this disemblance towards the world you live in, extending even to your own family, must bring with it a feeling of unreality; worse, a loss of energy in the sudden transitions from the one life to the other. Happily one thing is clear to me. This state of doubtfulness will not be of long duration, and the work that is done during that state will not be useless to me in whichever vocation my nature and my circumstances eventually force me into. I shall surely some day have the veil withdrawn and be allowed to gaze unblinded on the narrow limits of my own possibilities.

*30 April.* [Prince's Gate]
The time rushes and I accomplish nothing. Only three months more and I am only *beginning* work – joined the C.O.S. (Charity Organization Society) and about to make arrangements for physiology lessons, with but a poor prospect of much doing, considering all the social duties that are fast absorbing time and energy. If I can only get well

started in laboratory work, it would be easy to continue it in the country. It is hopeless to attempt to do much connected work in London, but one can just see the things which will explain and illustrate a whole course of reading, and learn the art of manipulation which will enable one to see more in the country.

As for the C.O.S. I proposed to join it when in a slightly different state of mind, but the experience I shall gain from it will work in well with my 'human' studies. One learns very little about human nature from society. It is too much clothed with the 'conventionalities and seemings'.

*5 May.* [Prince's Gate]
How comic this is, all this excitement about nothing. After a dinner where I have talked, I am absolutely useless in the way of brain-work. And one gets precious little by talking; let us hope one *gives* 'amusement'. Spent the whole day with Herbert Spencer at private view. He worked out, poor man, a sad destiny for one whose whole life has been his work. There is something pathetic in the isolation of his mind, a sort of spider-like existence; sitting alone in the centre of his theoretical web, catching facts, and weaving them again into theory. It is sorrowful when the individual is lost in the work, when he is set apart to fulfil some function, and then when working days are past, left as the husk, the living kernel of which is given to the world. On looking around and watching men and women, one sees how important a part instinct plays in their lives, how all-important it becomes in old age when the purely intellectual faculties grow dim, and one appreciates the barrenness of an old age where the instinctive feelings are undeveloped and the subject matter for them absent. There is a look of sad resignation on Herbert Spencer's face, as if he fully realized his position and waited patiently for the end, to him absolutely final. To me there is a comic pathos in his elaborate search after pleasurable 'sensations', as if sensations can *ever* take the place of emotions; and alas! in his consciousness there hardly exists an 'exciting cause' for emotional feeling. And yet there is a *capacity* for deep feeling, which every now and then one discovers, a capacity which has lain dormant and is now covered up with crotchety ideas presenting a hedgehog's coat to the outer world, a surface hardly inviting contact!

I see what it is in him which is repulsive to some persons. It is the mental *deformity* which results from the extraordinary development of

83

the intellectual faculties joined with the very *imperfect* development of the sympathetic and emotional qualities, a deformity which, when it does not excite pity, excites dislike. There is no life of which I have a really intimate knowledge which seems to me so inexpressibly sad as the inarticulate life of Herbert Spencer, inarticulate in all that concerns his own happiness. . . .

The reference in this entry to a quarrel about the large trees by the lawn at The Argoed is obscure.

*15 May.* [Prince's Gate]
Spent a dreary three days at The Argoed and Standish. Miserably seedy, walked about as if in an unpleasant dream reminding me of olden days when headache was habitual and life weariness my ordinary frame of mind. Fear I was not much good as companion to darling Father. His great and tender devotion to her who has gone and to those she has left behind strikes me every day more strongly. The grand simplicity of his nature, his motives transparent and uncomplicated, all resolvable indeed into one – desire to make those belonging to him happy. Read to me yesterday some of his journal in Rome, when he was courting Mother. Just the same mind as now – uncritical reverence for what was beautiful and good, no trace of cynicism or desire to analyse and qualify. Perhaps in his business career, in business matters, he has developed a shrewdness and sharpness of thought and action and with it a cynical depreciation of men and their ways. But this is foreign to his nature, has been acquired in the struggle for existence and never enters into his intimate relationships. With him the instinctive feelings are paramount. He would sacrifice all, to some extent even his self-respect, if he thought the happiness of some loved one were at stake. He is far away the most unselfish nature and most unselfconscious nature I know.

The Argoed building looked most melancholy, *actually* ugly and made still more dismal by the feeling that it was the work of a *dead will*, uncared for by any living person, rising up defiantly. All associations there are now painful. The nine withering Wellingtonias, the record of the *one* quarrel, reminding Father of the few *black days* of his happy otherwise married life. Curious fate. Poor little Mother clung to that place as something which belonged to her *exclusively*; which was to be *for her* entirely, to make up to her for much self-devotion to her family; and yet it was in this place that she met with death, in this place only that she has left the remembrance of self-will. Poor little Mother, in her youth twisted, and yet for all that her course was straight towards the good, in direction, with some swaying of the pendulum of motive. Only one year dead!

*18 May.* [Prince's Gate]
Have seen a little into the working of the C.O.S. . . . when one comes to consider the cases that come before the Committee for help, cynical doubt will arise as to the benefit derived by the Society from charity of any sort, except the great benefit of developing the benevolence and increasing the experience of those who give their time and substance. Even with my slight insight into C.O.S. work it seems clear that it is a decided improvement on the old state of things. That there is certainly *less harm done*, that in relieving cases the ultimate effect on society is recognized and considered as an argument for or against the case.

Still in the majority of the cases it *must* be a systematic favouring of the weak and helpless often to the positive detriment of the stronger and the more helpful individuals; though in some 'cases' no doubt society is directly benefited by the individual being helped over a time of trouble, started afresh in his work and saved from becoming a charge on the nation. But can these general considerations have any weight when we come face to face with individual misery? And do these economic facts bear any proportion in importance to the moral facts with which 'charity' is concerned? Does not the advisability of charity depend on the moral qualities which are developed in the relationship of giver and receiver . . .?

One thing is clear to my mind, it is distinctly *advantageous to us* to go amongst the poor. We can get from them an experience of life which is novel and interesting; the study of their lives and surroundings gives us the facts wherewith we can attempt to solve the social problems; contact with them develops on the whole our finer qualities, disgusting us with our false and worldly application of men and things and educating in us a thoughtful benevolence. Perhaps the worst result for us is that our philanthropy is sometimes the cause of pharisaical self-congratulation. I have never noticed this in the real philanthropist; he is far too perplexed at the very 'mixed result' (even if he can recognize any permanent result) of his work, to feel much pride over it.

Edward Lott (1822–86) was Herbert Spencer's closest and oldest friend.

*20 May.* [Prince's Gate]

Visited this morning Pavey (C.O.S. case). Had been dispenser, took to opium eating, now unfitted for work. Wife earning 15*s* a week, has to support him and three children, two provided for by relations, one boarded out at 4*s* per week. Still clings to her baby, poor woman. 'Why should I be separated from my children as if I were a bad woman? What will they think of me? They will hear whispers against me and I slaving all the while, night and day. I cannot bear it much longer; I must give way.' The wretched man, standing sulkily in the corner, twisting his thumbs, cursing the existing order of things, talking of his better days and good education, could write well, talk and translate French, had a smattering of Greek and Latin. All to no purpose! One is tempted to a feeling of righteous indignation against the man, but did he not make himself wretched and is he not on the whole more pitiable? Look at the two faces. An expression on the one of dogged discontent and misery, ever present disgust of the world and himself; marking the woman's face, deep lines of unselfconscious effort, of perhaps agonizing struggle, agonizing in those moments when she felt herself face to face with the fact that in the end she *must* succumb; but still she loved, and the little one for whom she is giving away strength, and maybe life, smiles sweetly and stretches its tiny arms longingly towards her.

I walk back down Piccadilly, meeting the well-dressed young men and young women who had been praying to Jesus of Nazareth that he should forgive them having twirled and whirled and chattered through the last week – 'sensitively' ignoring the huge misery around them. At home I find Herbert Spencer and his devoted friend, Mr Lott. The poor philosopher well-nigh weary of his life, finding no rest. Dare hardly speak or be spoken to, lest he should pay for each word with hours of sleeplessness. He having mastered thought is a slave to thinking.

Eleanor Marx (1855–98) was the youngest child of Karl Marx. She was much interested in the theatre and in politics. At the time when Beatrice met her she and her common-law husband, Edward Bibbins Aveling (1851–98), were still active members of the Social Democratic Federation, but they were soon to break away and join the poet and designer William Morris in founding the Socialist League. Eleanor Marx also played a part in the campaign to organize the unskilled workers into trade unions. Her life ended tragically when, despairing of her unhappy relationship with Aveling, she committed suicide. George William Foote (1850–1915) founded the *Freethinker* in 1881 and was imprisoned for blasphemy in 1883. He succeeded Charles Bradlaugh as President of the National Secular Society. He also founded and edited the monthly, *Progress*, and it was Aveling, not Eleanor Marx, who edited it when he was in prison.

*24 May (early morning).* [Prince's Gate]
Went in afternoon to British Museum and met Miss Marx in refreshment rooms. Daughter of Karl Marx, socialist writer and refugee. Gains her livelihood by teaching 'literature', etc., and corresponding for socialist newspapers, now editing *Progress* in the enforced absence of Mr Foote. Very wrath about imprisonment of latter. 'I couldn't see much joke in those particular extracts but there was nothing wrong in them. Ridicule is quite a legitimate weapon. It is the weapon Voltaire used and did more good with it than any amount of serious argument. *We* think the Christian religion an *immoral illusion* and we wish to use *any* argument to persuade the people that it is false. Ridicule appeals to the people we have to deal with, with much greater force than any amount of serious logical argument. The striking difference of this century and the last is that free thought was the *privilege* of the upper classes then and it is becoming the *privilege* of the working classes now. We want to make them disregard the mythical next world and live for *this world* and *insist on having* what will make it pleasant to them.'

It was useless to disagree with her – she refused to recognize the beauty of the Christian religion. She read the Gospels as the gospels of damnation. Thought that Christ, if he had existed, was a weak-headed individual with a good deal of sweetness of character but quite lacking in heroism. 'Did he not in the last moment pray that the cup might pass from him?' When I asked her what the socialist programme was she very sensibly remarked that I might as well ask her to give me in a short formula the whole theory of mechanics. Socialist programme was a deduction from social science which was the most complicated of all sciences. I replied that from the very little I knew about political economy (the only social science we English understood) the social philosophers seemed to limit themselves to *describing forces*, they were more or less necessarians. She did not contradict this. I do not know whether it is true or not. In person she is comely, dressed in a slovenly picturesque way with curly black hair flying about in all directions.

Fine eyes full of life and sympathy, otherwise ugly features and expression, and complexion showing the signs of an unhealthy excited life, kept up with stimulants and tempered by narcotics. Lives alone, is much connected with Bradlaugh set, evidently peculiar views on love, etc., and I should think has somewhat 'natural' relations with men! Should fear that the chances were against her remaining long within the pale of 'respectable' society. Asked me to come and see her. Exactly the life and character I should like to study. Unfortunately one cannot mix with human beings without becoming more or less *connected* with them. If one *takes* one must also *give* and a permanent relationship gradually rises up.

Chamberlain took 72 Prince's Gate as his London residence 1880–82, and lived at 40 Prince's Gardens from 1883 until his death. Beatrice met him at a dinner party given by a wealthy neighbour, Miss Williams. Beatrice was taking lessons in physiology.

*3 June*. [Prince's Gate]
Wretchedly wasted week. No hard work done. Sick headache from over-eating and under-exercising. Met sundry distinguished men, among others Joseph Chamberlain. I do, and I don't, like him. Talking to 'clever men' in society is a snare and delusion as regards interest. Much better read their books. If one could know them intimately, watch them at work and at home, and note the effect of the 'abnormal development', [that would be] quite another thing.

Lessons most interesting. . . . Before us on the table diagrams, microscopic sections, and various dissections – these last do not distress me but give me genuine pleasure to pick to pieces. One leaves behind all personalities, and strives to ascertain the constitution of things. . . . To me there is a deep and perplexing pathos in this study of Life and Death. . . . In me, such a study strengthens necessarianism; and as I hurry down Tottenham Court Road and jostle up against the men and women of the 'people' with their various expressions of determined struggle, weak self-indulgence and discontented effort, the conviction that the fate of each individual is governed by conditions born of 'the distant past' is irresistibly forced upon me. . . .

Herbert Spencer gave an annual picnic near Weybridge for his friends. Among them were Algernon Freeman-Mitford (1837–1916) who became Lord Redesdale, and Sir George Young (1837–1930), a distinguished administrator who strongly supported the higher education of women. Miss Chamberlain was Chamberlain's younger sister Clara (who later married Frederick Ryland). She and his daughter, Beatrice, were then part of his household.

*27 June.* [Prince's Gate]
Last Saturday spent at St George's Hill with a large party of somewhat elderly persons. [Mr and Lady Clementine] Mitford, [Mr and Mrs Charles James] Cropper, Sir G. Young, Sir W. Warrebus, Courtneys, Playnes and Chamberlains. Spent most of the afternoon with Miss Chamberlain – a really genuine woman, who is somewhat perplexed and bored by London Season life. Essentially provincial in the good and the bad sense. Mr Chamberlain joined us in the evening and I had much conversation with him. His personality interested me. Mr Mitford, aristocrat and diplomatist, with a 'divine' French accent and most charming manner, Lady Clementine (his wife) pleasant attractive woman and little else.

Gradually sinking into a do-nothing worthless life. Ah me!

*7 July.* [Prince's Gate]
Herbert Spencer called looking absolutely wretched. No better. 'I have no patience with what is disagreeable. I don't know what to do with myself. Even if I go fishing what can I do with my evenings without pleasant society? I am terribly bored.' Poor man, sinking into misery, with no loving hand to help him.

Seen more of C.O.S. work, visited various cases. What is wanted in London is a body of persons who would make it their business to know thoroughly each district, the capabilities and wants; and would have the means of getting at like information about other districts. London is so huge, and the poor are so helpless and ignorant, do not know even of those advantages which are open to them. The clergy, as an adequate organization, are worked out. Some secular body must take their place. Why do these hundreds and thousands of cultivated people go on boring themselves with unrealities when there is near to them this terrible reality of tortured life? If I could only devote my life to it I might do something, but that is not my fate! Perhaps I stand now on the eve of a new life, shall watch the sun rise and disappear behind a black cloud extending out into a grey sky cover. I shall not be deceived by its glory. If it is to be so, there is work and the influence that work brings, but not happiness. Am I strong enough to face that?

Galton's *Enquiry into Human Faculty* was published in 1883, being the third of the studies of heredity and intellectual capacity he published between 1869 and 1906.

*Sunday, 15 July.* [Prince's Gate]
If a future Francis Galton should ever invent a machine for registering thoughts as they rush through the brain, many humiliating reflections will be forced upon us during the London Season. He speaks in his *Enquiry into Human Faculty* of the mind 'mumbling over the old stories' but in the Society life one leads in this Babylon one's brain is for the most part engaged in 'chattering over its newest impressions'. Conversation becomes a mania, and a most demoralizing one. Even when alone, it is continued in a sort of undertone and the men and women one has met strut about on the ghostly stage, monopolizing in their de-materialized forms the little time and energy left. I suppose persons with real capabilities can take Society as relaxation without becoming absorbed by it; but then if it is to be relaxation one must not have much to do with all that elaborate machinery which moves it.

As it is, what between arrangements (which seem endless) and the strangeness of this disconnected companionship with many different minds, all superior in strength and experience to my own, the little mind I ever had is out of joint and useless. When I am not organizing, I am either talking with my tongue, or a lively conversation is going on within the 'precincts of my skull'. Reading and meditating are equally impossible. A train of thought is an unknown experience. A series of pictures in which the human beings represented have the capability of speech and gesture succeed one another. The mind seems for the time to lose its personality, to be transformed into a mirror of reflecting men and women with their various surroundings, one's own little ego walking in and out amongst them, looking small and insignificant beside them. Certainly 'Society' has carried the day – my own pursuits have gone pretty well to the dogs, but oh, how I long for rest. And for time to digest!!!!!!!!!!!

Interesting dinner here on the 18th. A Whig peer on one side and Joseph Chamberlain on the other. Whig peer talked of his own possessions, Chamberlain *passionately* of getting hold of other people's – for the masses. Curious and interesting character, dominated by *intellectual passions* with little self-control but with any amount of *purpose*. Herbert Spencer on Chamberlain: 'A man who may mean

well, but who does, and will do, an incalculable amount of mischief.'
Chamberlain on Herbert Spencer: 'Happily, for the majority of the
world, his writing is not intelligible, otherwise his life would have
been spent in doing harm.' No personal animus between them, but a
fundamental antipathy of mind. In what does it originate? I understand the working of Herbert Spencer's reason, but I do not
understand the reason of Chamberlain's passion. But then the motive
force which moves the man of action is seldom rational. Philosophers
will influence but never rule the world: at least not until the human
nature of the masses is fundamentally different, and then I suppose the
philosophers too will have advanced into a still calmer sphere! How I
should like to study that man!

I have come across many interesting individuals this season, typical
beings with special work to do in this world . . . work for which
human sacrifice must be made, of their own and others' happiness.
And those who would do the work, or would help others to do it, must
recognize this truth – for the days of self-renunciation and painful
conflict are not passed, and the great central idea of Christianity, the
sacrifice of the individual to the community, must still be the morning
star which leads to greatness. . . .

'If I have any vain regrets for absent opportunities it is exactly this,'
Beatrice reflected in *My Apprenticeship*, 'that I grew up to maturity as a
sociological investigator without a spell of observation and experiment in the
modern science of psychology.' It was, she said, 'the barren futility of the
text-books then current' that repelled her. 'Instead of the exact descriptions
of the actual facts of individual minds, reacting to particular environments
and developing in different directions, I seemed to find nothing but
arbitrary definitions of mind in the abstract. . . . For any detailed description of the complexity of human nature, of the variety and mixture in human
motive, of the insurgence of instinct in the garb of reason, of the
multifarious play of the social environment on the individual ego. . . . I had
to turn to novelists and poets.'

*23 July.* [Prince's Gate]
What is to be my work this autumn? I have got hold of a certain
number of physiological facts but what am I going to do with them?
What do I want with physical facts when my real interest is in
psychology? . . . Certainly the scientific mind seems to me the fairest,
the most *purely rational*. The only test it acknowledges is *truth* (in its
most literal and perhaps narrowest sense), a demonstrable accordance
of idea with fact. . . . But then when we come to human nature, and

to *human nature in combination*, is it possible to discern the chain or chains of events? And in practical politics, if we are forced to interfere through government with the sequence of events and to introduce new factors which will disturb the natural order of things, is it not safer on the whole to be governed by the instinctive cravings of society than by theories based on 'little knowledge'? Why should we not regard society as an individual, and acknowledge that it is natural and right that it should gratify the sensations and desires through the agency of self-government? Is it not possible that government is not a thing external and foreign to the community, but merely the external organ by which the society adjusts its actions to the conditions of the surrounding medium?

What is now my best course in the development of my own wee mind, the only question at present within the region of *my* practical politics? My power of *mastering facts* . . . is so minute that I cannot afford to spend much time and energy upon collecting and mastering facts from which I do not intend to reason. On the other hand, if life is a whole which begins with one thread and subdivides into many, or still better a tree of which each little twig . . . is only a reproduction as it were of the original trunk, shall we not better understand the *direction* of the growth by studying the main trunk than by looking curiously into some one mass of little twigs, all hopelessly intertwined with one another? . . . Therefore I shall go creeping up from the *ground*.

*27 July.* [Prince's Gate]
Last evening at Prince's Gate. Alone. Looking from this dismal back room on to the square garden. From behind those trees and distant houses I have watched many a sunrise, when sleepless from excitement. One in particular which I superstitiously remember.

'And so ends the London Season!' Beatrice wrote to Mary Playne at the end of July, 'and I shall return with a clear "social" conscience to my dowdy dress (black lace and all!), early hours, and dear books.' Number 10 Rutland Gate, Knightsbridge, was the London home of Beatrice's sister, Georgina Meinertzhagen.

*15 August. Rutland Gate*
Alas! Alas! the whirlpool!

Beatrice specified only one of the 'two books' – Renan's *Souvenirs d'enfance et de jeunesse*, on which she commented at length.

### 27 August. [Standish]
The whirlpool is past for the present – the current of my life may bring me again within the sphere of its attraction but now I again swim freely; with green banks of tangled verdure on each side I look dreamily into their depth and pick out for curiosity the quaintly coloured forms. Two books have at present fascinated me, and I will study and analyse them carefully before I set myself again to grapple with physiology, with a view of understanding the materialistic theory of psychology. My own individual life may be worthless, and if I am ever absorbed into another life I shall no doubt appreciate the pettiness of past existence, but today I feel as if I should regret it bitterly were I once to renounce it.

The Three Choirs Festival, which dates from 1724, is held annually at Gloucester, Worcester and Hereford in rotation. It lasts for several days and is a charitable fund raising event. Sir Richard Temple (1826–1902) was a notable administrator in India.

### 10 September. [Standish]
Said farewell to a curiously mixed party of acquaintances staying with us for the Gloucester Festival. Six or seven ordinary young persons . . . and a distinguished Indian governor – Sir R. Temple, distinguished most for his excessive ugliness. . . . Poor man. After generously orating to us for three days he tried in vain to gain information from Leonard Courtney, but our superior brother-in-law remains to all men inarticulate. I am now quite fond of him because I have ceased to expect to be interested by him. . . . Still, when those shaggy eyebrows are drawn together, and those capacious lips are parted, I listen breathlessly to the words of the oracle. . . . Alas! my thoughts run on politics now or, rather, wander hopelessly and aimlessly in the labyrinth of political problems, knocking up against fellow wanderers, who, unlike me, *seem* to be guided by some invisible thread.

Beatrice continued her study of physiology through the summer at Standish, using her diary to clarify her thoughts.

### 17 September. [Standish]
There is little doubt in my mind that comparative physiology, i.e.

knowledge of the development of animal life, is the only key to and the only basis for a science of sociology. . . .

*22 September.* [Standish]
I intend to work up those physiology papers and read (John) Stuart Mill's *Logic* [*A System of Logic*, 1843] and do as much practical work in the way of dissection and microscopic investigation as may be. In the meantime . . . refusing even to receive the impress of those pictures which are constantly passing before me, some of them passing away into the dimness of the irretrievable past. One such scene: in the Standish garden and the family life therein during the warm summer months. . . . It has been our nursery, and our playground, afterwards the place of our suffering, the half-hated, the half-loved, companion and confidant in our *ennui* and melancholy *dénouement*. We have wandered arm in arm along its paths, or moodily lounged under the trees hoping through companionship or through solitude to gain some rest and solace from that eternal question: 'For what good?'

And then the brighter days; and these more frequent as one grew in strength, when one revelled in delicious sensations and brooded over exciting thoughts arising from a sympathy with minds deeper and nobler than one's own — thought over past argument and dreamt of future achievement or perchance of — love. . . .

Beatrice was invited to stay in Chamberlain's London house.

*26 September.* [London?]
Spent the whole week with Miss Chamberlain. A quiet, genuine woman not attractive or interesting in person or intellect, sympathetic in character, valuing things truly and attempting honestly to guide herself and others by high principles. Threw more light on Joseph Chamberlain's character. Coming from such honest surroundings he surely *must* be straight in intention. He is one of many able minds who are all working for the same end and choosing the same means, yet all is darkness when I try to discover their meaning. Much might be learnt in studying the life and thought of such a man, discovering how *representative* he was, how much his convictions were the result of individual characteristics and how much they were the effect of surrounding circumstances. They are *convictions* passionately held, his whole energy is thrown into the attempt to realize them. Is the basis of those convictions honest experience and thought or were they origi-

nally the tool of ambition, now become inextricably woven into the love of power, and to his own mind no longer distinguishable from it? What is his principle? Is the government the interpretation of people's wants? Is it the business of the governing class to gratify the sensations of the great social organism, or should the advice of the more intelligent portion of the community be taken as the remedies, irrespective of the longings of the patient? If the government is an outside force to be directed by the ablest minds and, in remedial measures, against the dire disorder of society, then it is a question of correct diagnosis and of a most deeply thought out treatment; possibly the wisest physician will leave most to nature. If, however, government is only an organ of the body-politic, its function is the gratification of the instincts of the community. To resist this legitimate gratification would be to increase the hunger – until it could no longer be appeased without injury to the whole nature. Is that his principle?. . .

*5 November.* [The Argoed]
Three weeks thoroughly enjoyed at The Argoed, and some good work done. Solitude too has matured my plans for the future. *If* I remain free (which alas is a big if) I see pretty clearly where the work is which I *would* do. Whether I have sufficient faculty remains to be seen. Proof of incapacity will not be wanting if I am strong enough to see it. At present, in this phase of my work, my duties as an ordinary woman are not interfered with by the pursuit of my private ends. I doubt whether they would ever need be, if one chose to remain unmarried. It is almost necessary to the health of a woman, physical and mental, to have definite home duties to fulfil: details of practical management and, above all things, someone dependent on her love and tender care. So long as Father lives and his home is the centre for young lives, I have mission enough as a *woman.* If to this *most* important work I could join another work and work that would satisfy the restless ambition of my nature, then possibly I might remain content to know only through sympathy those feelings which absorb the energies of most women. A time would come when I should stand alone; destitute of those close intimacies, which become ever more precious as animal spirits and intellectual energies fail. If I could not honestly say, 'the work was good', I should bitterly regret the absence of human ties, the neglect and disease of those powers for good which belong to all women alike. Still, one must have courage, faith in oneself, trusting to

the sincerity of one's nature to tell one when it is misplaced. All I can pray for is vigour, freedom from petty self-congratulation, vain castles which hide from view the clear horizon. . . .

This next fortnight will show me pretty clearly whether or not I have the gift of social diagnosis, and the next entry in this diary will be the means of testing it.

Beatrice proposed to test her powers of social description by a visit to Bacup, a town of textile mills and steep terraced streets where the River Irwell runs out of the moors and south towards Manchester. The town is close to Rochdale where the Co-operative movement began in 1844, and Co-operation flourished equally among the self-respecting Nonconformist artisans of Bacup. It was here that Beatrice became seriously interested in the Co-operative alternative to individualist profit-making on the one hand and state socialism on the other. Beatrice's richer Heyworth relatives had long since moved away from Bacup, but there were still a number of poor connections living there – mainly Ashworths and Akeds – and Beatrice was introduced to them by Martha Jackson ('Dada'), who had become Martha Mills after marrying the Potter butler. Although Beatrice stayed in Bacup from 7 November to 20 November, she did not make any diary entries at the time. The only detailed reference in the diary is a long retrospective entry on 31 October 1886. But the vivid impression the visit made on her can be judged from the first and second letters she wrote to her father, which she considered to be a substitute for the report she never wrote in her diary. To avoid mutual embarrassment she gave herself the travelling name of Miss Jones.

[*First letter:*] We arrived at Bacup about 6.30 and found our way along very ill-lighted back streets to this old-fashioned house at the back of the chapel. We were received by a regular old Puritan and his daughter (a millhand) in the most hearty fashion; prayers being offered up for our safety and spiritual well-being while under their roof. After we had enjoyed some delicious tea and home-made bread and butter, various of the elders dropped in to welcome Mrs Mills, to whom they are evidently devoted, and who is quite a great lady amongst them. She introduced me with the most bare-faced effrontery as 'Miss Jones, farmer's daughter, who had come here to see town life and manufacturers', and they all showed themselves anxious to 'lighten my ignorance' on things material and spiritual. I have been quite received into the charmed circle of artisan and small-bourgeois life, and have made special friends with John Aked, a meek, gentle-hearted man who suffers from the constitutional melancholy of the Aked family. I hear that a brother and sister of Grandmama Heyworth committed suicide, and two or three of the family have been threatened with suicidal mania. Perhaps it is from that quarter that we get our *Weltschmerz*. This morning he escorted us through Bacup, and I saw Rose Cottage and Willow Cottage, where our grandmama lived and died. Also Bankside and Fern Hill, the houses of the great Heyworth and Ormerod families. We dined with John Wooded, his wife and only son (cousins of Da's) and I have been listening to one continuous kind-hearted gossip interspersed with pious ejaculations and shrewd remarks on the most likely method of getting the good things of this world. Certainly the way to see industrial life is to live amongst the workers, and I am surprised at the complete way they have adopted me as one of their own class. I find it less amusing and much more interesting than I expected; and I am heartily glad that I made the venture.

[*Second letter:*] I am going on most satisfactorily. I find a diary out of the question; one has neither the time nor the place for writing. These folk live all day in 'coompany'; there are always some millhands [cotton-weavers] out of work who spend their days chatting in each other's houses. This house, too, is the centre of chapel-goers, and is used by the relieving officer to distribute the poor-rate.

Bacup is quite a small manufacturing town. The 'old gentry', 'them as really was gentry', have disappeared, and the present manufacturers are self-made men, 'who are much more greedy like than the old lot'. The Whitakers still own the land, but they come only to drain the land of money, to the evident indignation of the inhabitants. The Ormerods and Heyworths were looked upon 'as real gentry'. John Aked told me yesterday (in a six-mile walk with him across the country; he is out of work) that 'Lawrence Heyworth was one of those men who married his servant, and she was my aunt; but I've heard tell by those who've seen her, she was a bonny one to look at'. I asked him what had become of the family, and he said: 'I've not heard mich of them, save Mrs Potter, and folk say she was an able, stirring body; you've a look of that, Miss Jones, far more like a male than a female to talk wi'.'

They have not as yet the slightest suspicion: the old hands look at me with admiration, 'as a right useful sort of body as would be a comfort to my father', and the young men with a certain amount of amazement and fear. One shrewd old man smelt a rat and asked me whether my father was not a Lord, and when I told him he was an honest farmer, he strained all my knowledge of farming by cross-questions as to stock, etc.; but at last he was disarmed, and remarked that if he came south he would 'coom un 'ave a chat wi' ye father', and he would like to see these Welsh lasses 'if they'd all got sich white teeth and glistening 'air' as I; but he thought we had it 'middling snod (smooth) wi' ye, e'en warty' (even on weekdays). The same shrewd old man told me a lot about the failure of the company mills owned by working men [Co-operatives]; how the managers were invariably tipped to take worse goods for the same money, and how the committees of working men 'got talkin' like'.

Many of these are shut up; in fact, trade here is worse now than it has ever been; but there is comparatively little poverty, and those who remain out of work move on to the big towns where there are more 'odd jobs'. The wife of the old man with whom we were 'ta in' was a jolly fat woman who talked such broad Lancashire that I could scarce understand her; but in the course of the evening she bashfully admitted that she 'summat took a bit of backy', whereupon I produced my cigarette-case and offered the company some 'Welsh cigars'. You would have laughed, Father, to see me sitting amongst four or five millhands smoking quietly, having been voted 'good company', 'interesting like' to talk wi'.

Under the benign influence of tobacco the elder ones came out with the history of their lives, gave me a list of their various successive occupations, and some of them of their series of wives. I was surprised at their fair-mindedness, and at the kindliness of their view of men and things; now they all recognize that men get on from having certain qualities and that 'na makin' of laws can alter that'. This class of respectable working man takes little or no interest in politics (they have no votes); their thoughts are set on getting on in this world and the next; their conversation consists chiefly of personalities and religion. The old man and his daughter with whom we were staying are a veritable study in Puritan life on its more kindly side; worth a dozen history books on the subject. We always have prayers in the evening, and I have been constituted the reader as I pronounce 'so distinct like'. It is curious how completely at home I feel with these people, and how they open their hearts to me and say that I'm 'the sort of woman "they" can talk straight away with'.

I can't help thinking that it would be as well if politicians would live amongst the various classes they legislate for, and find out what are their wishes and ideas. It seems to me we stand the chance, in our so-called representative government, of representing and working out the wishes of the idler sort of people, who, because they have no quiet occupation absorbing their time and energy, have time and energy to make a row, and wish to alter things because they don't fit themselves. Of course it would be absurd to generalize from such a narrow basis; but much that one sees and hears whilst living with the working men and women as one of them sets one thinking that a little more patient observation might be advisable before carrying out great organic changes, which may or may not be right. Mere philanthropists are apt to overlook the existence of an independent working class, and when they talk sentimentally of the 'people', they mean really the 'ne'er-do-weels'. It is almost a pity that the whole attention of these politicians should be directed towards the latter class.

*20 November.* [Standish]
I shall not write in this book the detailed account of Bacup and its inhabitants. Upon that account I shall rest my claims to an individual life and the Spirit of Truth grant that I may see clearly. The last evening at Bacup I heard a grand sermon from a Dissenting minister, without culture; who had been a farmer the first part of his life and had left his work only when called upon by the divine spirit. . . . I was strongly moved as I listened to the words of that thin spare-looking man whose whole frame seemed shaken by the earnestness of his spirit and in silence I renewed the vow that I would work for the cause of goodness and truth; and prayed that I might be shown my way clearly.

There had clearly been some discussion within the family about Chamberlain's intentions, for Beatrice wrote to Mary Playne in October in a manner that revealed her ambivalence. 'If, as Miss Chamberlain says, the Right Honourable gentleman takes "a very conventional view of women", I may be saved all temptation by my unconventionality. I certainly shall not hide it. He would soon see that I was not the woman to "forward" his most ambitious views.' At the same time, and despite the fact that both her father and Herbert Spencer disliked the man, she had invited Chamberlain and two of his children to visit the Potters at the New Year.

*24 November.* [Standish]
Alas! the whirlpool. Only two months and I shall be sailing past it for weal or for woe.

*7 December.* [Standish]
I began my account but a practical problem has intervened and I must keep all my strength of mind to deal with it. One thing I will *not* do. I will not give way to a feeling, however strong, which is not sanctioned by my better self. I will not desert a life in which there are manifold opportunities for good for a life in which my nature is at war with itself.

*27 December.* [Standish]
Rather a miserable dinner-party. Old philosopher very low, feeling his pulse and looking suspiciously at every morsel of food, speaking grudgingly every word. . . .

Yesterday better. 'It would never have done for me to marry,' he said. 'I could not have stood the monotony of married life and then I should have been too fastidious. I must have had a rational woman with great sympathy and considerable sense of humour.' 'Rather difficult to find,' I observed. 'Rational women are generally odiously dull and self-centred.' 'That is a very erroneous generalization; George Eliot was highly rational and yet intensely sympathetic, but there the weak point (which appeared a very important one to me) was physique.' 'I could not have married a woman who had not great physical attraction,' added the withered old philosopher, stretching his bony limbs out and leaving that patent theory-making machine on the side of the armchair, his upper lip appearing preternaturally long and his eyes preternaturally small.

Father, what between past remembrances and future prospects, was excited and really unhappy, though he did his best to appear genial and happy. Slight feeling of jar in the whole party, and consciousness of wide difference of opinion on a possibly *coming* question. When host and hostess are not at peace with themselves and the world there is not much chance of real geniality. However, my tortured state cannot long endure. The 'to be or not to be' will soon be settled.

Sir James Knowles (1831–1908) was the founder and editor of the *Nineteenth Century*.

*New Year's Eve. Standish*
Rosebud and I alone.

It is indeed an Eve for me. Two distinct ways open to me, one of which, it seems inevitable, that I must take. Herbert Spencer's last words: 'It is not only foolish but absolutely wrong of you not to publish your Bacup experiences. At the present time, a protest, formed on actual observation of the working man in his normal state against the pernicious tendency of political activity, would be invaluable. I shall arrange with Knowles about publishing an article from you.' And while the old philosopher is discussing with the editor of the *Nineteenth Century* the desirability of encouraging a beloved disciple to come into the literary arena, the same beloved disciple is entertaining with no *un*tender feeling the arch-enemy, the very embodiment of the 'pernicious tendency'.

And this horrible dilemma which appears to threaten me (principle versus feeling) renders all my thought egotistical. My own immediate fate stares me in the face wherever I turn. I seem to be moving onward amidst a company of phantoms, some pushing others restraining; but both parties equally ghostly in their powers, equally immaterial in their influence on the result. I, too, seem to be as in a dream, acting a part with my own family as audience, a part which *makes itself* as I go on, the final scene of which lies not within that healthy region of free-willing foresight. And as the time approaches I *dare* not *think*, but trust that the energy stored up in days of thought*lessness* will suffice for the last struggle; or that perchance some current arising within the 'whirlpool' will drift me outward. This truly is my last hope; if I do hope for continued independence of mind and body.

## ༀ 1884 ༈

*12 January. The Argoed*
Another small episode of my life over. After six weeks of feverish indecision, the day [of Chamberlain's arrival] comes. House full of young people and the three last days passed in dancing and games: I feel all the while as if I were dancing in a dream towards some precipice. Saturday 5th remainder of the ball party chatting round the afternoon tea table, the great man's son and daughter amongst them.. The door opens – 'Mr Chamberlain', general uprising. I advance from amongst them, and in my nervousness almost press six pounds just received into his hand. General feeling of discomfort; no one quite understanding the reason of Mr Chamberlain's advent. There exists evidently no cordiality between him and his host, for Father in a

few minutes returns to play patience with an absent and distressed look, utterly disgusted at the *supposed* intentions of his visitor.

At dinner, after some shyness, we plunged into essentials and he began to delicately hint his requirements. That evening and the next morning till lunch we are on 'susceptible terms'. A dispute over state education breaks the charm. 'It is a question of authority with women; if you believe in Herbert Spencer you won't believe in me.' This opens the battle. By a silent arrangement we find ourselves in the garden. 'It pains me to hear any of my views controverted', and with this preface he begins with stern exactitude to lay down the articles of his political creed. I remain modestly silent; but noticing my silence he remarks that he requires 'intelligent sympathy' from women. 'Servility, Mr Chamberlain,' think I, not sympathy, but intelligent servility: what many women give men, but the difficulty lies in changing one's master, in jumping from one *tone* of thought to the exact opposite – *with intelligence*. And then I advanced as boldly as I dare my feeble objections to his general proposition, feeling that in this case I owe it to the man to show myself and be absolutely sincere. He refutes my objections by re-asserting his convictions passionately, his expression becoming every minute more gloomy and determined. He tells me the history of his political career, how his creed grew up on a basis of experience and sympathy, how his desire to benefit 'the many' had become gradually a passion absorbing within itself his whole nature. 'Hitherto the well-to-do have governed this country for their own interests; and I will do them this credit, they have achieved their object. Now I think the time is approaching for those who work and have not. My aim in life is to make life pleasanter for this great majority. I do not care in the process if it becomes less pleasant for the well-to-do minority. Take America for instance; cultured persons complain that the society there is vulgar, less agreeable to the delicate tastes of delicately trained minds, but it is infinitely preferable to the ordinary worker.' I suggest meekly that this characteristic of American society does not appear to have any relation to a superior equalization of conditions, brought about by American institutions. That no doubt the working class are better off, but that that surely is due to the unlimited space and power of development of the American continent; on the other hand, huge fortunes are accumulated and *seem* to be more limitless than in England and to wield more power. That in fact the plutocracy, owing to the generally corrupt nature of American institutions, *is said* to be more powerful there than in any country.

And so we wandered up and down the different paths of the Standish garden, the mist which had hid the chasm between us gradually clearing off. Not a suspicion of feeling did he show towards me. He was simply determined to assert his convictions. If I remained silent he watched my expression narrowly, I felt his curious scrutinizing eyes noting each movement at if he were anxious to ascertain whether I yielded to his absolute supremacy. If I objected to or ventured to qualify his theories or his statements, he smashed objection and qualification by an absolute denial, and continued his assertion. He remarked as we came in that he felt as if he had been making a speech. I felt utterly exhausted, we hardly spoke to each other the rest of the day. The next morning, when the Playnes had left, he suggested some more 'exercise'. I *think* both of us felt that all was over between us, so that we talked more *pleasantly*, but even then he insisted on bringing me back from trivialities to a discussion as to the intellectual subordination of women. 'I have only one domestic trouble: my sister and daughter are bitten with the women's rights mania. I don't allow any action on the subject.' 'You don't allow division of opinion in your household, Mr Chamberlain?' 'I can't help people *thinking* differently from me.' 'But you don't allow the expression of the difference?' 'No.' And that little word ended our intercourse.

Now that the pain and indecision are over, I can't help regretting that absorption in the peculiar nature of our relationship left me so little capable of taking the opportunities he gave me of knowing him. The political creed is the whole man; the outcome of his peculiar physical and mental temperament played upon by the experiences of his life. He is neither a reasoner nor an observer in the scientific sense. He does not deduce his opinions by the aid of certain well-thought-out principles, from certain carefully observed, ascertained facts. He aims, rather, at being the organ to express the *desires* of those he believes to be the majority of his countrymen. His power rests on his intuitive knowledge of the wishes of a certain class of his countrymen, his faculty of formulating the same and of re-impressing these wishes forcibly on a mass of indifferent-minded men, who, because these desires are co-existent with their apparent or real interests, have them latent within them. Whether these desires are normal, and the gratification of them consistent with the health and well-being of the English body politic, is a question upon which I certainly do not presume to have an opinion. He is an organ of great individual force, the extent of his influence will depend on the relative power of the class he is adopted to represent.

By nature he is an enthusiast and a despot. A deep sympathy with the misery and incompleteness of most men's lives, and an earnest desire to right this, transforms political action into a religious crusade; but running alongside this genuine enthusiasm is a passionate desire to *crush* opposition to *his will*, a longing to put his foot on the necks of others, though he would persuade himself that he represents the right and his adversaries the wrong. In this belief, he, as a man with a vigorous reason, occasionally feels shaken. If it were to fail, the rationale of the whole tenor of his thought and action would be destroyed. Therefore he hates the moderate man, the man who refuses to allow that political principles are a question of morality and asserts that they should be the result of exercising your reason on certain disputable facts. He prefers the adversary who regards him as the incarnation of the evil one and answers his cold sneers with virulent abuse. Enthusiasm and self-will are the dominant forces in Chamberlain's mind. A keen, calculating intellect, admirable in manipulating practical detail and in adapting the means to the end, considerable diplomatic power and personal influence over men are the instruments whereby he effects his objects.

And now that it is all over, I have a stunned feeling as I gradually wake up to the old surroundings. . . . Plenty of practical work immediately in front of me, which will absorb my small bit of energy for the next six weeks. Then a return to the old work. Only everyday actual observation of men and things takes the place of accumulating facts from books and boudoir trains of thought. Undoubtedly the Bacup trip is the right direction. To profit by that kind of observation I *must* gain more knowledge of legal and commercial matters, understand the theory of government before I can appreciate the deficiencies in the practice. The time is now come for some defined object towards which all my energies must be bent. . . .

It was towards the end of January that Beatrice received her invitation to Highbury, the house which Chamberlain had recently built. The meeting at Birmingham was on 29 January. John Bright (1811–89), a Birmingham M.P. for thirty years, was a leader of the Free Trade movement, a member of three of Gladstone's cabinets. Though strong for parliamentary reform, his *laissez-faire* convictions led him to oppose government action to aid the poor. Yewtree was the name of Lawrence Heyworth's house near Liverpool. The Kenricks were related to the Chamberlains, and Joseph had married two of them. Arthur Chamberlain was Joseph's brother. Philip Muntz (1839–1908) was one of the three M.P.s who sat for Birmingham. The 'caucus' was the local Liberal Party organization set up by Chamberlain as part of his move to decentralize and strengthen the Liberal Party in the country. Francis Schnadhorst (1840–1901) was Chamberlain's main supporter in his bid to lead Radical Nonconformity. As secretary to the Birmingham Liberal Party he played a decisive role in the reorganization of the Party locally and nationally. He was appointed the first secretary of the National Liberal Federation when it was set up in 1877 and was the chief organizer of the Liberal victories of 1880, 1885 and 1892. George Melly was M.P. for Stoke-on-Trent.

*16 March.* [Standish]
Receiving a pressing letter from Miss Chamberlain, and feeling convinced that the negotiation was off, I saw no harm in going for two days to Birmingham to watch the great man at home. I am afraid there is a dash of the adventuress about me, and it struck me as rather comically interesting to investigate the top-most branch of the caucus under the circumstances.

Highbury is a very elaborately built red-brick house with numberless bow windows and long glass orchid-houses stretching along the brow of the hill upon which it is placed.

Inside there is very much *taste* and all very bad. At first you admire the bright softness of the colouring and general luxurious comfort of the rooms and furniture, but after four and twenty hours the whole palls on you, and you long for a bare floor and plain deal table. The two Miss Chamberlains sit ill at ease in the midst of the luxury. They are dressed with the dowdiness of the middle class, and are both of them simple and genuine, naturally inclined for hard work and simple fare, and loving the easy intercourse of family life and intimate friendships. From the great man they get conversation but little sympathy; possibly they don't give it. He comes and goes, asks his friends and entertains them and sees little of his womenkind. In Birmingham they make kindly homely hostesses and are useful to him; in London they are glum and sit silently between the distinguished men who dine with the future 'Prime Minister' and try in vain to interest and be interested in the fashionable worldly-wise wives who stay the correct time in the drawing-room. . . .

In spite of the luxury and brightness of the house, a gloom overhangs the 'Home'. The drawing-room with its elaborately carved marble arches, its satin paper, rich hangings and choice watercolours

105

has a forlornly grand appearance. No books, no work, no music, not even a harmless antimacassar, to relieve the oppressive richness of the satin-covered furniture. Here on Tuesday afternoon, 29 January, I find the whole family assembled (except its head) ready to receive me. Presently the great man himself emerges from his glass houses and gives me a constrainedly polite welcome. Are we about to take part in a funeral procession? think I, and sink oppressed into a perfectly constructed armchair. Enter John Bright. 'Miss Potter, I think you know her.' 'Not me,' say I humbly, 'but I think you knew my grandfather, Lawrence Heyworth.' 'Lawrence Heyworth,' replies the old man with slow emphasis, 'yes. Then you are the daughter of Lawrencina Heyworth — one of the two or three women a man remembers to the end of his life as beautiful in expression and form.' With this introduction our intercourse becomes naturally of the most kindly description. Immediately he dives into the memories of the past, tells me of his visits to Yewtree and describes the girl-hostess, who charmed the teetotal and Anti-Corn Law League enthusiasts who visited her father. This afternoon, however, the old man is too miserable and restless with the prospect of the evening to sink quietly into his favourite topic — reminiscences of the past — and presently he leaves the room. 'There is one consolation for me,' remarks Mr Chamberlain as he gets up to follow him, 'Bright in a terrible fidget is a good deal worse than I.' 'Miss Potter, I shall reserve the orchid-house for tomorrow and then I shall do the honours myself. I don't want my sister to take you there', and he forthwith retired to his library.

At dinner we are all subdued. The only stranger a certain George Melly from Liverpool, intimate friend of the Holts [Robert and Lawrencina], who fawns upon and flatters Chamberlain till I feel inclined to shriek with nervous irritation. Austen Chamberlain, a big fair-haired youth of handsome feature and open countenance and sunny sympathetic temperament, is deputed by his father to escort us womenkind to the town hall. We are placed in the front seats of the balcony overlooking the platform. A long row of Chamberlains and Kenricks continue our line. The men look earnest and honest, the great man's brothers perhaps have a bit of the cad in dress and manner; the women are plain and unpretentious, essentially ungrace-ful, might be labelled 'for use and not for ornament' and are treated accordingly. Arthur Chamberlain, by whom I sit, instructs me concerning the Liberal association, describes to me the *theory* of the

Beatrice with her parents 1865

*Above:* Lawrencina
Potter *c.*1860

*Right:* Richard
Potter *c.*1860

*Left:* Martha Jackson, date unknown

*Below:* Herbert Spencer *c.*1875

Beatrice in
Germany *c.*1881

Beatrice 1883

*Left:* Laurencina and Catherine
*c.*1862

*Below:* Mary, date unknown

*Left:* Georgina, date unknown

Blanche 1865

Theresa 1875

Margaret 1880

Rosalind 1880

Standish House, Vale of Severn, Gloucester

Rusland Hall, Cumberland. Inscription on photograph reads:
'*For my dear child Beatrice* Rusland Hall Bought at a flower show there
August 22 1885 by Richard Potter'

*Above:* York House, Kensington Palace Gardens, London

*Right:* Dried flowers in Beatrice's Diary collected as she left her birthplace. 'As I wandered this afternoon along the Standish walks and picked these flowers, all memories whether bitter or sweet, were cloaked with the beautiful sadness of the setting sun' 8 April 1884

Family group 1865; left to right: Georgina, Mary, Lawrencina Potter, Margaret, Beatrice, Richard Potter, Theresa, Blanche.

organization and points out proudly as proving the representative character from among the members (all ranged in raised seats behind the platform) strong-featured artisans and mechanics scattered amongst the sheepish-looking individuals who compose the majority. 'Not a good place for hearing, behind the speakers, but a place of honour, as Joe says if there were a row he would feel amongst friends.'

Below us, packed as close as may be, stand some thousands of men. Strong barriers divide the hall into sections, and as a newcomer tries to push himself in or a faint-hearted one attempts to retire, the whole section sways to and fro. A wonderful sight watching these thousands of faces upturned in eager expectancy. Faint cheers rise out of the general hum, as a favourite member of the 'nine hundred' seats himself; and friendly voices from the crowd greet distinguished members [M.P.s] of neighbouring constituencies and delegates from other caucuses as they take their places on the platform. The band strikes up, and the three Members for Birmingham enter. John Bright is received with affectionate and loyal applause as he stands for a moment before the children and the children's children of his old friends and contemporaries. Muntz, a feeble-looking elderly gentleman with rabbit-like countenance and shambling gait, forms an interval between Bright and Chamberlain; and in his weak mediocrity, looks comically out of place as a materialized vacuum between these two strong embodiments of humanity.

Chamberlain, the master and the darling of his town, is received with deafening shouts. The Birmingham citizen (unless he belongs to the despised and downtrodden minority) adores 'Our Joe', for has he not raised Birmingham to the proud position of one of the great political centres of the universe! . . .

I was disappointed in Bright as an orator. Still, there was something nobly pathetic in this strong echo of the past; this old old story of Tory sinfulness told by the stern-looking old man, who seemed gradually to lose consciousness of the crowd beneath him and see himself only confronted with the forces of the past. . . . While Philip Muntz meandered through political commonplaces and defended himself with feeble voice from charges of lukewarmness and want of loyalty to the Radical programme, the crowd once more became a concourse of disconnected individuals. . . . Laughter and loud-toned chaff passed from neighbour to neighbour. . . . As the time advanced the backmost portion became more and more unruly, whilst the eyes of those in front gradually centred themselves on the face of the next speaker. *He* seemed lost in intent thought. You could watch in his expression some form of feeling working itself into the mastery of his mind. Was that feeling spontaneous or intentioned? Was it *created* by an intense desire to dominate, to impress his own personality and his own aims on that pliable material beneath him, or did it arise from the consciousness of helpful power, from genuine sympathy with the wants and cravings of the great mass who trusted him?

As he rose slowly and stood silently before his people, his whole face and form seemed transformed. The crowd became wild with enthusiasm. Hats, handkerchiefs, coats even were waved frantically as an outlet for feeling. The few hundreds of privileged individuals seated in the balcony rose to their feet. There was one loud uproar of applause and, in the intervals between each fresh outburst, one could distinguish the cheers of the crowd outside, sending its tribute of sympathy.

Perfectly still stood the people's tribune, till the people, exhausted and expectant, gradually subsided into fitful and murmuring cries. At the first sound of his voice they became as one man. Into the tones of his voice he threw the warmth of feeling which was lacking in his words, and every thought, every feeling, the slightest intonation of irony and contempt was reflected on the face of the crowd. It might have been a woman listening to the words of her lover! Perfect response, unquestioning receptivity. Who *reasons* with his mistress? The wise man asserts his will, urges it with warmth or bitterness, and flavours it with flattery and occasional appeals to moral sentiments. No wonder the modern politician turns with disgust from the cantankerous debates of an educated 'House' to the undisputing sympathy of an uneducated and like-thinking crowd. Not extraordinary that the man of passionate conviction, or of *the will which stimulates it* and clothes it in finely-worded general principles, ignoring all complexity in things, should become the ruling spirit when the ultimate appeal, the moving force, rests with the masses whose desires are prompted by passion and unqualified by thought.

That evening at supper we entertained some twenty of the caucus. The Chief sat silent in a state of suppressed exaltation, acutely sensitive to sympathy or indifference even from an outsider. His faithful followers talked amongst themselves on local matters, questions of party strategy and discipline, and looked at him from time to time with respectful admiration.

The man's power as a leader and controller of men is proved by his position in his own town.

As far as one could judge from watching the large parties of adherents who humbly ate and drank at the great man's table, morning, noon and night, and from listening attentively to their conversation with each other and with him, his authority over the organization he has created is absolute.

He recognizes no distinction of class, and in this, as in all other matters, he is supported by the powerful clan to which he belongs. The Kenricks and Chamberlains form the aristocracy and plutocracy of Birmingham. They stand far above the town society in social position, wealth and culture, and yet they spend their lives, as great citizens, taking an active and leading part in the municipal, political and educational life of their town.

There is one eternal refrain in a Chamberlain–Kenrick household: Birmingham society is superior in earnestness, sincerity and natural intelligence to any society in the United Kingdom, and apparently the conviction remains unshaken by wider social experience, for the Cabinet Minister and his womenkind repeat with warmth the same assertion in the London drawing-room. Certainly, as far as my experience went of the family and its immediate surroundings, earnestness and simplicity of motive were strikingly present.

In living amongst the millhands of east Lancashire I was impressed with the depth and realism of their religious faith. It seemed to absorb the entire nature, to claim as its own all the energy unused in the actual struggle for existence. After the gratification of the simple animal instincts, the surplus power, whether physical, intellectual or moral, was devoted to religion. Even the social intercourse was based on religious sympathy and common religious effort, and it was this one-idea'dness and transparentness of life which attracted my interest and admiration. For a time it contrasted favourably with the extraordinary complexity of the mental activity which is formed by London and cosmopolitan life and which with some natures tends to paralyse action and dissipate thought. The same quality of one-idea'dness is present in the Birmingham Radical set. Political conviction takes the place here of religious faith, and intolerance of unbelief in the main articles of the creed is as bitter in the one case as in the other.

Possibly the Bible, from its inherent self-contradiction, is a more promising ground for individualism than the Radical programme, and less likely to favour the supremacy of one interpreter. Heine said

109

some fifty years ago: 'Talk to an Englishman on religion and he is a fanatic; talk to him on politics and he is a man of the world.' It would seem to me, from my slight experience at Bacup and Birmingham that that part of the Englishman's nature which has found gratification in religion is now drifting into political life, and when I suggested this to Mr Chamberlain he answered: 'I quite agree with you, and I rejoice in it. I have always had a grudge against religion for absorbing the passion in man's nature.' It is only natural then that, this being his view, he should find in the uncompromising belief of his own set a more sympathetic atmosphere wherein to recruit his forces to battle with the powers of evil, than in the somewhat cynical, or at any rate indefinitely varied and qualified, political opinions of London society.

The devotion of his electors no doubt springs partly from their consciousness of his genuine loyalty and affection for them. But the submission of the whole town to his autocratic rule arises from his power of dealing with different types of men; of enforcing submission by high-handed arbitrariness, attracting devotion by the mesmeric quality of his passion, and manipulating the remainder through a wise presentation of their interests and consideration for their petty weaknesses.

In his treatment of some members of the Association, (I noticed this particularly in his attitude towards Schnadhorst), he used the simple power of 'You shall' and 'You'll go to the devil if you don't'. The second power, of attraction, is shown to a certain extent in private intercourse with his most intimate friends, but chiefly in his public relationship towards his own constituency, and it is proved by the emotional nature of their enthusiasm.

It is to this power that Chamberlain owes all the happiness of his life, and it is the reaction of this power which intensifies his sympathies and also his egotism. Whether it will develop so as to assume a form which will extend beyond the immediate influence of his personality is one of the questions which will decide his future greatness. At present he fails to express it in his written words, except in the bitterness of his hatred and contempt, which is but one side of his passion.

His diplomatic talent is unquestioned and is manipulated in his administration of public and local affairs and in his parliamentary work – the only case in which he does not show it is in *la recherche d'une femme*; but then possibly he does not consider our sex worthy of manipulation.

Is it cold-blooded to write truthfully of one's relationship to a man? If one tells anything one should tell all. A diary is only the reflection of one's mind for one's own interest and amusement in after years: or, rather, it is, with me, an outlet for expression. I cannot feel, or think, or see, without a desire to formulate, and then desire is not satisfied unless the formula is as complete as I can make it and expressive of the whole experience. All the small *affaires de cœur* of past years I have left unmentioned, simply because they have not interested me. The commonplaces of love have always bored me. But Joseph Chamberlain with his gloom and seriousness, with absence of any gallantry or faculty for saying pretty nothings, the simple way in which he assumes, almost asserts, that you stand on a level far beneath him and that all that concerns you is trivial; that you yourself are without importance in the world except in so far as you might be related to him: this sort of courtship (if it is to be called courtship) fascinates, at least, my imagination. His restrained politeness gave way this morning after the first meeting. I had no longer any desire to dispute with him. I no longer cared to adjust my mind to his: I wished only to watch him. We wandered amongst his orchids and he seemed curiously piqued because I said that the only flowers I loved were wild flowers, and at dinner apologized to me for my own want of taste! That evening after the second meeting, I felt that susceptibility was increasing. It did not show itself in any desire to *please me*, but in an intense desire that I should *think and feel like him* (even in small details of taste), by a jealousy of other influences, specially that of the old philosopher, and in his serious attempts to drag me into his interests. I have not met him since except for a few minutes at an evening party.

I don't know how it will all end. Certainly not in *my happiness*. As it is, his personality absorbs all my thought and he occupies a too prominent position for me not to be continually reminded of him. At the best he will leave a present blank though a past interest. And if the fates should unite us (against *my will*) all joy and lightheartedness will go from me. I shall be absorbed into the life of a man whose aims are not my aims; who will refuse me all freedom of thought in my intercourse with him; to whose career I shall have to subordinate all my life, mental and physical, without believing in the usefulness of this career whether it be inspired by earnest conviction or by ambition. Beliefs are so much a matter of temperament, and my temperament (if it be not ridiculous to compare the nature of an ordinary young woman with that of an extraordinary man) is exactly

111

opposite to his. I hate every form of despotism. My admiration first for Goethe, then for Herbert Spencer, rested on their great faith in natural development. If I married him I should become a cynic as regards my own mental life. I should either destroy my intellectual individuality, and I can imagine doing that under the influence of strong feeling, or I should become a pure observer and throw up the ball of right and wrong in 'matters of opinion'. In the latter case I should separate, even more completely than I do now, my intellect from my feeling. When feeling becomes strong, as it would do with me in marriage, it would mean the absolute subordination of the reason to it, or eternal separation; and if life apart were impossible the 'pure intellect' would die. I should become *par excellence* the mother and the woman of the world intent only on fulfilling practical duties and gaining practical ends. And that, Mary would say, is a consummation devoutly to be wished for.

Richard Potter now gave up the family home at Standish and moved his London house from Prince's Gate to York House, a fashionable residence in Kensington Palace Gardens.

*8 April.* [Longfords]
This afternoon I drove from Longfords to settle up everything at Standish. A lovely spring day, with moisture and sunshine and soft sounds of nature's love and growth all around me.

The early spring months have always been sweet at Standish and the loveliest memories of my childhood gather round the first long days, when the dreary walks along the muddy roads directly after the midday meal were replaced by the scramble among hyacinths and ferns, the gathering of primroses and violets and the building of grottoes in the hours of sunset and dusk.

My childhood was not on the whole a happy one; ill-health and starved affection and the mental disorders which spring from these, ill temper and resentment, marred it. Hours spent in secret places, under the shade of shrub and tree, in the leaf-filled hollows of the wood and in the crevices of the quarries, where I would sit and imagine love scenes and death-bed scenes and conjure up the intimacy and tenderness lacking in my life, made up the happy moments. But long dreary times of brooding and resentfulness, sharp pangs of mortified vanity and remorse for untruthfulness, constant physical discomfort and frequent pain absorbed the greater part of my existence – and its *loneliness* was absolute.

It is only lately that I have known the true childish happiness, that I have experienced the *deliciousness* of life, known what it was to revel in my own sensations. But as I wandered this afternoon along the Standish walks and picked these flowers all memories, whether bitter or sweet, were clothed with the beautiful sadness of the setting sun, soon to be lost in the oblivion of night, a night which may be, to each individual mind, eternal. The garden seemed to breathe back the feelings and thoughts, thought and felt there; the struggles and strivings for bad and good ends, the plans of active minds for worldly happiness and the longings after a higher and purer life; and all these were blended into one and seemed as a departed being. The multitudes of memories weighed on me; I could have sat down and wept, if weeping were my habit! The air was heavily laden with scents and sounds, all nature seemed springing upwards: I, alone, looked towards the past, had a past growth behind me, a growth of endurance more than of action, still a growth full of discipline and leading to present happiness. Friendships made and happily not broken, ties of blood and constant companionship slackened but not destroyed by the diverse facts of active full-grown life. The nine sisters all in health and happiness, young ones growing from babyhood into childhood from childhood into youth, each a lovingly watched problem, the rightful working out of which the mother tries to discern and help forward. Husbands in the prime of life, each with his work in the world, true useful work honestly done. The cup of happiness seemed very full. And presiding over the group of human beings, all enjoying wealth and success and the happiness which both bring, the strong sweet nature of the father, loved even in his little failings, a nature ever changeful and yet persistent, one on which you dare not count and yet *in fact* found enduring in sympathy and help. And clinging to him the loved child of the mother.

This is the last scene to which the Standish garden has formed the background of *family home*.

The flowers and birds and the soft light of the setting sun as it gleamed through the mist and spread enchantment around seemed to say 'some day you will look back on this time spent here, as one of peace and achievement, one of promise and content; other days are coming, there may be the dazzling brightness of the midday sun, but there will also be a darkness which you know not. Past miseries have been but the chilliness of the grey dawn: future sorrow will have the blackness of night in which you will wander disconsolate if it be not

113

relieved by the inward light of hope and faith in the rising sun. Child, beware; if the stars of noble effort and noble faith shine not clearly in that night, if their light and the soft moonlight of clear conscience be over-clouded by indulged desire and muddy motive, that night will be dark indeed, will have the darkness of eternal death. You stand on the threshold of active life: ways open before you, each step must decide you. Fear not, but judge by the true light which is given you. Work and pray.

*22 April. York House*

Settled at last! I was thankful to read the other day in Bacon that it was advisable to keep some record of your motives and aims, that on the whole it helped forward consistency. Looking back through my diary I find that I have had a decided motive for work the last two years, over and above the practical aim of fulfilling my domestic duties and making the best of my position. This aim has been based on the belief that I have faculty for literary work. *Now*, I think this has been a delusion. Still I don't see how I could do better than keep up my own individual interests. There is so much spare time in my life, it must be filled somehow. If I were, in a fit of discouragement, to throw up everything (for if I gave up my aim it would mean this with me, I couldn't do purposeless work) I should become miserably restless, probably give way to some strong feeling and find my own nature too much for me. My nature is like a strong wilful ship; unless I keep it occupied it gives me endless trouble. If I once begin to humour it, give way to it and allow it to amuse itself in its own sweet fashion, it becomes unbearable and a curse to its owner. And lately I have allowed it free play, and must have a struggle with it, before I can again have peace. Can I begin this struggle bravely and instantly? What is the use of drifting, unless indeed I half desire to be where the current of my own feeling will bring me? And there is the trouble. My own mind is not made up. I have been meditating over the question for five months, have done little else but think about it; now I am no nearer solving it. Practically I have resisted, have refused to take the line of subordination and absolute dependence which would have brought things to a crisis. Possibly my refusal to consent to the conditions will have cured all desire on the other side. Then, though mortified, I shall be relieved. I shall have been only decently truthful and honest and can abide by the consequences. But if the question be put in another form?

114

Let me look facts clearly in the face and take counsel with myself. Ambition and superstition began the feeling. A desire to play a part in the world, and a belief that as the wife of a great man I should play a bigger part than as a spinster or an ordinary married woman. Let me analyse the part I should play. He has taken his line for better or for worse in politics; he has an overpowering ambition, he will not hesitate much as to the means of gaining his ends. He has told me distinctly that he will not bear his opinion being 'controverted' or his action criticized. He desires a woman who is personally attractive to him, who will sympathize and encourage him, be a continual rest to him, giving him the uncompromising admiration which the world withholds. His temperament and his character are intensely attractive to me. I feel I could relieve the gloom, could understand the mixed motive and the difficulties of a nature in which genuine enthusiasm and personal ambition are so curiously interwoven. The outward circumstances of the life of a politician's wife would be distasteful to me or, rather, they would be supremely demoralizing, unless they were accepted as a means to an end in which I myself believed. And here is really the kernel of the question. Do I believe in the drift of his political views and do I believe that the means employed are *honest*? If I do not believe that this line of political action is right, if I do not believe that the end is pursued without deviating from the first moral principles, and were yet to sign both aims and means with my signature, I should be selling my soul and should deserve misery. It is no use saying that my signature is of no importance. Certainly not to the world; but all important to me. The first duty of the individual is to live truly and honestly according to the nature which has been given to him. Once married, I should of course subordinate my views to my husband's, should, as regards his own profession, accept implicitly his views of right and wrong. But I cannot shirk the responsibility of using my judgement before I acknowledge his authority.

Social questions are the vital questions of today. They take the place of religion. I do not pretend to solve them. Their solution seems largely a matter of temperament. Still, the most insignificant mind has a certain bias, has an intellectual as well as a moral conscience. If we wilfully deny the laws of our special mental constitution, we must suffer the penalty of a diseased and twisted nature; we must leave this life conscious of faithlessness to the faith which is in us. And even if I put on one side the question of the right or wrong in the aims pursued in political action, as one on which I could form no opinion, and might therefore safely accept that of another person, there still remains the question of means. I *can* and *must* judge as to the honesty and straightforwardness of these. It requires no special knowledge, no great reasoning power to understand a lie: information withheld and falsified, false accusations advanced, passions appealed to, to attain other ends than those proposed. A higher standard of motive is asked for in social action more than in any other.

The social reformer *prefers* to be an uncompromising altruist. He solemnly declares that he is working for the public weal. His whole authority, derived from public opinion, arises from the faith of the people in his honesty of purpose and fine strength of understanding. If he uses his mind to manipulate facts, to twist them so that they shall serve his own personal interests, if the craving for power is greater than the desire for truth, he is a traitor to the society to which he professes loyal service. Interested as I am in the welfare of humanity (however incompetent I am to help it forward), I could not help judging each separate action according to the laws of my own mind, and if I could not express that judgement, had to sit silently and acquiesce in wrong-doing, not only acquiesce but help it forward with my devotion and sympathy, where could I turn to for peace, that peace which passeth all understanding, the peace of a satisfied conscience, the deep content arising from the consciousness that, however minute our intellectual and moral qualities may be, we are striving honestly to develop them and use them for the good of our fellow creatures? I should *not* influence him. He has shown me that distinctly. He has been straightforward all through, has told me distinctly his requirements. When I have been absolutely honest with him he has turned away. That is not what he wants and *I know it*. It is only when I have simulated *la femme complaisante*, turned the conversation from principles to personalities that he has desired me. He has pointed out to me plainly the hardships in the life of the wife of a man absorbed in public life, has not wished me to be influenced by any glamour that may surround it, has said in so many words 'only devotion to my aims would justify you in accepting it'. And I have not only no devotion to these aims, but have to twist my reasoning in order to *tolerate them*.

And now, what is the straightest course? It is not to cut the knot by refusing all further intercourse. I know how strong the temptations are which would entice me into it. Great personal attraction and the immediate gratification of a woman's instinctive longing for love and support and for settled and defined occupation. And beyond this, the

116

desire for the personal prestige and the importance I should acquire by becoming his wife. And if he no longer wishes for it what is the use of playing further with my own nature? Looking back on the whole affair, I confess to myself that my action and thought have been wanting in dignity and nicety of feeling. I have *chattered* about feelings which should be kept within the holy of holies. The only excuse has been the extraordinary nature of the man and his method and the interest which public position lends to his personality. But now I can make a fresh start; force my thoughts from their dwelling-place of the last five months, and devote myself vigorously to my duties and to the natural and true development of my own nature. Amen. . . .

The remaining months of the Season then I shall devote myself body and soul to my home duties, to settling Father and Rosy in their new life, making this house a centre to the family and of real sociability. I shall look about me for some permanent work, some sphere of practical usefulness. . . .

Mary Booth's father, Charles Zachary Macaulay, spent the last years of his life at Southsea, near Portsmouth.

*9 May.* [York House]
I shall not write again in this book. It is the close of a period with me. I began it with my old ambition strong upon me; working my little faculties to their utmost, in the full belief that some day I should have somewhat to tell to the world. This strange conceit was fostered by the retirement of a woman's life, living and striving by herself, shielded from all tests as to the real worth of her work. Midway in this period, another path seemed opened to me, another highway to prominence. That also is closed. I remain weakened and discouraged, my old ambition fallen irretrievably. I prayed for light and I *have it*. I see clearly that my intellectual faculty is only mirage, that I have no special mission. . . .

Strength too fails me now. I look hopelessly through the books on my table and neither understand nor care to understand what I read. My imagination has fastened upon one form of feeling. The woman's nature has been stirred to the depths; I have loved and lost; but possibly by my own wilful mishandling, possibly also for my own happiness; but still lost. Let me look that fact bravely in the face and learn by it. I may not again trifle with my nature: and yet – I would

117

not be without the experience of the last months. It has broadened the basis of sympathy, as all true experience does, even if it be the experience of our own gains, of our own craving for the devotion of another being. One must *feel with* (*mitgefuhl*) in order to understand, and to feel with, one must have felt before. One person stands out bound up with the last sounds of a departing day. Mary Booth's gentle and loving contempt for any *special* work outside the ordinary sphere of a woman's life; her high standard of excellence which should discourage any vain attempt to leave the beaten track of a woman's duty. And I having revelled in feeling, having yielded up my soul, believing that it was desired, found satisfaction in this. She made me ready to renounce my old aims and acknowledge the sway of the new feeling. Those three days at Southsea seemed designed to increase the sensitiveness to the blow. And when it came, when I realized by the tone and the expression that all was over, my whole nature gave way before it. Both ideals had fallen. Life alone, life together, remaining only the seemingly daily round of commonplace duties. And the blankness and weariness within my soul brought strikingly into relief by the luxury and enviableness of my surroundings. The whole seems a nightmare.

There is glitter all around me and darkness within, the darkness of blind desire yearning for the light of love. All sympathy is shut from me. I stand alone with my own nature now too strong for me. I clutch desperately at *my duty* to those around me, that last hope for the soul despairing of its own happiness. . . . Still there rises up before me, the misty forms of three maidens: Humility, Tenderness, Discretion, and they beckon me with loving pity to follow them. Amen.

*28 July.* [York House]
One last word. I have seen the great man once or twice this Season – there was a little flicker of feeling and then it died, died a natural death from the unfitness of things, and he was the wiser of the two. Perhaps I shall soon hear of his marriage to a woman who would suit him and his conditions. *I* was not equal to it. But we have parted friends and understand each other. A few years, possibly a few months, and I shall be a name to him, one of the many women he has liked, examined, found wanting in qualities and pliability of nature and dismissed from his thoughts. All his energy of thought and feeling is and always will be devoted to his great purpose in life; if I had from the first believed in that purpose, if the influence which formed me and the natural

tendency of my character, if they had been different, I might have been his helpmate. It would not have been a happy life; it might have been a noble one. Of the simple spontaneous love, there was naught between us. He has it not to give, and my feeling for him was gradually created within me by many mixed motives. It pained me cruelly to part from him in hardness and misunderstanding, not knowing whether I had offended him by word or deed, but now *that* bitterness has passed from me and I shall watch his career, and whether he rises or falls in the world's estimation I shall know that I am watching the struggle of an earnest mind.

On the back page of this manuscript volume Beatrice had written yet another testamentary note which emphasized her state of depression.

*1 August*. [York House]
In case of my death I should wish that all these diary-books, after being read (if he shall care to) by Father, should be sent to Carrie Darling.

BEATRICE POTTER

## *VOLUME 7*

In an effort to raise her spirits Beatrice went on a holiday to Bavaria with Margaret Harkness. From Munich they went to Mittenwald where Beatrice thought the piety of Catholic peasants seemed 'to satisfy all the needs of human nature and idealize all the relationships of life'. On a Sunday afternoon she sat in the churchyard 'and listened to the weird music of the village choir, and read Comte's catechism of Positive religion', she wrote in a letter to her father. Three days later she wrote again: 'I am beginning to feel that my small attempts at self-culture have been rather *mis*-directed and that analysis and criticism are rather poor stuff to live on . . . one ought to be going in for practical work if one is ever to do anything for one's fellow-mortals – it seems a pity that there is no way of teaching mortals humility early in life. . .'

*8 September. Munich*
'Our harmony as moral beings is impossible on any other foundation but altruism. Nay more, altruism alone can enable us to live in the

highest and truest sense. To live for others is the only means of developing the whole existence of man. Towards Humanity, who is the only true Great Being, we, the conscious elements of whom she is the compound, shall henceforth direct every aspect of our life, individual and collective. Our thoughts will be devoted to the knowledge of Humanity, our affections to the Love, our actions to her service.' Auguste Comte.

In 1884 Richard Potter rented a house at Summerhill, a few miles south of Coniston Water and close to his business interests in Barrow-in-Furness.

### 15 October. Summerhill

I don't suppose I shall ever again take that interest in myself to make me much care to tell my thoughts and feelings to this impersonal confidant – my diary. At any rate there is a long lapse in my habit of writing down what I see, think and feel. And yet I am loath to bid goodbye to an old friend, one who has been with me since I first had experiences, and wished to tell them to someone, though it were only to a phantom of myself. It would be curious to discover who it is to whom one writes in a diary. Possibly to some mysterious personification of one's own identity, to the Unknown, which lies below the constant change of matters and ideas, constituting the individual at any given moment. This unknown one was once my only friend, the being to whom I went for advice and consolation in all the small troubles of a child's life. Well do I remember, as a small thing, sitting under the damp bushes and brooding over the want of love around me (possibly I could not discern it) and turning in upon myself and saying – 'Thou and I will live alone, and if life be unbearable, we will die'. Poor little meagre-hearted thing! And then I said – 'I will teach thee what I feel, think and see, and we will grow wise together. Then shall we be happy.' So I went my own little way and noted diligently what I saw and began upon this to reason. Soon I found that there were other minds seeing and reasoning who would in their strength carry me on my way. I clutched at their help and they for pity's sake gave it me. But still I loved only the Unknown one, and my *feeling* was constantly looking inward though my *reason* was straining its utmost to grasp what was outside. Then came friendship in the guise of intellectual sympathy, in later years discovering itself in its true nature, affection gently putting reason with its eternal analysis on one side. And last of all came passion, with its burning heat, an emotion which had for long smouldered unnoticed, burst out into flame, and burnt down intellec-

120

tual interests, personal ambition, and all other self-developing motives.

And now the Unknown one is a mere phantom, seldom conjured up, and then not grasped. Reason and feeling alike have turned towards the outer world and no longer care to look within. Today I say humbly, 'we have learnt, poor thing, that we can neither see, think nor feel alone, much less live, without the help of others; therefore we must live *for* others and take what happiness comes to us by the way'.

And all the time I was travelling in Bavaria this was the eternal refrain running through my mind. I saw things; I wrote about them; I lived with an intimate friend, but day and night I cried secretly over the past, and regretted the form which my past life had given me. For who can undo the moulding work of years? We must bear with the self we have made.

The storm has swept over. I can once again go on my way, if I knew only which way to turn.

G. H. Lewes (1817–78) was a man of letters, actor and playwright, and editor of the *Fortnightly Review*, 1865–66. He was particularly interested in philosophic and scientific subjects and was sympathetic to the ideas of Auguste Comte. He was well-known in literary and bohemian circles and in 1854 he became the common-law husband of George Eliot. Beatrice was reading his *History of Philosophy*, and making notes on the works of Bacon, Descartes, Spinoza, Hobbes, Locke, Leibnitz and Berkeley.

*24 October.* [Summerhill]
Got back to books again: and stopped as usual by poor health. The whole of my life, from the age of nine (when I wrote a priggish little note on the right books for a child to read) has been one continuous struggle to learn and to think, sacrificing all to this, even physical comfort. When I think of the minuteness of my faculties (which so far as persistent work goes are below the average) and of the really herculean nature of my persistence, my own nature puzzles me. Why should a mortal be born with so much aspiration, so much courage and patience in the pursuit of the ideal, and with such a beggarly allowance of power wherewith to do it.

And even now, now that I have fully realized my powerlessness to achieve, have perhaps ceased to value any achievement which in my vainest dreams I thought open to me, even now my only peaceful and satisfactory life lies in the old lines of continuous inquiry. Endless questionings of the nature of things, and more especially of the nature of the queer animal, man, and of the laws which force him outside, heaven knows where to. Of the nature of that destination, whether it will answer the 'wherefore' of the sorry past of misery and struggle. That old dream of a bird's-eye view of the past and through it a glimpse into the future, that old dream now recognized as a dream, fascinates me still. With labour and pain I master some poor fact, I clutch it, look at it over and over again like a miser with his coin of gold. At times I pour before me my little hoard of facts – a tiny little heap it is – some of it base coin too. I pass them through and through my brain, like the miser passes the gold through his hands trying to imagine that before me lies the wealth of the world wherewith I may untie the knots of human destiny. Since I have been suffering from neuralgia and have been sitting up hours through the night, I have thought – this cannot long continue, thoughts are the shadows of actions. Where in thy life is the reality?

*24 October. Midnight.* [Summerhill]
Up with pain. The last sleepless nights I had were those terrible ones at York House. Sitting in blank misery on my sofa looking at the two candles burning lower and lower. Darkness is unbearable when in pain. But how much more difficult to bear mental misery than physical pain.

During the autumn of 1884 the country was convulsed by a crisis in the Sudan and attention focused on the expeditionary force which Gladstone had reluctantly and belatedly sent to relieve General Gordon and the garrison besieged at Khartoum. At home, a bill to widen the franchise in country constituencies, increasing the electorate from three to five million, was passed in June but was held up in the House of Lords until November when the Liberals agreed to the Lords' demand for a redistribution of seats. The Fourth Party was a clique of Tory Democrats led by Lord Randolph Churchill (1849–94) who advocated a new conservatism involving political and social reform and popular participation in party affairs. Mary (Polly) Playne had married a young lawyer named Erskine Pollock from a distinguished legal family.

*6 November.* [York House]
A week in London and Winchester. Stayed with the Alfred Cripps. Theresa, fascinating as ever, slightly depressed with poor health, but sweetly happy with that good husband of hers. Alfred keeps up his success at the Bar. Bought the family place and taken to farming in these bad times as a recreation! Evidently will not go into politics

except as 'a scholar and a gentleman'. He is not a leader of men. His opinions do not represent the *desires* of the masses; they are the result of an attempt to deduce laws of government from certain first principles of morality. His theory as to the present state of political life – that the tendency is to ignore principles and follow instinct, and that this is based on the fallacious belief that what the people wish is *right*. He believes in principle, believes in the possibility of reducing politics to a science. Many cultivated men think with him, that political action should be governed by principle, but there is no body of doctrine upon which they can agree; hence they cannot organize themselves into a party for working purposes. . . .

The state of political parties now in England is curious. The Liberal Party are still bound together (and this is shown strikingly in the present crisis) by that metaphysical doctrine that each responsible individual has an equal right to a say in the government of his country. But the man of principles is rapidly becoming aware that these may involve a disagreeable conclusion: the practical disenfranchisement of the upper classes when *their* interests clash with those of the lower and more numerous class of manual workers.

This conclusion he tries to avoid by proposing various artificial restrictions on the absolute power of the majority, and this is the issue upon which he is likely to split from the party to which he belongs by tradition. The democratic party on the other hand has transformed the doctrine of the equal rights of individuals into that of the absolute right of the majority, tacitly asserting the infallibility of the judgement of the great working masses on social questions. Practically this means that social laws are not discoverable by the scientific method, that the only guide to political action is the will of the people. And when you come to analyse this 'Will of the People' it must consist of their self-interest as a class (in so far as they are sufficiently intelligent and far-seeing to discern it), of the various *feelings* they have towards other classes. If their feelings are those of sympathy and desire for cooperation and not those of envy and antagonism, or leaving feeling out of the question, if their powers of reasoning as a class are sufficiently great to teach them their true interests, all may be well in the future. But there is this awkward sign of the times.

The political leaders who play for and gain the support of the masses appeal to the passions of envy and antagonism, and in their bad logic, their recklessness of statement, and their recourse to flattery and personalities, show pretty clearly *their* opinion as to the reasoning faculty of their clients. The Conservatives are wildly chaotic, running up and down senselessly between the two standards of class government and democratic Toryism. Up to recent years they have been the party of prejudice, but prejudice is well-nigh dead as a political force. It meant simply the self-interest of the upper classes, the naïve assertion by them that their well-being was the *raison d'être* of the body politic. Undoubtedly the opposition to the democratic party should be reformed on the lines of principle, but here comes in the disagreement of the doctors amongst themselves. *As a fact*, and this is another disagreeable sign of the times, there is seen to be developing within the smaller conservative party a spurious democratic party, which stimulates passion and prostitutes principle, and is more reckless both as to means and as to ends than its legitimate rival.

This fourth party has sprung up to meet the wants of the local provincial organization of the opposition. In their provincial organization lies the political power of the future. They are either the manipulators or the exponents of the Will of the People – probably partly one and partly the other – manipulating their apathy and expressing their passion. In the character of the men who dominate these political organizations will be seen the character of the masses, in its negative and positive aspect. Such is the authoritative statement of Beatrice Potter! . . .

I have seen something of Leonard Courtney lately. He and Kate stayed with us for a fortnight or so this autumn. A character you learn to admire and reverence for its high integrity of purpose and honesty of means. Wanting in sympathy and the humility which sympathy brings. A man who believes firmly in his mission as *teacher* – perhaps ignoring too completely the wisdom of learning from others and through others. And as this deficiency is not supplemented by any adaptability through worldly motive, he seems likely to fail in political life. His intellectual faculty does not show itself in conversation, except in the rugged integrity of his judgement. Faculty he *must* have had to have risen to his present position. But in his views there is a curious want of coherence. . . . He pleases no party, is representative of no class *interest* or school of *thought*. Unless of great value as an official, he will be spurned off the battlefield of politics. But his influence as far as it has reached will have been a noble one – sincere faith in his aims, absolute honesty in his means and a large-hearted pity for ignorance and vice and reverence for virtue. He is one of those few men to whom one would instinctively turn in adversity and sorrow.

The Playnes stayed a fortnight with us and seemed happier for their change. Life has changed for them since those Wiesbaden days we spent together. Arthur is now a hard-worked manufacturer, fighting for existence in these days of over-production. Mary full of schemes, not of social advancement, but of work amongst the millhands trying to inspire them with an *esprit de corps*. Polly married, Bill [Playne] at school, establishment reduced to women servants, interests commercial and rightly *social*. This man and woman are fighting their battle bravely. . . . The younger Mary married to a successful London barrister of 'the distinguished family of Pollock' – a typical London man. A hard-working self-controlled individual with no public spirit and a mild astonishment at the foolishness of any form of altruism. . . . The marriage has been a terrible trouble to the Playnes; they having got thoroughly wrong with Erskine, and exaggerating to themselves his deficiencies.

Becoming every year more intimate with the Booths, knowing now pretty well the story of their life. Their children, too, growing up with each character known to me and gradually unfolding itself. Indeed if it were not for a morbid horror of a certain physical deformity overtaking me, I could lead now a full and happy life, even without those closer ties which make a woman's life blessed. I have health – liberty – and love; with fair faculties to understand and sympathize with what goes on around me. It is true my personal ambition is dead and I feel now that the time and strength devoted to its fulfilment was wasted and that to some extent I have missed my vocation through placing my aim too high. But though I was deceived by my conceit, my motive was pure – sprang from a desire to do honest work and to live sincerely according to my nature. Perhaps, should all ways to the simple happiness of wifehood and motherhood close, I shall turn again and struggle onwards on the path chosen by my nature in the first enthusiasm of youth.

But nature is strong and cries out for its natural fulfilment [some words deleted in the original MS] while I suffer, I console myself with the faith that pain must have some equivalent in force; it rests with the will to direct this force rightly. We cannot triumph over difficulties, we cannot accept discipline with meekness and courage, without rising out of it more powerful for good.

*19 November.* [Summerhill]
A wild west wind, sweeping over the Old Man [of Coniston] towards

us. Mr Grayson just left. Brings back to my remembrance those Rusland days of work and simple enjoyment of nature. Ah me! Since then seems a whole epoch of my life — left me stranded in a desolate sort of country with no hope or faith. Must pick up and think of others. Altruism is after all the creed of those who are suffering personal misery and yet do not intend to sink into abject wretchedness. It used to be devotion to God, under one form or another; now this God is dead it must be devotion to other human beings. . . .


*26 November.* [York House]
Have seldom felt more strangely ominous than I do now; as if death were approaching. Personally it would be welcome. Had a strange dream, Mother, looking beautiful and young, put out her hand and then kissed me. I, sobbing the while, begged her forgiveness for lack of tenderness. 'It was my nature, Mother, I could not help it.' Then she bent over me and kissed me a second time. What would I give for a mother now; just to lay my head down, tell all — and cry. Perhaps the earth will be my mother — I sometimes think so — hope and pray so, but I would like to have someone by my side when I go.

It is curious this feeling of life being *ended*; at some moments scene after scene of times gone by seem to rush through my mind, as if that was all that concerned *me* personally. When I think of the future there are strange and confused things, but anyhow only for a short time. And the longing — the longing that the end may come.

Then I get up and look at myself: a strong healthy body looking as if it had centuries before it. No release yet; years of health before you. How is it that anyone cares for life? I have always hoped for better, and better has never come except perhaps those eighteen months after Mother's death when duty and faith still burnt clearly.

Tonight is as the end of the year — a year spent in much misery — and little action. Tomorrow will begin a new time for me. A life of noble usefulness lies before me, with the *freest* of conditions if I am really equal to them. *Spoilt* by circumstances if I cannot make use of them and *master* them. I once longed for power; I have it now. Every possibility of free thought and free action are open to me and influence that I have no right to. Shall I sink under the very vastness of my opportunities — or rise to them and fulfil them?

For many months my thoughts have wandered over and over the same old ground. Perhaps this terrible time of tortured feeling will

126

after all transform itself into good as all pain rightly taken should do. God grant it may be so.

Before Beatrice's sister Kate married Leonard Courtney she worked as a voluntary rent-collector in an experimental housing scheme for 'the poorest of the poor' just off Tower Hill, and behind the Royal Mint. Beatrice now took over this charitable work, collaborating with Ella Pycroft, who became a lifelong friend and later was responsible for the teaching of domestic economy in the London County Council schools until her retirement in 1904. Beatrice worked in a newly-built block called Katherine Buildings, five floors high; it had 281 rooms, and about 600 tenants; none of the rooms had running water, and there were 18 trough-like closets in common use. 'In short,' Beatrice wrote afterwards, 'all amenity, some would say all decency, was sacrificed to the two requirements of relatively low rents and physically sanitary buildings.' The lady rent-collectors, working to the principles of the housing reformer Octavia Hill (1838–1912), had to act as welfare workers and moral guardians of their tenants.

[December? York House]
If I take to this work, might as well keep account of it. Breakfasted with Kate. Of course her first thoughts are for Leonard. Met directors at the buildings, amongst them stumbled on an old lover. Discussion as to stoves and other fittings. Crowder, cut and dried philanthropist, with little human nature, determined that tenants *should* like nothing but what was *useful*. Paint and finish all rooms alike. Kate mildly suggests that tenants *have* taste, are immensely influenced by small things. . . .

∽ 1885 ∾

*4 January.* [York House]
Royal Academy private view with Herbert Spencer. His criticisms on art dreary, all bound down by the 'possible' if not the probable. That poor old man would miss me on the whole more than any other mortal. Has real anxiety for my welfare – physical and mental. Told him story of my stopping cart and horse in Hyde Park and policeman refusing to come off his beat to hold it. Want of public spirit in passers-by not stopping it before. 'Yes, that is another instance of my first principle of government. Directly you get state intervention you cease to have public spirit in individuals; that will be a constantly increasing tendency and the State, like the policeman, will be so bound

by red-tape rules that it will frequently leave undone the simplest duties.' . . .

At tea met Madame de Souvestre who had already taken possession of me at the R.A.P.V. [Royal Academy Private View] 'Is it true you are writing or publishing something?' 'Good gracious, no. I am an insignificant mortal, do nothing but keep a well-ordered house – if only the world will let me be so.' (Somehow or other – I suppose it is in my phraseology – people *will* think me extra-ordinary, which certainly I am not except it be extra-unsatisfactory.) Really a thoroughly objectionable woman; utterly unreal.

Anna Swanwick (1813–99) was a pioneer of women's education and one of the founders of Girton College, Cambridge. She was a translator of Greek and German plays, especially of Goethe's *Faust*. About this time Beatrice drafted a long letter to her in which she discussed Herbert Spencer's ideas and objected to the 'gigantic experiments' in state education which seemed to be based on 'inadequately thought-out theories – the most dangerous of all social poisons'. She did not send what she later called a 'priggish pronounce-ment', but she thought the draft was an interesting expression of 'the anti-democratic and anti-collectivist bias with which I started out to investigate the working of social institutions'. She lunched with Miss Swanwick, 'seventeen distinguished spectacled women and two men', she wrote to her sister Mary.

*8 January*. [York House]
Dear little Miss Swanwick. A nature of angelic purity and sweetness. Great faculty, mathematical and literary – great power of expression though her *reasoning*, when she leaves poetical assertion, I am unable to follow. An idealist in all things. Believing in that order of thought which ends in the 'Beautiful and the Good', without caring to test this order of thought by the order of things – at least so it seems to me.

Edward Bond (1844–1920) was a wealthy leader of the Charity Organi-zation Society, and he was much interested in housing reform. It was said that he was the object of hopeless love by Octavia Hill, and that he was the model for the character of Daniel Deronda in George Eliot's novel.

*16 January*. [York House]
Another day at Whitechapel. Met Mr Bond there, looked over fittings. . . . Afterwards talk with Mr Barnett. He is anxious that I should spend this unoccupied time in getting more general informa-tion, and find out particulars about medical officer, sanitary officer, relieving officer, School Board visitor, Voluntary Sanitary Committee

– and their powers and duties. . . . Miss Pycroft spent three days with me. Daughter of country doctor and one of two families, step-mother died. Plain, very strong-looking, and unattractive except for sincerity of expression. Free thinking – had somewhat similar life to ours, isolated from other country neighbours by opinions. Decided business capacity and strong will and placid temper. Devoted to her father, with whom she has same intimate companionable relationship as we have, and fond of all her step-sisters. Evidently suffered from feeling herself unattractive in comparison to a pretty sister. Very anxious for work and indifferent to life! We shall get on and we are anxious to have no other workers on the block.

Beatrice kept insisting that her relationship with Chamberlain was finished, yet she was unable to break it in fancy or in fact. In November she had been visited by Clara Chamberlain, who told her much about the Chamberlains, including anecdotes about 'little Joe's' childhood. 'It is a comfort to have come out of a painful affair with the respect and affection of his family,' Beatrice wrote to Mary Playne afterwards, 'and to have done no harm anyway.' She was whistling in the dark, for her depression was deepening; and there was a new crisis in the Chamberlain affair at the end of January 1885. On 29 January, Chamberlain delivered a powerful speech at the Birmingham Town Hall on 'The Fruits of the Franchise', the third in a campaign to launch a 'Radical Programme' of reform, provocative and wide-ranging in its scope and aimed at winning the support of rural voters newly enfranchised by the Reform Act of 1884. It is not clear whether Beatrice actually went to Birmingham for this meeting or whether it merely reminded her of the similar occasion she recorded in January 1884.

*George Eliot's Life as Related in Her Letters and Journals* by J. W. Cross was published in January 1885. 'He is a good, delightful creature and I always feel better for being with him,' George Eliot wrote of Herbert Spencer in April 1852. Two months later she wrote: 'My brightest spot, next to my love of *old* friends, is the deliciously calm *new* friendship that Herbert Spencer gives me. We see each other every day and have a delightful *camaraderie* in everything. But for him my life would be desolate enough.'

### 29 January. [?]

A warm moonlight night with soft west wind, thinking of a crowded hall, deafening shouts, dead silence except for one voice – the voice of the people's tribune; and between those vividly representing thoughts, reading snatches of George Eliot's letters, whose life has been curiously linked through the affection of one great man with mine. . . .

A strange calm over me, though tomorrow I shall know how my fate is to be unravelled. No longer in my hands. If the answer be yes I am in honour tied. If no, I am free and *will be* free in body and mind, free until another binds me. I will not bind myself again and wake up and find myself unbound. Do most people shut their eyes wilfully as *I* have done and drift, drift, drift they know not whither even with a dim dark dread of a whirlpool ahead. God help the child: this will be thy last childish day – tomorrow will make thee a woman, a woman to love or a woman to work while others love. Before this thou had an intellect and *thought*, suffering has born to thee a soul, in pain its childhood has been lived, present satisfaction or present renunciation will be its maturity. Amen.

In his *Life of George Eliot*, Cross quotes her notebook entry in which she explains the theme of her poem 'The Spanish Gypsy'. 'I saw it might be taken as a symbol of the part which is played in the general human lot by hereditary conditions in the largest sense, and of the fact that what we call duty is entirely made up of such conditions. . . . Tragedy consists in the terrible difficulty [of adjustment] of our individual needs to the dire necessities of our lot.'

*Sunday* [1 February. Birmingham?]
Long talk with Clara Chamberlain. Leaving her great position for a quiet working life with a man who has loved her for years past. 'At first I had a lonely life of it, very little companionship, Beatrice away, my brother absorbed in his sorrow and his politics, and only the little children to care for.'

My relationship to her is a peculiar one – intimacy begun on both sides for different reasons than mere natural affinity, but now grown into a steady friendship. Whether it will endure will practically depend on me. A perfectly true nature, possibly deficient in sensitiveness to fine shades of feeling and not sympathetic or over-tolerant of any form of want of self-control. *Very reserved.* To me this morning's talk seemed like the dropping of the curtain over the tragic end of strong feeling.

George Eliot's letters disappointing. Dull and pretentious in their style, wanting in spontaneity; strengthens the doubt I felt the other day in reading one of her books whether some of her grand paragraphs were not rubbish. But worse than falling short intellectually, they give me a painful impression of her character. It may be narrow-minded prejudice, still I feel that a woman who left the beaten track of

130

morality should have some 'inward searching' -- apparently not; posed as the great and good woman. Really self-indulgent? Took to herself all the good things of this world and, if one judges from J. Cross's *Life*, which of course may be quite misleading, did not seek the less gifted and fortunate, but chose from the first those for friends who could benefit her by thought, word or deed. Perhaps genius is always selfish – has a voracious appetite for the material and spiritual good things of this world.

Herbert Spencer deliciously conscious about the 'Miss Evans' episode – asked me seriously what was my impression of their relationship in reading those passages referring to him. Had wished John Cross to insert contradiction that there had ever been aught between them. Shows his small-mindedness in his extreme concern but, as George Eliot says, his friendship will always endure because of his truthfulness. . . .

Most interesting bit of George Eliot's *Life* to my mind is the description of the 'motive' for 'The Spanish Gypsy'. Most interesting to me, because this great question of inherited fate has been uppermost in my mind for some time past. Half the misery ( the misery of those classes who are not depressed in body and mind by the struggle for bare subsistence) comes from our own rebellion against this 'inherited fate', our ceaseless longing for advantages which do not belong to those qualities we have, want of gratitude for those arising from qualities we do possess. In one word, graspingness, which, because it grasps after spiritual and not material blessings, is sometimes dignified in our minds by the sense of righteous self-discontent – moral effort. But true *persistent* effort is only consistent with peace of mind – resignation – otherwise the pain of mortification interrupts and disturbs the effort, destroys the *straightness* of the aim. *Renunciation*, that is the great fact we all, individuals and classes, have to learn. In trying to avoid it we bring misery to ourselves and others.

That false metaphysical idea of rights, as some unalterable result determined in quantity and quality, due to all men alike, is working its wicked way in our political life. The right of a man, that is to say the natural right of a man, apart from what other men contract to give him as their fellow, is surely only the sum of external forces which react on the internal force, to put it pedantically, though possibly the socialist would distinguish between *inherited conditions* and *inherited qualities*. He would say we try to level the condition, we do not attempt to touch the result of the qualities.

But this distinction of *inherited conditions* and *inherited qualities* seems to me to be the distinction between the practical and the impractical socialist. Those social reformers who try to equalize the former may err in their method, but the *aim* has surely nothing contradictory to natural law. If it *could* be attained, this equalization of conditions, it would further the selection of the fittest. How far it is in the power of the State to do it is another question. But to equalize the result which is yielded to the presence or absence of qualities in the individual is impracticable and would be terribly injurious to the happiness of the race if it were to be accomplished. This seems to me to be the difference between the English socialism and the Continental communism. I know little about history but I *suppose* the State has until the last fifty years *accentuated* the advantages of the fortunate and that all the machinery of society – industrial, religious, educational and social – has been built on the basis of privilege. I *suppose* there is still higher class legislation or the effects of it unrepealed and unremedied. Now the power lies in the hands of the poorer classes, we shall watch their attempts to remedy the effects of past injustice and whether in their attempt they commit injustice of another sort. . . .

*8 March*. [York House]
I spend my time now in alternate days of work and rest. The physical part of my work absorbs so much energy that I have little left for thought and feeling. Work is the best of narcotics, providing the patient be strong enough to take it.

All is chaos at present. Long trudges through Whitechapel after applicants and references, and tenants tumbling in anyhow. A drift population, the East Enders, of all classes and races – a constantly decomposing mass of human beings, few rising out of it but many dropping down dead, pressed out of existence in the struggle. A certain weird romance, with neither beginning nor end, visiting amongst these people in their dingy homes; some light-hearted enough, in spite of misery and disease. More often feel envy than pity. Shall in the future, when other workers are found, and when once I am fairly started in the practical work, undertake less of the management and use the work more as an opening for observation.

Mean some day to master, as far as my power goes, what has been theoretically thought out in social questions. Earnestly hope I shall never get conceited again, or look upon any work I do as more than a means for remaining contented and free of pain. Relief to be alone, and have poor little Rosy off my hands and out of my thoughts for a short time. . . . Society constantly increasing – have none of that terrible nightmare feeling about it of last year. Real work brings society into its proper place – as a rest and relaxation, instead of an effort and an excitement. Trust I shall never make social capital out of my work. That with me a danger as I enjoy retailing my experience, independently of any effect I may produce, and the 'vanity motive' comes in to strengthen desire. Perhaps this past year of suffering will decrease my egotism, and instead of that cold observation and analysis, all done with the egotistical purpose of increasing knowledge, there will be the interest which comes from feeling, and from the desire humbly to serve those around me.

*11 March*. [York House]
Walking through the city met Professor Roberts, an interesting ugly little man, with artistic pretty 'bad-form' wife. He, coming from South Kensington Museum from a lecture. 'Is there a Professor Main at South Kensington?' I ask suddenly. 'Ah, I grieve to say, he has left us – an exceedingly able, brilliant young man, a charming fellow; but now in consumption – believe he has gone to the Engadine or Colorado.' And as I walk silently by the dowdy little professor's side through the dirty crowded thoroughfare with its noise and its bustle I think of a Sunday morning, the still calm alpine air, the exquisitely formed and coloured flowers close around us and beyond the 'Eternal Forms' bound to the heavens by soft ever-changing wreaths of mist. Two young human beings on the threshold of life and on the verge of an ever-uniting love. Parted for ever – one to die, the other to live a life of?

*13 March*. [York House?]
Feel rather depressed by the bigness of my work. When I look at those long balconies and think of all the queer characters – occupants, would-be occupants – and realize that the characters of the community will depend on our personal power, and that, again, depend not only on character but on persistent health, I feel rather dizzy. The home life and Rosy add to the strain. Have cleared away all 'instructive books'; taken to poetry and beautiful prose. Find the restfulness of *beauty* now that I have hard practical work and constant frictions. Emerson's essays delight me. . . .

133

*12 April. The Argoed*

Here for two or three days' rest. My work takes a good deal out of me, and sometimes wonder how much of it I shall eventually do. Feel so utterly *done* when I come back from Whitechapel. Too tired to think or feel, which possibly under present circumstances is the most comfortable state. So long as I have strength enough to go on, don't much care, but dread idleness as if it were Hell. Wonder how it will all end, or whether it will end me. Saw Maggie Harkness the other day. Back from Berlin again. 'I'm heartily sick of it' – that has been the text of her life since I first knew her, the text in these unbelieving days of many lives. Among the East Enders, in spite of their misery, misery which makes me sick to see, there seems little desire to leave life, on the whole a value in it. Perhaps they *expect* less than we do. What will the next entry be – in the rapids – or out of them? either *for ever*.

George Peabody (1795–1869), an American philanthropist, settled in London, spent large sums on schemes for housing the artisan class.

*4 June.* [York House?]

Working hard. Buildings unsatisfactory. Caretaker hopelessly inadequate. Tenants, rough lot – the aborigines of the East End. Pressure to exclude these and take in only the respectable – follow Peabody's example. Interview with superintendent of Peabody's. 'We had a rough lot to begin with, had to weed them of the old inhabitants – now only take in men with regular employment.'

The practical problem of management: are the tenants to be picked, all doubtful or inconvenient persons excluded or are the former inhabitants to be housed so long as they are decently respectable?

May have some rough work to do, but am gaining experience. When over-tired, the tenants haunt me with their wretched, disorderly lives. Wish I had started with more experience, and had taken the thing more regularly in hand. Half-hearted work is always bad. Altogether my life, though not so completely wasted as it was last year, has not turned into much good for others; the rapids are too dangerously near. But there must be an end to that.

Towards the end of July, in an effort to settle the matter one way or another, Kate Courtney arranged a country picnic in Buckinghamshire, inviting Chamberlain specifically to meet Beatrice. It was a disastrous occasion. 'The great man and I are painfully shy when we are alone and very anxious that nothing shall be noticed when others are there – a state of affairs which seems destined to lead to endless misunderstandings,' Beatrice wrote to Mary Playne afterwards. 'It certainly brings a good deal of unhappiness to me – and I can't imagine *he* finds much amusement in it. I should think that one or the other of us would break off this enigmatical relationship this autumn, by refusing to see more of each other.' When Beatrice later reflected on the picnic she was even more explicit. 'That day will always remain engraved on my memory as the most painful one of my life,' she recalled. (See entry for 12 May 1886.) The Courtneys shared her disgust. 'I wonder what you thought of yesterday,' Kate wrote to Beatrice; 'to me there was no sign or trace of any other feeling than an intense personal ambition and a desire to dominate at whatever cost to other people's rights. I do not even see any room in his nature for such an affection as would satisfy one of us. It would be a tragedy – a murder of your independent nature.' Leonard Courtney wrote to similar effect, and so did Mary Booth, in whom Beatrice had confided. 'You could never be happy and would be increasingly unhappy with that man. . . .'

Beatrice then went to Rusland to stay with her father and Rosy. 'During my fortnight's holiday', she wrote to Mary Playne, 'I have thought very seriously about my own future, especially about my relationship to Mr Chamberlain, and I think I have arrived at definite conclusions. I certainly do not intend to be forlorn. Heaven knows there is enough work to be done . . . to make life worth living even without personal happiness. . . .'


*7 August.* [Rusland]

I return to London tomorrow for five weeks' hard work. Exhausted and very miserable the first two days of my holiday. The old delusion returned in the spring – had a rude shake to awaken me. Now must face a working life bravely and make the best out of it. Work has only been half-hearted hitherto. Now shall keep regular account of it, written with care. Companionship with philosopher always refreshing – because of his *true-mindedness*. Either the bias of my character or his past influence is over-powering; always return to his view of the duties of the State – the free and right administration of *justice* between individuals. But because there has been no justice or, rather, injustice administered to great classes of men, owing to their powerlessness, great wrongs have arisen. Can these wrongs be redressed? Certainly not by the simple administration of justice – that must be based on the *status quo*. Ought we then to take from a whole class of individuals that which has been stolen (we will admit the theft) by past individuals of that class in past times from other classes – shall we not offend actively against the very principle we wish to establish? That is the crucial question.

135

Emma Cons (1838–1912), Beatrice said, was 'one of the most saintly, as well as the most far-sighted of Victorian women philanthropists'. She began her career in a similar fashion to Beatrice – rent-collecting, then a reaction against 'the self-complacent harshness' of the Charity Organization Society, then the management of working-class dwellings. She took over the Victoria Music Hall (known as 'the Old Vic') and made it a centre of popular entertainment without the customary vice or alcohol.

*12 August.* [London]
Visited Miss Cons at Surrey Buildings (South London Building Company, cost £20,887, pays 4 per cent, no depreciation fund). According to evidence before Royal Commission, only three-quarters let. Working-class tenements, shops and cottages, outside stair-case, balconies round pleasure-ground, water closets together, one to each tenement with keys, *no* sinks. Wash-house and drying-ground on roof.

Miss Cons trained by Octavia Hill. Not a lady by birth, with the face and manner of a distinguished woman, a ruler of men. Absolute absorption in work, strong religious feeling, very little culture or interest in things outside the sphere of her own action. Certainly not a lover of fact or theory. Was not clear as to total number of rooms, unlets or arrears. No description of tenants kept. Did not attempt to theorize on her work.

Kept all particulars as to families in her head, spoke to her people with that peculiar mixture of sympathy and authority which characterizes the modern class of *governing women*. I felt ashamed of the way I cross-questioned her. As far as I could make out from her books, her arrears amounted to within a £1 of her weekly rent – that is to say, on the working-class tenants. She lives on the premises; collects other blocks, but devotes much time to other work in connection with the amusement and instruction of the people. A calm enthusiasm in her face, giving her all to others. 'Why withhold any of your time and strength?' seemed to be her spirit. All her energy devoted to the practical side of the work – very little desire to solve the general questions of the hour. These 'governing and guiding women' may become important factors if they increase as they have done lately; women who give up their lives to the management of men, their whole energy of body and mind absorbed in it.

Unlike the learned woman, the emotional part of their nature is fully developed, their sympathy kept almost painfully active. Their eyes are clear of self-consciousness and bright with love and the pity

136

from which it springs. They have the dignity of habitual authority. Often they have the narrow-mindedness and social gaucherie of complete absorption, physical and mental, in one set of feelings and ideas. The *pure organizer* belongs to a different class. She is represented by the active secretary to a growing society or the matron of a big hospital – is to a certain extent unsexed by the justice, push, and severity required. Not that I despise these qualities; the former is indispensable in any work, but with the manager it is more moral; with the organizer more technical justice. Push and severity are not *prominent* qualities of the governing and guiding woman. For the *guidance* of men by personal influence, *feeling* more than thought is required.

Desirable that I should thoroughly master details of South London Building Company management.

Haselour Hall, a fine property in Shropshire, was taken as a temporary home by the Booths, being accessible both from Liverpool, where Booth had his shipping business, and from London, where he was being drawn increasingly into social investigation. Each Lord Mayor of London raised a winter subscription for the poor, known as the Lord Mayor's Fund, which was disbursed as an indiscriminate charity; but in 1884 the incumbent Lord Mayor took the unusual step of asking the Statistical Society to discover what methods of assistance had proved most successful in the past. Charles Booth offered his services, and began a study based on the 1881 census tables. The *Pall Mall Gazette* was an influential evening paper founded in 1866. When W. T. Stead (1849–1912) was promoted to editor in 1883 he made it an outstanding example of the 'New Journalism', noted for its radical temper and its exposure of social abuses.

*Saturday, 22 August.* [Haselour Hall?]
Delightful two days with Booths. Charles and I [took a] long walk among pines and Spanish chestnuts. Discussed the possibility of social diagnosis. He, working away with [a] clerk on the Mansion House Inquiry into unemployed, and other work of statistical sort. Plenty of workers engaged in examination of facts collected by others – *personal investigation* required. *Pall Mall* [Gazette] have started this but in worst possible way, shallow and sensational. . . .

Working very hard. Now that I have more or less mastered detail I can do with less time and energy. The idea of developing self-government among the tenants has to be gradually introduced. Should like for that purpose to go back to Bacup and learn Co-operative spirit.

*10 September.* [Cheyne Walk]

Oh so tired. Struggling through the end of my work with painful effort. The old physical longing for the night that knows no morning.

Maurice Eden Paul (1865–1944), the son of the publisher Charles Kegan Paul, was a medical student who went East Ending, became infatuated with Ella Pycroft – with whom he had a dismal love affair that he broke off just before their planned marriage – and later became known as a Marxist writer and translator.

Beatrice was currently staying in the Courtney house at 15 Cheyne Walk, Chelsea, and travelling down to Tower Pier by the regular river service.

*15 September.* [Cheyne Walk]

Boys club started by Maurice Paul. Reading-room carried on by same. Spent three evenings there, and started the idea in my own mind of introducing a committee of men gradually into the management of buildings. . . . Interesting conversation with Ansing family who came to tea at York House. Man – Prussian Catholic settled in Whitechapel twenty-five years ago. Woman English. Sweaters: i.e. middlemen between [retail] shop and hands for the making of men's clothes. Man with a rigid disapproval of Whitechapel population – no pity. Woman more heart (on her tongue), should think she was fairly kind, though naturally enough treating the 'hands' for her own advantage, not for theirs. Give melancholy account of their habits in regard to work. She told me, and one of the 'hands' corroborated it, that she frequently spent the whole day hunting up her 'hands' in public houses to *persuade* them to finish work for which she had contracted. The account she and her husband gave of the class we all have to do with is much the same as I should give with my small experience, *minus certain lovable qualities* which a lady rouses into activity and appreciates. We should all designate them as on the whole a *leisure* class – picking up their livelihood by casual work (poor in quality), by borrowing from their more industrious friends, and by petty theft. Drunken, thieving and loose in their morality. I should add, generous-hearted and affectionate, capable of self-control when once you have gained their affection. As a class, *not beggars* – do not expect you to give. Unlike the country poor in this. Also warm in their feeling for family and friends. As a class, in a purely business relationship in which no other moral principle enters but that of fulfilling contracts, hopelessly unsatisfactory. This great principle must be developed in them by other moral methods besides that of a cold enforcement of justice.

Outside my work, I had a pleasant life at Cheyne Walk. Journeys down the Thames in the ferry steamers, especially back by the evening light; the picturesque side of London lower-class life, the background of grand public buildings with their national historical associations. And then once back in that perfect house, Maggie Harkness fresh from her novel-writing to greet me to chat on all subjects, human and divine, and to play snatches of good music on the parliamentary piano; I, lying the while on the sofa, watching the river and the barges on it creeping by. Happy fellowship in work, rest, and also in memories. 'Who would have thought it', we said constantly to one another, 'when we two as schoolgirls stood on the moorland near Bournemouth, watching the sunset and the trees against it, discussed our religious difficulties and gave vent to all our world-sorrow, and ended by prophesying we should in ten years be talking of cooks and baby linen, boys going to their first school and other matronly subjects, who would have thought of our real future?' She, struggling for her livelihood with queer experiences of a working woman's life; of another with her cook and big establishment but also absorbed in work outside home duty; both passed through the misery of strong and useless feeling. . . . Who would have thought it! Will another ten years bring as great a change or have we settled down in the groove we are destined to run in?

Hippolyte Taine (1828–93), a French historian noted for his social determinist theories and his work on pre-Revolutionary France, had published a description of the Potter household in his *Notes sur l'Angleterre*, which appeared in English translation in 1872. 'In France,' he wrote at the end of an admiring comment on Lawrencina Potter's intellectual attainments, 'we believe too readily that if a woman ceases to be a doll she ceases to be a woman.' Beatrice was probably reading the evidence given to the Parliamentary Select Committee on Artisans' and Labourers' Dwellings Improvement, 1882.

*6 October. Crosthwaite* [Cumberland]
A pleasant holiday among the hills. Read Taine's *Ancien Régime* with real enjoyment after ten days of 'Artisan Dwellings'. These generalizing histories are most useful in giving a continuity of historical conception, in developing the historical sense, which one can afterwards use at one's own convenience and according to special affinities to certain portions of the man's history.

I do not know how little or how much my energy will be equal to, but while I hope to devote the greater part of it to my own subject, yet

I feel my knowledge of history is wholly inadequate even for my special purposes. At the same time, a thoroughly detailed knowledge of what actually *is*, will give me a much stronger imagination, will furnish me with the raw material, the knowledge of men and women in different conditions, with the aid of which, added to a knowledge of past circumstances, the history of former men and women may be instructive. A rigmarole way of expressing myself! When I was at Bacup, I felt as if I were living through a page of Puritan history, felt that I *saw* the actual thing, human beings governed by one idea – devotion to Christ – with no strength or forethought for this world; in every action of their daily life 'living unto God'. And I realized the strength of this power which the instructed believe is passing away. I realized its 'permeating influence' and wondered with sadness what would fill the void it would leave, what inspiring motives would take its place.

Except the Grecian history I have never studied any epoch. . . . I studied the speeches in Thucydides carefully and, I think, gathered from them a pretty complete idea of Greek political philosophy. I *lived* in Plato for two or three months, realized the social charm of Athenian society, and breathed in his idealism of human nature. . . . I felt inspired by those clear deep tones of Aeschylus, that grand necessarianism, the emotions of mankind summarized in poetry which is more like music in depth and comprehensiveness of feeling. . . . I followed Sophocles in his polished realism, Euripides in his rhetorical descriptiveness; Aristophanes can only be understood in the original, he must be untranslatable. Aristotle I have never attempted but intend to read his *Ethics* and his *Politics*.

Then of historical Christianity I know little beyond a general knowledge of the New Testament. A very careless reading of Gibbon has given me a general view of the *facts* of the Decline and Fall of the Roman Empire. . . . A slight acquaintance with Lucretius, Horace, Pliny (the younger), Juvenal. . . . Marcus Aurelius stands out from amongst them as having had a personal influence over me, determined to some extent my moral tone and action. . . . A sympathetic appreciation of Buddhism – I do not say in any way an adequate or thorough knowledge of it. But for a year or so it was the subject matter to the study and realization of which were devoted my whole thought and feeling. At a time, too, when this meant months of *brooding*. . . .

Of French thought I know little – my reading of Voltaire and Rousseau have stimulated appetite without gratifying it. Of English history and literature, I may say, as an Englishwoman I am *absolutely* ignorant. Goethe was read with care and love – but from the personal rather than from the historical point of view. He was read as a master, from whom I should learn the 'art of life'. I had no historical knowledge from which I could understand him relatively to his age. My relationship with him was too intensely *personal* – his influence over me was for the time supreme. After loving him so well I should hesitate before I tried to *judge him*. One feels tenderly towards a mind that has governed one.

As for scientific theories as to the evolution of society, main principles upon which to graft knowledge of special fact, I have none – except perhaps Comte's great generalization of the processes of human thought. I read with a sort of fervid enthusiasm Herbert Spencer's *First Principles* and accept his perfect formula of the course of life in all Being, accept it as the truest summary of it now attainable. His deductions from general theory, used as the first principles of social science, are to my mind suggestive hypotheses, not proven laws, but I have not studied them. He irritates me by trying to palm off illustrations as data, by transcribing biological laws into the terms of social facts, and then reasoning by them as social laws.

A deeper knowledge of his work based on a wider experience of life, may make me in the end his true disciple – at present I am not. I am *biased by his individualism*, not converted to it. I should like to understand clearly what his theory is . . . how he has worked it out.

I should like also to have mastered the general outline of the reasoning of the scientific socialist. But I will keep my *own* mind from general theories about society. Great experiments are being made – it is sufficient for the unphilosophical mind to watch carefully the result – and retail it. . . .

My special aim is to understand the conditions of the working class in the way of 'housing', by digesting the evidence of others, testing and supplementing it by my own observation and actual effort in that direction. To study state interference in its two separate functions is the special question: first of enforcing respect in the individual for the health of others, obliging the individual to fulfil the acknowledged contract with society; and secondly that more doubtfully natural function – its attempt to supplement by direct constructive activity the work of voluntary enterprise and of individual effort. . . .

On 8 October, Clara Chamberlain (now married to Frederick Ryland) wrote inviting Beatrice to visit her in Birmingham on 2 November. 'The election fever is absorbing everyone and I have, I fear, nothing more lively to offer you in the way of entertainment than a big meeting at the Town Hall when my brother addresses his constituents. . . .' Beatrice went to visit the Rylands, and while she was there she broke down and openly expressed her feelings about Chamberlain – only to be deeply mortified when Clara Ryland claimed that she had been mistaken about the whole affair, and that the 'brother had never thought of me'. (See the diary entry for 6 March 1886, when Beatrice recorded this visit.) Much distressed, she went to seek consolation in a three-day visit to Mary Booth.

*23 October.* [Crosthwaite?]
Tomorrow to London town to begin a new year of work. The report I sent to my directors had an effect, and has made them reconsider their plan for the new building. . . . I am back on the old lines, when shall I run off again?

In early November, Beatrice wrote to her father (who was away in Tadcaster, the original home of the Potters) that she was 'working hard at a book of all the tenants, past and present, with description of occupation, family, etc.'. She seemingly abandoned the project when she had to leave London suddenly a fortnight later. She had prepared a proposal for the better management of Katherine Buildings, and she was beginning to think of an association which would co-ordinate the various agencies concerned with the housing of the poor. She had in mind a body which would give the lady collectors better professional prospects. 'I admire and reverence women most who are content to be among the "unknown saints", but it is no use shutting one's eyes to the fact that there is an increasing number of women to whom the matrimonial career is shut and who seek a masculine reward for masculine qualities,' she told her father. 'There is in these women something exceedingly pathetic, and I would do anything to open careers to them in which their somewhat abnormal but useful qualities would get their own reward. . . . I think these strong women have a great future before them – in the solution of social questions. They *are not* just inferior men. They may have masculine faculty but they have the *woman's temperament* – and the stronger they are the more distinctively feminine they are in this. I only hope that, instead of trying to ape men and take up men's pursuits, they will carve out their own careers, and not be satisfied until they have found the careers in which their particular form of power will achieve most.'

*8 November.* [York House]
I meant this morning to have worked at my Katherine Buildings book, but unfortunately (fortunately!) my rent-books were away. I think I will keep Sunday for rest and writing a short account of my work for the past week. The past fortnight I have been struggling against

headache and physical depression: spent first three days with Mary Booth and the continual conversation upset me. . . . Two long conversations with Mr Barnett: I, making my suggestion of associating all agencies for housing the poor in one body. Have not thought this out and was rather astounded at the way he took it up and wanted me to elaborate a plan and to become the moving spirit. Shall I always disappoint myself and others when my strength comes to be tested – or will my strength increase and enable me to carry out what I initiate?

The Barnetts love new plans and purposes, are deficient in real power of organization and careful working out of detail.

And I am constantly weary; life is a continual struggle, a real battlefield, both physically and mentally. Still, if Rosy will only get strong, there is interest enough in life, and affection too, and this gnawing pain will cease in time. I have not yet fully realized the uselessness of it. As for work, I have done only my bare duty at Katherine Buildings, and have begun a careful account of tenants – but oh! for more energy. Went with two fellow-workers to the 'Vic', managed by that grand woman, Miss Cons. To me a dreary performance, sinking to the level of the audience, while omitting the dash of coarseness, irreverence, low humour which give the spice and the *reality* to such entertainments. To my mind the Devil is preferable, and in every way more wholesome than a shapeless mediocrity. . . .

*15 November.* [York House]
Worked well. Monday, Katherine Buildings, one to nine o'clock. Afterwards saw over Whittington Club. . . . Tuesday at Katherine Buildings book, 4 hours. Wednesday Albert and Victoria Docks from 10 p.m. to 6 a.m. Thursday, idle morning castle-building – afternoon, Katherine Buildings. Friday, 7 hours' work at Katherine Buildings book. Saturday, Katherine Buildings 12 to 7 o'clock. Forty hours' work including railway journeys.

On Thursday, 26 November, Richard Potter suffered a stroke. Sir Andrew Clark (1826–93), Chief Physician at the London Hospital, was a personal friend. Richard Potter was taken to stay with the Playnes at Longfords, then in the New Year Beatrice took him to Bournemouth with its milder climate. Her father's collapse, when her own emotions were under strain and her sister Rosy appears to have been suffering from *anorexia nervosa*, threw Beatrice into the profound depression in which she wrote the informal will which she included as the first entry in her diary for 1886.

Richard Potter was on his way to vote in the general election of November 1885. The Miss Darling mentioned here, and in ensuing entries until 1888, was presumably a sister of Carrie Darling but is not otherwise identified.


*19 December.* [York House]

A month ago today Father and Rosy returned from their little trip to York and Tadcaster. I had written to beg them not to take it, on Rosy's account. The reports of her state, physical and mental, brought to me by the servants and Miss Darling were most alarming and I had made up my mind to offer to take her away for six months. They came back both looking very ill – but apparently enamoured of each other. However, the next morning I broached the question with Father. I explained to him I felt very miserable about her and convinced that nothing short of separation from him would do much good. He, poor man, seemed quite relieved about the idea of getting rid of the responsibility and acquiesced in my vague suggestion I should take her away.

On Thursday, 26th, Father came down to breakfast late, very unusual for him. He looked to me strange, seemed so curiously slow in his movements. Still there was nothing to cause me much anxiety. He read the papers, but did not open his letters. I found them afterwards lying on the table. I had arranged an appointment with Dr Gee for Rosy at 11 o'clock. Father and she went out, he with the intention of voting. I watched him from the dining-room window fumbling with the lock of the dog's kennel. It struck me suddenly that he was fast becoming an old man. Then I went about my business – with a heavy heart, for six months' *tête-à-tête* with Rosy was not a refreshing prospect. Half-past ten and they had not come back – another twenty minutes I became nervous, opened the front door and walked to the big gate. There, some yards down the street, Father leaning heavily on poor little Rosy, dragging his leg, his face drawn down, but seemingly quite unconcerned at the change that had befallen him. I helped him into the house, hurried Rosy, who was pale and trembling, away with Miss Darling and sent for the doctor. Dr Tyrell, when he saw him, said immediately it was a stroke of paralysis and advised me to send for Sir A. Clark. His mind was not touched – it was as active as ever on politics, he talked in an excited manner with Sir A. Clark when he came that evening.

The 'beloved physician' spoke seriously to me that evening. 'The greatest proportion of these cases do not recover.' He seemed to get better the first three days, then a relapse. His mind became more affected, he was extravagant in his ideas and wishes. Saturday, 5th, was the '*black day*'. He dictated an extraordinary letter to Rosy and sent out for fifty or sixty pairs of slippers from different shops. Andrew Clark evidently thought the worst was coming, he feared softening of the brain and a rapid ending. Since then his tone of body and mind has become steadily healthier. He is happy and contented, slightly irritated with small things, but on the whole sweet and gentle to do for. It is a month now since he was struck down. His intelligence is singularly lucid on some questions and he is extraordinarily cheerful. But there is something gone – some part of his mind sleeping or dead? Tomorrow we move him to Longfords for the New Year.

Poor little Rosy had a terrible time of it. She reproached herself for worrying him into his illness, and she was not far wrong. But, as I told her, it was as much my neglect as her worry. Those were terrible days, complicated with business worries, Rosy's depression and temper and my own egotistical dread of the future. And the future does look gloomy indeed. Companionizing a failing mind – a life without physical or mental activity – no work. Good God, how awful. This time last year I was suffering from the same feeling – with other circumstances. There was hope for me then in work. Now I am *hopeless*. Except that this year I feel as if the end of my pain *must* come. Surely my cup is full.

little man, with a certain solid desire to advance his cause quite apart from his own prominence. He began life as a Methodist, became a free thinker, and rejoices in the greater freedom of London life from the personal supervision so dominant in provincial organizations. This question arose in our conversation discussing the attractions of London to the low-class labour drift, I noticing the absence of a strong *public opinion* forcing men to work and behave themselves. His wife is a more 'superior person' than himself, morally considered. She is unaffected and unselfconscious and much more thoughtful. Their family life is full of happiness and content.

*7 November. York House*
Is it this house with all its painful associations that drags me down again into this spiritless melancholy, or is it discouragement or ill-health? The dark autumn weather, the garden lonely and strewn with leaves, all the kith and kin out of London, the sight of the old work and the companionship of fellow-workers all bring a rush of the old memories. And of late I have given way to the old old feeling which sometimes I despair of ever shaking off. . . . The lot I have drawn in life is an evil-omened number. Still, there is freedom, freedom to do, to think and to feel the highest possible to one's nature. Happiness is a closed book – work is hardly opened. . . .

This undated entry was written when Beatrice was looking after the second of the pair of buildings which she managed with Ella Pycroft: her friend was away.

*Wentworth Dwellings*
It would not do for me to live alone. I should become morbid. I miss terribly the dependence of others on me, the happy necessity to seem bright, forcing one to put down depression sternly. And the East End life, with its dirt, drunkenness and immorality, absence of combined effort or common interest, saddens me, weighs down my spirit. I could not live down here. I should lose heart and become worthless as a worker. And practical work does not satisfy me; it seems like walking on shifting sand, with the forlorn hope that the impress of your steps will be lasting to guide others across the desert. . . .

Where is the wish for better things in those myriads of beings hurrying along the streets night and day? Even their careless, sensual laugh, the coarse jokes and unloving words depress one as one presses through the crowd, and almost shudders to touch them. It is not so much the actual vice, it is the low level of monotonous and yet excited life, the regular recurrence of street sensations in quarrels and fights, the greedy street bargaining, and the petty theft and gambling.

The better natures keep apart from their degraded fellow-citizens and fellow-workers, live lonely and perforce selfish lives. . . . Social intercourse brings out, and springs from, the worst qualities in East London; as a society it is an ever increasing and ever decomposing mass. . . . These buildings too are to my mind an utter failure. In spite of Ella Pycroft's heroic efforts, they are not an influence for good. The free intercourse has here, as elsewhere in this dismal mass, a demoralizing effect. The bad and indifferent, the drunken, mean and lowering elements overwhelm the effect of higher motive and nobler example. The respectable tenants keep rigidly to themselves. To isolate yourself from your surroundings seems to be here the acme of social morality – in truth it is the only creed one dare preach. 'Don't meddle with your neighbours' is perforce the burden of one's advice to the newcomer. The meeting-places, there is something grotesquely coarse in this, are the water-closets! Boys and girls crowd on these landings – they are the only lighted places in the buildings – to gamble and flirt. The lady collectors are an altogether superficial thing. Undoubtedly their gentleness and kindness bring light into many homes, but what are they in face of this collected brutality, heaped up together in infectious contact, adding to each other's dirt, physical and moral? And how can one raise these beings to better things without the hope in a better world, the faith in the usefulness of effort? Why resist the drink demon? A short life and a merry one. Why not? A woman diseased with drink came up screaming to me, in her hand the quart pot, her face directed to the Public [House]. What could I say? Why dissuade her? She is half-way to death – let her go – if death ends all. But with her go others, and they are only the first step downwards. Alas! *there* is the pitifulness of this long chain of iniquity – children linked on to parents, friends to friends, and lovers to lovers, bearing down to that bottomless pit of decaying life.

The bright side of East End life is the sociability and generous sharing of small means. These, of course, bring in their train quarrels and backbiting, for it is easier to give than to bear ingratitude, or than to be grateful. And as the 'Public' is the only meeting-place the more sociable and generous nature is led away even by its good qualities, while the crabbed and sickly constitution isolates itself and possibly thrives in its isolation. The drink demon destroys the fittest and spares the meaner nature, undermines the constitution of a family, and then passes on to stronger stuff. There are times when one loses all faith in *laissez-faire*, and would suppress this poison at all hazards before it eats the life of the nation. For hardworking men are tied to drunken wives, and hardworking women to drunken husbands, so that the good are weighted down and their striving after a better life made meaningless.

And yet there are glimpses into better homes – sights of love between men and women and towards little children – and rarely enough, devotion to the aged and the sick. And possibly it is this occasional rest from dirt and disorder that makes the work more depressing; for one must hear unheeded the sickening cry of the sinking man or woman dragging the little ones down into a poverty from which there is no rising.

In spite of the numberless out-o'-work it is difficult to find really good workmen; for they become quickly demoralized and lose their worthfulness. This again is depressing for how can one help these people if they are not worthy of life from an economic point of view?

*1 December. Kildare*
I have been so wretched during most of my seven weeks away that I am glad to get back to my home and my home duties. Intellectual work is the only occupation that absorbs my mind, prevents the constant brooding over the mistakes of the past and the dreary possibilities of the future. Perhaps too I was discouraged with the ill-success of my writing, though the idea was hailed as a good one. I must to it again. No one helps me with my idea: I must work it out more thoroughly alone. I also want to work out the idea of social research starting from personal observation and leading to laws which can be statistically stated, i.e. empirical laws.

There was as yet no English translation of Karl Marx's *Capital*, but Deville had published a French version of the first volume. Frederick Myers (1843–1901), poet, amateur psychologist and spiritualist, was one of the founders of the Society for Psychical Research in 1882.

*10 December.* [Kildare]
Ten days' hard work at Karl Marx ending in a cold in bed. Finished the first volume, that one translated into French.

Certainly our little party is not an enlivening one. Dear Father – merely a shadow – his intellect still clear though weak, but all his

187

moral responsibility and strong feeling gone. Sleeps, eats, is read to, and sleeps again; spending most of the 24 hours in a half-comatose state. Little Miss Darling, depressed and small-minded, melancholy, cross with her meaningless little life; still she is a loving little body and would have grown through love. And then Rosy! That sodden weight. Poor child, how I pity her life companion! Has she the power to develop? She is wonderfully improved and yet is not more lovable, only no longer detestable, for all her sins are of omission not commission. But there is not one spark of heroism, of self-ignoring love; it is all *passively self*. After all, what one reverences and admires, sometimes adores, *is* heroism of one kind or another.

But have I a right to criticize? For my life is contracted into a ceaseless regard for self, a petty regret for the past and fear of the future. Why this ceaseless grasping after that phantom – happiness? And as the only alternative why this desperate clutch at *Power* – power to impress and to lead? No wonder I gain only a powerless unhappiness.

Frederick Myers wrote an interesting article in one of the reviews the other day on multiple personality, giving pathological cases in which absolutely different personalities appeared in the same person according as different parts of their brain were physically acted upon. And surely this difference of personality in one person must not only be the result of physical agents, but must also arise with different mental agents, such as a change of ideas. We see these cases in sudden conversions, cases in which the mental agent is given an increased force by faith in supernaturalism, this change of personality sometimes dividing the life in two – an evil and a good part.

And certainly in my own case I have noticed a duplex personality, and have been happy or unhappy as one or the other got uppermost. The sadness and suffering of my early life brought out the *nether* being in me; the despondent vain, grasping person – (the Heyworth) – doomed to failure. Linked to this nethermost being was the phantom of Mother, the gloomily religious – affecting asceticism and dominated by superstition. Left under the dominion of this personality my natural vocation and destiny was the convent; for in this life the phantom would have been strengthened by religious exaltation, and the nethermost being soothed and deluded with hopes of another world where merit would be regarded by its true worth.

But there is in me another person. An enthusiast for Truth, regarding self only as a means to further Truth. Patient, faithful and light-hearted (because unegotistical), a lover of thought and ready to sacrifice all things to it. Essentially a *realist* in intellectual questions, a rationalist in metaphysics and therefore a sceptic of religion. This is the happiest and perhaps the highest expression of my Ego. But alas! this being has its life and origin in my sensual nature: it springs from vigorous senses and keen perceptions. If I were a man, this creature would be free, though not dissolute, in its morals, a lover of women. These feelings would be subordinated to the intellectual and practical interests, but still the strong physical nature upon which the intellectual nature is based would be satisfied. And as I am a woman: these feelings, unless fulfilled in marriage, which would mean destruction of the intellectual being, must remain controlled and unsatisfied, finding their only vent in one quality of the phantom companion of the nethermost personality, religious exaltation.

And so, in this ill-assorted round of disjointed circles, there is constant friction. And my intimacy with the great man brought about a deadly fight between the intellectual and the sensual, the sensual bringing forward the nethermost being and for a time overwhelming the higher part. But the intellectual has triumphed not by its own strength but by the force of circumstance; it has beaten the sensual and denied to it satisfaction. The nethermost being, however, stands there, vain, despondent, grasping, waiting only for physical depression to clutch and strangle the Ego. Such a being leads direct to suicide, for life with it is unbearable.

But if we recognize the existence of this duplex or manifold personality, surely we, by the added presence of the *Will*, may ensure success to one or the other? The battle was long and terrible because my *Will* was undecided which side to elect. Indeed for a long time it elected the lower and allowed Imagination to dwell on it and decorate it.

But now – Fate, that term for outside and independent forces, has built strong barriers and forced Will to be at least passive. And womanly dignity and reserve side with Fate and forbid the inroads of Passion. . . .

Two days in London with the Booths. Charlie absorbed in his inquiry, working all his evenings with three paid secretaries. I have promised to undertake the docks in my March holiday. Dear sweet little Mary, with her loving ways and charming motherhood. They become each year more near to me. Perhaps they are the only persons who really *love* me. It is sad, that my family for whom I have a strong

189

affection, are so distant from my real aims in life. Mary Playne I *do* love – and she loves me, for we have sympathized and helped each other's family life for eight years.

The Courtneys I have a strong affection for. Leonard has won my reverence – I feel the stronger for knowing him. He says little and he has no special regard for what I say, but his personality, perfect integrity and courage, stands out like a rock and his deep feeling binds me to him in the days of adversity. Kate is wonderfully happy, always in the highest spirits, strong in his strength and basking in his warm affection. It is a perfect union. Then the Alfred Crippses, with whom my relationship has been somewhat strained but who are always pleasant good-tempered companions, though difficult to deal with in business relations, not trustworthy. But Alfred and I have much in common and are naturally attracted one to the other, and Theresa is a warm-hearted creature with fresh ideas each day. Willy Cripps and I are old friends. In the dark days of his fortunes I believed in him and supported him; and he is loyal to me. For Blanche too I have a fellow-feeling, for we understand each other's melancholy madness. Daniel [Meinertzhagen] I am pleasantly connected with in business. He used to like me when I was a pretty successful girl – we still get on together, though I doubt whether I should see much of him if I took to a working life. Poor Georgie with her sad complaint and cynical view: 'Why don't you live like other people, instead of pretending to be a genius?' And that worthy couple, the Hobhouses. Maggie became utterly uninteresting, absorbed in her children, without friends, but without suffering. I felt those two days at Hadspen as if I were walking on an extinct volcano. As girls we had a passionate intellectual friendship. As women with the kindliest intentions we find nothing worth saying. With none of my sisters can I talk in the perfectly unconstrained way I talk to my friends – for they all secretly condemn my want of success and think my aim absurdly out of proportion to my capacity – that is to say, if they know my aim.

So I fall back on my friends. Let me arrange them: Charlie and Mary Booth, Maggie Harkness, Mr Barnett, Bella Fisher [see note for 15 July 1888], Ella Pycroft, Carrie Darling are those with whom I am persistently connected. . . . Clara Ryland and Beatrice Chamberlain, part of that black nightmare which still haunts me. It would have been wiser to have cut them off, but I could not, and I am still miserably entangled in the old feeling. Mme Souvestre, the clever passionate Frenchwoman – a good or an evil genius? She also intimately connected with that tragedy of my life. Ah! I forgot, the old philosopher, gradually sinking into his grave, sending me from time to time fresh instalments of his 'Reminiscences' to revise. A memory rather than a reality.

Then there is the home circle, to which I am bound fast. Poor sinking Father, my last tie to a loving life. Mrs Thompson, the capable nurse, little Miss Darling and poor incapable Rosy, with her heavy face and irritating ways. I cannot be loving with her. I can only be dutiful. . . . This old year wears out sadly – but it began *desperately*. Courage. . . .

Adam Smith (1723–90) was a Scottish economist famous for his book *An Inquiry into the Nature and Causes of the Wealth of Nations*, published in 1776. He was a pragmatist whose social insights influenced Ricardo and the nineteenth-century utilitarians. David Ricardo (1772–1823), influential British economist famous for the 'labour theory of value' – the value of goods are essentially a function of the labour needed to produce them – and 'the iron law of wages' declaring that wages tend to stabilize around subsistence level.

*20 December*. [Kildare]
Now to work! I want to sketch out my article before I finish the reading for it. It is to open with a demonstration that the proper subject matter for economic science is human nature. Social science being the science of 'men in combination', economics must be one section of this science, dealing with some special combining force. Then a sketch of the physical forces generated in social life – faculties and desires. I must show how social science includes all human faculties and desires, the history of religion with religious faculty and desire, and economics with those faculties and desires which have exchange value.

Then I must turn to the economists and show how they have defined the subject matter of their science to be *wealth* and I must show the absurdity of that, using physiology as an analogy. I must trace the historical origin of this in the mercantile theory – with the burst of true light in Adam Smith, the crystallization of falsehood in Ricardo and the development of that strange being, the man of the orthodox economists, the abstract man and his eventual fate in Karl Marx, his rehabilitation by the modern economists.

Turning back to my own theory, I must prove its practical usefulness; state economic problems in its terms and define the meaning of them. Show the importance of careful observation of

191

economic disease. Use the 1834 Blue Book to illustrate this and all the factory legislation. State problem of *laissez-faire* and of state help. Try my hand at the enigma of this production on the one hand and starvation on the other, and for this is needed a careful study of Depression of Trade Blue Book. . . .

*23 December.* [Kildare]
Made up my mind to do it. Anything would be better than this constant torture. Cut them [the Chamberlain family] all off. . . . After the next month, neither to hear of them, nor to see them. But the next month must be lived through and maybe I shall be obliged to entertain Clara Ryland. Then it shall be over.

ᗌ 1887 ᗍ

*21 January. 10 p.m.* [Kildare]
The beginning of another year – in another two hours I shall be nine and twenty!

A whole month lost in miserable uncertainty. . . . This year not altogether wasted but the last four months broken down completely. How shall this next year be spent? With courage and generosity? Surely there are not many more years to live. Why not give one's all? Life apart from the natural satisfaction to the human instincts must be more or less *brûler un petit feu* – it must be a constant joylessness – surely there may be the calm that comes from an absolute self-renunciation? Still, with a strong warm nature, it is not one crisis but always recurring crises.

*22 January.* [Kildare]
Written to put off my visit to the Arthur Chamberlains. It is like a load off my mind, for happily it is not too late to cut myself off entirely from that family. Only Clara to whom I owe aught; and I will see the last of her this time. Why should my life be spoilt simply from a feeling of loyalty? I shall always have a gentle feeling towards that family, for in a strangely blundering fashion they have tried to treat me well, to smooth down my hurt feelings by respect and admiration. And perhaps I have misunderstood them. Anyhow let them rest in peace.

In the meanwhile I am helpless with weakness and pain. Idleness and exercise have made matters worse. Neuralgia, tooth-ache, abscess, the complaints of a chronic ill-health – worse than illness. I am happier than I was this time last year, because I am less hopeless, more confidence in myself and faith in my work. This last month I have been under a heavy cloud, but I shall rise out of it into new energy. If only I can keep my health: and that can only be done by being resigned and happy, accepting life as the inevitable and guarding against those relapses into misery and useless feeling. All that feeling must be dedicated to work. I start better this year, for I know the pitfalls into which I may stumble – intellectual ambition and destructive feeling. Ambition must be crushed, feeling must be borne with and purified.

*5 February.* [Kildare]
An unpleasant week in London, broken down with neuralgia and weakness, both of which still oppress me. Perhaps I needed this terrible lesson of pain and weakness to teach me the suicidal effect of giving way to intellectual ambition and to strong feeling. Sometimes I have said to myself – these dreams are but dreams, why not indulge in them, why deny myself this harmless gratification? I have not counted the cost – the waking up, perhaps with weakened energies, to the dull routine of daily life. I wonder whether I shall bear my life through or whether, when the last remaining ice is broken, I shall break with life and end it in a sleep. How willingly I would yield it.

*25 February.* [Kildare]
Three weeks absorbed in my review of Karl Marx, which I have now nearly ended. It has cleared my own ideas, but whether it is written in a form that will be accepted and 'take' I do not know. Sometimes I feel elated, and think that I have got the right end of the stick; at other times, when I am depressed by fatigue, I see in my writing only disjointed half-truths. Anyhow, intellectual production makes life for a time enjoyable, lends to it a personal meaning. And now that I must face many years of this loneliness and absence of practical interests, constant intellectual endeavour is my only safeguard against morbid feeling. If only I could work from the pure love of my work and not need to stimulate my effort by vulgar ambition!

My spirits have risen into youthfulness. It is rare for me to feel youthful but just now I do! and am looking forward to my month in London.

193

I have enjoyed my three weeks' work: the peace of the *inevitable* has come back to me. The feeling is there deep down in my nature, lying dormant, but I have had the strength to resist all chance of exciting it. Will that strength continue? I think so.

And I will spend my time in London generously and well. I will try to sympathize with happiness as well as with sorrow and sadness. . . .

Began investigation of docks. . . .

Edward Spencer Beesly (1831–1915) was Professor of History at University College, London; a well-known Positivist, much interested in labour problems, he had helped promote the Trade Union Act of 1874. Most of the diary in this period was taken up with notes on dock wages and working conditions.

*12 March.* [London]
The Booths are delighted with my article. Charlie enthusiastic. They sent it to Professor Beesly. . . . He overlooks the whole point of the article, which is to distinguish between the labour that is useful and the labour that is useless. . . . However, if my idea is true it is unlikely that it will be accepted all at once, especially by men who are pledged by past utterances to contrary opinions. . . .

Long day at the docks. . . .

There was at this time a last prospect of a reconciliation between the Gladstonian Liberals and those who had followed Chamberlain's opposition to Home Rule for Ireland and broken away to form the Liberal Unionist party. Sir George Otto Trevelyan (1838–1928), historian and politician, had been Chief Secretary in Dublin 1882–84, and an opponent of the Home Rule policy, but, Kate Courtney wrote in her journal on the eve of this visit to her husband's constituency in Cornwall, he was now 'apparently seized with such a passion for Liberal Reunion' that he was expected to devote his Liskeard speech to that cause. W. S. Caine, another Liberal Unionist M.P., also spoke. Beatrice was reading Emile Zola's *Bonheur des dames*. *Princess Casamassima*, by Henry James, had been published in the previous year.

*15–17 March. Visit to Liskeard*
Leonard, Kate, Sir George Trevelyan and I left London on 15 March for Liskeard. Sir George Trevelyan is a tall, thin, nervous man, with a delicately courteous manner; one of the 'charming persons' of London society. Bred up in the midst of an aristocracy of intellect as well as of birth, he has always been mindful to fulfil not only the duties of a 'Trevelyan' but to carry on the intellectual calibre of the 'Macaulay'. The Trevelyans are one of the oldest English families,

distinguished for lack of distinction and for their luck in marrying heiresses. They have followed their wives from Cornwall to Northumberland, and the present representative married early in life a Manchester girl with a rent roll of £12,000 a year.

But Sir George is a Macaulay as well as a Trevelyan: his mother was the beloved and gifted sister of the great historian. He was born under the shadow of the great 'Uncle Tom' [Thomas Babington Macaulay], and trained by him in literary and political life. Essentially an aristocrat in his instincts, he has believed in the coming democracy, not from a sturdy fellow-feeling for the needs and aspirations of the people, but through an intellectual appreciation of the doctrine of individual liberty. He does not know, and is not interested in, the working classes – the realities of his life are bounded by 'Good Society'. But as I said before, he is distinctly a charming person, and it is in this capacity that we knew him on the downward journey.

Through the seven hours' journey I sat in the corner of the carriage and listened to the talk between the three. Politics lightened by literary reminiscences was the staple conversation. Kate with her genial emphatic talk, Sir G. Trevelyan determined to be pleasant, exclaiming every now and then 'I call this a jolly expedition', Leonard waking up from time to time to give an appreciative grunt to Sir George's light-touched reference to a past or present author.

Evidently Kate and Sir George were not congenial: Kate was unaware of it and chattered on, claiming him as a connection through 'our common uncle'. The 'charming person' was fully awake to the fact that Mrs Leonard Courtney, though doubtless a good soul and a wisely chosen wife, was not an attractive or well-bred woman according to the fastidious taste of a polished Londoner.

The connection was slightly recognized, and the conversation changed – but he was studiously pleasant, and attentive to the colleague's wife. Political personalities, to me the most tiresome of subjects, were the order of the day. One strong personal feeling uppermost, irritation with Chamberlain. 'Chamberlain is not loyal to his colleagues.' At which Leonard's eyes opened wide and he gave an unusually appreciative grunt.

A long cold journey, our train looking like Father Xmas with snow and icicles as we steamed into the West Country stations. A still colder drive in an open carriage at foot's pace, through a cheering crowd of genial Cornish folk up the high street of Liskeard. And at last a cosy room and comfortable dinner.

Kate surrounded by old friends in the large hall of the inn, shaking hands vigorously, her face beaming with happiness and a genuine warm-hearted interest in each individual supporter of the idealized husband, treating them all with the same emphatic geniality that jarred on the nervous fastidious temperament of her distinguished guest, but which warmed the hearts and roused the affectionate admiration of the strong-feeling and straight-thinking Cornishmen.

Sir George Trevelyan had written out his speech a fortnight since – the next morning he passed in a nervous awaiting of the luncheon. After we had finished breakfast the door opened, and in walked a hugely stout ugly man. The Courtneys both welcomed him warmly and introduced me to 'Mr Bolitho'. The Bolithos own everything in that part of Cornwall, from the land to the country-town banks. They are a sturdy Cornish family, energetic and dutiful, belonging to the tougher class of country gentlemen. Leonard Courtney began life as clerk in one of the banks; was encouraged and helped by the Bolithos and now they look upon him with a proprietary feeling, qualified by admiration for the personal distinction and knowledge of the great world they are unaccustomed to. This particular Bolitho, a man of 80, had journeyed up from a remote corner of Cornwall, had walked through the snow with his unmarried daughter at 12 o'clock at night in order to be present at the Courtney Demonstration. He talked the broadest Cornish and soon tackled the distinguished visitor. 'If I am not mistaken, Sir George, your great step-aunt married as second wife my great grandfather.' This in awkward slow tones. 'She happened to be a governess in his house.' 'Ah, really,' said Sir George (standing elegantly on one leg) with the politest intonation, as if he fully recognized the honour of the alliance. 'I knew I was a Cornishman, though my ancestors left Cornwall in 1520, but I was unaware of my connection with your family; I am delighted to claim it.' (The Bolithos are important to Leonard Courtney, thought Sir George, amicably glad to help on his colleague by politeness.) 'Yes,' continued old Bolitho. 'I remember my father telling me of the marriage. He was an enormously fat man and twenty years older than your great-aunt (distant cousin, thought Sir George), but in spite of the difference in their positions and ages it proved a most wise selection.'

The lunch was a great success. I sat between a Bolitho and a Plymouth editor, of whom more anon.

First-rate local speaking – Leonard's speech full of personal feeling for his fellow-Cornishmen – Sir G. Trevelyan, polished admiration for Leonard, clever suggestion as to procedure of the House, careful avoidance of the Irish problem. . . . He has a pleasant musical voice, a careful utterance, easy graceful manner – his language tasting a literary flavour. But he lacks *grip*: moral grip. He charmed his audience, he did not move it, for the simple reason that he was not moved himself. He stood at 'the meeting of the ways', and knew not which road to take. He quietly evaded the question and entertained the audience with a panegyric on Leonard, and a would-be enthusiastic denunciation of national extravagance and Jingo policy – the panegyric and denunciation cleverly linked together by reference to Leonard's career as an anti-Jingo and a careful Financial Secretary.

Far otherwise Leonard's speech. It was deeply religious in its tone, exhorting his fellow-citizens to grapple with the question, intellectually and morally to realize their duty to England and to Ireland. And when they felt they had gained a living faith, to spread it by earnestness and single-minded reasoning. And then he held up to them the ideal of unity between the sister kingdoms, each one helping the other with its special excellence.

His loud sonorous voice, awkwardly elegant gestures, his expressive ungainly mouth and powerful head and dark shaggy eyebrows gleamed energy and religious conviction; and he sat down amid a burst of Cornish enthusiasm, his face streaming with perspiration and his eyes rolling with tears.

A pleasant supper-party. I, especially interested in a local man – a Nonconformist farmer – who had spoken splendidly at the meeting. A deeply religious man, but admiring Herbert Spencer – and what is more, understanding him. Sentimental about the poor – and on this subject we talked at cross-purposes – our conversation another instance of the entire novelty of the scientific view of society, of the hopeless misunderstanding of the motto (my motto) *to know in order to act*. According to these excellent persons it is individual suffering that must be relieved not the common good considered. And I maintain that *I* am the *true socialist*, through my willingness to sacrifice the individual to the community. But this man had not thought of the social question, except from the religious and political point of view – charity and love of freedom were the qualities seeking expression in his earnest single-minded opinion.

Poor Charity and Freedom – what cruelties and tyrannical interferences are committed in your names!

Leonard and Mr Caine left by the morning train. Sir George

197

Trevelyan, Kate and I journeyed to Plymouth where we breakfasted with the aforementioned newspaper editor. He was an unpleasant-looking man desperately anxious to please, and with that social uneasiness characteristic of the smaller bourgeoisie in the act of climbing up the social ladder. Editor to a paper owned by a mixed body of conservatives and liberals, he represented privately and officially the moderate opinions which are destined to be adopted by the Dissenting lower middle class so soon as the Church is disestablished. His manner was disagreeably officious: his expression distinctly denoted the capacity for doing a dirty trick. His whole moral being might be summed up in 'sand the sugar, put the shutters up, and come to prayers'. And yet one has no right to say so; for the capacity for a dirty trick has not manifested itself in a concrete form – and men are hanged for deeds not for expressions. . . .

Anyhow, though perhaps unjustly unpopular, he gathered a goodly assembly of Plymouth worthies to meet the distinguished visitors. . . . Kate was as genial as ever, though conscious of class distinction – a consciousness that is present with her, as with many of our class, only when we deal with the smaller bourgeoisie. She would not have allowed the bright-minded bright-eyed girl to kiss her. I, on the other hand, was warmed by the spontaneous kiss and the 'Goodbye dear' after two hours' acquaintance.

I felt in the society of the Plymouth worthies the presence of inferior animals with smaller intellects and colder hearts – but none of the subtle antagonism and contempt of the wholesale trader to his retail brother.

Sir George Trevelyan was the polished London gentleman, scrupulously civil whether he talked to Dissenting minister, mayor or town councillor, and equally indifferent to and unconscious of the individual presence of one and all – but determined to behave as befitted the political leader. Kate left us at Exeter and I looked forward with some constraint to 6 hours' *tête-à-tête* with the 'charming person'. I was not the 'colleague's wife' but a 'Miss Potter' with whom he had unfortunately to travel. I begged him to go into a smoking carriage – and my prayer was genuine – for had I not in the pocket of my sealskin not only a volume of Zola, but my case of cigarettes! neither of which could I enjoy in his distinguished presence.

'I think I will have a cigarette. Oh! no – I won't. It would be ungracious.'

'Pray do not mind that, Sir George, I never notice ungraciousness,' exclaimed I with desperate earnestness. But it was a case of 'no go' with the model man – and we both subsided into our corners, he to read *Princess Casamassima* (with which he was highly delighted) and I to pretend to sleep and amuse myself with picturing the past two days – turning over in my mind what each actor had said, looked and done. . . .

Sir G. Trevelyan, agreeably surprised by my modest silence, thought at least he ought to address me, and read at short intervals bits from the paper about the snowstorm and an exhibition at Rome – to all of which I returned a polite 'How very interesting' and subsided back into my meditative doze. . . .

His want of any self-conscious, self-renunciating devotion to public duty, of the determined integrity which transcends personal loyalty, causes that absence of moral tone that has distinguished him in this terrible national crisis. . . . Even Chamberlain is more capable of it – *is* capable of the highest form of it – if it were not for his temper and line of domination.

Trevelyan's dislike of Chamberlain was evident. Scrupulous in his means and not *really* enthusiastic in his ends, Trevelyan perceives Chamberlain's bad qualities without understanding the moral force of his deep sympathy with the material misery of the world. Politics are a religion to Chamberlain. To Trevelyan they are a fitting occupation to a man of high breeding and literary culture – always to be subordinated to his chivalrous duty to those nearest to him and to his position as an English Gentleman. Chamberlain has brought passion into his work, Trevelyan has politely persisted. . . .

## VOLUME 11

Beatrice occasionally stayed at the house of her brother-in-law, William Cripps, who lived just off Portman Square.

*30 March. 2 Stratford Place* [Marylebone, London, W.1.]
Thoroughly enjoyed the last month. Have got statistical outline of dock labour for Tower Hamlets.

Certainly, inquiring into social facts is interesting work, but it needs the devotion of a life to do it thoroughly. I feel that the little bit of work I do will be very superficial, and that, until I could take to inquiry as a life-work, and not only as a holiday task, I should do very little good with it. But I need much preparation. A general but thorough knowledge of English history and literature – a skeleton, the flesh and blood of which I could at any moment gain by specialized study, a theoretical grasp of the growth of industry, and of the present state of industrial organization. . . . This, and a good deal more, I need before I am fully prepared for direct observation. A study of this kind is compatible with my home life, with its uniform duty of tender devotedness. Perhaps I shall be free before I am fit for freedom. Even now my freedom is considerable – more considerable than I have enjoyed since Mother's death. Quite four months of the year I shall be able to devote to actual observation, and if I take my rest in the country, that will not leave much more than six months to be spent in literary preparation. But as the observation will necessarily be disjointed and incomplete, it will serve more to clear my own ideas than to form definite pictures of life. My education is yet to come. In the meantime I am enjoying my life. I see more reason for believing that the sacrifices I have made to a special intellectual desire were warranted by a certain amount of faculty. As yet I have had no proof of this; my capacity has not been stamped as current coin; the metal is still soft and I know not whether it will bear the right impression. Still, I *feel* power, I *feel* capacity even when I discover clearly my own insufficiency, for I think I discern the way to overcome it. Alfred Cripps' criticism of my article made me aware how very far off it was from good work – but it was better than the last, and, unlike the last, I see how I can alter and make it good. *Nous verrons!* And the old faith in individual work is returning – in the sanctity of moral and intellectual conviction.

When I gave up my nature to the great passion of my life I denied this faith though I could not rid my nature of the effect of it. Even in those moments when I believed the time was come, when I looked forward to the joys of satisfied passion, a blank 'and after?' stared at me in the background. 'And after?', that cynical question asked by conscience of triumphant love.

The morning breaks and the cock crows, awakening the mortal paralysed by fear, or soothed by passion, to the old, old, question – And Peter is not the only man who turns round and weeps.

Beatrice had no home in London when her father gave up York House in September 1887. She stayed with relatives and friends, but she usually took a room in the Devonshire House Hotel, a quiet Quaker establishment near Liverpool Street Station and convenient for her work in the East End. Mr Hoffman was foreman in a shoe factory, a Methodist lay preacher and a socialist who had made a study of the sweating system in the clothing trade.

[April?] Devonshire House Hotel

Found it quite impossible to write in London and so wasted a week in attempting to do so. Interesting dinner with Benjamin Jones and Mr Hoffman. Hoffman is a Christian socialist. . . . Argues that all men have a *right* to live, and to live well . . . believes that socialism should be the result of public opinion and that socialists should preach at the corners of the streets the doctrines they believe in. . . .

[22 April. Brighton?]

Paid Mr Spencer a visit. Found him in a pitiable condition. Perfectly hopeless, thinks that he can neither eat, walk nor talk. Sent me away after I had spoken to him for a short time and told me to return to him in an hour's time as he wished to discuss an important business matter. . . . He asked me whether I should recommend Alfred Cripps or Charles Booth as trustees for the continuation of his sociological research. I advised Alfred Cripps. He then said that he wanted to consult me as to another appointment, that of Beatrice Potter as literary executor. I was taken aback, but it was evident that he had set his heart on it and longed, poor old man, that someone who loved him should complete his life. I was very much touched by his confidence in me, though I suggested he might find a fitter person from a literary point of view. I can quite understand his feeling. He instinctively feels that . . . the world will look back upon him as a thinking machine and not as a man with all a man's need for a woman's love and devotion and for the living affection of children. And my relationship to him represents in a way both the absent elements. Poor old man, he is paying the penalty of genius; his whole nature is twisted by excessive development of one faculty. In view of my respon- sibilities I must see something of his friends. . . . I have written to T. H. Huxley to beg for an interview. I should like him to write a sketch of Herbert Spencer as he was in the hey-day of his life.

Thomas Henry Huxley (1825–95), the eminent biologist who was the principal exponent of Darwinism and a dominant figure in English science and education, had recently retired for reasons of health. His eight children were brought up in a permissive manner. Arthur James Balfour

(1848–1930), Conservative politician and philosopher, was the nephew of Lord Salisbury and succeeded him as prime minister in 1902. Millicent Garrett Fawcett (1847–1929) became the non-militant president of the National Union of Women's Suffrage Societies in 1897. The movement for women's rights had been gathering momentum for half a century and there had been a few legislative successes such as the Married Women's Property Act of 1882. Suffrage resolutions had been presented in Parliament (in the Lords in 1851 and the Commons in 1870), and John Stuart Mill's *Subjection of Women* (1869) was a powerful argument in their support. There were now local groups all over the country.

*6 May.* [London]

Huxley to dine. The old lion is broken down: he has only the remains of greatness. Has lost that delightful spring of mind and living energy of thought that charmed those who knew him. He told me more about himself than about Herbert Spencer. How as a young man, though he had no definite purpose in life, he felt power, was convinced that in his own line he would be a leader. That expresses Huxley – he is a leader of men. I doubt whether science was pre-eminently the bent of his mind. He is truth-loving, a love of truth finding more satisfaction in demolition than in construction. He throws the full weight of thought, feeling and activity into anything he takes up. He does not register his thoughts and his feelings, partly because his early life was supremely sad and he controlled the tendency to look back on the past and forward into the future. When he talks to man, woman or child, he is all attention, and has or, rather, had the power of throwing himself into the thoughts and feelings of others and responding to them. And yet they are all shadows to him; he thinks no more of them and drops back into the unreal world he lives in. For Huxley, when not working, dreams strange things, carries on lengthy conversations between unknown persons living within his brain. There is a strain of madness in him; melancholy has haunted his whole life. 'I always knew that success was so much dust and ashes – I was never satisfied with achievement.' None of the enthusiasm for 'what is' – or the silent persistency in grasping truth; more the eager rush of the conquering mind, loving the fact of conquest more than the land conquered. And consequently achievement has fallen far short of capacity. Huxley is greater as a man than as a scientific thinker. The exact opposite might be said of Herbert Spencer. I ventured to put forward the idea that H.S. had worked out the Theory of Evolution by grasping the disjointed theories of his time and welding them into one. No, said Huxley, Herbert Spencer never knew them – he elaborated his theory

202

from his inner consciousness – he was the most original of thinkers though he never wrote a new thing. He never read, merely picked that which would help him to illustrate his theories. He was a great constructor. The form he gave to his gigantic system was entirely original – the component factors were not new – though he had not borrowed them.

And we disagreed on another point. I suggested that as I had known H.S. he was personally *humble*. Both the Huxleys exclaimed. They had thought him intolerant of criticism, though Huxley said he had always found him pre-eminently just, ready to listen to adverse criticism and adverse facts from those he *respected* or had affection for. But most men were to him the 'common herd'. There is some truth in that. After all, I must remember that in his attitude towards me there was sentiment, and sentiment breeds humility. I asked Mr Huxley whether he thought that it was a mistake for me to undertake the literary executorship. Oh no, said the great man benignly, all a man wants as a literary executor is a sympathetic friend – Herbert Spencer's autobiography tells its own story, it is intensely characteristic of the man. He said it kindly and I think sincerely.

All through the interview Huxley's past and present life interested me more than his opinion of Spencer. For to him Spencer has been one of the shadows crossing his over-filled life. Success sufficient to keep the family had been his one great personal aim – apart from his impersonal desire to elucidate, to *lead* men to see the truth. Huxley, considering his brilliant capacity, has failed as a scientific man – as a seeker after truth. He has gained what his nature sought after – personal pre-eminence, immediate power over the mind of his countrymen. Further, his warm, indulgent, loving nature has bound him down to the necessity of providing for a large and indifferently dutiful family.

He suffers in his old age from the melancholy of true failure; from the wearing anxiety of unself-controlled children – his brilliant and gifted child has sunk into hysterical imbecility, another daughter, mad with restless vanity, has taken without a care to public singing. Two daughters have married mediocrities. One son is gaining a modest livelihood, has failed to distinguish himself from lack of ambition or purpose. Another son is worthy but dull, lives at home without understanding his father. And the little daughter gads about to balls, and flirts away with inferior young men. Ah! these great minds, seldom fit for everyday life.

203

This morning I walked along Billingsgate from Fresh Wharf to the London docks. Crowded with loungers smoking bad tobacco, and coarse, careless talk with the clash of a halfpenny on the pavement every now and again. Bestial content or hopeless discontent on their faces. The lowest form of leisure – senseless curiosity about street rows, idle gazing at the street sellers, low jokes – and this is the chance the docks offer. . . .

Dinner in the evening with the Courtneys. John Morley, Mr Arthur Balfour (Secretary for Ireland), Mr E. Russell (editor of *Liverpool Post* and rising politician), Mrs Fawcett and Mrs Dugdale (Sir G. Trevelyan's sister). Arthur Balfour is a charming person. Tall, good-looking and intellectual. Says cynical and clever things, which are meant to be cleverer than they turn out to be. Easy and well bred – of the ancient type of gentleman politician, a type fast fading out of existence. Is connected with the world of science through his gifted brother who died some time since [F. M. Balfour (1851–82), Professor of Animal Morphology at Cambridge]. The party was most harmonious – John Morley evidently in sympathy with Arthur Balfour, in spite of their public opposition. John Morley amused and interested the whole company by his description of the front Opposition bench and repetition of Gladstone's remarks on the speeches made. The conversation, though easy and pleasant, was all froth. No one said what they thought and everyone said what they thought to be clever. But the individual who interested me most was Mrs Dugdale. She had asked to meet me and evidently wished to make my acquaintance. She is the fascinating widow sister of Sir George Trevelyan and lives for distinguished and interesting society. She is supposed to be a friend and possibly the future wife of Chamberlain, and that was the reason she wished to know me. I felt it instinctively, and as I looked at her charming person, with all the daintiness of a well-bred lady, I felt her superiority to me in attractiveness. She would suit him, but she would not suit his family. If he married her he would have to keep two establishments. She is a thin-natured woman, superficially sympathetic and with admirable tact – no vices or even queer faults – but with little generosity or depth of feeling. But she is adaptable, without conviction, and worshipping distinction.

She tried to book me to go to the House with her, but I would not. Even if she were not connected with me in that subtle way, I should not care to know her. It is not worth my while to know 'Society' – to meet it occasionally at the house of my distinguished brother-in-law refreshes me, makes me feel how little I lose in being out of it.

Beatrice inserted a number of pen portraits in her diary at this time, the subjects being tenants in Katherine Buildings, dock workers and others whom she met while doing research for the Booth survey. She was interested in family budgets and in the complex and often unsatisfactory ways in which working men's wages were computed. She was also beginning to take an interest in factory and other protective legislation.

*8 May.* [London]
Kerrigan, amusing Irish School Board visitor, Limehouse district (Stepney). Describes his casuals (about 900) as 'hereditary casuals' . . . . The worse scoundrel is the Cockney-born Irishman. The woman is the Chinaman of the place, and drudges as the women of the savage races. She slaves all day and all night. Describes the communism of this class. They do not migrate out of the district, they are constantly changing their lodgings, but if they like the circle of their friends they go round and round within a certain area. They work for each other – hence low ideal of work. Never see excellence. They never leave the neighbourhood. From the dock gates they lounge back to the street – 'treating' or being 'treated' according to as they have earned a few pence. Live chiefly on 'tobacco' which is a compound of sugar, vinegar, brown paper and German nicotine. The teapot is constantly going – bread and a supply of dried haddock which goes through a domestic preparation, dried in the chimney and acquiring a delicate flavour by lying between the mattresses of the beds. They never read; and, except the Catholics, never go to church. On the Bank Holiday the whole family will go to Victoria Park. . . .

*12 May.* [London]
Docks early morning. Permanent men respectable and clean. Casuals low-looking – bestial, content with their own condition. Brutal fight and struggle. (As a few men are given work for the day.) Sudden dissolution of the crowd, with coarse jokes and loud laugh. Look of utter indifference on their faces. Among them are one or two who have fallen from better things. Abject misery and hopeless determination to struggle on. The mass of rejected lounge down to another dock or spread over the entrances to the various wharves. . . . Some hundred of the lowest will congregate, waiting on the chance of a foreman needing an odd man. If a man weary with the *ennui* of an

empty stomach drops asleep, his companions will promptly search his pockets for the haphazard penny.

Robinson, socialist dock labourer, originally tobacconist. Emigrated, and returned to England because he became homesick. A rolling stone and very superior and interesting-looking. Bitter and hopelessly illogical. The *Right to Live* and to marry and to have children the basis of his argument. . . . Socialism making no progress among dock labourers. They are incapable of organization. Sees no remedy but a complete reconstruction of society. . . . State ought to supply *pleasant* labour for everyone. . . . Complains that women of working class are no companions to their husbands. 'When I was courting my wife I could not get a word out of her – it was just walking by her side and giving her an occasional kiss. If a working man gets a good mother, and a woman that doesn't drink, as his wife, that's as much as he can expect. And my wife wasn't the first woman I courted – they're all alike in not talking of anything but details.'

T. R. Malthus (1766–1834) was an influential English economist who maintained that poverty was unavoidable because the population would always increase faster than the means of subsistence. *The Fruits of Philosophy, or The Private Companion of Young Married Couples* was a pioneer work on contraception written by an American physician named Charles Knowlton, who was sentenced to three years in prison when he first published it in 1832. In 1877 the noted freethinker Charles Bradlaugh (1833–91) and his collaborator Annie Besant were prosecuted in London for selling the book. Bradlaugh's Hall of Science, which was the centre of Secularist and popular scientific education, was first opened in the City Road in 1868, and it was later moved to Old Street in the City of London itself. There were similar centres in a number of provincial towns, especially in the 1880s when the Secularist movement was at its peak.

*13 May*. [London]
Most amusing afternoon with Kerrigan, in Victoria Park. Victoria Park lies in the extreme east of London. It is surrounded by streets of small two-storied houses of the genteel type; a porch and one bow-window, venetian blinds and a lace curtain. These are inhabited by the lower middle class. Now and again there is a row of more modest little dwellings, without the bow or the porch, or with a bow of less publicity and consideration, the abode of the aristocrats of the working class, mechanics or permanent labourers.

Sunday afternoon is a great time in Victoria Park, not confined to local people, but the meeting-place of the enthusiasts and the curious-minded of the whole East End district. The first group we came to were congregating round a small organ. They were old men, women with children, and one or two stray youths, entitling themselves the Elder Branch of the ancient sect of Primitive Methodists. Verily they looked like the adjectives of their title! The second group, larger and more within the combative spirit of the age, 'The Christian Association of Young Men' [Y.M.C.A.], composed of city clerks, spotty, seedy and smelly, but one or two among them inspired with living enthusiasm. They were singing loudly, when we reached them, of the Blood of Jesus, and that eternal happiness which is to wipe away the feeling of grievance among the failures of this life, and to compensate for an existence of dreary half-starved drudgery. . . .

. . . facing another crowd there was a messenger from the Hall of Science. He was explaining to an attentive audience of working men that man was an animal, and nothing but an animal. His face was lined by sensuality and moved by shallow quickness and assertiveness of thought. He used scientific phrases, quoted freely from Huxley, Darwin and German physiologists, and assumed a certain impartiality in his treatment of rival religious theories of man's development. But the burden of his message from the domain of science was the animalism of man, the gross unreason of believing in a 'Higher Nature'. But the thickest crowd surrounded the banner of the Socialist Democrat. From a platform a hoarse-voiced man denounced the iniquities of the social system. His hearers were also working men, on their faces earnest attention. In one hand he held Malthus, in the other *The Fruits of Philosophy*. The subject was a delicate one, the two rival methods of checking the growth of the population – late marriage versus preventive checks. But he joined issue with both methods, for he declared that neither was needed. There was bread enough for all if it was equally distributed. Men starved while warehouses were stocked to overflowing – it was the commercial system that was at fault, not the laws of nature. The crowd was not enthusiastic, only interested and eager to listen to new suggestions. But for the most part they were men in full employment whose speculative interest in social reform was not whetted by positive hunger. Every now and then, when he denounced employers, there was a grunt of approval. When he pointed out the cul-de-sac of competition there was even slight applause. But when he turned from 'what is' to 'what should be' if the socialist dogma reigned supreme, there was simply scepticism, readiness to listen but not willingness to perform.

Some yards from these in the open grass space, a circle of the strangest individuals. 'Latter Day Saints' was inscribed on their banner. They seemed like beings from another world. Bearded, soft, illogical and illiterate, they stood there preaching alternatively, listened to by a scoffing crowd. They could not answer the rude questions and pert arguments of the bystanders. They offered, meekly, the other cheek, remained silent with closed eyes, or struck up a feeble hymn to drown opposition. . . . These and others gathered small crowds of curious listeners, intent only on whiling away the afternoon's holiday. The 'new thing', atheism and insubordination, the 'old thing', rabid religion, claimed equal attention. Sober sense and deep silent feeling were alone unrepresented and unfelt.

We wended our way back between the groups and crowds to Mr Kerrigan's lodgings. The back room of a small working-class dwelling – serving for dining, sitting, sleeping, working room of this humble individual, with the most ingenious arrangements for all his functions. Mr Kerrigan is the most amusing Irishman. A seaman by profession, taken to School Board visiting as a livelihood. Intensely interested in his fellow-men and very extensive though uncultivated knowledge of science and literature. Lover of books. His language is picturesque and descriptive; he has the knack of ready generalization which makes his personal experiences among the East End poor fall readily into a definite picture of different classes. . . . There was something pathetic in his intense pleasure in our visit and our conversation. He gave us excellent tea, and afterwards first-rate cigarettes.

Ah! what would the conventional West End acquaintance say to two young women smoking and talking in the bed, sitting, working, smoking and bath room of an East End School Board visitor? It is quite sad leaving the homely Quakers' hotel. Ella Pycroft and I have found each other excellent company. We have entertained freely and thoroughly enjoyed our life in working-class society. . . .

The next section of the diary deals with Beatrice's final exchange with Chamberlain, and the proper sequence has to be re-established because she tore out the entries 1 June and 11 August and sealed them, together with five letters from Chamberlain, in an envelope which she did not open until three years later. When she did open it, she added a comment. The diary entries, together with the relevant letters, are here restored to their proper sequence; and the subsequent comment will be found between 29 and 31 May 1890.

Chamberlain had been intermittently in touch with Beatrice through his sister and daughter, and on 19 May he wrote her a letter saying that he had met Charles Booth at breakfast at the Courtneys' and that he had subsequently read a paper written by Booth, for the Statistical Society, on 'The Inhabitants of the Tower Hamlets'. Once again he asked Beatrice what might be done, since he was equally sceptical about large-scale charity, state employment schemes and emigration. It is clear from the following diary entry that Beatrice responded to this letter and agreed to visit Birmingham again. The second Chamberlain letter, dated 5 June, accepted an invitation from Richard Potter to visit The Argoed on 23 July; and in a third letter Chamberlain, who wished to go to the Queen's golden jubilee naval review, postponed the visit until 30 July – a decision confirmed by the fourth letter on 21 June.

## 9 June. The Argoed

I spent a week with the poor old philosopher in Brighton. A small house with sunny aspect and glimpse of the sea to enliven the poor old philosopher as he lay on his couch bemoaning his own weakness. His companions, a chattering old maid and a weak young man just recovering from brain fever, engaged as secretary and acting as attendant. There lies the great thinker in a living death – apparently brought on by his own excessive self-consciousness. Doctors say there is nothing the matter with him; he persists that he would die if he were to exert himself. Facts are these. Suffers from intermittent pulse and sleeplessness and a modified form of indigestion. All these symptoms certainly increase when he has any form of excitement and he apparently lives through periods of better health and then recurrent weakness, each time sinking to a low level. Whether these facts are caused by his mental state or whether the mental state is a sign of some definite physical disease could only be gauged by an omniscient intelligence. But there he exists, a living tragedy of an unnaturally developed intellect, to whom all rest and placid peace is denied. I had little talk with him except bright chaff to enliven and cheer him. Most of the time I spent sleeping or wandering by the uninteresting sea. I meant to have worked but I dreamt instead.

I dreamt of the scene I was soon to see; another act of the old, old story. A week from the day I left the old philosopher lying wearily in bed, I sat in a crowded hall in Birmingham. Within a few steps of me stood the great man on the platform. He was supported by his brother and the few of the faithful still left in the fold. He was white and agitated, for this was a crucial time, whether or not these meetings would be successful. He has lost none of his old charm of voice and manner, less arrogance and a touch of stern sorrow at the defection of

209

friends, the breaking-up of friendships. But his speech showed no hesitation. Resist unto death was his true motto. And after he sat down it was natural our eyes should meet in the old way.

The town hall was still more crowded in the evening. It was not the crowd of 4 years ago, nor the intoxicating enthusiasm of those brilliant days. It was a gathering of sensible folk, who had determined on supporting the leader of the town or who pooh-poohed Irish powers of self-government. And the speech also had a different flavour. Sentimental sympathy for the wrongs of the down-trodden masses was exchanged for a determination to preserve law and order. The statesman had overcome the demagogue.

Refused to dine at a man's political dinner at Highbury. Met the great man and his daughter at the Arthur Chamberlains'. Result – invited him to come and see Father and enjoy bracing air and beautiful scenery. In six weeks the great man comes, and before then I must have my article written. Now to work, try to forget that which it is useless to remember, and work while the day lasts for who knows when. . . ?

His aims are denoted by enthusiasm or ambition – in his means he is not scrupulously honourable or loyal and he is indifferent to the morality of his associates so long as they serve his purpose. In his relation to me there has been a strange lack of chivalry and honour. In mine to him, of womanly dignity.

Beatrice could not contain her misery any longer, and when Chamberlain went The Argoed she told him how strongly she felt for him and at the same time insisted that they should not meet again. Chamberlain kept his emotional distance, saying that they could remain friends, but Beatrice then wrote to say this was impossible. On 7 August he sent his last letter.

I thank you sincerely for your kind letter. I cannot help feeling depressed and discouraged at times and I value greatly the sympathy which you have shown me.

The concluding part of your letter has given me much pain. Did I indeed do wrong in accepting your invitation? If so forgive me and allow me to tell you frankly what I feel. At your own request I destroyed your letter of March 1886. There was one passage in it on which I did not presume to put a definite interpretation, and which I thought at the time was rather the outcome of a sensitive mind, overstrained by suffering and work, than the expression of settled feeling. I thought you had forgotten it and wished me to forget it also.

So much for the past – now as to the future. Why are we never to see each other again? Why can not we be friends – 'comrades' – to use your own expression? I like you very much – I respect and esteem you – I enjoy your conversation and society and I have often wished that fate had thrown us more together.

If you share this feeling to any extent why should we surrender a friendship which ought to be good for both of us?

I have so much confidence in your generosity as well as in your good sense that I am encouraged to make this appeal to you in what I feel to be a very delicate matter.

The circumstances of my past life have made me solitary and reserved, but it is hard that I should lose one of the few friends whose just opinions I value and the sense of whose regard and sympathy would be a strength and support to me.

I cannot say more. You must decide, and if it is for your happiness that we should henceforth be strangers I will make no complaint.

I return your letter, as you wish it, but there is surely no reason why you should be ashamed of feelings which are purely womanly and for which I have nothing but gratitude and respect.

I am always

Yours very sincerely
J. CHAMBERLAIN

At the end of this letter Beatrice wrote the following comment.

This letter after I had, in another moment of suicidal misery told him I cared for him passionately. This after he had pursued me for 18 months and dragged me back into an acquaintance I had all along avoided. To insist on meeting a woman who had told you she loved you in order to humiliate her further.

*8 August.* [The Argoed]
A week's unhappiness added on to the long chain of misery already forged – seemingly impossible to break. But I have health and intelligence and a warm heart and I have suffered pain – surely these shall not be wasted. And after all, all my crime has been being too much a child of nature, saying what I thought and felt too simply. Feeling has over-ridden dignity. And now to work again. . . .

Gracedieu was the Booths' country estate in the Charnwood Forest in Leicestershire where they moved in 1886. Beatrice and Charles Booth visited the exhibition at Manchester Art Gallery.

[August?]. *Manchester*
I shall not forget the misery of that day's journey up to London. The nerve was not killed! And added to pain was the feeling that I could no longer respect the man. Since that correspondence of 1886, he has tried every means to renew the acquaintance. Six or seven times in the

year I have refused his overtures, made directly or through his family. At last I gave way. If he had treated me with simple respect when we met at his brother's house, there would have been a reason in his advances. He could well have said – you told me to forget and I thought you wished me to mark my continued respect for you. But he behaved towards me as the triumphant lover, as a man who is sure of his conquest. And then after that visit to The Argoed with another proof that I cared for him deeply and desired that we should not see each other again, to appeal to my 'generosity' to be his friend; of course I was weak and gave way again, weak and romantic. But he did not like the tone of my letter. Perhaps that has saved me from more entanglement.

The visit to the Booths followed up by two days here has recovered my spirits. The beautiful old place, filled to overflowing with happiness and youth, checked my egotistical suffering. The Booths' home life at 'Gracedieu' is perfect. Mary says her life is one continual sunshine. Charlie has the three sides of his existence complete – profession, home, intellectual interest. His business, he says, is the most important to him of the three, but I expect he under-rates the constant happiness of satisfied affection. He and I have spent two evenings here alone, principally at the pictures [exhibition of nineteenth-century English paintings]. We are very fond of each other, a close intimate relation between a man and woman without sentiment (perhaps not without sentiment but without passion or the dawning of passion). We are fellow-workers, both inspired by the same intellectual desire. Only in his life it is only an etc.; in my life if it becomes anything it would become the dominating aim.

The exhibition of pictures is well worth seeing. The striking feature of it taken as a whole – the variety and range of thought and feeling covered by the English nineteenth-century school. Undoubtedly the pre-Raphaelites stand out as the greatest individualists. Walker, Burne-Jones, Rossetti, Watts – all expressing suffering in one form or the other, significant of the passion or weariness of mental development as distinguished from physical development. No age which has produced these men as the leading artists can be called materialistic. It is a reaction from materialism. The pictures that gave me most pleasure were Walker's 'Plough', Leighton's 'Summer Moon', Burne-Jones' 'Pygmalion', Calderon's 'Aphrodite', Mason's 'Harvest Moon', Millais' 'Victory' and 'The Vale of Rest'.

Settled with Charlie on the autumn's work. The sweating system is to be the subject of my next paper. I have it in my mind to make it more of a picture than my article on 'Dock Life' – to dramatize it. I have great opportunities, working with him, of acquiring all the information. I could not get at the picture without living among the actual workers. This I think I could do. But most assuredly if I am to do work of any value, I shall need to develop morally as well as intellectually.

*21 August. The Argoed*
Spending these days in reading English literature with a view to gain the ease and simplicity of style which Leonard says I lack; also in order to discover the secret of great writing, whether prose or poetry. To me it seems as if the art of presenting pictures to the mind were the aim of writing. Not only the conception of the whole work should be a representation of life, but the expressions through which this is attained should mirror some concrete thing or specific movement. . . .

Henry Mayhew (1812–87): his sketches of London life are fascinating and unique source material for the social historian. Frederick Denison Maurice (1805–72), Anglican divine, professor of English literature and history at King's College, London, was influential in the Christian Socialist Movement and founder of the Working Men's College in London in 1854.

*29 August.* [The Argoed]
Visit of three days from the Barnetts, which has confirmed my friendship with them. Mr Barnett distinguished for unself-consciousness, humility and faith. Intellectually he is suggestive, with a sort of moral insight almost like that of a woman. And in another respect he is like a strong woman; he is much more anxious that human nature should *feel rightly* than that they should *think truly*; *being* is more important with him than *doing*. He told me that Comte, F. D. Maurice and history had influenced him most; but evidently the influence had been more on his character than on his intellect, for intellectually he has no system of thought, no consistent bias. His thought is only the tool whereby his feeling expresses itself. He was very sympathetic about my work and anxious to be helpful. But evidently he foresaw in it dangers to my character, and it was curious to watch the minister's anxiety about the *morale* of his friend creep out in all kinds of hints. He held up as a moral scarecrow the 'Oxford Don', the man or woman without human ties, and with no care for the

213

details of life. He told his wife that I reminded him of Octavia Hill, and as he described Miss Hill's life as one of isolation from superiors and from inferiors, it is clear what rocks he saw ahead. I tried to explain to him my doctrine of nervous energy, that you were only gifted with a certain quantity, and that if it were spent in detail it could not be reserved for large undertakings. But as he suggested, very truly, if all the thought and time spent on egotistical castle-building or brooding were spent on others, your neighbourly and household duties would be well fulfilled without encroaching on the fund reserved for your work.

Mrs Barnett is an active-minded, true and warm-hearted woman. She is conceited. She would be objectionably conceited if it were not for her genuine belief in her husband's superiority, not only to the rest of the world (which would be only another form of conceit) but to herself. But the good in Mrs Barnett predominates and her constant flow of spirits, her invigorating energy, is uncalculably helpful to her husband. Her nature is saturated with courage and with truthfulness; her sympathies are keen and her power of admiration for others strong. Her personal aim in life is to raise womanhood to its rightful position; as equal, though unlike, to manhood. The crusade she has undertaken is the fight against impurity as the main factor in debasing women from a status of independence to one of physical dependence. The common opinion that a woman is a nonentity unless joined to a man, she resents as a 'blasphemy'. Like all crusaders, she is bigoted and does not recognize all the facts that tell against her faith. I told her that the only way in which we can convince the world of our power is to show it! And for that it will be needful for women with strong natures to remain celibate, so that the special force of womanhood, motherly feeling, may be forced into public work.

In religious faith Mr Barnett is an idealistic Christian without dogma; Mrs Barnett an agnostic with idealism. In social faith the man a Christian Socialist, the woman an individualist. The woman is really the more masculine-minded of the two. Mr Barnett's personal aim is to raise the desires of men and women, to cultivate their higher tastes, to give the poor the luxuries and not the necessaries of life. The danger which I foresee of mental strain, and thence melancholy, he looks upon as imaginary. And I think myself that in my fear of melancholy for the race I am governed by the bias of my own rather peculiar constitution. It was not an overstrained mind which made our Aked relations suicidal – they were innocent of intellectual effort. And I have inherited the suicidal constitution, and, naturally enough, I connect it with other qualities of my nature, whereas it may be only co-existent with these qualities.

The Barnetts' visit braced me up to further effort and stronger resignation. But in my work of observation, I must endeavour to get in front of my own shadow – else I shall end by disbelieving in sunshine!

Mayhew's *London Labour and London Poor* (1851) is good material spoilt by bad dressing. It is a mine of information, both of personal observation and of statistical inquiry, but there is no opening to it, nor any destination reached. It is overloaded with descriptive detail. . . .

A week staying with the Courtneys. It is delightful to watch their happiness. Success has made Leonard more cordial and open-minded. As chairman of committees all the finest points of his character are brought into play, and his deficiencies are not seen. He could not be influential in party politics. He lacks the sympathetic understanding of the opponent's view – cannot even appreciate the striking features of his own argument. And his principles and opinions are really the result of fine moral qualities and of the personal experience of life, not deduction from observed facts. The only great defect in his nature is an unconscious contempt for any opinion which he himself does not hold . . . and this defect, I take it, arises more from a want in his intellect than from narrow-heartedness. . . .

Kate has become 'the wife of Leonard Courtney'. She basks in the sunshine of happiness. Her life is a purely social one and not demanding much self-sacrifice or self-devotion. . . . She has lived a good deal apart from her family but since her happy and successful marriage she has always tried to welcome them, though she has been unwilling to take more than her share of family duty, and perhaps even to shirk this. She is benevolent and worldly, a good citizen of the world but not a heroine. . . .

Benjamin Jones to dine here. Kate kept the conversation *conversational* so I did not thrash the question out I meant to. B. Jones is in a queer position – his experience as [a Co-operative] organizer and employer battling with his desire to retain working-class sympathies. . . . It is almost amusing to see his perpetual desire to keep himself 'right' with his own class. He is spoilt as a thinker on social questions by lack of humility and absence of imagination. One of his leading doctrines is that there is more luck than ability in success, and that one man is as good as another. He thought I had taken upon myself 'a task' in proposing to deal with the sweating system in two months. He suggested that I ought to go to Leeds and inquire into the sweating system in practice there, that the reverse process was going on in the provinces from that going on in London – viz. in provincial towns factories were overcoming sweating, whereas in London sweating was overcoming factory production.

It is strange, living in close correspondence with all sorts and conditions of men, how one observes the same fact about classes as about individuals. Each class seems to have a certain range of ideas, out of which it seems incapable of growing, unless it ceases to be a class. And so it is with the individual. Few individuals are capable of continual growth. It is the gift of perpetual youth. Most of us sink, early or late in our lives, into a state of intellectual self-complacency, or into indolent doubtfulness. We settle down to one point of view, and naturally enough our intellectual horizon remains eternally the same, and we gaze constantly on one side of each object, forgetting that there are at *least* four others, and may be an infinite number of sides.

*30 September. The Argoed*
The day (yesterday) we gave up York House, my article on 'Dock Life' appeared in the *Nineteenth Century*. Exit a hateful association, enter a promising beginning. This summer has been very mixed in its thoughts and feelings, but it ends hopefully, if only I felt stronger and more equal to the hard work before me. The home life has settled down into a satisfactory existence as far as work is concerned. So long as I can get four or six months away, no life could be better for the work which I have at last drifted into. It is strange that it is *the* work I have always longed to do; it is the realization of my youthful ambition. And yet, on the other hand, I have been forced into it by circumstances. At one time, if it had not been for events, I should have married because I longed for happiness and doubted my own capacity. At another time I seemed quite settled into practical work and acquiring considerable position in it. There I should have remained if it had not been for Father's illness and leaving London. At the time, that withdrawal from active life seemed to me almost a warrant to withdraw from life altogether. I had lost all faith in my ability for purely intellectual work, and looked to the future with blank despair. Those winter months of 1885–6, I shall never forget their silent agony. It was literally a fear of madness, that made me pull myself

216

together and take to books and go back to my study. A very little encouragement gave me sufficient strength to go on *manfully*. Last summer I heartily enjoyed. I worked hard and wrote an article with enthusiastic diligence. It was condemned by my friends. This summer I could scarcely have lived through if it had not been for the traditions of work. I dawdled and wrote my paper with no enthusiasm and with little effort. It was accepted by the leading review and is now printed, two months after its acceptance. I should have trembled with delight – two years ago. Now I look upon it as only the natural result of my labour, and go forward with calm persistency. I know now that I have no talent, that I am almost lacking in literary faculty. But I have originality of aim and method, and I have implicit faith that I am on the right track, and I have a sort of persistency which comes from despair of my own happiness. My success will depend on my physical strength, and on whether I have sufficient moral backbone to banish self and its dark shadows, to enable me to see things in their true perspective and without morbid exaggeration of that which is painful. . . .

Goodbye, little home, with your picturesque surroundings and all-expressing scenery, goodbye, summer of 1887 with your cross-purposes and crooked ways. Enter, persistent, patient work, with faith but no hope! Next year we shall be here again, not altered in one condition, but *grown*.

In October Beatrice started to research into conditions in the boot and shoe and tailoring trades, interviewing officials and workers about conditions and pay. It was all part of her inquiry into the sweating system, which was to lead into a wider and sympathetic study of Jewish life in the East End, undertaken in the course of the Booth investigation and published as part of it. She was encouraged by the Chief Rabbi and helped by prominent members of the Jewish community in London. As her evidence in the House of Lords committee of inquiry shows, she was to shift the line of attack on the sweaters away from personal and racialist explanations and to demonstrate that both sweaters and sweated were victims of a more complex system of exploitation. Olive Schreiner (1855–1920), author and feminist, was best known for *The Story of an African Farm*, published in 1883. The Akeds were Beatrice's relatives from Bacup. Arnold Toynbee (1852–83) was an economic historian and reformer who urged university students to study the miseries of the poor. Toynbee Hall, opened at the end of 1884, was named after him. It was the first 'settlement house', where resident volunteers provided community services and sought to promote understanding between the classes. Samuel Barnett was the first warden and he soon established a programme of educational activities which later developed into the Workers'

Educational Association. Other projects launched from Toynbee Hall were the Guild of Handicraft, the Hampstead Garden Suburb and the Youth Hostels Association. Many residents afterwards became prominent in public life.

*14 October.* [Devonshire House Hotel]
The Akeds, mother and son, have been staying with me. They are simple, true-hearted people, strong Christians. I love these Lancashire folk. I showed them all over London; the one thing they delighted in was the endless galleries of books in the British Museum. Olive Schreiner was staying here. She is a wonderfully attractive little woman, brimming over with sympathy and thought. Titus Aked lost his heart to her; her charm of manner and conversation bowled over the true-hearted 'Lancashire laddie' with his straight and narrow understanding. He looked at the wee little woman with a mixture of reverence and tenderness and listened intently to every word she said. . . .

Very favourable notice of my article in the *Daily Telegraph.* . . . Secured one of the Toynbee men to work for me.

John Burnett (1842–1914) was the general secretary of the Amalgamated Society of Engineers and after 1886 he was employed to report on trade union matters to the Board of Trade.

*18 October.* [Devonshire House Hotel]
In bed with a cold – two days lost. Burnett, labour correspondent, dined here last night. Comes from Northumberland. Hard-headed man with no sense of humour. Excellent manners and very dignified. Was engineer and belongs to Amalgamated Engineers, and is leading trade unionist. Believes in socialistic legislation, increased inspection of workshops, free education, etc., and 8 hours work day. Says socialistic wave is sweeping trade unionists along with it; they would lose their influence with the working classes if they did adopt socialistic programme. Would start public works for the unemployed, though he believes that most of those who 'show up' are loungers; thinks it would satisfy public opinion if they were proved not to be able to work. . . . Had read my 'Dock Life' and was evidently more inclined to treat me seriously.

Sir Walter Besant (1836–1901), novelist and critic, was concerned with the social problems of East London; he helped to set up the People's Palace in the Mile End Road, which became a centre for cheap, elevating and popular entertainment, and he proposed to undertake an impressionistic survey of London Life.

*19 October.* [Devonshire House Hotel]
First morning learning how to sweat; Mrs Moses, 78 Oxford Street, Stepney. Four rooms and a kitchen, one room let for 3s. Deserted street during the daytime. Public house at each corner. Small back yard. Three rooms on ground floor, two used as workshop. Large room with two machinists – Polish Jews – and master who acts as presser.

In back room, mistress, first hand who was a Scotch woman and two girls learning the trade. Coats turned out at 1s 2d each, trimmings and thread supplied by the sweater. Buttonholes 4½d a dozen by woman outside. Mistress said the women by working very hard could earn 10s a week, with 2s deducted for silk. Evidently these people worked tremendously hard, a woman working from 8 a.m. to 10 p.m. without looking round, and master working up to 2 o'clock and often beginning at five in the morning. The mistress was too busy to give me much information and I did nothing but sew on buttons and fell sleeves in. They all seemed very pleasant together. . . .

Afternoon had interview with Besant, the novelist. Evidently nothing to be got out of him and his 1,300 investigators. Had no idea how they intended to classify their information. One idea, to prevent early marriages. Struck me as a quack, so far as investigation is concerned.

Later on, came in to the Barnetts' in time for committee about casual wards and workhouse accommodation. . . .

*20 October. Devonshire House Hotel*
Spent over a fortnight here, five days of which have been spent otherwise than in work. At times terribly despondent and disgusted with my own, impulsive, mad behaviour. At other times enjoying my spectator's life and successful in my attempts to forget the immediate past. After all, it will soon be like a dream – to him and to me.

Goodbye, little book. Enter another record and painful effort.

## *VOLUME 12*

*1 November. Kildare, Bournemouth*
Again the comfortable lodgings. Father's step on the landing with the

drag of the foot on the oil-cloth. From the sitting-room windows the broad cliff walk; immediately behind it, the sea, the same everlasting beat of the waves on the shore, sometimes a soft rhythm, at other times a loud break of the in-rolling ocean. The pine-wooded town, smart young ladies and delicate narrow-chested men, and an occasional weather-beaten admiral or retired general, men and women, for the most part, whose interest is centred in gossip over five o'clock tea. The social life of Bournemouth is not invigorating, even to look at from the outside; to live in would be purgatory. But I come down to rest, and to think over the material gathered while at Devonshire House. Now that observation is my work, I find it as necessary to have two books as when reading was my source of information.

Otherwise the autobiography is eaten up by statistics of wages, hours of work, and names of employers – no room for the general history of a woman's life. And without any egotistical brooding, it is still necessary to keep a record of individual growth, not only as a stepping-stone to higher life, but as a help in the future. So often have I found strength in turning over the back pages of my life, in watching the inevitable work its way, in spite of my desperate clutches after happiness, which were seemingly foredoomed to failure. Now the struggle is finally over. Passion lies at my feet, dead. At first, I stood over it and wept bitter tears. Now, I have buried it and think of it tenderly. I have lived through my youth – it is over. But I am only on the threshold of working womanhood – as Bella Fisher said to me the other day, 'You are just beginning your life'. And how must I equip myself for this new life, the outward form of which will be literary expression? First and foremost I must be warm-hearted and just. No one can write that which they *are not*. No one can perceive and calculate the larger currents of thought and action, unless their mind be dominated by far-reaching and far-seeing sympathy. Secondly, to do much I *must* be strong. It is here I fail, missing opportunity after opportunity because I lack the strength to grasp them. And here comes a difficult question. I do not wish to forgo the Society of my own class and yet to enjoy means wasted energy. Late hours, excitement, stimulants and unwholesome food all diminishing my small stock of strength available for actual work. And Society has another drawback; it attracts one's attention away from the facts one is studying, so that the impression is not so keen and deep. To take a clear impression, the intellect must be in a peculiar state, strong and yet for the moment blank. That is why I find so much difficulty in working at two subjects at the same time – the facts of the one efface the facts of the other. And when striking personalities intervene with the complicated problems of their lives it is so hard to drive them out of one's thoughts. For the men and women of Society are, naturally enough, more interesting, as psychological studies, than the men and women with whose circumstances one is not familiar and whose phraseology one does not quickly understand. Gradually, if you give way, that ogre Society sucks you in and you are lost to the bigger world of common life.

I see before me clearly the ideal life for work. I see it attainable in my present circumstances. Love and cheerfulness in my home life; faithful friendship with a few – to those tied to me by past association, to those bracing me by moral genius, to those who will aid me to judge truthfully, and lastly charity and sympathy towards women of my own class who need it, whether they be struggling young girls, hard-pressed married women or disappointed spinsters. Every woman has a mission to other women – more especially to the women of her own class and circumstances. It is difficult to be much help to men (except as an example in the way of persistent effort and endurance in spite of womanly weakness); do what one will, sentiment creeps in, in return for sympathy. Perhaps as one loses one's attractiveness this will wear off – *certainly* it will. At present it is only with working men one feels free to sympathize without fear of unpleasant consequences. And besides this continual guarding of oneself from bitterness, untruth, and lack of sympathy; persistent and well-planned effort in work and constant self-control to secure health. It is only by realizing religious purpose in work that one's life can be sufficiently concentrated to achieve worthfulness. The times at home must be spent healthily, the free time away must be economically used so as to get the most out of my very small ability. I see quite clearly I have no talent, but for all that I shall succeed in a quiet way, or rather I may open the pathway for others' success, cut a way into the forest of facts which sooner or later must be used to build up society on a scientific basis.

On the whole I am encouraged by the publication of my article. It made no great sensation and was snubbed by the *Spectator* and ignored by the other papers except the *Daily Telegraph*. But it was thought *painstaking and thorough*, and showed that I understood my subject. Some careless work I regret, some words were thoughtless.

I lunched with Knowles. He was very polite, and not only offered to take the article on the 'Sweating System' but proposed one on Co-operation, the very subject I had thought of writing on in the summer. I expect I shall do the 'Sweating System' for Charles Booth, and that 'The present state of Co-operation in England' will be my next paper in the *Nineteenth Century*. Altogether I am hopeful. I have made a steady rise in literary capacity as my diary shows. There is no reason why I should not rise further.

*13 November*. [Kildare?]
A very happy peaceful fortnight, with one drawback, tooth-ache. Wrote out my notes and shall tomorrow decide on my plan of campaign with Charlie for the coming month in London. Read four volumes of Macaulay's history. It interests me, not only as a standard work, but as the writing of Mary Booth's uncle. In the seven volumes there is only one chapter devoted to the 'condition of the people' question. Not one word, except in this chapter, about home industry, the growth of foreign commerce, literature, art, or the habits and occupations of the various classes of the English people. . . .

*16 November*. [Devonshire House Hotel]
Delightful evening with the Booths. Charlie looked tired and worried. . . .
    Dined at Toynbee Hall and attended conference on women's wages. There was very little information elicited. The Sanitary Inspector for the district got up and told us his personal experience of success! He and all his family had succeeded because they chose to work, and it was a man's own fault if he did not succeed. This was the burden of his song and did not interest the assembly. I was induced to speak in spite of my dreadful nervousness. I *must* conquer it – it is necessary for me to be able to speak on occasions.

    Annie Besant (1847–1933), Secularist, Fabian, trade union organizer, Theosophist and later a founder of the Indian nationalist movement, had a disastrous marriage with the clerical nephew of Sir Walter Besant. Arnold White (1848–1925) was a journalist and minor politician who stood for a strong imperial policy. Ben Tillett (1860–1943) founded the Dockers' Union in 1887, and was a leader of the great strike in 1889.

*27 November*. [Devonshire House Hotel]
Nearly half my month past. A certain amount of definite information and a confused impression of men, women and places, a jostling of images each seeking to efface the other. I am sorry I have not seen

Mrs Besant again. We met and [I] felt interested in that powerful woman, with her blighted wifehood and motherhood and her thirst for power and defiance of the world. I heard her speak, the only woman I have ever known who is a real orator, who has the gift of public persuasion. But to *see* her speaking made me shudder. It is not womanly to thrust yourself before the world. A woman, in all the relations of life, should be sought. It is only on great occasions, when religious feeling or morality demand it, that a woman has a right to lift up her voice and call aloud to her fellow-mortals.

Mrs Besant came to supper here to meet Mr Barnett. She was artificial and had evidently one aim in view – to get a footing in Toynbee Hall. She refused to discuss social questions to their bitter end and gave me the impression of a want of candour. If she had been perfectly straight-forward she would have had more chance with Mr Barnett. The impression she left on his mind was of acting a part; and I think the impression was a true one. She is loved by her friends and seems capable of strong friendship so that there must be genuine worth in her. Her position among the socialists is uncertain. Socialists are not characterized by devotion to leaders, and men are jealous of women who assume leadership. Whether Mrs Besant's capacity will overcome these two antagonistic currents of feeling remains to be seen. She is a woman unsexed by the loss of her child, embittered by the fact that the law robbed her of her child, but she has many fine qualities, has been lifted by work and trouble out of all pettiness of nature and smallness of aim.

Meeting at the Tabernacle, Barking Rd, Canning Town. I was advertised to appear at this meeting of dock labourers. The hall was crowded and the men were fine, determined, though a quiet-looking set – far superior to the run of dock labourers at the dock gates. I was the only woman present and as I made my way up to the platform I enjoyed the first experience of being 'cheered' as a public character. In the little room behind the platform were assembled the speakers of the evening, minus the renowned Arnold White. The chairman, Alderman Phillips, was a pleasant good little fellow, with the small commonplace mind and kindly features which denote hard-working philanthropy. Two or three councillors, among others a self-important little man who butted into the room exclaiming: 'Well, what's it all about? what's one to say?' and then, without waiting for an answer: 'I suppose the usual thing, elevation of the working class, grandeur of unity, etc., etc.' There was a considerable confusion in the minds of the other speakers as to what they *were* to say, for, with the exception of the secretary of the newly formed association, they none of them knew anything about dock labour or dock trade. I was pressed to second the resolution, but absolutely refused to speak. We came on to the platform. Secretary Tillett opened the proceedings. He is a light-haired little man with the face of a religious enthusiast, might have been a revivalist. Honest, undoubtedly, but ignorant and unwise. He ranted against 'white slavery' and the form of sub-contract and irregular hours. I do not think the meeting were 'taken in' by his rant; they applauded his denunciation of sub-contract. He went on indefinitely, until the chairman checked him, and whispered that he had better keep to the point and propose the resolution. Then came a series of the 'councillors' who certainly hardly justified their titles. A small man with a loud voice, a professional speaker, accustomed to fill up gaps at public meetings, pranced about the platform and shouted loudly: 'When I see on one side of me the starved dock labourer with his face marked by indelible lines of overwork and surrounded by a wretched family, a wife worn by strain, worry and labour, and on the other side of me, the bloated official of the dock company with his brougham, his great house and his servants, I feel and I say that it is, etc., etc., etc.'

Happily at this moment the bulky form of Arnold White was seen wending its way to the platform. No one knew him except the secretary. . . . He is a big man with a red and somewhat bloated face and an equally corpulent body, black eyes, with a suspicious tendency to fiery blood-shot, and a heavy black moustache and a somewhat unctuous voice. . . . He dwelt on the iniquity of pauper immigration, but to this audience of dock labourers his denunciation produced little effect, for foreigners do not patronize the dock gates. He spoke fluently with the customary three adjectives at every turn. No sooner had he sat down than he offered to take me back in his brougham, which offer I promptly accepted. He was considerably cheered as we left the platform and I followed meekly in the train of the hero who had given £20. The man who opened the door of his brougham refused to take the tip offered, which Arnold White characterized as 'noble'. The interest of the conversation on our long drive homeward was slightly spoilt by the strong smell of spirit which the philanthropist transferred to the atmosphere of the closed brougham. I suggested that the night air was pleasant, and he forthwith opened the window to my intense relief. His talk was the usual philanthropic sympathy with the troubles and cares of the lower classes, interspersed with 'When I saw Gladstone the other day', 'Only this week I was staying with Tennyson', 'The day I had worked at the docks I went to lunch at Lord Rothschild's'. We touched on the population question, and he said somewhat alarmingly: 'I need a noble woman to help me', at which I started back, as just previously he had asked me to supper with him, which I refused. Whether it was the effect of the public meeting or of the spirit or of the long drive back with a not bad-looking young woman, Mr Arnold White became rather too confidential. I was disgusted with his reference to 'family life' as a curse to a man; a delicate wife, it seems, expected him to live with her for seven months out of the twelve. 'Of course if your family sympathizes with your work it is all very well' was his response to my assertion that family life was the only thing worth living for.

I dare say he is in his way a sincere man, but to my mind his view of society is mischievous and illustrates the strict individualist doctrine that every man had better stick to his own family and his own duties and not meddle with others.

*6 December*. [Kildare]
Father's illness has taken a turn for the worse. He has completely lost his memory. He asks question after question: whether Mother is dead, where he lives, and why he is living here.

*13 December*. [Kildare]
Father much better: memory returning. . . . Intend to spend these two months in reading history and studying composition. Hope to read through Gardner, Lecky, Walpole; to translate Chaucer into modern prose; and to write from dictation selections of various writers.

Francis Buxton (1847–1911) was Public Works Loan Commissioner and a member of the London School Board, 1889–1904. Beatrice was inclined to see slights where none were intended. She had first welcomed Professor Beesley's reaction – 'I think one of the monthlies would very likely take it,' Beesly wrote to Mary Booth on 9 March 1887; and, apart from one short remark about Marx's definition of labour, there was nothing in the letter to 'squash' the Marx article except an understandable comment that was to echo down the years among Beatrice's friends and acquaintances: 'Miss Potter's writing is often very difficult to read. It might be well to have it copied before sending it to an editor.'

225

*Christmas Day.* [Kildare]

The first Xmas for five years that I have been in a peaceful, happy frame of mind. It seems a whole lifetime since that Xmas at Rusland (1882) when Maggie Harkness and I amused ourselves with teasing Leonard Courtney, then fiancé to Kate. And yet, though I have travelled far in thought, feeling and experience, I am back exactly at the same point. Then my ambition was individual work – the direction determined on, the scientific description of society. If only I had been true to my ambition! I tried to push it from me, and to clutch at other things, but all in vain. I lost the one without gaining the other. And I had my punishment: four years of misery tempered only by humiliation. Even now a foolish, quixotic generosity urges me not to turn my back on the figures of the past. Happily a feeling of contempt for dishonourable and unchivalrous conduct has killed all other feelings except sadness that the same qualities which wounded me have, perhaps irretrievably, injured his career. 'Let him rest in peace.'

Outward circumstances are sad enough at the present time. Father, sweet as ever, but his mind failing rapidly; his companionship naught but the answering of disjointed questions. Rosy, the same poor creature. The old philosopher downstairs, to whom I am tied by pity and reverential gratitude, the victim of a strange disease of mind and body, sits in his chair not desiring to move body or soul; one day passes like another, and yet no improvement. He waiting with patience for returning strength, pursued by the desire to finish his *System of Philosophy.* I can give him no help. I sit in his room reading or writing, now and again saying some kind word, a bright anecdote or a stray reflection. Yesterday as I sat there, I heard a sudden moan, as if he were in pain. 'Are you suffering?' 'No,' groaned the poor old man. 'A momentary fit of impatience. Why suffer more todays?' A question I could not answer.

But while one is young and strong one lives in the future. I have been tossed on the ocean of passionate feeling; but now I am safe in smooth water. I think it must be a Dutch canal. Certainly the scenery is not romantic, but through the landscape, starting from close about me, and all running towards a distant horizon, are satisfactory lines. . . . I have liberty to follow those lines as far as the tether of faculty and strength will allow me. Surely this is a great privilege, more than the ordinary lot of unmarried womanhood? God give me strength!

The year's work has not been great. I may safely put down 2½ months as wasted in misery. This is the toll I have paid to feeling. Four months spent in observation and society. About five weeks on that 'Review of Karl Marx' which was squashed by Professor Beesly's unfavourable criticism. But I elaborated a theory which I still cling to and towards the elucidation of which all my work is directed. One month in writing my article on the docks and the better part of the other two or three in reading and study of one kind or another, in visits and journeying to and fro. No new friends. Charles Booth a working intimacy. Barnetts, Ella Pycroft's friendship confirmed. Benjamin Jones beginning to take his place as a friend, John Burnett (Board of Trade) likely so to do, the Francis Buxtons becoming more than friendly acquaintances, otherwise the old circle unchanged. A very pleasant feeling to all my family – my position with them improved by the success (relative to their appreciation of me) of my article. So the old year dies, and the new year, with her yet unbroken promises, steps on to the scene. I have forgotten one charm of the old lady: the amazing adventures, old acquaintances and strange experiences she has led me into.

PART IV

# The Working Sisterhood
*January 1888–December 1889*

## Introduction to Part IV

'TO BE THOUGHT OF as a sound and conscientious worker, with ability guided by conscience, is my one ambition,' Beatrice wrote early in 1888, as the search for professional satisfaction gradually led her to a new kind of life. 'My work is all in all to me,' she noted during the winter months she was caring for her father and preparing for the next phase of her work with Charles Booth by reading 'all the volumes, Blue Books, pamphlets and periodicals bearing on the subject of sweating that I could buy or borrow'. When she went back to the East End after Christmas she followed up her autumn interviews by disguising herself as a working girl and getting employment as a trouser hand.

It was much like her visit to Bacup where she had passed herself off as 'Miss Jones', and the experience was a valuable complement to her more conventional inquiries. When she described it in 'The Pages of a Workgirl's Diary' published by the *Nineteenth Century* in October 1888, the episode caused quite a stir — 'a cheap triumph' she called it because the article was no more than an expurgated version of her diary-entries.

Before the article was printed, Beatrice was called before a committee of the House of Lords which was investigating the sweating system. She disliked giving evidence, found the newspaper comment on her appearance 'offensive' and was much upset by charges that she had distorted the facts. She had, through nervousness, exaggerated the number of days she had actually worked as a trouser hand, and this figure was widely reported. When she came to read the galley proof of her remarks she felt obliged to amend what she had said to the much less dramatic truth. 'This double sin of saying what was not true, and then altering it in what seemed a sly way', she wrote in *My Apprenticeship*, 'caused me many sleepless nights.' That was an

231

understatement. Conscience-stricken by this lapse from her own strict standards, she almost worried herself into a collapse, and the sense of shame which troubled her through the rest of the year was so lasting that she never recalled the incident without embarrassment.

As Beatrice began to make her way in the world, particularly a man's world of public affairs, there was a growing contrast between the self-searching entries in her diary and the cool professionalism which so impressed her contemporaries. 'A rather hard and learned woman, with a clear and analytic mind', was the way the journalist H. W. Nevinson saw her at that time. The most striking examples of this contrast during the next two years are the brief yet profoundly pathetic references to Chamberlain when Beatrice heard him speak in the House of Commons, read of his courtship and heard of his marriage. She saw the link between 'a life of loneliness and work', and Mary Booth was sufficiently in her confidence to see it, too. 'I am sorry, dear, that the old thing still shows signs of its deep root. I don't like and can't manage to get to like the idea of a future of work for you,' her cousin wrote in the summer of 1888. 'I mean a lonely future of nothing but work. . . . If it is so, darling, it can't be helped, but I think it is a pity.'

Beatrice also thought it was a pity. She did not easily turn her back on the idea of marriage. 'God knows celibacy is painful to a woman,' she exclaimed in 1889, but she was trying to come to terms with her prospects as a working spinster. She wrote a revealing and touching letter to Beatrice Chamberlain. 'If you should ever think of joining the working sisterhood (I mean work in its narrow sense) remember that you already have an elder sister established in a flourishing business. In my heart of hearts I wish you a different fate: but a working life has its attractions. It is full of interest and sympathy, and it has its own peculiar charm of an impersonal way of life. Anyway, it has the element of growth – one is always growing in a working life. Remember, *that if you ever need it*, it is one of the keenest pleasures of life to help those who are beginning the same life-journey as oneself: but you have so many near friends and relations that you will be independent of your faithful old maid friend.'

Despite Beatrice's vision of 'the working sisterhood', and her belief that 'every woman has a mission to other women', she was reluctant to make the state of female labour her special mission in life. That was what Charles Booth proposed when she had completed her study of the immigrant Jewish community in the East End, and he was supported

232

by the eminent Cambridge economist Alfred Marshall, but Beatrice could not be persuaded. For one thing, she was ready to move on from a subordinate role in Booth's great survey to work of her own choosing; and, for another, she was both uncertain of her own views on the matter, and concerned about an ill-considered intervention in the growing debate about female suffrage.

Her subsequent explanation in *My Apprenticeship* is so relevant to her general views on the status of women, and so illuminates what she wrote in her diary at the time, that it must be read in full. Mrs Humphry Ward (1851–1920) was a social worker and noted novelist, whose anti-suffrage 'Appeal' was published in the *Nineteenth Century* in June 1889.

'In the spring of 1889', Beatrice wrote,

I took what afterwards seemed to me a false step in joining with others in signing the then notorious manifesto, drafted by Mrs Humphry Ward and some other distinguished ladies, against the political enfranchisement of women, thereby arousing the hostility of the ardent women brain-workers, and, in the eyes of the general public, undermining my reputation as an impartial investigator of women's questions. When pressed by Frederic Harrison and James Knowles to write a reasoned answer to Mrs Fawcett's indignant reply to this reactionary document, I realized my mistake. Though I delayed my public recantation for nearly twenty years, I immediately and resolutely withdrew from that particular controversy. Why I was at that time an anti-feminist in feeling is easy to explain, though impossible to justify. Conservative by temperament, and anti-democratic through social environment, I had reacted against my father's overvaluation of women relatively to men; and the narrow outlook and exasperated tone of some of the pioneers of women's suffrage had intensified this reaction. I remember at a luncheon given by an American lady to American suffragists (who had not given me a cigarette to soothe my distaste for the perpetual reiteration of the rights of women) venting this irritation by declaring provocatively – 'I have never met a man, however inferior, whom I do not consider to be my superior!' My dislike of the current parliamentary politics of the Tory and Whig 'ins' and 'outs' seemed a sort of argument against the immersion of women in this atmosphere. But at the root of my anti-feminism lay the fact that I had never myself suffered the disabilities assumed to arise from my sex. Quite the contrary; if I had been a man, self-respect, family pressure and the public opinion of my class would have pushed me into a money-making profession; as a mere woman I could carve out a career of disinterested research. Moreover, in the craft I had chosen, a woman was privileged. As an investigator she aroused less suspicion than a man, and, through making the proceedings more agreeable to the persons concerned, she gained better information. Further, in those days, a competent female writer on economic questions had, to an enterprising editor, actually a scarcity value. Thus she secured immediate publication and, to judge from my own experience, was paid a higher rate than that obtained by male competitors of equal standing.

Beatrice did not wholly reject the idea of reviewing the disqualifications and disadvantages of her sex, as she told Frederic Harrison in a letter declining to answer Mrs Fawcett. 'I look upon all my present study of labour and trade questions', she wrote, 'as leading up to an investigation of the industrial and social position of women in England which I hope to begin some 8 years hence (!) when I am sufficiently educated to undertake it.' In the meantime, however, she had moved from the specialist studies in the East End to a much more general interest in social problems. Ever since she had been impressed by the sturdy self-sufficiency of the Co-operators of Bacup she had been thinking of writing about a movement which apparently combined individualism and the abolition of the profit motive; and during the months she spent with her father in 1889 she worked over 'an arid mass of print' – reports of Co-operative congresses and files of Co-operative journals – to equip herself for the new task. Whenever she was able to get away from home, she recalled, she 'wandered through the Midlands, the Northern Counties of England and the Lowlands of Scotland, attending sectional conferences and members' meetings, and settling down for days or weeks at such centres as Leeds, Newcastle, Glasgow and Manchester' to interview Co-operators, to visit their stores and workshops, and to go through the archives of their societies. She learnt a great deal, and quickly; her preliminary work had given her, she said, 'a bunch of keys' which opened all doors to her, including the smoking-rooms in conference hotels, and she used her intelligence, her charm and her private means

Portrait of Sir Charles Booth by William Rothenstein 1908

*Below:* Eleanor Marx *c.* 1886

*Below right:* Leonard Courtney 1883

Joseph Chamberlain speaking at Birmingham Town Hall, January 1884

Highbury, Chamberlain's house in Birmingham

The main street of Bacup, Lancashire, about the time of Beatrice's second visit

Katherine Buildings in the East End of London, 1885

Whitechapel High Street in the East End of London

*Below left and centre:* Henrietta and Samuel Barnett at the time when
Toynbee Hall was founded, 1883. *Below right:* Alice Stopford Green,
date unknown

*Above:* The Dock Strike 1889

*Right:* Ben Tillet *c.* 1900

*Far right:* Tom Mann 1889

*Right:* John Burns 1889

*Far right:* Henry Broadhurst *c.* 1900

*Facing page:* Portrait of Joseph
Chamberlain by John Singer
Sargent 1896

*Right:* Sidney Webb 1885

*Below:* 44 Cranbourne Street,
London WC2, Sidney's birthplace

Sidney Webb 1891

Beatrice Webb 1891

to make the most of her opportunities. She had become a truly independent woman, able to go where she pleased and to do what she liked, and constrained only by her continuing obligation to her ailing and aged father.

Beatrice made the most of that personal freedom and, though she continued to collect material for her pioneering book on Co-operation, she was soon led to take an equally strong interest in the trade unions, for the two movements were clearly enmeshed, especially in the industrial districts of the North where the artisans, like Beatrice's relations at Bacup, were chapel-going, temperance enthusiasts, strong on self-education and self-improvement, and Co-operators and union men as a matter of course. It was, moreover, a propitious moment to discover the trade union movement, for it had come quite suddenly to a turning-point in its history.

Trade unions had hitherto been small bodies of craftsmen, more concerned with friendly society benefits than the class struggle, and their leaders had been more interested in playing a minor role in Liberal politics than in striking out on their own to form a party of working men who would seek to put their own representatives into Parliament. Small groups of socialists or labouring men had tried to run their own candidates, though the cost of elections and the limited male franchise had made most of such attempts a forlorn hope; and it was only in 1893 that the Independent Labour Party was formed. Seven years later a significant part of the trade union movement broke away from the Liberals, and in combination with the I.L.P. and the Fabian Society founded the Labour Representation Committee which was to become the modern Labour Party.

The first important sign of a new mood was the wave of militancy which swept through the unskilled and unorganized trades in the summer of 1889. Its first victory was in the London dock strike where the wretched casual workers held out for a month behind Ben Tillett and John Burns (1858–1943), a former engineer and a leading member of the Social Democratic Federation who became the outstanding leader of the 'New Unionism', and eventually President of the Local Government Board in a Liberal Cabinet. At the end of August, when the men had won, Beatrice noted the 'solidarity of labour' in this decisive strike. This 'revelation' she said, had 'shown me that in my desire to master commercial and financial facts as the only key to the labour problem I was guided by a true instinct: that in my capacity to master these facts will rest my power to influence for good the condition of my people'. It was in that mood that she went to the Trades Union Congress in September 1899 where the militants began their campaign to oust the 'veteran' leadership and to commit the unions to independent political action.

# ᑲ 1888 ᑭ

Francis Bacon (1561–1626), statesman and philosopher, sought a new interpretation of nature to replace the Aristotelian system, using an inductive method based upon investigation and observation.

*2 January.* [Kildare]
From life to grammar! For the first time looked through 'English grammar and composition'. These are new ideas to me. . . . I read for 3 or 4 hours daily and have been for the last fortnight steeped in Bacon – his Life and Works. . . . He was a great *failure*; he failed in all his aims, both personal and public . . . he failed as a politician, as a judge, in friendship and in married life. And yet he is one of those who have moved humanity a step forward, in spite of failing to advance it in the ways he had decided on. His faith, hope, patience and devotion had their effect; the great central idea of his life that 'we must know in order to act' was impressed on the minds of future generations through his words. But he ignored the office of morality in guiding action, of genius in guiding thought. And in return the morality of his own time condemned him to ignominy; and the scientific inquiries of all ages have left his pathway untrodden. . . .

Auberon Herbert (1838–1906) was younger brother to the Earl of Carnarvon, the Colonial Secretary, and had himself been a politician of increasingly unorthodox opinions. After serving in the Army, and standing as a Conservative candidate for the House of Commons, he became a vegetarian and a teetotaller, an agnostic, a student of psychic research, a republican and a sympathizer with organized labour. While at Oxford he had become a friend and disciple of Herbert Spencer, and was later one of the philosopher's three trustees. After he gave up politics in 1874 he retired to farm at Ashley Arnewood Farm, near Lymington, and at Dalmally, near Loch Awe in Scotland.

*8 February.* [Ashley Arnewood, Hampshire]
In the midst of the most beautiful part of the New Forest there are a few acres of poor pastureland enclosed by a wooden fence. . . . On the higher part of this ground stands a little colony of queer red-painted buildings, two large cottages and various small outhouses, huddled together, yet distinct from one another, and quite free from architec-tural plan. No attempt at a drive or even a path, not even a gate. To

237

enter the back yard the visitor must needs dip under a wooden paling. But once inside the larger cottage, there is comfort, even taste. The floors are bare and clean-scoured; here and there warm-coloured rugs thrown across; while the monotony of the panelling is broken by draped eastern hangings. In the dining-room, the old forest hearth, bringing with it the commoner's rights, stands intact; the only part of the 'Old House' (still the name of the colony) left unchanged. It forms a half-circle, the chimney rising straight from the stone hearth, whereon a fiery mass of peat and wood burns brightly. . . . Refined eccentricity, not poverty, lives here. . . . In the smaller cottage live three maidservants. Two men (formerly Shakers) serve in all capacities, for ponies, cows, drawing of water, hewing of wood and as messengers to the civilized world.

Mr Auberon Herbert, head of this little home, is a tall, stooping man; he is already quite grey (though only fifty years of age) and the look of failing physical strength is stamped on his face and figure. His bearing, manner, voice – all tell the courtesy and sensitiveness of good breeding; his expression is that of an intellectual dreamer, tempered by the love of his fellow-creatures whether human or otherwise, and in the truthful sympathy of his grey eye and in the lines of his face the quick observer reads past suffering and present resignation. The younger son of a great English peer, he was brought up to the amusements and occupations of his own class – the quick succession of public school, university, Army, sport and racing, and lastly politics, with a background of big country houses and sparkling London drawing-rooms. But his choice was not here. He married a woman of his own caste, but, strangely enough, sharing his own tastes; and these two refused to move in the groove of aristocratic custom and they settled down in a country farm to carve existence according to their own conscience. Strange stories floated up to 'London Society' of their doings – Shaker settlements, gypsy vans, spirit rapping and medium-hunting and, to the horror of Mrs Grundy, eating with their own servants! Now and again the literary world was charmed by brilliant articles in the *Fortnightly* or letters in *The Times*; and the political set was half offended, half amused with the outspoken and well-worded dialogue *A Politician in Trouble about his Soul* (1884) which actually seemed written for the purpose of disproving the usefulness of politicians! But generally Auberon Herbert was looked on as an enthusiast, a Don Quixote of the nineteenth century, who had left the real battle of life to fight with a strange ogre of his own imagination, an *always Immoral State Interference*; a creation the uncouthness of whose name was a sufficient guarantee of its non-existence.

Now the life-companion is dead. Two little girls, one thirteen, the other seven, a boy away at a grammar school, are the beloved of this solitary man. Both the girls are dressed in grey smocks, worsted stockings and thick clump boots. . . . A young Oxford man, pleasant, fairly intelligent, but no way out of the common, lives in the house as tutor. Here, in the midst of great natural beauty, far away from all human interest, these three lives slip slowly onward, the man towards old age and death, the girls towards the joys and the troubles, the risks and the fortunes of mature womanhood.

Across the forest and moor we rode on that February day, the man, the elder girl and I myself, to this home in the wilds. . . . After our long ride, fourteen miles roundabout from the station, we were tired; lunch over, we sank into comfortable chairs round the blaze of peat and wood fire, sipped coffee and smoked cigarettes. Religiously minded individualism disputing with scientific fact-finding! Discordant tendencies, it is true, but mutually tolerant. 'A woman without a soul,' said Auberon Herbert playfully, 'looking on struggling society like a young surgeon looks on a case, as another subject for diagnosis. Cannot you see it is moral law that should guide our action; and that the only moral axiom in social life is free action for every man's faculties.'

*12 February.* [Kildare]

Last days at Bournemouth; hardly expect to return here. If Father lives we shall move to Wimbledon for next winter. Very happy during these peaceful months; read English history and literature, long rides and short walks, listening to the band. . . . And now I enjoy my life. I have fair health, faith in my own capacity to do the work I believe in, and I have regained my old religious feeling without which life is not worth living to one of my nature. Intend to spend ten days of my holiday in the West End before I settle in to work; and then a hard pull and a long pull to get the material wherewith to make a really graphic picture of the London tailoring trade. Thirty years is a good deal of sand in the hour-glass; I must justify all this long period of silent intellectual seed-time by fruit.

One good thing done; Herbert Spencer cured — at least for the present. Living with us gave him courage to rise out of his state of lethargy and take to active life again. Now I hear he is running about

London and thoroughly enjoying Society. Poor old man, it is a comfort to think one has been a help to him (though he does not acknowledge it and says it's a new drug!). It is a small return for his constant intellectual guidance and sympathy. . . .

Shall turn my back on Society; except in so far as it is likely to be useful to my work. So mighty is even a small success! Great ladies want to know me – and yet, I have not proved *ability* but only a certain originality in thought and expression.

'Neo-Malthusianism' was then the polite phrase for advocacy of birth control.

*22 February.* [London]
Staying with the Hobhouses and wasting time! Spent afternoon and evening with Benjamin Jones in their happy little home at West Norwood. They live on £400 and are as happy as others on £4000. Three boys and a girl; have taken measures to prevent others from coming, and advise others to do so. 'Four I can bring up with comfort; eight or ten would have strained both Annie and myself!' If it were not for conceit and the intellectual shallowness which springs from this, Benjamin Jones would be a big man. . . .

The question of Neo-Malthusianism is coming to the fore; the underground growth of it is unquestioned; the open discussion of it is every day more permitted. I see it practised by men and women who are perfectly pure. I cannot see *reasons* against it; yet my moral instinct is not with it.

*4 March.* [London]
Trying to grasp my subject – the trade and labour question of East End tailoring. Wish I had more strength and pluck.

Beatrice prepared herself for work in an East End sweatshop by training at a Co-operative tailoring workshop.

*28 March. Good Friday.* [Devonshire House Hotel]
So the first six weeks of my inquiry ends. Think I have broken the crust and am now grabbing at the roots of the subject. But much definite work I have not done. Most of my time spent in training as a 'plain hand', and it remains to be seen whether my training will be of real use. Anyway, it has given me an insight into the organization, or, in this case, into the want of organization, of a workshop, and into the

actual handicraft of tailoring. Otherwise my life has been extremely interesting, and I am more than ever assured that, *if I have capacity*, I have found the life that suits me, in which I am happiest, in which I can be of most use to my fellow-mortals. My work now absolutely absorbs me. When I am too tired to work I pray; when I am too exhausted to pray I simply rest in the faith that my work is useful if I give it my best energy and my whole heart. And now there are no conflicting desires and few conflicting duties. Society, even now that it is unusually gracious and flattering, has no charm for me, and the other night after I had come back from a distinguished party to which I had been enticed, I felt that I should not regret the loss of attraction (as I shall inevitably lose it), for I did not care for the result. Only in work should I fear the loss of a woman's charm, for undoubtedly it smooths out obstacles, but then I am so planning my life that the work I need it for will be done before I lose it!

Of my family I see less and less but that is unavoidable in my present hurried life – every bit of spare time must be devoted to work.

Arthur Dyson Williams (1859–96) was a barrister and nephew of the wealthy Miss Williams in whose house Beatrice had first met Chamberlain.

*9 April.* [Devonshire House Hotel?]
Rosy engaged to Mr Williams. He is a respectable young man with fair abilities and I should think a good fellow. A barrister, not likely to do brilliantly, with a small income of his own. He is not up to the mark of the other brothers-in-law, but then Rosy is the least gifted, mentally and physically, of the whole sisterhood. I wonder how her little nature will thrive under it; whether this the greatest crisis of a woman's life will make her grow into a 'Soul', whether it will lift her out of the tiny part played by a little Ego grasping after personal happiness. . . .

*11 April.* [London lodgings]
Settled at 56 Great Prescott St, to begin life as a working woman. With a very queer feeling I left the house in my old clothes and walked straight off to Princes Street and Wood Street, a nest of tailors. No bills up, except for 'good tailoress', and at these places I daren't apply, feeling myself rather an imposter. I wandered on, until my heart sank within me, my legs and back began to ache, and I felt all the feelings of 'out o' work'. At last I summoned up courage and

knocked at the door of a tailor wanting a 'good tailoress'. A fat and comfortable Jewess opened the door.

'Do you want a plain 'and?' said I, trying to effect a working-class accent.

'No,' was the reply.

'I can do everything except buttonholes,' I insisted.

'Where have you worked?'

'With my father, a master tailor. I've come from Manchester.'

'Rebecca,' shouted the fat Jewess to her daughter down the street, 'do you want a hand?'

'Suited,' shouted back Rebecca, to my mingled disappointment and relief. 'You will find plenty of bills in the next street,' she added in a kindly voice.

So I trudged on, asked at one or two other places, but all were 'suited'. Thought I, 'Is it because it's the middle of the week, or because they suspect I'm not genuine?' and looked sensitively into the next shop window at my reflection; certainly I looked shabby enough. I pass by a shop where a long list of 'hands wanted' is nailed up; but I have neither pencil nor paper and cannot in my dazed nervousness remember addresses and names – and how can I walk any longer? I feel quite strained. So in a fit of listless despair I take the top of the tram down Mile End Rd. It is warm and balmy, and with a little rest from that weary trudge I pick up my pluck again. A large placard strikes my eye. 'Trouser and vest hands wanted immediately.' I descend quickly and am soon inside the shop. A large crowded room with a stout, clever-looking Jewess presiding at the top of the table, at which some thirty girls are working.

'Do you want trouser hands?'

'Yes, we do,' answers the Jewess.

'I'm a trouser finisher.'

The Jewess looks at me from top to toe; and somewhat supercili-ously glances at my draggled old dress.

'Call tomorrow half-past eight.'

'What price do you pay?' say I with firmness.

'Why, according to the work; all prices,' answers she laconically.

'Then tomorrow, half-past eight', and I leave the shop feeling triumphant to have secured a place, but a little doubtful of my power of finishing trousers. So I hurry back to my little room, throw off my disguise, gulp down a cup of tea and rush off to a friendly Co-operative workroom to 'finish a pair of trousers' which I accomplish without difficulty in two hours. If they only expect 'finishing' I'm safe. Basting I have not really mastered.

*12 April.* [London]

Thursday morning I reappear at 198 Mile End Road. It is a long irregular-shaped room running backward from the retail shop to the kitchen. Two small tables by the gas jets (used for heating irons) serve for the two pressers. Then a long table with forms on either side and chairs at top and bottom, for the trouser finishers. Two other tables for machinists and vest hands and a high table for the trouser-basters complete the furniture of the room. It is barely 8.30 but the 30 girls are crowding in and taking their seats in front of their work and boxes on the tables. The 'missus' has not yet come down; the two pressers, English lads of about 22, saunter lazily into the room a little after the half-hour. The head woman calls for a pair of trousers and hands them to me. I look at them puzzled to know what to do; I have no materials wherewith to begin. The woman next to me explains: 'You will have to bring trimmings, but I'll lend you some to begin with.' 'What ought I to buy?' say I, feeling very helpless. At this moment the 'missus' bustles into the room. She is a big woman, enormously developed in the hips and legs, with strongly Jewish features and only one eye. Her hair is crisp and has been jet black; now in places it is quite grey. Her dress is stamped cotton velvet of a large flowery pattern; she has a heavy watch-chain, plentiful rings; and a spotlessly clean apron.

'Good morning to you,' she says good-temperedly to the whole assemblage. 'Esther, have you given that young person some work?'

'Yes,' replied Esther. '3½ trousers.'

'I have not got any trimmings. I did not know that I had to supply them. Where I worked before they were given,' I ejaculate humbly.

'That's easily managed; the shop is just around the corner, or Esther,' she calls out across the table, 'you're going out; get this young person her trimmings. The lady next you will tell you what you want,' she says in a lower tone bending over between us. The lady next me is a good-tempered married woman of a certain age. She, like all the other trouser-hands, works piecework; but in spite of that she is ready to give me up a good deal of time in explaining how I am to set about my work.

'You'll feel a bit strange the first day. Have you been long out 'o work?'

'Yes' I answer abruptly.

243

'Ah, that accounts for your feeling awkward like. One's fingers feel like so many thumbs at first.'

And certainly mine do. The work is quite different from the Co-operative shop [in which I learnt the work?]; much coarser and not so well arranged. And then I feel nervous, very much 'on trial', and the heat of the room, the crowded table and the general strangeness of the position, all these circumstances unite to incapacitate me for even decent work.

However, happily for me, no one pays much attention. There is plenty of row, what with the machines, the singing of the girls at the other end of the room, the chattering that goes on at the upper end of one table, at which sits the mistress. Chaff and bad language is freely thrown from the two lads at the pressing-tables to the girls at our table. Offers of kisses, sending to the Devil and his abode, and a constant repetition of the inevitable adjective form the staple of the conversation between the lads and the workgirls; the elder women whisper bits of gossip or news in each other's ears. There is a free giving and taking of each other's trimmings, and a general super-vision of each other's work, altogether a hearty geniality of a rough sort. The missus joins in the chatter, encourages or scolds as the case may be.

'The missus has 16 children,' says the Mrs Read (the woman next me), '8 of her own and 8 of her husband's. All those girls at the last table are her daughters.'

I look down the room: the girls there are smartly dressed, but are working quite as hard as the others and appear on terms of equality.

'They are a nice-looking set,' say I in a complimentary tone.

'Yes, it's a pity some of the girls are not like them,' mutters the woman. 'They're an awful bad lot, some o' them. Why bless you, that young woman just behind us has had three babies by her father, and another here has had one by her brother.'

'Yes,' remarks the person next to her (a regular woman of the slums), 'it's ill thinking of what you may have to touch in these sort of places.'

'Well,' replies Mrs Read, 'I've worked here these eight years and never yet had any words with anyone. There's regular work and no one need grumble who wishes to work. There's no need to mix yourself up with others whose look you don't like. There's some of all sorts here.'

'I'm one of those sort', continues the slum woman, 'that answers a person back when they call me bl—y names. I'll give the last word to no one.'

'I don't choose to hold conversation with such as they,' replies Mrs Read with conscious superiority. 'It isn't as if I 'ad to work for my living. My 'usband is in regular work; it's only for the extras that I work; and just for those times, per'aps three or four weeks, when the building trade is slack.'

This effectually silences the woman of the slums. Her husband comes home drunk every night, and spends his time lounging about the publics (so [I] was afterwards informed by Mrs Read). She has an ill-looking daughter next her, with whom she exchanges work and bad language and shares victuals.

So we go on; my attention divided between my work and picking up bits of conversation. Evidently much of the work is for export, chiefly for Parnells [a wholesale house]. Other work is for sale in the front shop; the trousers we are finishing for 3½ up to 5d are sold from 4s 6d up to 8s 6d. Coats and vests for 17s up to 22s. Coats must be made out. The coarser trousers are also made out in large quantities and are probably paid 2½ for finishing.

'One o'clock,' shouts a shrill boy's voice. 'Stop work,' orders the missus.

'I wish I could finish this bit,' say I to the woman next me.

'You mustn't. It's dinner-time.'

So I put on my bonnet and jacket and go out into the Mile End Road heartily glad to get a breath of fresh air and a change from the cramped position. I take the tram up and down to Aldgate and end by turning into a clean shop for a cup of tea and a bun. Back again at two.

'You must work a little quicker for your own sake,' says the missus, who has been inspecting my work. 'We've had worse buttonholers than this,' she says in a kindly voice, 'but it don't look as if you have been 'customed to much work.'

But now begins the drama of the day. The two pressers come in ten minutes after hour. This brings down upon them the ire of the Jewess. They, however, seem masters of the situation, for they answer her back in even choicer language than she has advanced to them. They taunt her with putting the 5s she rings out of them on horses; they declare their right to come when they choose, and if they want a day off, to take it. And then begins a perfect volley of abuse, in which the girls at one of the tables join in, taking the 'missus'' side against the pressers. At this critical point enter the master.

Mr Marks is a somewhat sleepy-looking well-dressed Jew, with an evident desire to keep the peace. I think also he has himself suffered from the missus' tongue and feels the masculine side of the question with the bevy of women shouting on all sides. Anyway, he is inclined to take an impartial view of the row. 'Now just you be quiet,' he shouts to the two pressers. 'Go on with your work and don't speak to my wife.' And then to his wife in a lower tone, 'Why can't you leave them alone and not answer them?' and the rest of his speech I cannot hear but it is evidently taking the form of expostulation.

'Why, if you were only a bit of a man,' says the missus, raising her voice so that all may hear, 'you would throw these two bl—y rascals out. Why, I'd throw them out at any price. The idea of saying how I spend my money. What's that to him? And that Joe says he'll call the Factory Man in. He may call the Devil in, if he likes, and the only person as he'll notice will be himself. The idea of his saying that I spend my money on horses; as if I couldn't spend my money on anything I like. As if you wouldn't give me money, as I earn, when I ask you, Mr Marks; and never ask where it goes to,' she adds, looking threateningly at Mr Marks. The betting on horses is evidently a sore point.

'It's not their business what you do with your money,' says the master soothingly. 'But just let them alone, and tell the girls to be quiet.' But the pressers have caught the word 'devil' and reply in due form. The quick firing of words between missus and men goes on: the tall young man, Joe by name, shouts the loudest and the longest, but as Mrs Read remarks to me, 'It's Harry as makes the bullets; just listen to him; but it's Joe that fires them.'

At last it subsides. Women (outdoor workers) come in and turn the mistress' attention off the pressers on to their work. They, like most of the indoor hands, are Christians but, unlike the former, they are nearly all married women.

'Come in on Monday, Mrs South. But mind it's Monday morning and not Tuesday morning. You understand English, don't you? Monday morning.'

A boy comes into the shop with a bundle of trousers unfinished.

'What do you think of this, Esther? Mrs Hall says she was washing on Monday, cleaning on Tuesday, and I suppose the Devil on Wednesday; for here on Thursday the work is sent in undone', and the missus, as she throws the bundle on to the table, says, 'Now, girls, be quick with your work; there's all this to be done extra before Friday for Parnells. Strike her name off the book, Esther.'

At last tea-time breaks the working day. All, or nearly all, the women have their own teapots on the gas stove and have with them bread as a relish. The missus takes her tea at the top of the table. The obnoxious pressers have left for the half-hour. The missus' feelings break out. 'Pay them 5s a day to abuse you; as if I couldn't spend my money on what I like; and as if Mr Marks would ever ask – I'd like to see him ask me how the money had gone.'

All the women sympathize with her, and exchange abuse of the absent pressers. 'It's awful, their language,' says the slum woman. 'If I were the missus, I would give the bl—y scoundrels tit for tat.'

'As for the Factory Man', continues the mistress, turning to another sore point, 'just fancy threatening me with him. Why, they aren't fit to work in a respectable shop – they're d—d spies. I'd throw them out, if I were Mr Marks, if it cost me £100. If he were half a man he would.'

'You have nothing to fear', venture I, 'from the Factory man. You keep the regulations exactly.'

However, the pressers are not 'thrown out'. The truth being that in the busy season it would be difficult to supply their place.

The women on either side of me offer me tea, which I resolutely refuse. An hour afterwards I have finished my second pair of trousers.

'This won't do,' says the missus, pulling the work to pieces. 'Here, take and undo that one. I'll set this one to rights. Better have respectable persons who know little to work here than blackguards who know a lot and a deal too much too,' she mutters, still smarting over the taunt of money laid on horses.

'Eight o'clock by the Brewery clock,' cries out the shrill voice.

'Ten minutes to,' shouts the missus, looking at her watch. 'However, it ain't worth while breaking the law for a few minutes. Stop work.'

This is most welcome to me. The heat, since the gas has been lit, is terrific and my fingers are horribly sore and my back aches as if it would break. The women bundle up their work and one or two take it home. Everyone leaves their trimmings on the table with scissors and thimble.

The freshness of the evening air is delicious, and as I walk up Mile End Road the physical sensation of free movement and rest to the weary eyes and fingers is keen enjoyment. Back in my little lodging and eat my supper and tumble into bed.

*13 April.* [London]

Friday morning I have trimmings to buy before I sit down to work. But this morning I feel hopelessly tired, my fingers clammy and a general shakiness all over. The needle will not pierce the hard shoddy stuff; my stitches will go all awry and the dampness of my fingers stretches the linings out of place. Altogether I feel on the brink of deep disgrace as a needlewoman. . . .

'This will never do,' says the missus as she looks over the work. 'This work won't suit me. You want to go and learn somewhere first. This will never do. This won't suit me,' she repeats slowly. All the women at the table look at me pityingly and I retire to my place feeling very small. There is a dead silence, during which I arrange my trimmings so as to be ready to take my leave if the missus persists. Presently she beckons to me. 'I'll see what I can do with you. You sit between those two young ladies and they'll show you. You must help one another,' she says to the two girls. . . .

Tea-time the missus addresses me: 'Now I am very much interested in you; there is something in your face that is uncommon. The women here will tell you that I have made an exception for you. I should have bundled you out long ago if it had not been for your face and your voice. Directly you open your mouth, anyone can see that you are different from others. What have you been?'

'I used not to have to work for my living,' I reply, evading the question. 'I am looking out for different work now, but I had to take to something.'

'A nice-looking person like you ought to get married to a respectable man; you're more fit for that than to earn your living,' says the shrewd Jewess. 'But since you have come here, I'll see what I can do with you.'

I have my cup of tea. The pale weary girl is munching her bread and butter.

'Won't you have some?' she says, pushing the paper towards me.

'No, thank you,' I answer.

'Sure?' she says. And then, without more to-do, she lays a piece on my lap and turns away to avoid my thanks. A little bit of human kindness that goes to my heart and brings tears into my eyes. Work begins again. My friend has finished her trousers and is waiting for another pair. She covers her head with her hand and in her grey eyes there is an intense look of weariness, weariness of body and of mind. Another pair is handed to her and she begins again. She is a quick worker but, work as hard as she may, she cannot make much over a 1s a day, discounting trimmings. A shilling a day is about the price of unskilled woman's labour.

Another two hours and I say 'goodnight' to the mistress and leave this workshop and its inhabitants to work on its way day after day and to become to me only a memory. . . .

Leonard Courtney's speech was to advocate Proportional Representation in county elections.

*15 April.* [London]
An interval. Spent the afternoon in the Speaker's Gallery. Debate on local government. Eloquent speech of Leonard's, full of fine feeling and earnest thought, ignoring party politics and striking into the heart of the question of representation. Followed by Chamberlain – by taunts and jeers at his proposals. And then a rattling party speech – out and out defence of Tory Government. Certainly Chamberlain is not a half-hearted fighter. He has adopted the Tories as his hard and fast allies and he sticks to them through thick and thin. What a change in that man's position! Only three years ago he was the idol of the democracy and the *bête-noire* of the well-to-do classes. Now he is the darling of the aristocracy and the much abused 'traitor' to the people's cause. His American mission has been eminently successful, but it is a success which will bring flattery and consideration from the 'classes' and not from the masses. And socially he is absorbed by the aristocratic set. He is flattered and spoilt by all the fine ladies of London Society; and has a pleasant enough life of it – if he is satisfied with Society and does not awaken to the consciousness of loss of real power. Society is a magic looking-glass; it often reflects past and not present position, and if you are agreeable, it will not cease to reflect the past, even magnifying it. And so a man lives on in a fool's paradise, forgetting that the ladder is destroyed by which he rose and upon which he might have risen higher.

It did me good to hear these two men this afternoon. The contrast between Leonard's tone and his was another death-knell to feeling. Courage, courage. My present life, though lonely and at times wearisome, is better than it would have been by his side. For there is growth in it. Only I must keep humble and devoted. Humility, devotion and truth-desire – my three guardian angels. *True to myself.*

Still, if I believed in prayer for others, I would pray for him – for his true success.

249

Mary Endicott (b. 1864) was the daughter of the American Secretary of State for War. Chamberlain met her in November 1887 when he was in America to resolve a fishing dispute between the United States and Canada.

*26 April.* [Devonshire House Hotel?]
Large dinner at the Adlers' (Chief Rabbi) to meet me. The Jews have opened their arms to the dark-eyed Christian who is studying their East End life, and at least two threaten me with 'intentions'. I am a wonderment in their well-regulated social life, a strange thing curious to behold and pleasant to look upon.

'Chamberlain's marriage' placarded all over the city. Engaged to an American girl and shortly to be married. I had heard of the rumour for some time, but I hardly believed it. Now it is an established fact. It is good for me, and good for him – may be the saving of him yet and shows him in a better light. A gasp, as if one had been stabbed, and then it is over. Fortunately for me, it comes now that I am happy and settled in my own working life. Poor Beatrice Chamberlain, it is hard on her.

'To be or not to be.' *Pall Mall* [*Gazette*] 29 April. No one knows. 'Miss Endicott has at last acknowledged, etc.' To be. *Pall Mall* 31 May.

*5 May.* [Devonshire House Hotel?]
The last few days of my active life for some months to come. On the whole I have been very happy, full of interest and blessed with *content*. I have not felt living alone. My work is now all in all to me. When I am not actively engaged in it, I sit and dream over it – chew the cud of all I see and hear. And then, when I am utterly exhausted, I am not depressed, only satisfied, like the child-bearing mother, to wait for returning strength. Prayer is a constant source of strength. I like to sit in that grand St Paul's with its still silent spaces; there is a wonderful restfulness in the great 'House of God'. And I enjoy the life of the people at the East End – the reality of their effort and aims, the simplicity of their sorrows and of their joys. I feel I can *realize* it – see the tragic and the comic side of it. To some extent, I can grasp the forces which are swaying to and fro, raising or depressing this vast herd of human beings. I feel that my painstaking study of detail will help me towards that knowledge of the whole, towards which I am constantly striving. Anyway, I shall leave steps cut in the rock, from the summit of which man will eventually map out the conquered land of social life. Amen.

*12 May*. [Devonshire House Hotel?]
Gave evidence yesterday before the Lords Committee [on sweating]. A set of well-meaning men, but not made of stuff fit for investigation. As they had forced me to appear, they treated me very kindly, and lunched me in the middle of my examination. A few Peeresses came down to stare at me! Arnold White was there – very uncomfortable. With all his accusations [against sweaters using foreign labour] he has brought down any number of lawyers' letters on his devoted head. But when you come to pay witnesses, you must expect them to swear facts to please you, and for those they libel to be more than indignant with you.

On 12 May 1888 the *Pall Mall Gazette* published an article entitled 'The Peers and the Sweaters.'

In the morning the only witness was a lady – Miss Potter – dressed in black and wearing a very dainty bonnet, tall, supple, dark, with bright eyes, and quite cool in the witness chair, who was fluent on coats and eloquent on breeches. Unfortunately, though her voice was a little shrill, it was very difficult to hear sentences, which were very sharply delivered.

*16 May*. [The Argoed?]
Disagreeable consequences of appearing in public; description of my appearance and dress, and an offensive notice in the *Pall Mall [Gazette]*. The economic side of the question is an unattractive one, and draws down abuse of all kinds from the least scrupulous class of men.

*25 May*. [The Argoed?]
Detestable mis-statement of my evidence brings down libellous imputations, all the harder to bear as I was pressed into giving evidence and was unwilling to speak of my personal experience of the workshops. Perhaps what made it still worse is that Maggie Harkness, taking for granted that all the newspapers told of my evidence was true, has been spreading a report that I had been telling stories. A false friend, not intentionally so, but actually. How differently the Booths have acted! However, I suppose I shall weather the storm as I have weathered others. God help me! My intention was to tell the truth and nothing but the truth and there was as a fact only one small inaccuracy (either on my side or on that of the shorthand writer) – exclusively instead of inclusively three weeks' work. Both statements

would be inaccurate, the one more than covers, the other does not cover, the length of time I worked but I altered the proof so that it will now be an understatement.

*28 May.* [The Argoed?]
Foolish to have allowed myself to be so thoroughly upset by false reports and *Pall Mall* libels. Suffering from attack of nervous exhaustion from the intensity of my misery. I must have a strain of mania in my nature which needs all my self-control to overcome.

*31 May.* [The Argoed]
Delightful ride through the country; shaken off distemper and feel more inclined to work. But cannot forget this time last year! [Beatrice's break with Chamberlain.] It is hard for a woman to bear. Courage. That is the one meaningful word of my life; think I have almost a right to adopt it as an acted-up-to motto.

*1 June.* [The Argoed]
We regret deeply and passionately many things we have done or left undone, but we fail to rejoice (because of our ignorance) over the evils we have avoided and the terrible possibilities we have escaped.

*4 June.* [The Argoed]
Why look everlastingly at the past that is irretrievably gone, its facts engraved on eternity? In the present it is the future that is the living reality, for it is the child we are creating. These last few days, days of humiliation (haunted by memories) have brought vividly to my mind the meanness and pettiness of gratified vanity; of the miserable little excitements in noting one's own tiny successes. Even one's humiliation, the 'Scarlet Letter', is of small significance if one looks at it relatively to the great movements round about one – how much less important therefore the little spasms of admiration in the tiny set one lives in. Now that I am started in public work I must try to avoid the valleys and hills of Egotism – intense depression at failure or loneliness, elation in success.

*6 June.* [The Argoed]
Busy writing my paper on the tailoring trade. It is a horribly stiff bit of work, all the more so as I am not physically strong at present, ought really to have had a fortnight holiday before beginning it; but then I

work so slowly that I dared not take it. I feel as if I were hammering it out of me, not writing it. Fear it won't be a success.

*29 June.* [The Argoed]
These latter days [I] constantly think of Mother: sometimes the feeling of her presence is so strong that I am tempted into a kind of communion with her. We knew each other so little in life-time, and, strangely, I love her better now. I understand her more completely. I feel that she at last knows me, tries to cheer my loneliness and to encourage my effort, now that her outward form lies decaying in the earth. She seems now to belong more to me than to the others; the others have their husbands and their children; I have nothing but my work with the fitful warmth of friendship. So Mother seems to stand by my side, to be watching me, anxious to reach out to me a helping hand, at any rate to bless me. I have been wounded, horribly wounded, and the scar can never leave me, but I can fight through the rest of the bullets of life with courage. And perhaps, when it is over, I shall know that she has been by my side.

Arabella Fisher, sister to Lord Wrenbury whom Beatrice had met years before at San Remo, had been secretary to the eminent geologist Sir Charles Lyell (1797–1875), whose development of evolutionary science preceded that of Charles Darwin (1809–82) and Alfred Russel Wallace (1823–1913) in the field of biology. She was now married to an elderly retired doctor and lived in the country.

*15 July. Gracedieu*
The charming home of my best friends. The Booths are satisfied with my paper and are, as usual, full of wise and temperate encouragement. Charlie likes me as a fellow-worker, Mary regrets me as a possible married woman, but both alike are constant and warm in their friendship, in times of trouble and days of success. And their full, happy, dutiful lives fill one with peace and satisfaction as one watches them. They and their family are the bright spot in my life, a continual source of strength, an everlasting upspringing interest. And Charlie and I make admirable fellow-workers: he has the cautious, careful intellect with an ingenious touch of detail, while I paint in broader colouring, caring more for the general effect of the picture than for *exactness* in representation. Perhaps I get an undue amount of credit. But he is absolutely generous, never thinks whether he gains the credit so long as good work is done. After this year is over our fellow-working ends – at least for the present.

Bella Fisher staying here for two or three days. She and I have perhaps more in common than I and Mary Booth, for she is essentially the *unmarried* woman, though she happens to have married late in life. But the struggle, work and success of her existence have all belonged to spinsterhood. Her marriage, as she once quaintly put it, was a 'provision for old age', entered into after she felt that the best part of her work was over. She is not original intellectually, simply strong and clear with a dash of literary talent that enables her to translate hard scientific fact into simple and graceful language. She is the very soul of conscientious and industrious work; her work is the best part of her intellectually and seems to be inspired more by her moral nature than by her intellect. Duty cheerfully and heartily accepted is the motto of her life, warm-hearted devotion to the great masters of her work – Lyell, Darwin, Wallace – and constant sympathy for fellow-workers. These have been the charm of her somewhat grey-toned existence (if judged by circumstances) and the result has been a broad stream of universal optimism with a deep undercurrent of strong religious faith in the moral government of the world and in future existence. Only one flaw in her moral nature and that superficial; a certain self-satisfaction, a perhaps legitimate conceit that she has done well by God and man. She is a self-made woman, who has gained livelihood and position by hard work and has yet fulfilled all her home duties, and she is fully conscious of this and is apt to put down all the suffering of the world to the fact that other persons 'do not likewise'. In this she may be right, but the problems of life, whether from her own nature or from outward events, have always come before her in a clear, unconfused light. Since her marriage to the kind old doctor her power of work has fallen off. I am not quite certain that now and again she does not regret her freedom. Her marriage is one of deep affection but with no intellectual companionship and at times her life is lonely and needs the stimulus of other minds. . . .

*21 July.* [The Argoed]
I wish I could rid myself of self-consciousness and ambition in all its forms. Life is so short and there is so much that needs doing that it is a sin to waste a thought or a feeling on self. Some days I seem to rise above it, to look down on my own struggle, failures and little successes as something too small and insignificant to be noted, to see it all in proportion to the great currents of life, of all kinds, that surround one. But at other times I brood over what will be thought or said about

me, now feel elated by appreciation and praise, then down in the depths of misery from a sense of indifference or blame, think one day I am a genius, another day an utter failure. Still, I believe the religious spirit growing within me, the consciousness that I am but an instrument to be handled, or thrown on one side, by a greater power, with the one clear duty in either case to submit with love and cheerfulness. . . .

*29 July.* [The Argoed]
This day last year I spent with J.C. Now we have each gone on our way – parted for all Eternity (?)

*6 August.* [The Argoed]
[John] Burnett thoroughly approves of my paper. 'Tone admirable', but considers it is written for those who already know the ABC of the question. The *Spectator* is kinder to me this time than last and I should think expresses the general opinion of those who take the trouble to wade through it. 'Heavy reading but full of sound and valuable information.' That is exactly what I wished it to be. I knew I could not make it brilliant, but I hoped to give a clear and exhaustive account of the much-talked-of 'sweaters' in the tailoring trade, more especially after my somewhat sensational appearance before the House of Lords. I shall be curious to see how my enemy the *Pall Mall* treats it, or whether it simply ignores it. I *am* so glad that the general opinion is that it *is sound work*. To be thought a sound and conscientious worker, with ability guided by conscience, is my one ambition. I do not care to be thought 'talented' or brilliant. . . .

Dr Mandell Creighton (1843–1901) was Professor of Ecclesiastical History at Cambridge, Canon of Worcester, and later Bishop of London. He was the author of a five-volume *History of the Papacy*. Marie Souvestre introduced Beatrice to the Creightons.

*15 August.* [The Argoed]
Pleasant stay with the Creightons at Worcester. Friends of Miss Souvestre, they asked me to stay with them so that I might come down to Cambridge (where Canon Creighton is Professor of History) to 'address' a social meeting. I refused that honour but have promised to go to Cambridge. Canon Creighton is a scholar and a priest with wide and tolerant social sympathies. He is small and unimpressive as a person, with a somewhat paradoxical conversation at first going off,

but with the quick apprehension and the love of learning for its own sake characteristic of the true student. I have not read or heard of his History. I should gather from his nature and from his estimate of other historians that he belongs to the German school and dislikes the popular form given to the study of the past by Lecky and Green. Perhaps he is more a Scotch antiquarian than a German student. He is strong in contempt (too strong in that direction to be very strong in any other) of any work that is not more or less on his own lines, though liking all agreeable interested persons as friends. He is a bit of a flirt, at least I think so, but quite a harmless one. On the other hand he despises feminine efforts, and tacitly insists that woman's mission is to charm and not to instruct. 'Women cannot take the discipline that is needed in order to do good work; they are perpetually making short cuts.' He professes contempt for university life and its 'talk without action'; in fact he is slightly contemptuous of all human effort. Here his theology helps him, for, in spite of his paradoxical and extremely secular conversation, the Canon is deeply religious. I take it his religion is the finest part of his nature. As a preacher he is earnest and simple. . . . He and I 'skirted' questions; we did not thrash them out.

His wife is an attractive woman with a sound intellect whenever she chooses to use it. She has seven children and is preparing for another. She is a devoted wife and an equally devoted mother – somewhat after the Mary Booth type. But her cultivation of mind is of the sound sort and the little literary work that she has done has been well done. She does not share her husband's slight opinion of women's faculties, thinks that they could do as much if they tried but that while the men are there the work might as well be left to them and women content themselves with culture and children. She has, I think, a warmer heart and a larger mind than her husband's but naturally enough she has not the faculty of acquisition so fully developed. There is a serenity, an unself-consciousness, a trustworthiness in her face that is exceedingly attractive. Altogether she is lovable, a woman with many abiding friendships both with men and with women. The home life is perfect, the outside life full of intellectual interest and moral refinement. Neither husband nor wife are in the least interested in industrial questions and their society in this way is purely restful. We parted affectionately with hopes of future meetings. One never knows how relationships will develop but if mine with them is favoured by circumstances it may become one of the more attractive friendships of

256

my life. On both sides there is, I think, cordial liking and perfect ease in each other's company.

*17 August.* [The Argoed]
Tomorrow our Monmouthshire farmhouse fills with wedding guests. Rosy and Dyson on Monday to be made man and wife. The last marriage of the Potter girls – 'for you know that other Miss Potter is a confirmed old maid and has taken to writing and statistics, etc.; you would have hardly thought it, would you, from looking at her ten years ago. Some say she was the prettiest of the lot, but then she took to queer ways and that never pays.' 'Ah, but it wasn't that,' says a spiteful mother of unmarried daughters. 'She wanted to make a great marriage and failed.' So thinks the world. Meantime the two young people go on their way rejoicing – Rosy blushing and blooming, Dyson somewhat nervous as behoves a good young man about to become a husband. Good in that way I believe the young fellow is, and quite harmless in other ways – would break none of the ten commandments except the 1st, 3rd and 4th of the subject matter of which he knows naught. He has even the milder virtue of kindliness in his judgement of men and things, a certain shifty tolerance of this shifty world. Small and of insignificant build, weak-eyed and rapidly going bald with features and manners betokening infirmity of purpose rather than deficiency of mind, an intellect wrapt up in the cant of current agnosticism and radicalism, with no aims, no God, no nothing, except a certain warm affectionateness of disposition and a form of cleverishness. Depressed, chronically depressed as a man who lacks a God, a life-purpose, or animal spirits of the kind and the degree to play the Devil must needs be. In short – a nonentity. . . .

In this entry Beatrice is referring to her first meeting with Chamberlain.

*21 August.* [The Argoed]
The wedding passed off very happily. Old Miss Williams, the virtual mother (the real mother is a nonentity), who is the fairy godmother endowing the young people with means of livelihood, is a pleasant sociable old lady who has seen a good deal of the life of her own class. She is rich and loves to be acquainted with *interesting* men and women (Ah! how well I remember that dinner at her house – the introduction before dinner – the sudden attraction on both sides – the first beginning of years of misery!). . . . A shy boy (brother to Dyson), a smart semi-Russian cousin and his sister, Kitty Holt [Beatrice's

niece], the Leonard Courtneys and the Hobhouses made up the party. Dyson distinguished himself by a clever little speech at the breakfast and during the whole time showed to advantage. The parishioners and tenantry gave Rosy an ovation: the wedding itself was the prettiest of sights and she and her young man departed with the good wishes of all, of high and low degree.

Now the Williams family have left. The Courtneys and Mary Playne, Kitty [Holt] and Bill [Mary Playne's son] are here. The Courtneys are thoroughly satisfactory. Leonard's presence is always bracing though I never speak to him except in chaff. . . . So I bask in his presence! and he in return has an affection for me though not equal to his affection for the charming young Kitty. Miss Kitty is a slim, graceful girl. . . . She longs for a Career (with a big C) little knowing, poor child, the strain, the loneliness, the patient endurance needful to make even a little headway in work. Evidently just at present she envies me! Poor child! Bill is 6ft 3 and broad in proportion. With his black eyes and swarthy complexion he is attractive, even at the most unattractive age of 17. It is impossible to say what he will become. . . . He is perfectly straight in all ways: loves games and sport, has ambition in his work with plenty of sense and the signs of ability. His weakness is love of popularity, [a liking] for tip-top people, [and] a general easy-goingness of disposition (which comes from being universally liked).

Mary and Kate talk personalities all day. The more I see of other people the more I realize how utterly unintellectual we are as a family, considering of course our (great!) ability. Mary, though strikingly clever in all she does and says, simply dissipates in outrageous personalities and personal feelings. She worships *success*, though possibly as years go on the higher forms of success monopolize her reverence. I know she would always be loyal and affectionate, but her judgement would entirely and exclusively depend on the world's verdict. She listens to that first, and then with her great ingenuity argues that in all instances it is always just – if there is failure there is always moral deficiency, if success always moral greatness. And her success and failure are the success and failure of today – the floating on the surface of public opinion, not the deep undercurrents which determine the directions of the world's thought, feeling and action. 'I like to be *de mon temps*' is her characteristic phrase.

And now I am left alone – the last and only Potter! I am well started in work. My beginning is not brilliant, but it is sound. . . . The next

paper is of a different sort and will probably attract more attention –
possibly too much attention for my comfort! There is nothing in it but
bright description of an audacious adventure. Unhappily it is connected in my mind with a false step: the inaccuracy of my evidence
before the 'Lords'. The fear that this may be dwelt on by my enemies
in the Press haunts me vaguely. . . . Self-consciousness and vanity –
absence of a sensitive conscience in questions of truth – are still the
great stumbling-blocks of my nature. Can I overcome them? Watch
and pray.

*27 August.* [The Argoed]
The clouds look as if they were gathering. God help me!

*28 August.* [The Argoed]
Early morning. One of those horrible nights of self-torture: heart
palpitating the night through, the mind one mass of whirling
possibilities all of them of the nightmare type, the mouth parched.
And then, unless I conquer it by turning my mind vigorously to other
things, a day of restlessness haunted by the fears born in the morbid
hours of the night. I shall not easily forget that time at Dewsbury after
I had realized my 'false step' (for at first I thought it a slight
inaccuracy of no consequence). I was living in the midst of new life,
apparently in the highest of spirits, listening and talking with avidity.
But throughout a horrible pain was gnawing at my consciousness. I
tossed about during the night, if I sank into a doze I woke up in a cold
perspiration. All day I rushed from my own thoughts only to meet
them at every corner. At last, on that journey down to Monmouth I
had become a prey to mania. I lost all control and the laudanum bottle
loomed large as the dominant figure. Then there was a reaction: and in
a few days my work and the effort it needed had turned aside the
current of self-torturing energy. And yet there is no outward sign of
this inward misery. I seem to others calm, collected and usually in the
highest spirits. In the end of course I bear the signs of extreme
physical strain written on my face, but no one could tell that the
physical strain arose from mental misery.

As a child I had it – once during my girlhood – and then for four
years I was simply a prey to it. Twice it has led me into deep waters of
humiliation which will be an everlasting memory to me. It is my
nethermost being of despairing self-consciousness. There is only one
spirit that quells it – religion, the consciousness of a great Father, the

judge of all things, the consciousness of an immortal soul chastened by suffering, strengthened by repentance. . . .

It is strange that the spirit of religion always dwells on an unmarried life devoted to work rather than on the restful usefulness of wifehood and motherhood. Sometimes I wonder whether it is inflation, but the consciousness of a special mission, of duty to society at large rather than to individuals, is constantly present with me in my better moments, ceasing only when I am a prey to passion, self-consciousness or egotism. . . .

And it is partly the consciousness of a special mission, this faith in my own capacity, that brings a strained feeling into many of my relationships, even to my nearest and dearest friends. To them, whenever I hint at it, the whole idea seems ridiculously out of proportion with what they know of my abilities. And their perception of the incongruity is reflected in my mind, and I wake up to moments of self-dissatisfaction and cynicism which are keenly painful. But for the most part I hide this faith away and my best friends know not the nature of the spirit that moves me slowly but inevitably to Special Usefulness or to Life-failure. Work while it is yet day: for the night tarrieth not.

Multitudes of men and women must have this consciousness of a special mission. . . . In too many cases it *must* be mere self-will, a desire to avoid the daily duties of life and claim more exciting and pleasurable occupation. And yet, in my own case, however sternly I examine myself I cannot dissociate the desire to do this special work with the spirit of religion, with all that is best and highest in me. It needs to be chastened, to be freed from ambition and vanity, but it must still remain the central motive of my life.

*30 August.* [The Argoed]
I feel as if I could not set to work until the suspense is over. Oh, how hard any kind of publicity is to a woman, and yet how can one avoid it? It is a sort of fact that follows me in my work, in my friendships, even in the depth of passion.

An unsigned article entitled 'The Glorified Spinster' appeared in the issue of *Macmillan's Magazine* of September 1888.

*3 September.* [The Argoed]
A bundle of nerves truly!

Have started another note-book, portraits of the men and women I meet – their appearance, gesture, style of conversation, and as much of their history and character as can be jotted down. Someday it may be useful, for I intend to relieve my statistical and economic studies with 'sketches from life'. Anyway it is intensely interesting to *realize* other lives: to make men and women into moving figures within your mental vision, always to be summoned when you are weary of work, when you are lonely – or still more – in those dark hours of egotistical brooding. . . .

I am idling, idling away my time. The very consciousness that there is work, and plenty of it to my hand, inspires me with an intense longing to dream away my days over miscellaneous reading.

Just parted with Ella Pycroft at Tintern [railway station in the Wye valley near The Argoed] and a bitter, cold drive back. She and I have read with amusement a cleverish paper on 'glorified spinsters' in *Macmillan's*. 'A new race of women not looking for or expecting marriage.' 'Self-dependent, courageous, and cool-headed.' Ah, poor things.

*14 September.* [The Argoed]
My 'Pages of a Workgirl's Diary' has been very successful, and no unpleasant consequence has resulted from the publication of it. The success, indeed, has been out of all proportion to the literary merit. It was the originality of the 'deed' that has taken the public, more than the expression of it. However, it seems clear that the little literary faculty I have is of the narrative and picture-making form.

This little success has made me very happy, and if I can only keep my head and heart devoted to work, if I can resist all inclination to rest on my oars, all inflation from a tiny success coming after years of depression, I may be both happy and useful while I have health and freedom to work.

'Glorified spinsterhood' is at present gilded, gilded by the charm of novelty and youth. Dark times will come again; days of weary loneliness, of physical depression, of the decay of all personal charm (the most precious gift of womanhood), times when work and relationships grow every day more and more prosaic. Then both happiness and usefulness will depend on the consciousness of good work done and good work doing. I need the prayer more in success than I did in failure: God help and guide me!

*15 September. Standish*
Across the fields from the station every step I take reminds me of some

other time. One memory is deeply engraven. An afternoon in the summer after Mother died: then as now I came from The Argoed. It was a glorious evening . . . all this beauty without – and within? The first enthusiasm of youth tasting the delights of the passion for truth. I stood still; it seemed as if a voice from above blessed me and bid me go on my way and turn neither to the right nor the left. And today I am again standing on that same spot . . . the whole scene the same – and yet how changed! And I myself? No longer in the first enthusiasm of youth: in the middle years of womanhood. The life dedicated to the search after truth no longer an aspiration but a fact. The illusion . . . rolled away. And in their place? The peacefulness of resignation, the passion of a woman's nature burnt out: in its stead – persistent effort for an unknown humanity.

*9 October*. [The Argoed]
Gave up my papers for Charles Booth in despair, and spent the time in reading Lecky and Burke instead. Half from indolence, and half from a feeling that I had secured all I wanted from that bit of work and that I ought to turn my attention to reading up the past for my 'History of Co-operation'. Accepted an invitation to read a paper at Oxford to a women's trade union. Written long letter to *Times* on home-work and the sweating system.

Robert Holt was Beatrice's brother-in-law. Lord Granville (1815–91) was an eminent lawyer and judge, Foreign Secretary under Gladstone and leader of the Liberal Party in the House of Lords. Arthur Hobhouse (1819–1904) was a Q.C. who was given a peerage in 1885 and became an alderman of the London County Council in 1889. He was uncle and guardian to Henry Hobhouse.

*21 October*. [Liverpool]
Three days at Liverpool. Robert as chairman of the Liberal Association entertaining Lord Granville, Lord Hobhouse and a Mr Cross. Liverpool worthies in and out all day. It is amusing to see our dear genial, ugly and essentially middle-class sister talking at cross-purposes with the urbane and polished ex-Foreign Minister. He is an inconsiderable man, pleasant enough. But mental insignificance, joined to great political position, is irritating to a democratic mind. He, like most 'Society men', doesn't care for the likes of me, and until last night he had not addressed me. But he came up (I having appeared in a pretty black gown) while I was discussing vehemently labour

questions with Mr Cross, with whom I had struck up a friendship. Lord Granville listened with a sort of puzzled air, and when I, out of politeness, tried to bring him in, and explained to him the actual point we were thrashing out, he looked still more utterly at sea, as if I had asked him to join us in conversing on Chinese metaphysics. What could a woman, who really by night light looked quite pretty, want with such questions! Still less, how could she expect a polished man of the world to know what she was talking about? So the noble Earl stood silently gazing in mild surprise. . . .

With Lord Hobhouse I had a great deal of conversation – sympathetic conversation. Liked him better than I have ever done before, and I think he returned the compliment. There is a genuine ring about him. He is dull, wanting in play of mind, and totally deficient in humour, but he is thoughtful and conscientious to an almost painful degree. He interests me as Henry's uncle and as a more typical and finer example of the *genus* Hobhouse.

*25 October.* [The Argoed]
Two friends soon to be married, both of whom I looked on as settled in 'glorified spinsterhood' – Ella to Maurice Paul, and Carrie Darling to her old love, Mr Murdoch, each marrying a man many years younger than herself. Ah, women!

*26 October.* [The Argoed]
Five months here have passed quickly and happily, half in work, half in idleness. It has been a very happy time – Rosy married (what a blessing!), Father happy, and the family plans matured (whereby I get six months' freedom for work) and I, with my foot well on the ladder. . . . My life must be summed up in the two words: Work and Pray. . . .

*31 October.* [Stratford Place?]
First night in London. For these months of coming work, I take as my motto: Singlemindedness, humility, discretion. These three virtues shall be my moral aim. God help me.

*3 November.* [Stratford Place?]
The paper for the Oxford trades union meeting has cost me sufficient. It ought to be successful. It took at least a week's hard work writing it. . . . I do it principally to give myself confidence in public

263

speaking, and if I failed I should lose all heart. It is needful for my work to be able to speak on occasion. . . .

In dreadful perplexity about my work. Charlie wants me to do 'Women's Work at the East End' and have it ready by March, which means sacrificing part of February to writing. . . . It would indefinitely postpone Co-operation. On the other hand, 'Female Labour' is a subject of growing importance, one which for practical purposes is more important than Co-operation. It touches very nearly on home industries, a subject fraught with interest considered by the light of the steady cry for labour regulation. Then the work is needed to complete Charlie's book and I owe him consideration. I have already a mass of material in my head which could be used for it and it would be doing the work which lieth to my hand instead of seeking far afield for it. . . .

Chamberlain's marriage to Mary Endicott was to take place in Washington on 15 November.

*7 November.* [Stratford Place?]
The blow has come. I thought the nerve was killed: it was only deadened, deadened and dying, dying in the life of new and growing interests. Another fortnight or three weeks and it will be dead. And instead of pain slight contempt and good wishes for their happiness.

*8 November.* [Oxford]
The *reading* of my paper was successful and I have broken the ice and now feel free to speak when the spirit moves me. The paper itself was a little above and beyond the working women's comprehension and it was not *popular* in its tone. But my nervousness left me and my voice sounded well. If I have something to say I now know that I can say it and say it well.

*10 November.* [Oxford]
Delightful two days at Oxford. Far more beautiful than I expected. Leisure, culture, historical association, architectural beauty and the eternal youthfulness of the University with the immortality of the past – all that makes life charming and attractive. . . . Still, the whole time I walked about with a bit of cold steel in my heart and at nights I tossed about with the heat and discomfort of feverishness from a festering sore. Oh, it is hard to bear.

And yet when one looks at it, it is better for me. My work will be the better for it. And it is better for him. Surely it is pure egotism to suffer so intensely. . . . The past affects only me, personally, not my work, and though there is much to regret deeply and eternally, yet it was not any sin on my part; it was too much candour, too much feeling. The whole thing, no doubt, arose from faults, grave faults, but the pain will be worth suffering if it cures these, if it cures them before they interfere with my work. That, and that alone, I have now to live for, day and night.

*14 November.* [Stratford Place?]
The eve of his marriage. This afternoon I spent in Westminster Abbey listening half-dazed to the solemnly intoned prayers, and to the heights and depths of the anthem. . . . I prayed for their happiness, that the love of a good woman might soften and comfort him, inspire him with pure motive in the days of success and tenderly protect him in the hours of gloom and depression. And that she, poor child, might resist all temptation to become hardened with the glare and glamour of great position and great possessions. It is almost happiness to think that he is happy after these long years of hard suffering and hardening ambition. The pain to me – for alas we are all human – seems at times melted into a glow of satisfaction in his softened feeling. If he could only *feel* my sympathy and *understand* it. God bless them.

*15 November.* [Stratford Place?]
2 a.m. Awake – thinking of their future. This marriage will, I think, decide his fate as a politician. He must become a Tory. The tendencies of his life are already set in that direction: hatred of former colleagues, sympathy with the pleasure-loving attractive class of 'English gentlemen' with which he now associates. She will see entirely through his eyes; by her sympathy with his injured feelings against his old party she will intensify the breach; by her attraction to the 'good society' she will draw him closer to the aristocratic party. She is, besides, an American aristocrat, and like the aristocrats of a new country is probably more aristocratic in her tastes and prejudices than the aristocrats of the old country. Her ambition, too, will be social rather than political. Politics are at a discount in America. Society is everything. All this if the marriage be happy, as I think it will be as far as they two are concerned. If it is unhappy, if it means friction, God only knows where he will go to. Morally he would be utterly

ruined. In despair and bitterness of heart, he might become the reddest radical, and sit again as an 'English Robespierre'; politically this would mean hopeless discredit. Unless she be a woman of real genius the middle course, the quiet re-adoption of the old [friends?], will be impossible to him.

5 p.m. It must be over: and they are man and wife. . . .

### [16?] *November. 2 Stratford Place*

Willie Cripps is wonderfully kind to me; he sees that I am suffering acutely and nothing can exceed the delicate consideration with which he treats me. . . .

A long morning at the British Museum reading up *Jewish Chronicles* and suchlike. The Reading Room has a 'homey feeling': it was there in the spring of '85 that I first recovered my thirst for knowledge and again felt the passion for truth overcoming all other feeling. It is filled with ugly nonentities, the 'failures of life', but for the most part they seem mesmerized by the atmosphere of untold knowledge and unfathomable experience (which haunts the home of millions of books) into a sort of listless content. There you see decrepit men, despised foreigners, forlorn widows and soured maids, all knit together by a feeling of fellowship with the great immortals. . . .

### 18 *November.* [Stratford Place?]

A long morning at St Paul's: the Holy Communion afterwards. Lunched at the Cathedral Tavern and walked from the city to visit Maggie Harkness alone in her little bedroom in Gower Street. Tomorrow intend to 'pull myself together' and begin work in good earnest.

### *Epitaph* [on Chamberlain]

Courage: masculine strength: ability to execute and manipulate: intense egotism, showing itself on one side by a strong desire for personal power, on the other by a love of ease, luxury and splendour. Bitterly resentful of personal slight or personal injury. Originally religious and enthusiastic. The loss of his dearly loved wife seemed to him a death warrant to his faith in a personal God: a clear and sufficient proof that no God, who treated him so badly, could exist, or if he existed, deserved worship. A second loss matured his bitterness. From lost happiness he turned to love of power. All forces, within and without, were bent to his object. But his intense sensitiveness to his own wrongs was not tempered by any corresponding sensitiveness to the feelings and the rights of others. Right and left, as he ascended the ladder of political life, he kicked at those beneath him and flung those above him to the ground if they interfered with his progress. On the other hand his personal charm won him a few friends, devoted and true. To these friends he has always been loyal. But he made secret enemies on all sides. The working-class leaders saw in him an instrument of great power, and for a time they looked upon him as their future leader; but they never trusted his single-mindedness, they always suspected his ambition. The time came when he thought himself strong enough to try on the Crown. He over-rated his position – the democracy remained faithful to the old leader. Hisses and groans now greeted the name of Chamberlain. He turned with wounded feelings from his love of power and pursued pleasure. The democracy like God Almighty had shown itself oblivious of his claims, ungrateful for his sacrifice. In his pursuit of personal pleasure he has ignored utterly the feelings of others. He has gained present happiness. Will he rest in it? Has he found a mate to his nature, one who will see only with his eyes and believe firmly and implicitly in the single-mindedness and purity of his aims, one who will attract him back to the old lines of activity for without power he will be restless and discontented, without happiness he will be bitter? His whole life has been a grasping after personal power and personal pleasure: he has seemed to *attain*, but in each instance he has won, not to possess, but to lose.

One great quality, warm devotedness to those who devote themselves body and soul to him. *This* is the secret of his family's devotion: this may secure to him married happiness.

*24 November*. [Stratford Place?]
A week of utter nervous collapse. It is strange that a being who will henceforth be an utter stranger to my life should be able to inflict such intense pain – pain which cannot be controlled but only silently borne with. . . .

*28 November*. [Stratford Place?]
Hard at work at the Jewish community, seeing Jews of all classes all day long. Now that Charles Booth has no more work for me to do, I feel much inclined to work out my original idea – the actual nature of economic science. I shall have to read up for it for about a year. . . .

Then Co-operation must be looked into – trade unionism too. Plenty of work before me if I have only the courage, strength and ability to do it.

*1 December. Devonshire House Hotel*
A whole month of my free time gone, and only just begun work in good earnest. It is refreshing to be back again at the old quarters, with purely working associations. November is always a bad month for me. I suffer from the depths of physical depression, and this November the most exquisite mental torture has been added to it. However, it is over. Onward!

*8 December.* [Devonshire House Hotel]
Making a certain headway with my subject, and settled on my work for the next two years (!) – a thoroughly exhaustive study of Co-operation. I shall work under Benjamin Jones. The last fortnight has been uphill, lonely work, with strength hardly sufficient to bear up against the mental misery, but I am beginning to feel peaceful about it and to lose my bitterness, which at times has been horribly intense. . . .

Hubert Llewellyn Smith (1864–1945) was an Oxford statistician, a resident of Toynbee Hall, and one of Charles Booth's collaborators; he became an eminent civil servant in the Board of Trade. The 'runners' were touts for labour agents and lodging-house keepers who battened on the ignorance of immigrants, and they were normally paid on commission.

*16 December.* [Devonshire House Hotel]
A fiasco! A cold winter's morning at 6 o'clock. I sally out into the streets with Llewellyn Smith (a Toynbee man and fellow-statistician) under the guidance of an official of the Jewish Board of Guardians. Our object is to see the arrival of the immigrant Jews; the official who conducts us spends his life in meeting trains and boats to save the young women from extortion (or worse) at the hands of the runners who make their livelihood by preying on incoming foreigners. . . . Llewellyn Smith is a clever, ambitious young Oxford graduate, has worked his way to college and kept himself from an early age. He is formal-minded but has ability, and is generous in his helpfulness to others working on the same lines. He and I are good friends and working *camarades*, with that pleasant cordial relationship that is possible with a young fellow many years younger than oneself. So,

after all, the time of waiting from 8.30 to 12 o'clock, of fruitless waiting, passes not unpleasantly. We talk a little . . . we laugh a great deal. . . . At last 12 o'clock – and we give up. Our poor little guide looks pathetically sorry for our bad luck. We leave him walking to and fro. 'I dare not sit down, I should go to sleep. The boat *must* come in – but I may have to wait here all day.' The runner wrapt in a warm coat trimmed with astrakhan comfortably ensconced in an armchair by the waiting-room fire, like a fat spider waiting for his prey.

[Don was Beatrice's dog.]

*Xmas* [The Argoed]
Alone! At the Argoed: Spending my Christmas Day with Don.

*29 December.* [The Argoed]
In bed with tooth-ache and neuralgia, after a somewhat melancholy attempt to write the first page of my Jewish Community. Obliged to go to London to have the tooth attended to before I can hope for peace. As I am too feeble to write on a 'subject' let me end this volume of my diary with the personal reminiscences of the year.

Well! my dear, if notoriety be desirable as a preliminary step in a literary career, you have achieved it! Enough and to spare of mention of you in the daily papers: why, even a bogus interview with you telegraphed to America and Australia. But how much of that is the frothy foam raised by your plunge into an original adventure? . . . But anyway you have learnt one lesson: personal notoriety with its attendant social distinction, with its little train of would-be friends and acquaintances, proves to be as much an 'illusion' as the charming house in London turned out to be in 1884, for a slightly different reason. A working life means to a woman with little strength seclusion from society; you cannot enjoy what you have won in the way of social position, even if you cared to. On the other hand, there remains the solid satisfaction in the *doing of the work*, the growing and widening interests, the delight of the handicraftsman in the tools he is beginning to handle with ease. With a juster estimate of your true strength, with a certainty that you can do marketable work, and yet with an effectual cooling of those exalted dreams of possible achievement, the element of Peace enters into your life. . . .

So, Friend, you have every reason to write to me cheerfully with regard to what you are pleased to call your Work. As for the life of Feeling during the last year; you have suffered some terribly sharp twinges. But even here you have reason to be grateful. That black cloud which has overhung your life these six years has at last rolled away, bursting, it is true, with a terrific flash and peal of thunder. Ah! it began as a small speck on a bright summer's day. Those warm sunlit hours of qualified vanity and growing passion – how you revelled in them! To you the first burst of spring after the dull cold time of an unloved and struggling youth. And then cruel mortification, ending in mutual disgust and permanent separation. Still, in spite of painful reminiscences, in spite of tooth-ache and loneliness, you begin the New Year with courage and hopefulness. You are at peace with your own conscience. You try to do your best, neither God nor man can ask for more. And in return, pray for the strength that will enable you to work, for the guidance which will inspire you to work well and wisely. Implore the help of the three guardian angels of intellectual effort – truth-desire, patient work, humility. God help you!

## VOLUME 13
### ∽ 1889 ∾

*8 January.* [The Argoed]
The best wishes to you, Book 13 of my life! May you be fuller of interest, less egotistical than former volumes. Hard at work on the paper on the Jewish community and more than halfway through. Resting for 24 hours before I begin the second part in good earnest.

On 9 January, Beatrice inserted a cutting from an unnamed newspaper about the new Mrs Chamberlain, and wrote: 'Every Romance has a conclusion. This is the end to the romance of four volumes of my life!'

*14 January.* [Longfords]
Invalided: brain sickness, cold, loneliness, and the horrible stench of a dead rat have driven me from my mountain home into the comfortable house of my 'Playne' sister. Arthur and Bill rescued me, cheered me with their companionship and brought me back with them. Ah me! The wound will heal, time only is needed; the scar will remain there.

*21 January.* [London]
A pleasant time at Longfords and back to London with my paper not

quite finished but in a hopeful condition. Think it will more than satisfy Charles Booth and will prove one of the 'attractions' of the book.

Alice Green (1847–1929) was the widow of the historian John Richard Green (1837–83) and she also wrote on historical themes. Irish-born, and a keen Home Ruler, in 1921 she became a senator of the new Irish Free State. After the introduction of public elementary education in 1871 control was vested locally in elected school boards. The campaign for the eight-hour day was now winning considerable support among trade unionists. Herbert Spencer was boarding with Mr and Mrs Grant Allen at Dorking for nine months until March 1889.

*11 February.* [London]
56 George Street, Portman Square. Pleasant little lodgings with the faithful Neale [her maid] to look after me. Just beginning Co-operation: a two years study! Seeing a few friends in a quiet way. I had a long talk the other day with John Morley. He is anxious about the Socialists at Newcastle. Up to now he has treated them with indifference, not to say contempt, but they mustered good votes at the last School Board election and John Morley began to take them seriously. When I talked to him he was preparing for an interview at Newcastle and was full of the eight hours movement and other social questions. In his speeches he says 'social question' is the one thing to live for. . . . And yet he has evidently never thought about 'social questions': he does not know even the ABC of labour problems. Oh! ye politicians!

A week with the poor philosopher. In the same state of body, but his mind is acclimatized to it and I think on the whole he is happy. Long walks I had over the Downs at Dorking, watching the effects of cloud, storm and sunshine.

Mrs Johnny Green, the historian's widow (and a lady of intellectual as well as social distinction) is courting me! poor little me! She has called twice in one week and seems to wish to see me every day – suggests I should live with her. She has a wizened face – ugly usually, attractive at times – reminds me of a mediaeval picture; only, unfortunately, one knows it is not only 'bad drawing' that distorts her features. Colourless hair and an acid expression, perpetual discontent written on her face, the rest of her nature an enigma. She has a weird mind, seldom speaks well of her friends, describes their faults with more sharpness of outline than is charitable and submerges their virtues in sentences implying personal affection as the origin of her appreciation.

Miss Souvestre, the brilliant Frenchwoman, comes to see me. She was for a time an intimate friend of Mrs Green's, now has broken with her, says she is not to be understood, has only one characteristic – vanity. Her sudden affection for me, Miss Souvestre says, is a wish to meet a rising sun! Oh, charming Frenchwoman. However, you are at other times frank. '*Mai oui: vous avez fait un succès avec 'Pages of a Workgirl's Diary'; mais comme le Public Anglais est bête!!*'

*21 February.* [London]
Sad the drifting away of friends. Maggie [Harkness] who is offended that I am offended at her publication of a silly story about me and Herbert Spencer. It was an unpardonable act, but still I have forgiven her and she might forgive me. Probably we shall be firm friends again, for though I do not trust her, I love her and she loves me: we have the same troubles and the same difficulties, the same eternal struggle without result. Then the Booths. It would be strange if the close personal friendship between me and the husband had not ended. Mary has been generous, thoroughly generous, but for the last year the warm affection between us has been cooling. She has discouraged me from coming to them when they are alone, and I, sensitive to the least feeling on her side, have kept away. We have both been in London for some months and I have seen Charlie once. Mary and I have seen each other but I feel it is *forced* on her side and no longer a pleasure. I went yesterday by appointment for a chat with her, but she had filled the room with other friends, probably she forgot that she promised me a free afternoon. I felt it the more as I wanted to ask her advice and needed comfort, but she was absorbed in a new friend for whom she has the same feeling as she used to have for me. So after an hour's desultory talk I left, choking with disappointed and wounded feeling, for I am very fond of her and hate breaking ties. Charlie I could have given up but *she* has been so much to me. Now it rests with her whether or not the friendship is to be renewed – if she does not *really* wish it, it will be dropped.

Indeed it is doubtful whether warm sentimental friendships even with women are desirable. When you must face life alone, it is better not to deceive yourself with an apparent one-ness of thought and feeling. It can only be temporary; the circumstances of life are too utterly different; there is no real communion of interests and therefore there can be no permanent tie. With another unmarried or childless woman the circumstances of life are much the same as yours; there is a similarity, if not a communion of interests, so the tie is likely to be more lasting. But in the nature of things it cannot be secure, and when the breach comes it is all the more painful. Religious feeling, communion with unknown spirits, beings without ties, creatures of your own imagination who are to you always what you would have them be, are the only safe companions to the lonely mind.

Beatrice Chamberlain had written to Beatrice in November 1888 asking to see her, but Beatrice had put her off. Arabella Fisher wrote to Beatrice on 21 February advising her to see Chamberlain's daughter – 'but do not draw the tie too close'; to ask the Rylands to visit The Argoed late in the year; and to allow the new Mrs Chamberlain to call if she wished. 'The mere fact that you hate seeing any of them is a proof that you should do so in its proper time and place and live it down,' she added; and she gave Beatrice stern advice. 'You have something to *kill*. Kill it deliberately, and you will gain strength for future work and happiness.'

*28 February*. [London]
I have acted on her advice and written to ask Beatrice [Chamberlain] to come and see me. I wonder whether she would have said the same had she known all. I think so. Anyway I will obey her instructions as if they were words from on high. In the great crisis of life one willingly accepts the judgement of another: if I had only been guided by some strong perceiving woman. If I had had a mother or a sister to whom I could have confessed all! As it is I will struggle through as a self-enforced penance, as an atonement for the vanity, vulgar ambition and want of womanly reticence and self-control. God help me, and make it not *too* hard for me.

Alfred Marshall (1842–1924) was appointed Professor of Political Economy at Cambridge in 1884 and he became a leading authority on labour economics. His *Principles of Economics* was published in 1890. H. S. Foxwell (1849–1936) was Professor of Political Economy at University College, London.

*8 March*. [London]
Delightful visit to the Creightons at Cambridge. The interesting part of my visit was a long talk with Professor Marshall, first at dinner at the Creightons', then at lunch at his own house. We began by chaff about men and women, he holding that woman was a subordinate

being, and that, if she ceased to be subordinate, there would be no object for a man to marry, that marriage was a sacrifice of the masculine freedom and would only be tolerated by male creatures so long as it meant the devotion, body and mind, of the female, and no longer. Hence the woman must develop in no way unpleasant to the man: that strength, courage, independence were not atttractive in women, that rivalry in men's pursuits was positively unpleasant. Therefore masculine strength and masculine ability in women must be firmly trampled upon and 'boycotted' by men. *Contrast* was the essence of the matrimonial relation: feminine weakness contrasted with masculine strength, masculine egotism with feminine self-devotion. Naturally enough I maintained the opposite argument; viz. that there was an ideal of character in which strength, courage, sympathy, self-devotion, persistent purpose were united to a clear and far-seeing intellect: that this ideal was common to the man and the woman, although the qualities composing it might manifest themselves in different ways in the man's and the woman's life, that what you needed was not different qualities and different deficiencies but the same virtues working in different directions and dedicated to the service of God in different ways.

At lunch we struck on serious ground. He said that he had heard that I was about to undertake a history of Co-operation. 'Did he think I was equal to it?' 'Now, Miss Potter, I am going to be perfectly frank. Of course I think you are *equal* to a history of Co-operation, but it is not what you can do best. There is one thing that *you*, and only *you* can do — an inquiry into that unknown field of female labour. You have (unlike most women) a fairly trained intellect, and the courage and capacity for original work, and yet you have the woman's insight into a woman's life. There is no man in England who could undertake with any prospect of success an inquiry into female labour. There are any number of men who could write a history of Co-operation, and who could bring to the study of a purely economic question more strength and knowledge than you possess . . . if you devote yourself to the study of your own sex as an industrial factor, your name will be a household word two hundred years hence; if you write a history of Co-operation, it will be superseded or ignored in a few years. . . .'

Of course I disputed the point, and tried to make him realize that I wanted this study of industrial administration as an education for economic science. The little man with bright eye shrugged his shoulders and became satirical on the subject of a woman dealing with scientific generalizations – not unkindly satirical but gently so. . . . Altogether I came away liking and liked (?), with gratitude for the little man's kindly way of stating his view, refreshed by his appreciation, and inclined to agree with him as to the slightness of my strength and ability for the work I had undertaken. Still, with that disagreeable masculine characteristic of a persistent and well defined purpose, I shall stick to my own way of climbing my own little tree. 'Female labour' *shall* be one of the principle inquiries of my life, but I will not undertake it at present. My peculiar qualities will grow of themselves; my weakness I will try to obviate.

*7 March.* [The Argoed?]
Ran down to see Father, who has had a slight apoplectic attack. He lies in his bed in a state of complete apathy. His life can no longer be a pleasure to him or to those around him; it would be merciful if he should be taken. But the breaking of the tie would be sad, inexpressibly sad to a lonely life like mine. Still, I long for a complete holiday which his death would enable me to take. . . . At present my strength seems worked out. It is with painful effort that I begin on Co-operation. I look at the detail to be mastered with positive repulsion, and I long every day more for the restfulness of an abiding love. And yet I cannot sacrifice work for which all the horrible suffering of six years has fitted me, and cannot forget the past. But I must not let myself get morbid over it. I must check those feelings which are the expression of physical instinct craving for satisfaction; but God knows celibacy is as painful to a woman (even from the physical standpoint) as it is to a man. It could not be more painful than it is to a woman.

*8 March.* [Devonshire House Hotel]
It is all right with the Booths. Mary and I had a long talk over the keeping and repair of friendship; the tendency of the freshness of interest of two people in each other wearing out and leaving them indifferent to each other's society and unconscious of each other's new growth. . . . My friendship or, rather, my companionship with Charlie is for the time dropped – our common work is ended. His brave vigorous life with its varied interests and unself-conscious and disinterested pursuit of them will always be an encouraging thought; his thoughtful kindness and true affection will always be one of the comforting memories of my life. But my friendship with him had run in advance of my friendship with his wife and it is good now it should

drop behind, for a time at least, and possibly take a permanent 'back place' in his mind.

J. J. Dent (1856–1936) was a bricklayer who became secretary of the Workingmen's Club and Institute Union. He was closely connected with the Co-operative Movement.

*10 March.* [Devonshire House Hotel]
My stay in London nearly at an end, and no work worth speaking of finished or even begun. These last months have been full of silent suffering. I have been unable to raise myself from a state of intellectual torpor, from a certain indecision and indifference. . . .

Seen something during my London stay of Burnett, Benjamin Jones and Dent – the three most distinguished of my working-men friends. My friendship with the two former is becoming a close one, and likely to endure as future work will bring us together. For Burnett I have a strong admiration. He is singularly disinterested with a reserve of thought and feeling, a dignity of manner which makes him attractive. Jones is on a lower plane, but he also is an enthusiast for the service of Humanity. . . .

Dined last night at the Frederic Harrisons and went with them to the Positivist Hall in the City. Frederic Harrison spoke on the text 'Live For Others'. He spoke bitterly of the jibes and sneers with which Comte's doctrine had been received. He pointed out that Positivism was the only sincere religious form of the present day; that all religions and sects were making the service of Humanity the keynote of religion, but they refused to recognize that they did so. The whole address seemed to me *forced* – a valiant effort to make a religion out of nothing, a pitiful attempt by poor Humanity to turn its head round to worship its tail. Practically we are all Positivists; we all make the service of Man the leading doctrine of our lives. But in order to serve Humanity we need the support and encouragement of a superhuman force above us towards which we are perpetually striving.

Beautiful communion service at St Paul's. While I knelt before the altar I felt that I had at length made my peace with my own past, that the struggle with bitter resentfulness which began as I knelt at the same altar the Sunday after his marriage had at last ended. . . . Auberon Herbert dropped in before lunch yesterday (Sunday). He was excited with the prospect of converting Mrs Besant to Spiritualism. She had written to him on his article in the *Pall Mall* and it will end probably in a visit to Old House. Strange an intimacy between these two natures; Mrs Besant, with her rabid socialism, embittered by personal suffering against both the morality and the creed of Christendom; Auberon Herbert, with his idealistic individualism, a nature softened, perhaps even weakened, by a perpetual dwelling on spiritual influences. While he and I were chatting in a friendly way, enter Miss Souvestre. The brilliant irreligious Frenchwoman looked with cold critical contempt on that strange figure of a man seated on the sofa, advancing in his soft weak voice untenable propositions. It ended in a heated discussion in which I hardened into the French-woman's style of quick logical dispute. Poor Auberon Herbert left with a pained expression and with not a favourable impression of the clever French schoolmistress and her influence on his friend.

After he had gone, Miss Souvestre softened into affectionate admiration and loving solicitude. She is a remarkable woman. Purely literary in her training, with the talent of brilliant expression, and the charm of past beauty and present attractiveness. She is a student of individual human natures, but she is deficient in the personal experience of religious feeling and public spirit; she watches these qualities in others with a strange combination of suspicion, surprise and unappreciative admiration. You feel that every idea is brought under a sort of hammering logic, and broken into pieces unless it can be sound metal, and if it belongs to the religious order and is proof against ridicule, it is looked at critically and laid carefully on one side for some future hostile analysis. In her frankly expressed and lucid criticism (from her own standpoint) she is a useful friend, more especially to those who live in a different world and who are liable to the self-deception of religious conviction. And then her warm-hearted and disinterested affection for many friends, her courage and original-ity in her own profession, her dependence on personal ties and the unsatisfied passion of her nature, trying to find relief in vivid intellectual interests – all these qualities render her attractive to those whose friendship she chooses to cultivate.

After a visit from Beatrice Chamberlain who, Beatrice said, 'tried her best to start intimate relations' and 'found a perfectly cordial determination to keep to the *status quo*', Beatrice fell to musing about the new Mrs Chamberlain. Claude Joseph Goldsmid-Montefiore (1858–1938) was a Jewish scholar and philanthropist. Sir Edward Grey (1862–1933), states-man and bird-lover, was a rising star in the Liberal Party and later became foreign secretary.

*13 March.* [London]

Society is full of talk about the bride. Maggie Hobhouse describes her as a perfectly dressed woman, with quiet, dignified manners, frank blue eyes, retroussé nose, lovely skin, pleasant smile, but with not much behind – in fact, insignificant. If she were not Mrs C., says Kate (who invited her to meet the nobs of the Unionist world) she would be a pleasant nobody, and even in her present position she will never become somebody. 'A little Puritan' the world dubs her; 'charming but not pretty', 'might have come out of a country Rectory', 'a strange choice for Chamberlain to make, looks a mere child' – these are the remarks that fly to and fro. Everywhere she goes the world flocks round her, finds nothing to criticize, but nothing especially to remark about except the absence of anything striking and a certain charm of modesty and simple goodness. 'He is so happy that he cares no longer for Society'; 'I congratulated him but he did not seem "hearty" over it'; 'the affection is most on her side' – these are the contradictory statements as to his view of his charming bride. 'Have *you* seen her?' asks everyone I meet, with a quick glance at my expression. 'No, I have not seen her, but I hear she is charming,' I answer with placid indifference. But if I am taken unawares my feeling is one of sick faintness.

Dined in the evening with the Francis Buxtons and met a party of aristocratic young people and one Jew whom I asked especially to meet – Claude Montefiore. I think I told him more about his East End fellow-religionists than he told me. 'It is a lower race, raised by a unique religion – this fact seems to warrant the faith in a supernatural origin' his one contribution. There was a good deal of brilliant talk. A young aristocrat, Sir Edward Grey, a charming fellow with a pretty wife, came and sat down by my side and plunged into essentials – described the intoxicating passion for sport, the constant friction in his life of the love of physical enjoyment and a true desire to lead a useful, purposeful life. He is amongst the most independent and upright members of the House of Commons and as universally respected as he is universally liked.

This morning I am weary with this existence of chatter, and shall go back to my simple working life with true delight though with little strength. So ends my stay in London!

*15 March. The Star Hotel, Manchester*

A commercial inn. Delightful to get in harness again. The Booths think my paper on the Jewish community the best thing I have yet accomplished. Courage!

John Mitchell (1828–95), Beatrice said in her autobiography, was 'the most remarkable personality who emerged from the Co-operative movement'. A textile worker, strong temperance man and lay preacher, he served for more than twenty years as president of the Co-operative Wholesale Society, receiving a salary of £150 a year for running what may have been the largest business enterprise in the country. J. C. Gray (1854–1912) came from Hebden Bridge where he was active in the Co-operative fustian mill. He became general secretary of the Co-operative Union in 1891. Beatrice was attending a Conference of the Hebden Bridge Fustian Society, then the most successful of the Co-operative production societies. In the second paragraph Beatrice was proposing a trade union for celibate working women: she had originally written 'college' and made an incomplete correction.

*25 March.* [Hebden Bridge, Yorkshire]
Three days at Hebden Bridge staying with the widow of an iron founder. . . . Hebden Bridge resembles Bacup in its fusion of the working and lower middle class. Upper class it has none. My interest was in the vigorous Co-operative life, and I saw much of Co-operation. . . . Back to Manchester by afternoon train and ran up to see Maggie Harkness in her lodgings. Poor Maggie gets bitterer and bitterer with the whole world – does foolish and inconsiderate things and then is vexed that she loses friends. Poor Maggie! with her lonely tortuous life and envious temper. And yet for those in trouble she has plenty of warm sympathy – true *mitgefuhl* – for the failures of society. If only she had religion, that haven of rest and peace for the lonesome worker, the one anchor in this life of strange dreams and feverish feelings. . . .

Boddington a small manufacturing village: works owned by large capitalist proprietors of old manufacturing family: is the direct opposite to Hebden Bridge and Bacup. Here is practically an aristocracy of manufacture. . . . It is a sort of patriarchal establishment. . . . People are contented and are fond of their masters. It was with one of these that I spent today. A bachelor of some forty years' standing, a good-natured dutiful man, with that sort of unsatisfactory cheerfulness peculiar to elderly bachelors. . . . Poor fellow! He evidently thought that I might be in the same plight, for our eight-hour interview ended up by a suggestion that I should consider partnership, that a life of investigation might well end in an active participation in the business I investigated. There ought to be a trade [union?] for the new celibate order of working women: otherwise with the best intentions one repays kindness by causing 'emotional perturbation' as the old philosopher calls it. This is the second one this year! About two a year who develop *serious* intentions. One consolation, a few years more and that sort of thing will cease. I shall not regret it, for it has always bored me, an unnecessary stumbling-block to a working *camaraderie* with men of all kinds and conditions.

Bacup. Among my dear old friends with their kindly simplicity. Cousin Titus is now married to a young girl, with sweet modest expression and gentle ways. . . .

Mitchell, chairman of the Wholesale, is one of the leading personalities in the Co-operative movement. Belonging to the small trading class, Mitchell is an enthusiast for the consumer's interests. . . . He supports himself on the past proceeds of a small woollen business, and draws perhaps 30s a week from the Wholesale to which he devotes his whole energies. . . . Taken as a whole he is a good fellow, and in his inflated way a true patriot, according to the lights of his one idea: the consumer's welfare. His Board are entirely subordinate to him; they are corpulent, heavy eaters but for the most part they are neither more nor less than simple tradesmen. They strike me as an honest set of men, above corruption and proud of their position of directors of the central organization of working-class capitalists.

Three or four times have I dined with the Central Board. A higgledy-piggledy dinner – good material served up grossly and shovelled down by the partakers in a way which is not *appetisant*. But during dinner I got at a lot of stray information through chaff and discussion. Occasionally I am chaffed in a not agreeable way about matrimony and husbands, and pointed allusions are made to the propriety of a match between me and Mitchell! But it is all good-natured, and I take it kindly. After dinner, in spite of the chairman's disapproval, we smoke cigarettes and our conversation becomes more that of business *camaraderie*. I am a general favourite with these stout, hard-headed but true-hearted men and they look upon me as a strange apparition in their midst, the why and wherefore they have not fathomed. . . .

Gray is the working secretary of the Co-op Union. He is a nice young men, that is your first impression; scrupulously turned out in Co-operative clothes made by a Co-op tailor. He is an idealist, looking at Co-operation not as a huge organized consumer's interest, but as a true and equitable co-operation between capital and labour. He is not a self-seeker; he is a refined and modest-natured man, though at times he has flights of ambition for a seat in the County Council or perhaps even in Parliament. . . . He and I have cigarettes together in spare moments of office work and talk philosophy, religion and politics as well as co-operation. He has an insignificant little wife whom he treats kindly but who is vastly inferior to him in general calibre – his children ditto. His home-life, like that of so many of these leaders of the working class, is a separate thing, satisfying just the domestic instinct and quite unconnected with the world of higher thought and religion or semi-religious feeling. Indeed, it is exactly this fact which accounts for the extraordinary hold which an attractive cultivated woman can get over superior working men; her friendship is a revelation to them of the most inspiring relation of man and woman. The working man has still the eighteenth-century idea of a wife for the relief of physical nature, for the bearing of children, and the ministering to his personal comforts. Suddenly he is introduced to the nineteenth-century woman with her masculine interests and her womanly charm, a womanly charm cultivated by her as an instrument of power in public life, in the movement of the masses, not as a means of satisfying personal vanity and love of admiration. To the woman who unites charm, ability and religious enthusiasm there will someday open out a great future in power for good. Possibly future generations may see a woman step out of the ranks as a saviour of humanity, a supreme incarnation of the Mother's instinctive wisdom for the welfare of her children and their descendants.

*12 April.* [Manchester]
Just one month of my Co-op investigation over. Beginning to see my way, though have hardly got over much actual ground. The last week I have been watching with acute interest the drama at Birmingham. It has a morbid fascination for me, watching exactly those qualities in his nature which gave me so much acute pain gradually undermining his political career. What will be the end of it? Will he succeed in spite of temper, vanity and absence of honourable dealing, or will his public life end in a complete collapse and utter failure? His temperament will hardly allow of his accepting a secondary role in any party. And if he fails, will the restful happiness of his home-life compensate him for loss of power?

*13 April.* [Manchester]

Leaving Manchester for Oldham tomorrow. Have on the whole enjoyed my life here: gained strength and vigour and determination. It has been interesting too to come on the track of the Potter brothers. Certainly they must have been remarkable men, for after half a century has passed away there are still strong traditions of public spirit, large benevolence and keen business ability gathered round their homes. Descent from the old stock of the first mayor is a passport to confidence and respect from business and working men. There is now only one thing I need to make my life satisfactory – to rule out of my consciousness two personalities, *Beatrice Potter and the man she cared for.*

Beatrice's visit to Oldham fell through: she went to Burnley to attend a Co-operative meeting of shareholders, and then returned to Manchester.

*17 April.* [Manchester]

I come back dead tired. As I sink into the armchair in my little lodging the old maid lodging-house keeper says exultantly: 'See, you are completely knocked up. You're only a woman: in spite of your *manly* brain, you're just as much of a woman as I am.' Poor genteel celibate! For days back you have been envying me my energy, and peering into *Life and Labour* on my table with my name standing out as a contributor. Still more, you have been reading the leaders in two London papers sent me by friends and you have been hardly able to contain yourself with silent envy. Now you have your revenge as I roll, tipsy with fatigue, up to bed. 'You're only a woman after all,' I hear her muttering as she collars my bag to save me exertion, feeling herself for once a superior. *'Poor weak woman with a man's brain,'* adds the old maid, trying to define the exact nature of her distinguished lodger.

While Beatrice was in Manchester the first volume of Booth's survey was published. It included Beatrice's papers on the docks, tailoring and the Jewish community. *The Times* called it the 'grimmest' book of the day. Its first volume was originally called *The Labour and Life of the People* and the more familiar title was adopted in 1892.

*21 April. Gracedieu*

'The book' a great success and Charles Booth delighted. Leaders in all the principal papers, and C.B. quite the head of the statistical tree!

*7 May. The Argoed*
Lovely dreamy weather: back to work, dictating notes to Miss Darling in the morning, reading two hours in the afternoon: four days a week my 'subject', two days English literature with a view to construction and the true meaning of words. . . .

*25 May.* [The Argoed]
Began my early-morning readings. This is my day: tea at 6 o'clock, study from 6 to 8 o'clock. Notes and chat till 11; Father till lunch. Cigarettes and bask in the sun, and a siesta after lunch. 3.30 to 5.30 study. Then a delightful walk or ride: supper, cigarette with Father; saunter in the moonlight or starlight; to bed at 10 o'clock. An alternation of vigorous study and dreamy restfulness – of sleep, exercise, food (including in food the delicious and well-beloved cigarettes!) and the enjoyment of natural beauty, the whole softened and humanized by devotion to that loving gentle nature with its gradually decaying power of body and mind. But the one inspiring influence is Faith – faith in the worthwhile of individual effort for the common good.

Francis Ysidro Edgeworth (1845–1926) became Drummond Professor of Political Economy at Oxford in 1891, and editor of the *Economic Journal*. Maria Edgeworth (1767–1849), the Irish novelist, spoke out strongly for the education of women. Beatrice reported Professor Alfred Marshall's patronizing comments to the Booths and received consoling responses. On 16 June, Charles Booth wrote to say, 'don't be alarmed at Professor Marshall's bogeys but go on quietly'; and four days later Mary Booth spoke of 'his fads in all that concerns the destinies and capacities of his sex'. Marshall himself sent a pleasant letter on 2 July regretting that Beatrice's energetic and thorough methods of work were not to be directed into a path 'on which the broad and heavy masculine foot cannot tread'.

*4 June.* [Devonshire House Hotel]
Francis Edgeworth (nephew to Maria Edgeworth) Professor of Political Economy at King's College, London: eminent statistician of the mathematical type, a gentle-natured and intellectual man with queer cramped nature, excessively polite and diffident in manner, formal and exact in phraseology – an old admirer and a present lover! Even if I had not my work, the prospect of a matrimonial engagement, and the preliminary receipt of addresses, bores me intolerably, a horrible sense of unreality in a relationship which seems to spring from chance and ripens without occasion for intimate knowledge on

either side. This man is pathetic: his somewhat pedantic and thoroughly conventional conversation, his starved affections, the furtive glance of unsatisfied desire peering through the old bachelor habits and appearance of forty-four years of celibate continence, the little stories from *Punch*, the correct literary reminiscences, the greenness in all that appertains to emotional experience – and yet, withal, a hidden fire burning within, which might burst forth and burn down conventional barriers and dry sticks and leave the ground free for a new spring growth of thoughts and feelings. Poor fellow! He bores me. And those relations with men stimulate and excite one's lower nature, for where one can give no real sympathy strong feelings in another seem to debase one and drag one down to a lower level of animal self-consciousness. How one despises oneself, giving way to those feelings (and over thirty too, – it would be excusable in a woman of twenty-five), but that part of a woman's nature dies hard. It is many variations of one chord – *the supreme and instinctive longing to be a mother*.

Beatrice went to the Co-operative Congress, held annually at Whitsuntide. Mrs Marshall was Mary Paley (1850–1944), one of the first students at Newnham College. She was a noted scholar, who was self-effacing in the interests of her husband's career.

*7 June.* [Ipswich]
A whirl down to Ipswich in a crowded excursion train. Arrived at the White Horse Inn with Burnett and Fielding (manager of the tea department). At the door my old friends of the Wholesale, with Mitchell at their head, welcomed me warmly. In the commercial room I find other Co-operators; an American professor and his wife, and the unfortunate lover [Edgeworth] who has followed me hither. . . . Forty of us were installed in this romantic Pickwick inn with its rambling passages and covered courtyard, and here other leading Co-operators congregated, drank whisky and smoked tobacco. At the Co-operative Congress there is an absolute equality. All live together on the freest of terms – food, excursions and business are all given and taken under the democratic co-operative system. . . . It is Sunday evening and we are all assembled in the long coffee room, scattered up and down in knots round the long table, some of us devouring cold beef and tea, others chatting together. In one of these parties, behold the hero of this year's Congress, the distinguished man whom working-men Co-operators have elected to give the inaugural

address – Professor Marshall of Cambridge. He looks every inch the professor. A small, slight man with bushy moustache and long hair, nervous movements, sensitive and unhealthy pallid complexion, and preternaturally keen and apprehensive eyes, the professor has the youthfulness of physical delicacy. In spite of the intellectuality of his face there is a lack of the human experience of everyday life which begets the full maturity of man. Not that the professor is a lonely celibate. That gentle unassuming lady, badly dressed with protruding teeth, weak eyes and quickly changing colour – a former student of Newnham [College] and present lecturer – who sits by his side, selects his food and guards him from obtrusions, is his wife. . . . Tonight his desire to gain information outweighs his nervous fear of a sleepless night, and he is listening with mingled interest and impatience to the modicum of facts dealt out in the inflated and involved phrases of the chairman of the Manchester Wholesale – Mitchell.

As I approach I am greeted by my old friend. 'Now, Miss Potter, come and join me in a cup of tea. I haven't seen anything of you this time. I was just telling the Professor my view of the true nature and real use of the great Co-operative movement'. . . . I turned to the group on the other side, including Benjamin Jones, astride a chair, Burnett leaning back with stately dignity, and Dent with his head half buried between his brawny arms and large, powerfully made, workman's hands. Dent and Jones were discussing vigorously. Burnett was listening with the weighty and responsible silence of a government official. These three men are typical and representative of the three great working-class movements. Jones of associations for trading purposes, Burnett of trade unions, and Dent of workingmen's clubs and of productive side of Co-operation. . . . 'Now, look you here, Dent' says Ben Jones in his confident, cheery manner. . . . 'The sooner we get out of our head that the Co-operator is the most unselfish of men, the better. . . . Come, Miss Potter, leave Mitchell to his tea, and come and help me to make Dent understand our view of the question.'

'There is another question Miss Potter has to explain to us, one for which she is far more responsible,' Dent remarks in a gruff tone but with a kindly light in his grey eye. 'Why she lent her influence to that appeal against the suffrage. I believe it is just this: she is satisfied with her own position, because she is rich and strong. She does not see that other women need the power to help themselves which would be given by the vote.' This I feel to be an unpleasant accusation especially as

Dent and I are old friends and he speaks seriously. But before I have time to advance in sober procession my arguments the little Professor in tones of nervous irritability intervenes:

'Miss Potter sees what the women's suffrage people don't see: that if women attempt to equal men and be independent of their guidance and control, the strong women will soon be ignored and the weak women simply starved. It is not likely that men will go on marrying, if they are to have competitors as wives. Contrast is the only basis to marriage and if that is destroyed we shall not think it worth while to shackle ourselves in life with a companion whom we must support and must consider.'

There are two sides to that question, think I, and the celibate condition of the human race can be begun by either party to the matrimonial contract. However, catching sight of the poor little wife's agonized look, (for female suffrage is a red rag to the Professor's somewhat feminine nerves and shrewish temper), I laughingly reply: 'Mr Marshall, I pity you deeply. You are obliged to come to the rescue of a woman who is the personification of emancipation in all ways, who clings to her cigarette if she does not clutch at her vote. Why do not you leave me to my fate? Convicted of hopeless inconsistency, I might even give up smoking in the hope of protecting myself against my rights.'

'That's just it,' whispers Jones, 'that's why these women are so bitter against you. It is pure perversity on your side, to say one thing and act another.' 'Surely, Mr Jones, I am simply taking a hint from your admirable method of controlling the Co-operative body, signing resolutions in favour of one policy, and acting according to another.' 'She's got you there, Jones', but the smile which plays across Dent's face gives way to the perplexed expression as he adds: 'I believe you are in earnest with your views. I should like some day to have it out with you; a clever strong woman like you must have some reasons to give, and I can't say I think much of those in the protest. Will you come down into the courtyard? Maxwell is there and some of the Scottish delegates: you might like to ask them some questions.'

'I will go anywhere for a cigarette', and the company disperses, the Marshalls retire to bed, we to the smoking-room where I spend the rest of a late evening in telling fortunes from hands, and in a stray search after facts in the chaff of a smoking-room conversation.

On the whole the Ipswich Congress is to me personally unsatisfactory. There is the queer, pedantic, unhappy statistician [Edgeworth] who dogs my steps, makes elaborate speeches on formal matters, and jerks out, every now and again, agonized expressions of romantic regard. I hesitate to dismiss the man with rude coldness, for I feel that intimate friendship with an outspoken sympathetic woman might transform him from a statistical measuring machine into a human observer. But a lover has an evil effect and makes me self-conscious. The little clique of 'exceptional women' with their correct behaviour and political aspirations give me most decidedly the cold shoulder; this in a company of men annoys me more than it should do. But the supreme discouragement of the Congress is in the growing consciousness that I am unfit for the work I have undertaken, and that I am not even at the beginning of my study. The little Professor frightens me with asking in sinister tones whether I have considered the effect of 'the appreciation of gold in the years '71–'74 on the Production Societies then started', and tells me quite frankly that I have got the wrong end of the stick. Still, I got a good deal out of him in my long interview in his Cambridge study, and though disheartened, I came away more than ever determined to grasp my subject firmly.

*29 June.* [The Argoed]
Just ten days' reading at Co-operative periodicals. Tiresome work with apparently little result, except a gathering of disjointed facts, none of which one can verify. It is especially tiresome as, so far, I have no clear idea of the exact facts I am searching for, no settled plan of the scope of my work. Two ideas have settled down in my mind: (1) that the Co-operative movement means an association of labour to secure a large share of the profits from the middleman and the trader and the manufacturer, but that it fails entirely to check the fall of prices brought about by competition for the custom of the consumer; (2) that the idea that the present Co-operative movement actually arose from the sentimental propaganda of gentlemen idealists is false. It grew up on the basis of self-interest, and the idealism was grafted on to it. I am still in doubt as to whether this idealism has done much good. The one use of the gentlemen connected with the movement has been promoting legislation to legalize co-operative societies. Also profit-sharing was *not* considered a *sine qua non* in the earlier times of the successful movement begun at Rochdale. . . .

Ah me! I wish I had more strength and more ability. I have no lack of desire, nor of determination to use the little strength and ability I have to its very utmost extent.

Extract from letter of a lady: 'I pay rent and taxes – £130. I have nothing but what I earn by painting, teaching and writing: and naturally I have to work exceedingly hard. My stepmother and I let the ground floor to reduce our rent. Now here is the absurdity. Our lodger, a young man doing absolutely nothing but amuse himself has a vote. The owner of the house, working early and late (somewhat useful I hope in her generation, at all events not useless), because she is a woman is not allowed to vote. Again I may vote for parish guardians of whom I know nothing, but for an M.P. of whose opinions I can judge, I may not vote.'

Mrs Fawcett's indignant reply to the 'Appeal' does not convince me: but the above extract contains the pith of the argument in favour of women's suffrage, and as such is valuable. One must realize the strongest argument of one's opponent before one is fit to controvert the whole position. But at present I am anxious to keep out of the lists. I have as yet accomplished no work which gives me a right to speak as representative of the class Mrs Fawcett would enfranchise: celibate women. And, to confess it frankly, I am not sure of my ground. I am not certain whether the strong prejudice I have against political life and political methods has not influenced my judgement on the question of introducing women into politics.

*29 July.* [The Argoed]
Shall always consider this day as sacred [anniversary of Chamberlain's last visit], a sacrament of pain fitting me for a life of loneliness and work, a memory of deep humiliation, and a spur to unremitting effort to gain for others the peaceful joy which I have lost myself. [The next eight pages of this comment on Chamberlain were torn out from the diary and have not survived.]

*4 August.* [The Argoed]
Mrs Johnny [Alice] Green has been here for the last fortnight. In appearance she is a slight woman with neat figure and, if only she had more freedom of movement, with a graceful bearing. Her hands are small, white and well formed; her dress is natty though with the negligence of a woman with intellectual pretensions. Her hair and complexion are colourless, the colour worn from out of them by a strained and excited life. . . . She has the originality which springs from a lonely, unhappy and self-absorbed youth, from the enforced independence of a friendless womanhood. Bred up in a remote part of

Ireland in a poverty-stricken home, she struggled at self-culture against every imaginable adverse circumstance. A brief married life with a man of talent and she was left without a friend but with a distinguished name. Now she has climbed up the social ladder, social success based on her husband's achievements does not satisfy her. She aims at the position to be gained by personal merit. But she does not love her work for its own sake, but only for what it brings her, not for what it may bring to others. . . .

During the fortnight's companionship she has taken the inventory of my mental experiences, and has found something which suits her. She is in search of a confidential friend who will be a stay and support to her intellectual aims, who will encourage her to believe that she is governed and controlled by great motives. . . . Such is the woman who has chosen me as her friend, and to whom I am attracted by interest and pity, and by a willingness (bred from indifference) to enter into relations desired by others. . . .

*20 August. The Argoed*
A grind and no mistake! Six hours a day reading and note-taking from those endless volumes of the *Co-operative News*, a treadmill of disjointed facts, in themselves utterly uninteresting, appallingly dry, and not even complete enough to be satisfactory. . . .

The movement to organize the unskilled and casual workers of London had been gathering momentum since the successful 1888 strike of the match girls at the Bryant & May factory, which had been led by Annie Besant. The strike in the London docks began when a few men thought they were being cheated of a halfpenny an hour. It was soon given effective leadership by socialists who had been agitating in the East End for several years. The demand for 'the docker's tanner' – a rate of sixpence an hour – attracted much public support.

*29 August. The Argoed*
The dock strike becoming more and more exciting – even watched at a distance. Originally 500 casuals marched out of the West and East India Docks – in another day the strike spread to the neighbouring docks – in a week half East London was out. For the first time a *general* strike of labour, not on account of the vast majority of strikers, but to enforce the claims to a decent livelihood of some 3,000 men. The hero of the scene, John Burns the socialist, who seems for the time to have the East London working man at his feet, with Ben Tillett (my

friend of two years) as his lieutenant and ostensible representative of the dockers. The men's demands: 6*d* an hour, to be taken on at fixed intervals of four hours, and a revision of the contract system or a minimum wage of 8*d* an hour under it, are just – that is to say they ask for only the possibility of a decent existence, a standard of life which ought to be the lowest in the kingdom. The dock companies maintain the trade of London will not stand it, the public of all classes declare that it must. Since the amalgamation of the two companies rates have been jumped up from 6*d* to 1*s*. Why not another penny? says Burns. And then there is the widespread feeling that the companies are abominably managed – an idea which I, from my personal acquaintance of dock officials, should cordially endorse. . . .

The strike is intensely interesting to me personally, as proving or disproving, in any case modifying, my generalizations on 'Dock Life'. Certainly the 'solidarity of labour' at the East End is a new thought to me – the dock labourers have not yet proved themselves capable of permanent organization but they have shown the capacity for common action, of temperate and reasonable action. And what is more important, an extraordinary manifestation of practical sympathy, of effectual help, has been evoked among all classes at East London, skilled artisans making common cause with casuals, publicans, pawnbrokers and tradesmen supporting them. In truth, instead of showing less public spirit, East End society has suddenly, under the inspiration of a strong leader, roused itself to struggle against an evil growing in its midst to which it has shown itself hitherto absolutely apathetic and indifferent, and has proved itself more capable of concerted action than any other district in England. This most assuredly is a new idea and one that requires thinking over. Two facts the strike has brought out clearly – facts which when once completely recognized may influence the relations of capital and labour in the metropolis: first, that through the agency of a powerful press, public opinion is more sensitive to London's troubles, more likely to feel and express strong opinions one way or another (this was already manifested in the success of the Bryant & May strike); secondly, that commercially and financially an extended labour disturbance in London is far more disastrous than in any other part of England, and that therefore an organized labour party would have in London a lever for working its own will that provincial labour does not possess. I still doubt whether East End labour is capable of the permanent organization in times of peace, of the steady upholding of a definite standard of life by the rank and file, whether it will produce and sustain the leaders who will watch the causes of trade, seizing opportunities and bending to facts, by which alone the gradual advance in the conditions of labour will be ensured. It is doubtful whether the strike of [engineers in] 1872 (though it was successful) did any permanent good: it is equally problematic whether, even if the dock companies capitulate, the great struggle of 1889 will effect any permanent advance.

Constantly the last week, as I have eagerly read every detail of the strike, I have been depressed by my own powerlessness to suggest any way out of the difficulty. I have been disheartened by a consciousness that my little mite of knowledge is not of much avail, that the great instinctive movements of the mass are perhaps, after all, more likely to [have an] effect than the carefully reasoned judgements of the scientific (or pseudo-scientific) observer. And then I have realized that if we are to form a *basis for action* by a knowledge of fact, that knowledge must be far more complete and exhaustive than it is ever likely to be in my time, certainly than it is likely to be with me. . . .

Beatrice left for Dundee on 30 August to attend the Trades Union Congress. George Shipton (1839–1911) was one of the leaders of the 'Old' or craft unions, opposing the campaign for the eight-hour day and the socialist leaders of the 'New' unskilled unions. He and other members of the Parliamentary Committee virtually controlled the T.U.C. and were the political spokesmen for the T.U.C. as a whole.

*1 September*. [Dundee]
Twelve hours' journey *en luxe* treating myself to a first-class fare. . . .

This morning while I was breakfasting Shipton, the chairman of the Parliamentary Committee of the Trades Congress and secretary to the London Trades Council joined me. His view of the dock strike is strongly adverse to the men, and is visibly biased by his antipathy to, I might almost say hatred of, Burns. Ben Tillett is, he says, an enthusiast who, however, has made a good thing of his enthusiasm. 'The way the strike was begun', he remarked, 'was illegitimate. No responsible official of a trade union which had funds of its own to lose would treat employers in that fashion. Ben Tillett drew up a letter demanding certain concessions and sent it with a letter assuming that if these demands were not conceded by 12 o'clock that morning the men would come out. Just fancy expecting a manager to decide a question of enormous financial importance without consulting his directors!

Then Burns came on the scene with his intense desire for notoriety and his foreign ideas of the solidarity of labour which he is trying to foist on trade unionists. But it won't work. Each trade has its own interests and technicalities, and all organizations to be permanently successful must be based on an appreciation of these interests and on a knowledge of the facts of the special trade concerned. . . .' Clearly, whatever might be his sympathy for dock labour, his dislike of a socialist victory was the stronger feeling. . . . I should imagine that in his heart of hearts he has little sympathy with the workman, that he prizes his position as an official for the power it brings.

*2 September.* [Dundee]
My first day's holiday has been a hard one! At half-past nine I started off with two Co-op officials to inspect the Dundee store. A shrewd manager, a dividend-maker and nothing less but agreeable to give all information. Two-hour sitting of the Congress (in which the socialist party after all their exertions number only some 15 votes) and then a sail down the river with the trade unionists, a fine-looking, able set of men. The evening entertainment tiring but most amusing. The editors of the three leading papers of this part of the world entertained some four hundred delegates, Dundee notables and their wives. . . .

Henry Broadhurst (1840–1911) was the leading figure on the parliamentary committee of the Trades Union Congress, Liberal M.P. and holder of a minor post in the 1886 Government. Robert Cunninghame-Graham (1852–1936) was a colourful eccentric, elected as a Liberal M.P. though he was a convinced socialist. He became a famous traveller and author. H. H. Champion (1859–1928) was an army officer who resigned to devote himself to socialist propaganda. For a time he was secretary of the Social Democratic Federation and a leader of the dock strike. He campaigned for independent labour representation in his journal *The Labour Elector.*

*3 September. Dundee*
A battle royal at Congress between the supporters of Broadhurst and old-fashioned methods, and the socialists led by Burns and Mrs Besant. These two leaders, however, were absent, and the socialist party was led by two somewhat foolish young men, delegates of the London Compositors, and suffered in consequence. The battle raged round personal abuse of Broadhurst. The socialists have apparently spent the last year in spreading calumny of all sorts besides trying to persuade the rank and file that Broadhurst is a reactionary. But I think

they have driven it too far. Among English working men of the better type there is a rooted dislike to desert old leaders, an intense suspicion of the mere talker who has not proved his faculty for steady work. Then the socialists at present labour under the disadvantage of relying on outside money and outside brains. 'Why should I be dictated to by an ex-artillery officer?' [Champion] was one of Broadhurst's most effective points. Trade unionists are jealous of interference and intensely exclusive. (Why are you here? I am asked frequently. 'Come with mischief in your pockets? to plot and plan?') So the whole Congress set its back up; the socialists diminished down to eleven, while Broadhurst's supporters number 177. A brilliant victory for the conservative section (conservative not in politics but in the methods and aims of their own organization).

With Broadhurst I lunched and afterwards smoked a cigarette. His suspicions of my intentions were completely dissipated when he heard I was an anti-suffrage woman. He immediately thought me sensible and sound. 'When I hear a woman's name talked of I am immediately prejudiced against her, but I can see you are as different as pitch from diamonds.' So he chatted on about socialism, trade unionism and his own complaints and showed every sign of being confidential. A commonplace person, hard-working no doubt, but a middle-class philistine to the backbone, appealing to the practical shrewdness and the high-flown but mediocre sentiments of the comfortably off working man. His view of women is typical of all his other views: he lives in platitudes and commonplaces.

But in spite of the prejudice and exclusiveness of the leading trade unionists, the frank fellowship, the absence of personal animus and personal rivalry, the general loyalty to leaders and appreciation of real work as distinguished from talk is refreshing. Then among the veterans, the officials of the largest, oldest and most influential unions, there is a knowledge of facts, a realization of industrial problems, a full appreciation of commercial and financial matters which makes one feel hopeful of the capacity for self-government of the working-class. Very different from the socialist leaders with the dirty personalities with which they pelt each other, with their envy and malice against any leader and with their ignorance of, one might almost say their contempt and hatred for, facts – a crew of wrecked reputations, politicians 'on the make', and paid intriguers from the Tory causes, interspersed, it is true, with beardless enthusiasts and dreamers of all ages and conditions, redeemed by a John Burns who seems to be a man with a conscience and a will. But is he not departing from the socialist camp?

Just as the scandal of the Crawford divorce case in 1886 was blighting Sir Charles Dilke's career he married Emilia Pattison, widow of the notable Oxford scholar Mark Pattison (1813–84). Lady Dilke was the leader of the Women's Trade Union League, and she campaigned vigorously to rehabilitate her husband politically. Thomas Birtwistle and James Mawdsley were traditionalist leaders of the cotton-workers' unions. Prince Peter Kropotkin (1842–1921), the Russian anarchist, spent almost thirty years of exile in England. *Looking Backward* (1888) was a socialist utopia written by the American author Edward Bellamy (1850–98).

*18 September*. [The Argoed]
I had not time to write up day-by-day notes on the Congress. Scenes flash across my memory. A 'baronial mansion', in the fashionable suburb of Dundee across the water, recently created by the editor as an outward sign of the prosperity of the *People's Journal* – gorgeous and comfortable. Luncheon served by an old Scotch maid. Present: prosperous editor, depressed son, popular preacher, Unitarian minister, respectable maiden cousin, Lady Dilke, her pretty secretary and myself. Her ladyship is a hard-looking but attractive woman of 45: thin lips, large glassy eyes, a complexion which has been clear but which is now powdered – manners something between the *grande dame* and the adventuress – with that unpleasant desire to please which springs from a struggle with a doubtful position. She exerted herself to please me – poor woman! and I was kind enough to accept her attentions and breakfasted with her the next morning; but I 'cooled off' when she mentioned 'London'. Poor woman! How she must hate us – we respectable women who allow her to be gracious to us so far but no further. Evidently she can afford to neglect no one in her desperate struggle to recover her husband's footing in society and in the political world. A brilliant woman: with strong sense, great industry and capacity for manipulating – but coarse – coarse to the back-bone: a born intriguer with an unswerving faith in 'cleverness'; an utter cynic as to 'righteousness'. One good feature: her pretty secretary is devoted to her, so are all the women with whom she is connected in the trade union propaganda – she has distinctly the milk of human kindness.

Another scene. Breakfast table: on my right Broadhurst beaming over his ham and eggs and the delightful memories of yesterday's triumphs over his enemies. 'Yes, we are now going to take our stand against intrusion of strangers into our body on false pretences. They

294

have made us ten times more exclusive: we have cleared the platform of outsiders, we will now clear the press table from intriguers.' All this is muttered loud enough for my neighbour on the left to hear – Cunninghame-Graham who is poring over the *Labour Elector*. (C.-G. is a cross between an aristocrat and a barber's block: he is a *poseur* but also an enthusiast, above all an unmitigated fool.) 'I have a letter from Kropotkin,' C.-G. whispers to me. 'He says – and I agree with him – if Burns with 80,000 men behind him does not make a revolution it is because he is afraid of having his head cut off. Burns is a grand fellow, though: different from those miserable slaves of bourgeois trade unionists,' he adds with a contemptuous wave of his hand towards Broadhurst, a wave of the hand which gradually settles down on a loaf of brown bread which C.-G. believes to be common property, but which unfortunately happens to be specially prepared by Mrs Broadhurst for her great man's overtaxed digestion. The 'bourgeois slave' watches with indignation the delicately tapering fingers of the anarchist clutch hold of 'personal property' and with the large perspiring palm of his outstretched hand grasps the whole thing – bread and fingers. 'No, Sir, not that,' he roars, 'that's my *own* bread made by my *own* wife in my *own* house and carried here in my *own* portmanteau; *that* you cannot have.' C.-G. withdraws with the apologies of a gentleman. 'Not my bread; I'd rather he destroyed my reputation than he took my bread,' growled the dyspeptic but somewhat gluttonous Broadhurst. C.-Graham looked unutterably disgusted with the contaminatory contact of the perspiring palm and wiped his aristocratic hand in soft cambric.

Other scenes in the private smoking-room of the leading trade unionists to which I was introduced by Broadhurst's favour. Not altogether a nice atmosphere, hard, with a good deal of lobbying apparent in the background with the result of the return of the old Parliamentary Committee with only one change. 'Dirty work,' says Burnett with a look of unutterable contempt in his clear grey eyes. . . . Altogether the latter scenes of the Congress did not impress me so favourably as the opening days, when loyalty to the old leader only was apparent. The trade unionists are a fine body of men, but they are lacking in the naïve enthusiasm and open-hearted cordiality of the Co-operators. They are officials, and officials who live by manipulating their constituencies: they have the vices of officials combined with those of popular representatives.

The upshot of the Congress was the rehabilitation of Broadhurst and the old set and the discomfiture of the socialist outsiders. There are signs that the victorious leaders, warned by the socialist attack, will try to tighten their hold by placing the Congress on a more representative basis with regard to numbers and payment. At present every delegate has one vote, and a union may send any number of delegates irrespective of their membership and contributions. This gives an undue influence to mushroom unions, which may be created in order to swamp true trade associations. On the other hand, if membership were duly represented the great conservative unions of Lancashire would exclude from all power the new blood. The officials of these old standing unions have become intimately connected with the employers – many of them are J.P.s – and most of them conservative in politics. They believe in arbitration and conciliation and in dealing with each trade separately, all action to be based on technical knowledge of the special trade. They are fully alive to foreign competition and versed in all the intricacies of the currency question. With them trade unionism is rapidly assuming the form of a union of producers in one trade against the outside world, the differences between the two great classes of producers, capitalist brain-workers and manual wage-earners, to be settled by exports from both sides. Ideas such as the *solidarity of labour* are to them absurd: 'We lived through all that,' said Birtwistle, the veteran leader of the cotton-weavers. 'They imagine themselves the advanced guard, they are really the babies of trade unionism.'

Thus one of the cleavage lines in the Congress between the Old and the New school was the question of sending representatives to foreign and international congresses. On the other hand, the younger school maintain that the very difficulty of foreign competition would be solved by the 'solidarity of labour' and that the 'fossil' trade unionists are diverted from vigorous action by the mere pedantry of technical knowledge of the ins and outs of one tiny specimen of industry. . . .

It was a hard week, scarcely a holiday. When I arrived early on Sunday morning at Auberon Herbert's little cottage on the banks of Loch Awe [north-west of Glasgow] I was thoroughly exhausted, with a bad cold in the head into the bargain. A somewhat dreary little plastered cottage, with none of the charm of 'Old House', sup-plemented by two wooden shanties; low brushwood and unkempt grass surrounding it. . . . The children . . . most attractive. The elderly idealist interesting and becoming an intimate friend. But with his nature, distance lent enchantment to the view! . . . courtesy and

idealism cover subtle egotism and waywardness of nature. His little
fads about his health are ludicrous. . . . What between vegetarianism
and valetudinarianism he is rapidly sinking into old age, though he is
a healthy man of 50.

I enjoyed my days there. Between us we started a novel, *Looking
Forward* – an answer to *Looking Backward* – for which I supplied the
plot and the characters, while he is to work out a reformed world on
individualist lines. He told me during the long evenings, looking on
to the moonlit lake, the story of his life and we drifted into discussion
on marriage, and I suddenly perceived with intense amusement that he
was considering, with much doubting, 'possibilities'. He will doubt
too much to make the offer, so the friendship is safe. But as we pushed
off from the landing-stage to join the steamer on Saturday and I
watched the self-conscious expression of slight sentimentality – a
sentimentality of a somewhat inhuman character on the face of the
elderly Don Quixote of modern society – did I laugh or did I shudder?

A solitary day at Stirling feeling unutterably sad – a long night
journey – the exquisite beauty of the early morning spread over the
Monmouth valley as I drive up to our mountain home; the faithful
Neale with all things prepared, the breakfast table with a family party
of Playnes – cordial welcome – long gossip. The darling old Father
is delighted to see 'my little Bee', in one word *Home*. And now to
work.

*22 September*. [The Argoed]
The dock strike has ended in a brilliant victory to the men; all their
demands (with the exception of fixed times for taking on) conceded –
the concessions come into force in November. Burns' parting words
'Be good to your wives and your children and remember what a man
who drinks water can do.' Fifty thousand pounds subscribed (£24,000
from Australia), pressure from all other capitalist interests, and public
opinion of all classes have carried the dockers through to victory. But
there are already signs that the actual men concerned will be bitterly
disappointed, that this great effort to help the casual labourer, if it be
successful in retaining what has been won, will mean the gradual
extinction of the class, depriving the individual of the little he had
before. If so, the lesson should be brought out vividly, for the
movement has been led by the socialists, who have always denounced
the trade unionists for raising the standard of the favoured few to the
detriment of the many. This time they have adopted trade union

methods: it remains to be seen whether they arrive at trade union ends. . . .

### 30 September. *The Argoed*

This last month or so I have been haunted by a longing to create characters and to move them to and fro among fictitious circumstances – to put the matter plainly, by the vulgar wish to write a novel! In those early-morning hours when one's half-awakened brain seems so strangely fruitful, I see before me persons and scenes; I weave plots, and clothe persons, scenes and plots with my own philosophy of all things, human and divine. There is intense attractiveness in the comparative ease of descriptive writing. Compare it with work in which movements of commodities, percentages, depreciations, averages and all the ugly horrors of commercial facts are in the dominant place, and *must remain so* if the work is to be worthful.

But then I reason with myself: 'Who knows that you have any faculty for this new work? And grant you have, is it worth *your* while? Is it for that you have sacrificed your happiness?'. . . Still, I have in my mind some more dramatic representation of facts than can be given in statistical tables and in the letterpress that explains these – some way of bringing home to the hearts of the people, rich and poor, those truths about social organization that I may discover – illustrations of social laws in the terms of personal suffering, personal development, personal sin. But this must be delayed until I *have* discovered my laws, and as yet I am only on the threshold of my inquiry, far enough off, alas, from any general and definite conclusions.

Meanwhile my diary shall serve for those titbits of personal experience which are representative of the special peculiarities of the different phases of society I pass through. . . . But in this lighter work, this recreation of my imagination, I will not forget that, though in Art the representation of one individual instance may tell the whole, in Science to *know* the Whole we must observe countless instances – diverse and similar. And in my work Science must precede Art; Art must be the perfect representation of *facts and of their proportionate values*. Science and Art should be One, an Ideal towards which we creep blindly. Poor weak woman – comedy and pathos are in the chasm which lies between you and your goal.

Dear sweet Carrie [Darling]: seven years since we parted on the Victoria platform. A true woman though for many years she was an enthusiast for celibacy in her profession. A strange career. The child of the illegitimate son of a squire married to a woman of refinement and education, her breeding was somewhat mixed. Early in life she had to seek her own livelihood. But that necessity did not keep her from love-making. Twice or three times she was engaged or 'kept company', for her lower-middle-class origin showed itself in her love affairs if nowhere else. Jilted or jilting, she lived through them all with little display of passion: her whole enthusiasm centred in learning. At twenty-eight she was helped by friends to spend two years at Newnham: there made friends with the knot of distinguished women who were the first students at the University. From that time for some eight years her thoughts were absorbed by culture and by an immense desire to impart it, her feelings in friendship with women. Just in the middle of this period I first knew her; she came as a highly-paid governess to Bill and Polly. How I remember that first time I met her: I can now see her tiny form, beautiful eyes and delicately chiselled features all set in a Quaker-like simplicity of dress and manner as she sat in the Longfords schoolroom. Six months together in Germany confirmed our friendship. At Wiesbaden our rooms opened into each other: in her room we used to sit late into the night with our feet cocked high on the china stove . . . smoking cigarettes and talking philosophy, for we were then both in the metaphysical stage, or poring over some bit of puzzling German, or delighting in some verse of *Faust* or prose epigram of Goethe. It was my first friendship outside my own family, for my feeling for Margaret Harkness was one of pity not of liking in those days. . . . I recollect one walk we had in Kensington Gardens during a London Season, when I and the other sisters were in full swing of seeing men with a view to marriage. I remember giving her a description of a week's round of riding in the Row, dinners and balls and the Sunday calls from eligible young men. I remember the slight expression of contempt on that mobile mouth, the gleam of pity and sympathy in those large brown eyes. 'Oh, Beatrice, I would rather lead my life, hard though it be, than yours!' At that time she was second mistress at Dulwich, delighting in her work and living in the midst of a society of hardworking and interesting women. . . . In those days she enjoyed life immensely.

Then came the great crisis. One sister was supposed to be in consumption, three other sisters were doing poorly as governesses. She was offered a headmistress-ship in Australia with a good salary. . . . With a terrible wrench she threw up her position in

England. . . . It was just then that Mother died so that a great change in both our lives began at the same time. I remember the little woman's intensely sorrowful and anxious expression as she bade farewell on the Victoria platform the night Father, Rosy and I left for Switzerland. . . . Then came letters from her: her sisters were satisfactorily settled, she was working up the school successfully. But she was living in a society she hated. A year after began the story of the passionate attachment to a married man, the young English master of the boys' grammar school, probably the first really cultivated and attractive man she had come across, for her old lovers were of the lower-middle-class type. Four years of struggle and misery, then he left. Another man came on the scene and she seemed to be descending into a series of sentimental friendships, the feeling for the young Englishman looming in the background. Suddenly last autumn we heard with dismay she had thrown up her school, her lover had got a divorce or was getting one from his wife and, poor and ill, appealed to her tenderness to come to him in Japan. . . . On the way out she falls in with a bluff sea captain, apparently a man of sense and decision. In a few days he is desperately in love; in a few hours she has confided in him her whole story. 'What! Going out to a man who is still married, not yet divorced and may never be. You are not fit to be at large: marry me, but if you won't, for God's sake go back to your friends in England.' Meanwhile Robert (the old lover) seems queerly half-hearted and does not meet her as he promised. Then all becomes enveloped in mystery. The captain interviews Robert, extracts a promise from Carrie she will not correspond with him, and seemingly persuades her to become engaged in a sort of queer way to him. . . . Oh, woman, you are passing strange. God preserve me from a lover between thirty-five and forty-five. No woman can resist a man's importunity during the last years of an unrealized womanhood. That to me is the moral of Carrie's story.

### 11 October. Box House

Our new, and our last home. A pleasant little house with wide verandah giving it a comfortable, homely look; small rooms but with large windows and with a general air of dignity and self-respect in the passages and the staircase, the whole compactly built and well designed. Immediately behind Minchinhampton Common; from our front windows a wide view across the valley of beech trees to the Cotswold hills beyond, the delicate outlines losing themselves in the fields and woods of the middle distance. One great attraction: an expanse of western sky. From my bedroom windows I can watch the sunsets of each season of the year. Five minutes' walk and I am in the hall of Longfords listening to Mary's bright personality and consoling Arthur for Pollock's enormities, or I am wandering on the common with its glorious sky and distant hills. . . . This is to be our home until I lose the last tie of duty to another life and become an outcast from domesticity, a worker following her work whither it leads, like an animal following its food.

*25 October.* [Box House]
The Rylands' came this evening; morally a *tour de force* on my part, a determination to pay the utmost penalty of a want of perfect sincerity, of worldliness, of vanity, to adopt and maintain a dignity in my relations with the family which I so woefully lost in bitterly remembered days. . . . I want by my continued friendliness to that woman to put behind me all unworthy thoughts and feelings, to clear my mind of dross, and to work, so far as God gives me strength, in pure gold. God help me.

*27 October.* [Box House]
The strain is over and the task is done. Alice Green, with her extraordinary vivacity of intellect and brilliant powers of expression helped me over it, unknowing of the service she was rendering. . . .

*30 October.* [Box House]
Hard at work mastering every detail, technical and commercial, at the Longfords Mill. Made up my mind at The Argoed that the chance of seeing right into one business was not to be missed especially as the woollen trade is one in which Co-operative and Joint Stock have been tried and failed. . . . How inexpressibly ugly are the manners and ways of a typical middle-class man, who has been brought up in the atmosphere of small profit making. With the small manufacturer and retail tradesman business is a matter of driving . . . workers and customers, and an experience of this class makes one wonder whether 'profit' is not, on the whole, a demoralizing force, whether a system of standard salaries and standard wages such as is being gradually evolved in Joint Stock and Co-operative enterprises is not a higher form of industrial organization. Should not the use of a man's faculties after he has received sufficient to keep him in full working order be

301

dedicated to society? And are we not, through the force of public opinion and the natural evolution of industry, tending that way?. . . . Is not profit-sharing a sharing of unlawful gains?

Some such conclusion I am coming to in my study of the Co-operative movement. It seems to me to have been a movement *not* towards the sharing of profits by workers, but towards an unconscious realization of the socialist ideal of officially managed business on the basis of voluntary association: the difference between it and mere Joint Stock association lying in the fact that the religious element of work for humanity has entered into it and made it a vivifying force: that it has embodied in its creed the ethics of industry, purity of goods, equal payments, and care for the workers. And yet I am slow to accept a theory which ignores the whole idealism of the actual leaders.

James Keir Hardie (1856–1915) was a Scottish miner and trade union organizer who became a leading advocate of independent labour representation in Parliament. He fought a notable by-election in Mid-Lanark in 1888. The Liberals were angry because he split the vote, and it was rumoured that he had received a large Tory contribution towards his election expenses. When H. H. Champion was suspected of being the intermediary for 'Tory gold', as had been the case with two socialist candidates in 1885, Margaret Harkness tried to throw his critics off the scent by claiming that she had given Hardie a hundred pounds, though this was only a third of the sum involved (*North British Daily Mail*, 28 June 1888). Her letter in the *Star* on 16 September 1889 was an excited defence of Champion's political virtue and a flat denial of any complicity with the Tories. Tom Mann (1856–1941) was a member of the Amalgamated Society of Engineers who became a professional organizer, a leader of the 'New' unions and a key figure in the dock strike. Active in the Social Democratic Federation, later secretary of the Independent Labour Party, he became one of the founders of the Communist Party.

[14 November?]. *Devonshire House Hotel*
Arrived for a fortnight's holiday in London. Maggie Harkness came in to supper. Sad to feel that I more and more distrust her. The last blow to my confidence, a letter appearing in the *Star* at the time of the victory of the dockers, a letter mad with vanity, claiming to have paid Keir Hardie's electioneering expenses. Afterwards to account for borrowing money she tells me that the money was hers 'for that purpose and that purpose alone' which simply means that she served as go-between. The last year she has been hand in glove with the underground labour party, with Champion, Burns, Mann, etc. 'The only way to observe them is to pretend to be immensely interested, but

aren't they suspicious; mind you don't mention me if you meet any of them', and then she throws out hints of all kinds of mysterious intrigues. 'I can tell you nothing now, but I shall get out of the whole thing someday – then I can tell you all.' I look at her with blank amazement: in face of such utter deficiency of sense of honour there is nothing to be said, for there is nothing to appeal to. She is going to bring it all out in a book. If only her observation were not twisted by her methods she has splendid opportunities, but then it is doubtful whether a crooked path can ever reach the observer's goal – truth; whether insight is not as much a moral quality as an intellectual habit. Poor Maggie! A strange weariness and chronic depression adds pathos to her curious contortions: there is still pity in her suffering, admiration for her pluck, and appreciation of her kind-heartedness towards others' suffering, but can there be real friendship where there is no respect, no confidence? At times I feel that the pretence of the old feeling is a hollow sham, that a relationship in which one is perpetually trying to guard oneself against betrayal cannot be healthy or lasting and must end in death. But pity will keep me her friend until I cease to interest her and she slips from me, not I from her. She is typical of the emancipated woman who has broken ties and struggled against the prejudice and oppression of bigoted and conventional relations to gain her freedom but who has never been disciplined by a public opinion which expects a woman to work with the masculine standard of honour and integrity. A few more years and women will start alike with the freedom and with the standard of men.

*17 November.* [Devonshire House Hotel]
This Sunday last year I took the communion at St Paul's and prayed earnestly against bitterness and evil feelings. This day I take it again. Many of my thoughts during the last year have been unworthy. Can it be otherwise this coming year? I have work before me, work which will need all the devotion and energy of my mind, all the sincerity and warmth of my nature. Without help from the great spirit of Truth and Love I cannot do it. I pray earnestly that the help may be given me and that my life may be a 'living sacrifice' to the work that lies before me. Is it possible for me to lead an absolutely religious life without inflation, to keep my motives and methods perfectly pure without the self-consciousness that tends to a disproportionate and therefore untrue valuation of the importance of my life and work? . . . Beautiful service. Realized the unworthiness, mean unworthiness of the last

year. Morning and evening I will pray for humility, love, faith and energy. Let me suffer if by suffering my nature be purified and strengthened. . . .

*19 November.* [Devonshire House Hotel]
Meeting at Toynbee Hall: Tom Mann, Eight Hours movement. Fine fellow, absolutely straight and a warm enthusiast. He opened his speech by reference to Co-operation (the audience were Co-operators): Socialism means the *Co-operative organization of industry when no one shall be outside.* This was the ideal state towards which they were all striving. But so-called Co-operation like the trade unionism of the fossil unions had denied this faith. From this point he went on to argue that the only method of reducing the great army of unemployed was to reduce the hours of the workers so as to divide the employment among all persons in the trade. 'Statistics prove,' he said, and then followed some astounding statistical statements. 'Get the reduction of hours by any means; by combination, by local authorities, by parliamentary interference – but get it. *Reduction of hours never means reduction of wages:* you may exact more wages but the employer will get them back if you do not raise the *status* of labour and this can only be done by the increased mental and moral training which follows leisure.' (This seemed to me a fair argument, justified hitherto by facts – whether it can be applied to eight hours as well as to ten hours is a question of all-important detail.)

Then he referred to the docks, described the abject subservience of the dock directors: 'We can wring anything out of them now,' he cried triumphantly (a mischievous reaction from the incompetence and cynicism of the brainless directors – this triumph of inexperienced labour leaders, inexperienced in trade facts). 'But we are determined to eliminate the riff-raff, the wretched wastrels that have disgraced the docks. The end of this week we close our books. We must be hard-hearted and clear-headed; it is no use gushing over the out-o'-works. We want men who grasp the problem, who see that if we are to raise the status of our members we must keep them with sufficient wages to provide food, to keep up their physical strength, with constant employment to prevent them from becoming loafers. The other men at the dock gates must "clear off"; with us there is no room for them; no doubt there are other social movements to provide for them, but our movement is to eliminate them.' A strange interpretation of his opening ideal: 'an organization of industry which leaves no one outside'. . . .

*Laura Gay* was the title of the novel written by Beatrice's mother. The house of Joseph Priestley (1733–1804), scientist and reformer, was wrecked in 1791 by a mob objecting to his sympathy for the French Revolution.

## 26 November. Box House

Hastily summoned from London. Father sinking – he may linger a few days, a few months, but death is waiting for the body struck down this day four years ago. The spirit is fading away from our sight, gradually withdrawing itself to another world. Darling old Father, at last you are leaving us and we ourselves are far advanced on the road along which you have travelled with courage and loving kindness. May we do likewise.

He was in middle age when I was born. I can remember little of his life in its prime, except from hearsay and family traditions handed down the long line of daughters. But stories of his childhood and youth, told but yesterday, are fresh in my memory. First the Manchester street boy, a street boy by inclination not of necessity (for in those days his father had become a wealthy man) – shaking the oil out of the street lamps, the policeman appearing the next morning, his father's attempt at solemnity, the warning of prison which kept 'Dicky' for some days under self-restraint. Another time, the school-boy returning to the motherless home finds his darling sister shut up in the coal-hole by an inhuman governess. The chase after the woman with a riding-whip to thrash her, finally locked in her room, she not daring to face the fury of the outraged brother. The letter from school to the poor patient father: 'I will not return till she is dismissed.' The pitiful glimpse into that early home: the mother a lunatic, the father broken-hearted, three younger sisters and the vigorous sympathetic boy growing up undisciplined and untrained but with the whole family clinging round him. Then the London life of the radical politician's eldest son, in the thick of the political movement, associating with the élite of the radical world of the day, the attempt to become a Manchester warehouseman being thwarted by a somewhat avaricious uncle (Sir Thomas, the first mayor of Manchester) who wished to keep the golden goose for his own sons, and perhaps by the young man's own aspirations towards a larger and fuller life.

For Dick Potter had other blood, of a wilder stem than that of his grandfather, the hard-headed Yorkshire farmer. His mother was a beautiful woman of gentle family – a Hebrew prophetess to look at – married against her will to the wealthy Manchester warehouseman some 20 years older than herself. For the thickset form and colourless hair and complexion of the Potter was not attractive, not even in the gentle-natured persevering Richard, a loving parent and public-spirited man, the least able and the most amiable of the Potter brothers.

These Potter brothers live still in the hearts of Manchester folk as the energetic pioneers of Manchester radical politics, as the founders of the civic life of the town. But to the dark-eyed fiery-natured woman, with her fastidious tastes and highly strung feelings, the bourgeois conventions, the gross ideals of the *parvenu* were intolerable. Her husband was simply 'vulgar Mr Potter', her coarse-grained dictatorial brother-in-law Sir Thomas she hated, [she] went mad from sheer hatred. After the birth of her youngest child she was removed to an asylum: some years afterwards she recovered sufficiently to live with her mother – to her husband and children she never returned. She became sane on all but one subject – her special mission to lead the Jews back to Jerusalem. And after a life of internal tempest she lives in the memories of her grandchildren as she appeared the last few years of her life: a calm majestic woman, simple as a child, fervent as a priestess in her piety and assurance that 'God was near', doing all she did excellently – knitting and delicate fancy work, music and Hebrew translation, in peace with all men except with the memories of 'that vulgar Mr Potter' and of Sir Thomas whom she could not mention without a shuddering memory of the horrors of an old-fashioned lunatic asylum with its penal discipline.

This weird figure of the beautiful mad mother loomed large in our father's childhood and youth: it darkened with tragic helpless sorrow the closing years of the active radical politician. . . . Before young Richard was 21 years old, his father became a hopeless invalid; for some years he lingered, dying slowly of tumour on the brain, his son nursing him like a daughter, standing in his stead towards the three young girls, giving one as wife to Captain Anson, another to Charles Macaulay and caring tenderly for the beautiful youngest sister, the beauty and the fool of the family. At 26 he was left with many friends, a fair fortune, and life before him.

Though Dick Potter inherited a slim figure, aquiline features and dark piercing eyes from his mother he owed those qualities which made him a success in life to the commoner stuff of the Potters. The

Seddons were a decaying race: vain, passionate, eccentric, contorted in their aims and views. The Potters, on the other hand, were pushing their way upwards by fine temper, a sort of brutal persistency and above all an indifference to the world's opinion (unless it were to handle it) and an absolute *directness* of aim. Old John Potter, the farmer of Tadcaster, had his windows broken by a mob for refusing to illuminate in honour of a defeat of the Americans; his milder son Richard became a Unitarian when the Birmingham mob sacked Priestley's house. By nature the Potters were Radicals, Dissenting and individualist, believing instinctively that success always meant merit, unconscious of their own and others' feelings so long as they reached their aim. This was the type: Richard the elder had inherited from some other family an angelic sweetness of disposition, a temperament which he handed on to our father. Many a time Father has spoken to us of his tenderness, of the depth of his suffering at his wife's estrangement, of his self-forgetful devotion to his children – and now as I look at my grandfather's picture I see my father's loving kindness beaming from his eyes.

With these qualities the younger Richard began life. He had matriculated at London University, he had been called to the Bar, he had mixed freely in political society at a time when being an M.P.'s son carried prestige. . . . Before settling down to the Bar he decided on taking the 'grand tour' with his pretty sister Kitty. At Rome he met Lawrencina Heyworth. In 1844 they married. Their love story idealized with Mother's conception of her own and Father's character we have in *Laura Gay*, except that their love story with its sunbeams and storms continued throughout their united lives and ended only on her deathbed.

I will not attempt to describe Mother's character, and the effect, in this all but perfect union, the two natures had on each other, for I knew neither character until both had acted and reacted on each other some thirty years. Through Mother's precepts and prejudices Father became after their marriage isolated from his old friends (many of whom were 'irregular' in their views and actions). Discouraged from any serious attempt to succeed at the Bar, and after a year's wandering he settled down with his young wife to live on their income at a country place in Herefordshire. Four years afterwards, in the French Revolution of '48 he lost the greater part of his capital and at 32 years of age he had to cast around him for means to support the quick-coming family.

307

This loss of fortune became the great turning-point of his life. Physically indolent he would never have worked unless he had been stimulated by his passion for his wife and children, and by his ambition for a place in the world. Once engaged in business his life became one long series of varied enterprise, Mother's fertile imagination and ingenuity of intellect prompting him, her restless ambition spurring him on. Truly the little woman had both spurs and a bit – and kept a whip in reserve. She was dutiful, ambitious, ascetic, and restrained the natural self-indulgence, easy-going and undisciplined impulses of the far nobler nature she guided and governed. But withal Father had a latent will, and it is difficult to say in spite of apparent yielding whether with whip, spurs and bit she moved him further than one side of the road upon which he had determined to travel. I was no spectator, but when I appeared on the scene with eyes opened it was hard to judge whether Father's diplomacy had not check-mated Mother's temper.

Diplomacy, that doubtful virtue, was Father's great business talent, diplomacy and an instinctive knowledge of men. If he had had early training, if he had acquired as great a control over himself as he had capacity for handling others, it is difficult to know how far he might not have risen in power. And here he lacked the help of a judicious-minded wife. Mother kept him from animal self-indulgence, but in some ways she stimulated by her excited imagination his mental passions. As a child I remember many a time watching the two pacing up and down the Standish drawing-room denouncing an opponent as guilty of every form of malice and dishonesty: it was in these fits of personal irritation that he threw up the chairmanship of the Great Western, the Presidency of the Grand Trunk [Railway of Canada], that he sold out of a colliery investment of some magnitude. Here Mother was his evil genius, her family throwing mud at him when he was down, he turned round to load them with gifts when he was prosperous and they abject with fear of poverty. And yet he worshipped with reverential love the daughter of a man who had broken faith with him, the sister of the men who insulted him and then whined out for favours. Never a word of blame or resentment from him: they were the loved ones of the 'Darling wifie', the treasure of his life.

Was it the necessity of 'managing' his wife's temper (since from love he dared not defy her) that made him an intensely reserved man, though outwardly he seemed overflowing with spontaneous geniality?

'We do not know whether Mr Potter is very simple or very deep,' said one Gloucestershire lady to another. Which of his daughters could count on his actions, could lay bare the secret intentions of his heart? He told all, he left all untold. Who can read the paradox of Father's nature: was it intentional reserve, or absence of personal motive, was it utter unself-consciousness or was it diplomacy?

On all general questions he had a largeness of view, a certain noble philosophy, a childlike reverence for the Good, the Beautiful and the True – and yet in the aims of life he was a materialist. Here again a strange paradox: the evening prayer 'Gentle Jesus meek and mild, look upon a little child' said with childlike humility – who would have recognized the shrewd railway man bribing and manipulating a bill through the American Senate?

The elder sisters say the railway world with its jobbery, loose commercial views, with its guzzling and low ideals of enjoyment, injured his morale. I do not know as I did not see. When first I knew him he was already in the thick of it, an eminent man in his way. He took his wife and all his children into his confidence: to each and all he showed the cards he held in his hand, described to you exactly the reason for each move, for his suspicions and calculations as to the cards of his opponents. And yet to see him with these men, to watch his sympathetic smile and apparent want of purpose in all he said and did, the natural way in which they themselves were made to suggest what he wished – the absolute unself-consciousness of his effort – one felt one was in the presence of a born diplomatist. It flashed upon one: is he not handling his family in the same way? And certainly, judging by results, he handled it effectually, for it was he who married seven headstrong self-willed women to men he thoroughly approved and considered suitable, and prevented, without forbidding, all other marriages.

Companionship with him was a liberal education in human nature and in the affairs of the world; near relationship to him was a tie of extraordinary tenderness and charm owing to the absolute self-devotedness of his character. His own comfort, his own inclinations were unconsidered before the happiness of his wife, the welfare of his children. With him the domestic instinct was a passion to which all else was subordinated, except an occasional outburst of physical self-indulgence from which he recovered penitent, prostrate before the ascetic purity of his wife.

Darling Father, how your children have loved you, loving even your weaknesses, smiling over them tenderly like so many mothers. How we have all combined to blind you to the realities of your illness: nine diplomatists sitting round the old diplomatist, hiding things, smoothing things; and you all the while perhaps the most polished diplomatist of the lot, accepting the illusion as pleasanter than the fact, delighting in the diplomacy that you have taught us. With what gentle dignity you have resigned your grasp on life, though not without an internal struggle, but all hidden from view. 'I know you do it for my good, dear child, but it is a little hard'; these were his only words when, a year after his first stroke, I refused absolutely to post his letter ordering his brokers to buy for speculation. He tried it again, but this time I check-mated him by writing privately to the brokers urging them on their honour to discourage it. I remember the queer expression when he read their letter, the passing look of irritation, then the bright glance at me when he perceived my move, the affectionate tone in which he next addressed me on some indifferent matter, the silent acknowledgement of my good intention, the inward chuckle over the smartness of his offspring, and from that moment the absolute and entire resignation of his affairs into Daniel's [Meinertz-hagen] hands, betaking himself exclusively to the contracted routine of a shadow-like existence. His content would have been painful, if one had not felt that it was reasoned out of his large unselfish philosophy of life, an idealized Epicureanism, the happiness of the world (i.e. of those around you) and of yourself as a unit of the world.

And now that he lies helpless, the vitality flickering nigh to extinction, his limbs motionless, his breathing laboured, the last pleasure in his sleep, food and cigarette gone, he still brightens up to welcome his 'bright-eyed daughter', to compliment a middle-aged married woman on her good looks, to inquire how each husband is doing, to ask how much he will leave to his children. In the long hours of restlessness he broods over the success of his children and finds reason for peace and satisfaction. 'I want one more son-in-law', (a proof that he frets near his end, as he has discouraged the idea of matrimony for me, put it off as something I could easily attain). 'A woman is happier married. I should like to see my little Bee married to a good strong fellow', and the darling old father dreams of the 'little Bee' of long ago; he does not realize that she has passed away, leaving the strong form and determination of the 'glorified spinster' bending over him as a mother bends over her sick child.

But the happiness of these last four years he owes principally to a strange woman. I shall always feel deeply grateful to Mrs Thompson, 'dear old nursie' as he calls her. . . . To him she has been the personification of tenderness: always patient, always watchful, always ready to sacrifice her health and comfort to his infirmities. To me she has been a sympathetic companion; helpful with Rosy and fully alive to the difficulties and trials of my position as the centre of an active-minded and critical family. . . .

## PART V

# A Frank Friendship
*January 1890–July 1892*

## *Introduction to Part V*

As RICHARD POTTER'S health failed Beatrice was increasingly frustrated by the need to spend so much time with him. 'Without help from the great spirit of Truth and Love I cannot do it,' she said, as she struggled to reconcile her personal obligations with her sense of duty to society at large. 'I pray earnestly that the help may be given me and that my life may be a "living sacrifice" to the work that lies before me.' The help she needed was to come, early in the New Year, though not in the form she expected.

Since Beatrice had joined the Charity Organization Society in 1883 she had moved from philanthropy through economic theory and social investigation to reject both the motives and the consequences of unregulated capitalism. Over a period of seven years her professional and political development had thus recapitulated the evolution of social reform over as many decades, and she did not shirk the conclusion. 'I dimly see the tendency towards a socialist community in which there will be individual freedom and public property instead of class slavery and the private possession of the means of subsistence of the whole people,' she wrote in a decisive diary entry at the beginning of January 1890. 'At last I am a socialist.' And she added a phrase that showed how she was still rather surprised at the chain of events that had led her to a conclusion so distant from the teachings of her first mentor, Herbert Spencer: 'this is where observation and study have led me in spite of training and class bias'. The scientific method, after all, had shown how virtue and welfare could be achieved in a well-ordered society.

It was in the spring of 1888, Beatrice said, that John Dent 'talked to me, in tones of mingled admiration and suspicion, about a group of clever young men who, with astonishing energy and audacity, were haranguing the London Radical Clubs; contributing innumerable articles and paragraphs, signed or unsigned, to the *Star* and the *Daily Chronicle*, and distributing, far and wide, *Facts for Socialists* and other subversively plausible pamphlets'. These young men were in fact, the leaders of the Fabian Society, and at this time they were trying to infiltrate their collectivist notions into the official Liberal programme. It was still a very small society, only five years old, but it had been fortunate enough to attract some remarkable talents and to make a distinct mark on the political life of the metropolis. The volume of *Fabian Essays in Socialism*, published in 1889, had an immediate and continuing influence, for it put the intellectual case for gradualism against the utopian, Marxist and anarchist publications which gave such an apocalyptic tone to the socialist propaganda of the 1880s; it demonstrated, said Bernard Shaw, that Socialism might be preached 'without forfeiture of moral credit by a bishop as well as a desperado'.

George Bernard Shaw (1856–1950), who had not yet begun to write plays and was at that time making a bare living as a critic, devoted much of his time to public speaking on behalf of the Fabian Society, which he had joined in the summer of 1884; Graham Wallas (1858-1932), then a schoolteacher, was to become a noted professor at the London School of Economics; and his friend Sydney Haldane Olivier (1859–1943) was a civil servant in the Colonial Office who rose to be Secretary of State for India. Shaw, Wallas and Olivier, together with Sidney James Webb (1859–1947), were known among Fabians as 'The Four Musketeers', and it was chiefly to them that Dent was referring. They were all clever speakers, Dent said, 'but the man who organizes the whole business, drafts the resolutions and writes the tracts, is Sidney Webb'.

Beatrice had heard of him. She read *Fabian Essays* when it appeared, and told her friend J. C. Gray that 'by far the most significant and interesting essay is the one by Sidney Webb; *he has the historic sense*'. Sidney Webb had also heard of her. When he reviewed the first volume of the Booth survey in the *Star* he had observed that 'the only contributor with any literary talent is Miss Beatrice Potter'. But they had never met, although the political world in London was still quite small and they had a good number of acquaintances in common. 'I had entered the field of controversy from the standpoint of big enterprise, party politics and metropolitan philanthropy, and was biased against socialist solutions of political and economic problems', Beatrice said later by way of explanation, 'whilst the Fabians entered this same field as Radicals and rebels, drawn by a vision of a new social order, from every vocation and many parts of the country.' She and Sidney, in short, came from very different backgrounds – she was well to do and well connected, he was a shopkeeper's son, and he had almost nothing to commend him except his talent and his character.

He was little more than twenty when Bernard Shaw heard him speak for the first time and decided that he was 'the ablest man in England'. Shaw was given to hyperbole, yet his description of the youthful Webb was impressive. 'He knew all about the subject of debate,' Shaw recalled, 'knew more than the lecturer; knew more than anybody present; had read everything that had been written on the subject; and remembered all the facts that bore on it. He used notes, ticked them off one by one, threw them away, and finished with a coolness and clearness that, to me in my then trembling state, seemed miraculous.' Sidney was rather humourless, for he had been solemnly brought up, and he lacked the spark of imagination in his writing, but he had a prodigious memory, a clear and logical mind, pertinacity, and an astonishing capacity for work; he was, perhaps, a model civil servant, and he certainly became an ideal collaborator for Beatrice, who had all the attributes of a successful politician and the manner of a Cabinet minister.

Sidney James Webb was born on 13 July 1859 at 44 Cranbourne Street, just off Leicester Square, in the heart of London. His mother, Elizabeth Mary Stacey, was an orphan who had been brought up in Essex, and then had used money from a relative to open a hairdressing and millinery shop. His father, Charles Webb, came from an innkeeping family in Kent, and he may have come to the shop as an assistant of some kind before he married the somewhat older proprietor in 1854. He was interested in politics, having worked for John Stuart Mill in the Westminster election of 1865; he was a great reader of pamphlets and newspapers; he sat upon the local Board of Guardians, which administered the Poor Law, and on the local vestry, which was the municipal authority; and he was a sergeant in the Volunteers. He was, all the same, the frailer partner, overshadowed by his vigorous wife.

Mrs Webb ran the shop, and brought up her two sons and her daughter with sensible but frugal habits: Sidney was always considerate and polite, though he had no grace of speech or movement, and he spoke with the nasal reediness of a genteel Londoner. He was fortunate in his education. He first went to a decent middle-class academy near his home, and then – surprisingly for boys of their social background – he and his brother were despatched abroad for two years, first to learn French in Switzerland and then to acquire a thorough knowledge of German in a small town on the Baltic. He started work at the age of sixteen as a clerk in a City broker's office; but he did not care for a commercial career, and he began attending evening classes in an effort to better himself. He had so much ability, and he studied so assiduously, that he passed every course with distinction and became a notable prizewinner. In 1881 he sat the Civil Service examination and was appointed to a Lower Division clerkship in the Inland Revenue. In the following year he tried for the more difficult Upper Division, and though he came second in the list he declined the post he was offered in the War Office. In 1883, trying again, he once more came second, this time to his future friend Sydney Olivier, and they both became resident clerks in the Colonial Office. The work was not arduous, and Sidney continued to study: in 1886 he took an external degree in law at London University and was called to the Bar in Gray's Inn.

Sidney was thus the epitome of the scholarship boy, coming forward at a time when the public service was just opening to able young men; and that experience made a lasting impression, for he became a reformer in technical, secondary and higher education. He was also one of a new social class that Shaw neatly called 'intellectual proletarians' – educated young men and women who had talent but no means, who were at odds with established society and equally distanced from working-class life; and Sidney's political apprenticeship was spent in the literary clubs and political societies which catered to such young people. From the start he was interested in political economy, and he was both a Radical and an agnostic by the time he was twenty. But it was only after he met Sydney Olivier, who had spent some time tutoring the son of a leading Positivist, that Sidney was directly influenced by the ideas of Auguste Comte. That phase lasted well into 1887, when he gave a lecture suggesting that Positivism, Collectivism and Anarchism were all acceptable forms of socialism, and Comte's teaching about the moralization of capitalists and government by an enlightened élite had a strong influence on the Webb doctrine of gradualist socialism which had a lasting effect on Fabian and Labour policy. Webb always saw the Fabian Society as the means to a new moral order as well as to an improved social system.

From a different start in life, and by quite another route, Sidney Webb and Beatrice Potter had thus come to much the same conclusion

– society must be regenerated, and there was no better way of life than public service; and it was that common interest that led to their first meeting.

Beatrice was in a gloomy mood over Christmas, and her sister Kate suggested that she should go to London and accompany Leonard Courtney to the funeral of Robert Browning in Westminster Abbey on 2 January. 'Rather a grim diversion, thought I' Beatrice remarked, 'but I could go to the British Museum and get what I want – I will get Margaret Harkness to introduce me to someone there who will put me on the track.' What she wanted, since she was working on the first chapter of her book, was someone who could advise her on the historical origins of the Co-operative movement, and Margaret Harkness suggested Sidney Webb. 'He knows everything,' she told Beatrice. 'When you go out for a walk with him he literally pours out information.' On 8 January 1890, Beatrice went to meet Sidney in Margaret Harkness's 'little lodging' at 45 Great Russell Street, close to the British Museum. Beatrice's initial reaction was mixed. She found him physically unattractive. Sidney was not a Jew and Beatrice was not consciously anti-semitic but in her first description of Sidney in her diary Beatrice expresses the casually prejudicial attitude of her time and class. She was, however, much impressed by his intellect and enthusiasm. He immediately drew up 'in a faultless handwriting' a list of sources she needed to consult. They met again a month later, when Beatrice was back in London, and it was after this meeting that Sidney sent her what she wryly called 'the first token of personal regard' – the draft of a Fabian tract on the municipal inspection of industrial premises.

It was, from the first, an odd relationship; and it was even odder than the diary suggests, for Beatrice made relatively few comments on it. The most revealing material is in the fairly complete set of the letters they exchanged over the next two years (see the Passfield Papers and *The Letters of Sidney and Beatrice Webb*). For these letters, emotionally cool and intellectually intimate on her part, ardent on his, chart the chequered course of their emerging partnership, and in the following pages the key passages are summarized or quoted.

Sidney seems to have formed an attachment to Beatrice at their first meeting, and time only strengthened his affection and loyalty. Five years before meeting Beatrice he had been disappointed in love, and the marriages of several acquaintances had left him despondent at his failure to find a partner. 'I have often envied the ease with which others "catch on" to congenial spirits where I simply remain outside,' he wrote to the fiancée of a friend in December 1888. 'I am of course very busy, somewhat serious, very analytic and introspective – but I hope passably honest, sincere, and not obviously hateful or repulsive. Yet I seem "left out" in more than one department of life.' That state of mind accounts for the tone of desperation in which Sidney often wrote during the year in which he was trying to persuade Beatrice to marry him; and both her diary and her letters show how such pressure bothered her. The more he pressed his case, the more she assured him he could expect nothing but the frank friendship of collaborators in a common task, and it was only when he became depressed, and their common work seemed at risk, that Beatrice felt able to unbend towards him and to envisage something closer than a working agreement. Their courtship, in fact, was the last phase of their long apprenticeships, and it was in those troubled years that they learnt how to live and work together in a true and most remarkable partnership.

*1 February.* [Devonshire House Hotel]

Already one month of the new year past. Father lying in a half-conscious motionless state, recognizing his children but not realizing ideas or feelings; his life a flickering shadow which at times seems to disappear, then to gather substance, and for a while you imagine that it is the dear familiar spirit lighting up the worn-out frame.

I am, in the meantime, so long as life lasts, chained to his side. . . . Sometimes I feel discouraged. Not only am I baulked in carrying out my work, but with the lack of all accomplishment I begin to doubt my ability to do so. Continuous reading makes me feel a mere learner, entangled in my own growth, helpless before this ever-accumulating mass of facts, which must be carved into some intelligible shape indicative of its main characteristics. At present, the facts are heaped up around me, oppressing me with their weight.

I feel, too, exiled from the world of thought and action of other men and women. London is in a ferment: strikes are the order of the day, the new trade unionism with its magnificent conquest of the docks is striding along with an arrogance rousing employers to a keen sense of danger, and to a determination to strike against strikes. The socialists, led by a small set of able young men (Fabian Society) are manipulating London Radicals, ready at the first check-mate of trade unionism to voice a growing desire for state action. And I, from the peculiarity of my social position, should be in the midst of all parties, sympathetic with all, allied with none, in a true vantage-ground for impartial observation of the forces at work. Burnett and the older trade unionists on one side, Margaret Harkness with Tom Mann, Tillett, Burns on the other, round about me Co-operators of all schools, a new acquaintance with leading socialists, and as a background, all those respectable and highly successful men – my brothers-in-law, typical of the old reign of private property and self-interested action. There is Daniel Meinertzhagen, a great City financier, earning his tens of thousands each year, upright and honourable but cordially hating 'the social question', describing frankly his ideal: English capitalists retired from business living on an income of foreign investments, the land given over to sport, the people emigrated or starved out, no inhabitants except a few dependants to serve in one way or another the fortunate capitalists. Willie Cripps would add a pauper's hospital as a school for surgical experiment and observation and a limited number of surgeons and doctors to bleed an income out of the capitalists. Alfred Cripps (the youngest Queen's Counsel at the Bar) would maintain the need for legal advice, and the charm of a well-cared-for peasantry dependent on benevolent and wealthy barristers who might choose to spend the recess in the country. And then I turn from the luxurious homes of these picked men of the individualist system and struggle through an East End crowd of the wrecks, the waifs and strays, or I enter a debating society of working men and listen to the ever increasing cry of active brains doomed to the treadmill of manual labour – *for a career in which ability tells* – the bitter cry of the nineteenth-century working man and the nineteenth century woman alike. And the whole seems a whirl of contending actions, aspirations and aims out of which I dimly see the tendency towards a socialist community in which there will be individual freedom and public property in the stead of class slavery and private possession of the means of subsistence of the whole people. At last I am a socialist!

And this is where observation and study have led me, in spite of training, class bias, etc.

Lord Thring (1818–1907) was a distinguished parliamentary lawyer; Lord Monkswell was a Liberal and much interested in London municipal politics; Lord Dunraven (1841–1926) was an Irish politician and prominent Liberal who was chairman of the Committee on Sweating in 1889–90.

*9 February. Devonshire House Hotel*
Up here for a fortnight's change. Dined with Lord Thring to meet Lord Monkswell and discuss Lord Dunraven's draft report, and help to draft an opposition. Lord Thring is a dried-up little lawyer, upper-middle-class in origin, made a peer for many years' faithful service as head of the Parliamentary Drafting Office. His views are strictly economic, a bias against sensationalism, against state interference; in fact, the high and dry orthodoxy of 1850. The whole 'Sweating' business he regards as so much 'gas'. But with the present combustible state of public opinion safety-valves must be provided. Hence in the Opposition report he will deny all Dunraven's sensational premises, but declare that there *are* evils to be remedied (which he does not believe). The remedies he suggests are utterly insufficient to cure the evils – if they did exist – and he knows it. His attitude is typical of the

time. He dare not *dare* public sentiment, so he suggests remedies which are absolutely roundabout and bound to fail. 'Of course we must pat trade unionism on the back,' said he, 'but I will die on the floor of the House before I see trade unions made absolute by driving all workers into factories where they have unlimited opportunities for combination.' Lord Dunraven is playing the card of Tory Democracy: representing the middle classes as the tyrants of society, and representing himself and the Tory aristocracy as the only guardians of the interests of the poor. 'That is why it won't suit us to be quite frank,' he adds with cynical candour. 'We must go for the evils as strongly as he does; but we must cut the ground from under his remedies.' After dinner when we three were reading over and recasting Lord Thring's notes, I managed, 'in cutting the ground from under Lord Dunraven's remedies', to prepare the ground for my special erection, which will appear as a review of the two reports in the *Nineteenth Century*. If I can make them retain my suggestions to transfer the Factory Inspectors to the Labour department of the Board of Trade or to the Local Government Board, I shall have laid the foundation for a thoroughly efficient Labour Bureau. The enforced publicity of all business accounts will be one step further – that done, we shall be on the right road to making all property holders *voluntary* officials of the State, paid 'by results' instead of by salaries, and compelled by self-interest to inspect each other's work, the landlord the employer, the employer the landlord. Though I am suspected of socialism, my anti-sensationalism gives me a footing among the sternest school of *laissez-faire* economists, and this position I must guard jealously if I am to be of even little use as a reforming agency.

The *Labour Elector* expired on 1 May when Champion left for Australia. The entries for the month of February are confusingly dated in the original text.

[12?] *February*. [Devonshire House Hotel]
Margaret Harkness spent two nights here. She is in a much more satisfactory state. Her position with the new trade unionists, and the genuine affection the leaders have for her, has softened and enlarged her life. . . . From her I catch a glimpse into the inner workings of the movement. Champion, with his Tory sympathies, his money troubles and his somewhat crooked ways, is losing his hold on Burns and [Tom] Mann. The *Labour Elector* which started as the organ of socialist trade unionists is likely to become a Tory Democrat organ in

which Lord Randolph [Churchill] and Lord Dunraven will fly their state socialist rockets. The picture she gives of Burns and Mann, of their hard work, single-mindedness and strain is very fine – and it may be true. As usual she represents the society she lives in as a huge whirlpool and her friends seem like monsters (of virtue or wickedness) in a nightmare, but this time they are lovable.

*14 February.* [Devonshire House Hotel]
Sidney Webb, the socialist, dined here to meet the Booths. A remarkable little man with a huge head on a very tiny body, a breadth of forehead quite sufficient to account for the encyclopaedic character of his knowledge, a Jewish nose, prominent eyes and mouth, black hair, somewhat unkempt, spectacles and a most bourgeois black coat shiny with wear; regarded as a whole, somewhat between a London card and a German professor. To keep to essentials: his pronunciation is Cockney, his H's are shaky, his attitudes by no means eloquent, with his thumbs fixed pugnaciously in a far from immaculate waistcoat, with his bulky head thrown back and his little body forward he struts even when he stands, delivering himself with extraordinary rapidity of thought and utterance and with an expression of inexhaustible self-complacency. But I like the man. There is a directness of speech, an open-mindedness, an imaginative warm-heartedness which should carry him far. He has the self-complacency of one who is always thinking faster than his neighbours, who is untroubled by doubts, and to whom the acquisition of facts is as easy as the grasping of matter; but he has no vanity and is totally unself-conscious. Hence his absence of consciousness as to his neighbour's corns. [Last words torn and scratched out.]

Broadhurst lunched here: asserts that trade union officials are a lower class than formerly but from the context of his complaint I should judge that he feels he is losing ground and therefore being a vain man blames others. He is an intensely common personage, but shrewd and I should imagine he had served his class well according to his lights, and according to his degree of honesty. Capacity for work he most assuredly has. But party politics, and the six months' office, have roused too much jealousy and antagonism for a man without unsullied reputation to stand. The secretaryship of the Trades Union Congress has seemed to bring with it political and social prestige and office with £1200 a year, enormous prizes in the eyes of working men and every general secretary has coveted it. . . . The man is played out, used up in the trade union movement and ready to be cast on one side. Strange the capacity of movements to make use of individuals, to suck the good out of them and cast them off as husks or empty shells!

[15] *February*. [Devonshire House Hotel?]
Delightful evening with the Booths – an evening of the old sort of triangular discussions.

'I have found a new definition of socialism' said Charlie, after we had dismissed the 'Sweating Report', Sidney Webb and various other subjects. 'The prevention by a paternal state of the consequences of a man's action: *the substitution of a new set of consequences for the natural set of consequences* following upon a man's action.'

Mary looked doubtful and critical and I burst forth with indignant positiveness. 'I don't agree with you one little bit, Charlie. Quite the contrary, under state socialism, supposing it be possible, which I do not assert; but supposing it were to take place, every man would suffer the exact consequences of his action; he could not protect himself with private property as he does now. Instead of the great class of property holders who need not use their faculties, and who may yet receive the product of other persons' faculties, this class of persons would, under a socialist system, suffer the consequences of their action or their inaction. There would be only one exception – the individual or individuals who were incapable of serving the community in any way whatsoever. Those persons would, I suppose, be dealt with as they are now, by a Poor Law: that is to say they would be protected as they are now from the consequences of their absence of ability, which in a perfectly barbarous and natural state would mean starvation. But with the exception of this one class of paupers – or of incapables – all other men and women will be drawn into the most perfect form of competition. Socialism, as I understand it, instead of destroying competition, will bring about the most perfect and universal form of it, for the simple reason that no class will be able to protect themselves from communal service by the possession of private property.

'But surely, Beatrice, you take a very peculiar view,' said Mary (with the doubtful critical way in which she handles her husband and her friend alike), 'that is not the view of Marx, of Bax, of Morris. To them socialism means the giving according to the needs, the equalizing of conditions, the levelling of all classes to one standard of comfort.'

325

'And the substitution of the will of the State for the wishes of the individual,' added Charlie. 'For instance, instead of becoming a barrister, a doctor, a merchant as I felt inclined, I should be allotted a place by a state official in return for my food and lodging, and be forced to remain in that place until Death or the State Official removed me. And if I refused to do good work, I should be still given board and lodging, and whether I did excellently, well, middling or badly, the same food and lodging would be assigned me – that's why I define socialism as the substitution by a paternal government of artificial consequences for the natural consequences of a man's action: defining "natural consequences" as the reward a man would get under a strict competitive system.'

'I think you misunderstand socialism altogether,' say I (with, I fear, an increased positiveness of tone as I feel my ground firm under me). 'First, let us define socialism; for we may be talking about entirely different things. *I* mean by socialism, not a vague and sentimental desire to "ameliorate the condition of the masses", but a definite economic form; a peculiar industrial organization – *the communal or state ownership of Capital and Land*. This stands in the front place of the programme of all socialists: Morris, Bax, Webb, Marx, Schaeffner, Schaffle, down to the author of *Looking Backward*. These men would all agree what they mean primarily by socialism, whatever else they may mean besides, is the transference to the community of the *means* of production as distinguished from the *faculty* to produce. They assert that owing to the monopoly of these means of production (land and capital) it lies within the power of a certain class to dictate whether the rest of the nation shall use their faculties or not, whether they shall be worked day and night or be unemployed. I am not for a moment endorsing their assertion. I only give their view of the present individualist system as a proof that the one thing upon which they all agree is state ownership of capital and land. I say that under this system there would be absolute freedom of individual action. . . . I have become a socialist not because I believe it would ameliorate the conditions of the masses (though I think it would do so) but because I believe that only under communal ownership of the means of production can you arrive at the most perfect form of individual development, at the greatest stimulus to individual effort; in other words cmplete socialism is only consistent with absolute individualism. As such, some day, I shall stand on a barrel and preach it.'

[16] *February*. [Devonshire House Hotel]
By a morning train to Harrow to visit M.H. [Margaret Harkness] in her convent, a bare unlovely place, with a perpetually smiling buxom old prioress. . . . Afterwards to Prince Kropotkin's, a former chamberlain to the Czar of all the Russias, now a poverty-stricken nihilist picking up a living at journalism. A hero in his way, but a very unwise one. Chattered nihilistic economics at an overpowering pace: anarchist so far as central government is concerned, antipathetic to socialism of the opportunist type, believing only in the revolution of the proletariat of all countries. It was he who wrote to Cunning-hame-Graham at the time of the London strike: 'If Burns with 100,000 men at his back does not make a revolution it is because he fears his head will be cut off.' It is the same man who declared to me that the Spaniards are in a state of higher political evolution than the English! and ended up with a vehemently expressed paradox: 'Wisdom is the greatest curse imaginable in political life.' This was gesticulated at the window of the train in which I was steaming off to Baker Street after an entertaining afternoon.

Beatrice was considering ways in which sanitary and factory legislation could be applied to sweatshops.

[22 or 23] *February*. [Devonshire House Hotel]
Am collecting my ideas for the remedies for the Sweating system, and what I do not get inserted in the Lords' Report I shall use myself in my *Nineteenth Century* review. . . .

Sidney Webb called in in the afternoon with his draft proposals and practically a proposal to transfer the Factory Inspection to the County Council in London, adopting Charles Booth's dual registration of workshops by landlords and employers, and advising some rather absurd provision of dining-rooms by employers. The County Council's inspection of workshops and factories is good and I accepted it, but I persuaded him to give up his idea of increasing the requirements of the Factory Act with regard to larger workshops and factories lest we should drive the trade into a lower channel. . . .

The *Fabian Essays on Socialism* are making way: it is curious how many persons wake up to the fact that they have always been 'socialists'. The delicious *positivism* of the authors, their optimistic conclusion that the world is most assuredly going their way, the plausible proof they bring in favour of their confidence, the good temper and the moderation, all impress the ordinary English reader.

It is curious too how they bolster themselves up with the abstract economics formerly used by the extreme *laissez-faire* school; I say 'bolster' advisedly for I believe the basis is false, whichever superstructure, socialist or individualist, may be true.

Enjoyed my stay in London; two nights at the Creightons' and then to Birmingham.

*29 March.* [Box House]
Am labouring with my paper on the Lords' Report, have been for the last three weeks. Stuck in the middle; oppressed with a constant headache and sick to death with grappling with my subject. Was I made for brain work? Is any woman made for a purely intellectual life? Then the background to my life is inexpressibly depressing – Father lying like a log in his bed, a child, an animal, with less capacity for thought and feeling than my old pet, Don; with no intelligence of passing events, crying out only for his animal wants, for his food, for rubbing, for mechanical reading to soothe the restlessness of his wandering mind. In spite of the coming spring with its gladsome sounds and sights, the consciousness of his presence falls like a black pall overhanging all things and deadening all thought and feeling. One longs for release and yet sickens at the thought of this weary desire for the death of one's father.

*22 April.* [Box House]
Finished my paper and sent it off. Spent a week in London, and dawdled a week away here with Alice Green. Decided to go for a real holiday, and then make up my mind what work I had better turn to; whether to struggle on with Co-operation without my six months [leave from home duties], or settle down to a course of reading for the winter, and start off in the spring whatever happens, whether he lives or dies. Incline to the latter. I may never get another chance of six months' hard reading – the conditions here are perfect for study, while it is doubtful whether I can get the liberty for a sufficiently long spell to do the work well, besides the doubt as to affording it.

Every day my social views take a more decidedly socialist turn. Every hour reveals fresh instances of the curse of gain without labour, the endless perplexities of the rich, the never-failing miseries of the poor. In this household [there are] ten persons living on the fat of the land in order to minister to the supposed comfort of one poor imbecile old man – all this faculty expended to satisfy the fancied desires of a being well-nigh bereft of desire. The whole thing is a vicious circle, as irrational as it is sorrowful. We feed our servants well, keep them in luxurious slavery, because we hate to see discomfort around us. But they are consuming the labour of others, and giving nothing in return, except useless service to a dying life, past serving. Here are 13 dependants consuming riches and making none, and no one the better for it. . . . It is wrong, wrong, wrong.

Though Sidney Webb won a Whewell law scholarship to Cambridge, he did not take it up.

*26 April.* [Box House]
Sidney Webb, the socialist, spent Sunday here. The son of a small London shopkeeper. Father isolated from his own class by his superior tastes: disciple and political supporter of J. S. Mill. Scrimped his own expenditure to educate his two sons and one daughter, the two former sent to Germany and allowed to run wild at a pastor's. Here the elder boy took to novels, Sidney to history, metaphysics and German economics. At 16 and 17 respectively they went 'into the City'; Sidney into a colonial broker's. Disgusted with the petty cheating of a low-class broker, the boy worked [in] his spare hours for the Civil Service examination, passed into the second division, spent 16 months in the Inland Revenue, passed into the first division, second, abided his time until a good position was open, passed second again through the first class into a good position at the Colonial Office; became a barrister, took his London degree, won the second Whewell scholarship – all in his leisure hours at the Colonial Office. 'I have done everything I intended to do,' said the little man. 'I have a belief in my own star.' 'Take care, Mr Webb,' say I in a motherly tone, 'don't be complacent about small successes.' Poor Sidney Webb. I surprised him by my sympathy and 'unholy knowledge' (as he termed it) of men's feelings into a whole history of his life, his thought, feeling, and action. 'You reduced me to a pulp by your sympathy, and then impressed your own view on me; you have made me feel horribly small – you have given me an altogether different sense of proportion – and yet I don't believe that I looked at things in a disproportionate way,' says the little man defiantly. 'Come, Mr Webb, you can feel you have humbled me – by making me a socialist.'

I am not sure as to the future of that man. His tiny tadpole body, unhealthy skin, lack of manner, Cockney pronunciation, poverty, are all against him. He has the conceit of a man who has raised himself out of the most insignificant surroundings into a position of power – how much power no one quite knows. This self-complacent egotism, this disproportionate view of his own position, is at once repulsive and ludicrous. On the other hand, looked at by the light of his personal history, it was inevitable. And he can learn: he is quick and sensitive and ready to adapt himself. This sensitiveness, combined as it undoubtedly is with great power, may carry him far. If the opportunity comes, I think the man will appear. In the meantime he is an interesting study. A London retail tradesman with the aims of a Napoleon! a queer monstrosity to be justified only by success. And above all a loop-hole into the socialist party; one of the small body of men with whom I may sooner or later throw in my lot for good and all.

*5 May.* [Box House]
About my work: suddenly started on a new idea. That I will spend this winter in elaborating my old theory of economics. It seems to me that it is needed, some new view, that now is my time to work it, since I am thwarted in practical work. . . .

It is strange how absolutely *alone* and *independent* my life has become: not *lonely*, for I have many friends and fellow-workers and do not feel the need for more sympathy than I get; quite the contrary, in most of the relationships I willingly give more than I receive. But that terrible time of agonizing suffering seems to have turned my whole nature into steel – not the steel that kills, but the surgeon's instrument that would save. My whole thought and feeling has drifted far out into the future – present persons seem to me so many shadows. It is for future generations, for their *noble* happiness, that I live and pray. . . . I have staked all on the essential goodness of human nature, on that which maketh towards righteousness. If this be mere illusion, mere cant, then my own little life is a wretched failure, an absurd bubble pretending substance. . . .

The spring months, since I returned early in March, have passed happily. Those delightful early mornings, my window wide open, reading in bed, looking from time to time out on the glorious wooded valley, with the calm lines of hill behind, the walks on the common, the rides on the highland, the hours of reading and meditation with the bright soft colours and glad sounds of spring – the spirit of peaceful energy within and without.

Beatrice had been sympathetically encouraging to Sidney in the first months of their acquaintance, and at the end of April she invited him to Box for a day. The visit, he wrote to her on 30 April, made 'a very deep impression', and the 'frank friendliness' of his reception made him tell her that 'I really must have a mentor outside the working circle, a looker-on who sees most of the game, and I hope you will not refuse to repeat the experiment (as opportunity serves)'. Beatrice responded that 'this desire to be helpful' was 'part of the mother's instinct' and that when it was joined to intellectual dependence ('a curious trait in even the most intellectual women') it lends to friendship between men and women that subtle usefulness which will always make such friendships one of the greatest factors in life – so long as it is not blurred by the predominance of lower feeling, when I think it becomes a source of pure evil. The antithesis between 'intellectual dependence' and 'lower feeling' was to be the source of much difficulty in the relationship between Beatrice and Sidney over the next twelve months, for she saw him essentially as a fellow-worker, while he was in love with her from their first meeting, though any attempt on his part to say so brought a stern rebuke.

They travelled together to the Co-operative Congress in Glasgow, and what she called 'a critical 24 hours' began with a letter from Sidney which she inserted in the diary.

You tortured me horribly last night by your intolerable 'superiority'. Surely an affectation of heartlessness is as objectionable as an affectation of conceit. And you blasphemed horribly against what is highest and holiest in human relations.

I *could* not speak my mind last night, but this agony is unendurable. You will at any rate not be indifferent to my suffering. I do not know how to face another night such as I have passed. I believe you are free in the morning: come off somewhere and let us clear up what is more important than all congresses.

Now you know why I could not confess to frank speaking. Even with you.

### 23 May. Glasgow

Exquisite Whitsun weather. A long journey up in third-class saloon, I in one of the two comfortable seats of the carriage, with S.W. squatted on a portmanteau by my side, and relays of working-men friends lying at full length at my feet, discussing earnestly trade unions, co-operation, and socialism. S.W.'s appearance among them surprises, and, on the whole, pleases them. . . .

In the evening S.W. and I wandered out through the Glasgow streets. A critical twenty-four hours followed, and another long walk by glorious sunset through the crowded streets, knocking up against drunken Scots. With glory in the sky and hideous bestiality on the earth, the two socialists came to a working compact. 'You understand you promise me to realize that the chances are a hundred to one that nothing follows but friendship. If you feel that it is weakening your life, that your work is less efficient for it, you will promise me to give it all up?'

'I promise you. However it ends I will make it serve my life – my work shall be both more vigorous and higher in tone for it. I will *make* you help me, and I will insist on helping you – our relationship shall be judged solely by the helpfulness to each other's work. Forgive me, if I say that I believe that if we were united we could do great things together. I will not bother you with that; but I will vow solemnly that, even if after a time we part, I will do better things for our friendship than I could have done without it.'

'One word more,' say I. 'Promise me not to let your mind dwell on the purely personal part of your feeling. I know how that feeling unfulfilled saps all the vigour out of a man's life. Promise me to deliberately turn your mind away from it – to think of me as a married woman, as the wife of your friend.'

'That I can hardly promise. But I will look at the whole question from the point of view of health: as you say, I will not allow myself to dwell on it. I will suppress the purely personal feeling. I will divert my imagination to strengthening the working tie between us.'

One grasp of the hand, and we were soon in a warm discussion on some question of economics. Finis. . . .

Margaret Llewelyn Davies (1861–1944) was a well-known Co-operator and social reformer.

## 24 May. Glasgow

The event of the day was the sudden springing on a Congress of hard-headed Co-operators of advanced socialist theories. Margaret Davies's paper, literary and thoughtful, was listened to with respectful perplexity; then Benjamin Jones came forward and in his sonorous tones announced the conversion of socialists to a due appreciation of Co-operators, and the 'new compact' whereby socialists and Co-operators should work together as far as they could go, and then separate in good will. Whereupon Sidney Webb sprang forward and in the name of London socialists apologized for taunts and sneers, accepted with warmth the proffered hand, etc. All the while the audience of grey-headed men were evidently equally perplexed at the problems raised, and at the sudden appearance of socialism as a movement with representatives – the idea of socialist persons sufficiently important to conciliate or apologize for had evidently never occurred to them. . . . The whole scene gave one the feeling that socialists had hardly begun their propaganda.

On 29 May, Beatrice wrote to Sidney to say that she had been reflecting uneasily 'about all that had passed at Glasgow' and telling him not 'to build up a hope'. 'Personal happiness to me is an utterly remote thing; and I am to that extent "heartless" that I regard everything from the point of view of making my own and another's life serve the community more effectively. . . .' Sidney replied next day with the first of many letters urging her not to commit 'emotional suicide' by sacrificing everything to her vocation. 'Whether we are ever destined to be united or not, you are a source of life and work and happiness to me. . . . Will you simply let things alone and see what happens?' Beatrice wrote back at once. 'I will not withdraw my friendship unless you *force* me to do so, by treating me otherwise than as a friend. . . . Your letter has touched me deeply but it must be the last word of *personal feeling*.'

After the events in Glasgow, Beatrice unsealed the packet of letters from Chamberlain which she had put away in the summer of 1887: she read them over and added the following note in her diary.

I sealed this parcel up nearly three years ago. I have opened it to try and rid my mind of the whole story by seeing the actual facts. I succeeded in my effort to rise out of the agony of that relationship into a life of vigorous work – may it not be possible to cast even the memory of it from me? It has haunted me day and night. I watch his life with feverish interest, tracing with a horrible ingenuity those qualities that pained me, undermining the public usefulness of his life. I observe narrowly from all the tiny details I can gather from newspaper paragraphs and personal gossip the effect of his marriage on his character. It has seemingly withdrawn him from all active sympathy with that mass of struggling poverty; he has become a man of society, enjoying wealth, leisure, social position and a charming young wife. The stern enthusiast with his uncompromising policy who dictated his views to me in the Standish garden has been transformed by circumstances into the man of pleasure, the darling of fine ladies, the centre of half a dozen London drawing-rooms. And this in spite of an overpoweringly strong will which would dictate to the world the manner of its government.

But all this is unworthy of me, this brooding over his ill-success is a heaven-sent vengeance on my deep humiliation, on the humiliation which he seemed to glory in and wish to prolong. After all there may have been misunderstanding on his side – on mine there was eccentricity bordering on madness – the pride and independence of a strong man, the simplicity of a child, and a total absence of the reserve and dignity which should characterize a woman. I was willing to offend him by refusing to yield to his opinions on questions of common weal. I was ready to humble myself by telling frankly of my deep and abiding feeling, how was it possible for a man, bred up in conventions, to see me as I was and to realize all the horrible suffering I was passing through. First I appeared to him as a self-opinionated person, too full of her own ideas to sympathize with his, at other times as an uncontrolled emotional woman, now refusing to see him, then expressing in naked written language the depth of her feeling. Naturally enough he was puzzled – dreading to be refused – frightened of being caught – and amazed with my perfect self-possession in conversation and argument. In short, whatever may have been his faults towards me, there were ample in myself to account for all the sufferings I passed through. Can I be brave and sensible and once for all vow that I will forgive and forget?

*31 May*. [Devonshire House Hotel?]
It is a very solemn thought to feel you have a man's soul in your keeping. This afternoon at Westminster Abbey I prayed I might be worthy of the trust, that it might raise my life and his to a higher level of 'service'.

Beatrice now left with Alice Green for a holiday in Bavaria and the Dolomites. While she was away she and Sidney corresponded with high-minded intimacy. 'A very fearful responsibility has been laid upon us both – unexpectedly, undesirably,' Sidney wrote on 16 June. 'We have the ideas which can deliver the world. . . . You have it in your hands to make me, in the noblest sense, great. I, even I, have it in my power to help your own particular work. . ... Between us two let there be at any rate perfect soul union.' Beatrice wrote back a cautionary letter from Trento on 22 June. 'You are expecting too much from me – if you do not take care – you will frighten me back into acquaintanceship,' she reminded him, and though Sidney accepted the reproof he persisted. 'Our ends are the same, our views are the same; surely out of so much identity there must come harmony,' he wrote on 24 June.

*1 June. Cologne*
A long afternoon spent in prayer, kneeling alone in the Minster. Eight years ago, about this time of year, we passed through here – Mr

Spencer, Father, Rosy and I. Then I was in the pride of life, in a whirlwind of striving after personal happiness and personal success. I prayed – but with only half my heart. I was not ready to lay my life down – I had no conception of personal service. Six years ago, I passed through again, alone and broken-hearted. I prayed, but I prayed the prayer of despair. I sought relief in work for others – not simply the good of others. And even then there lurked a desire deep down in my heart that the cup might pass from me. Still, I remember well, that in an ecstasy of devotion, I prayed I might pass through the fire, that the evil might be burned out of me, slowly if need be, inch by inch. Today, as my eyes followed the grand lines and rested on the gorgeous colours, my mind travelled back through those six years and noted each stage of that long agony ending in utter humiliation – realized that my prayer has been granted. I had passed through the fire; I had been chastened but not purified; that none of us can hope to be without love as well as suffering – the dark and the bright side of tenderness. But am I chastened? I prayed, I implored help and guidance to be humble and pure, to be worthy of the position of influence I have gained. . . . And thus I thought of the worship a man is giving me – not me – but Woman through me – and I prayed again that I might make my life a temple of purity wherein to receive it. And I, so vain, so impure – God help me.

That summer both Beatrice and Sidney saw the Passion Play presented every ten years by the villagers of Oberammergau.

*27 June*
The last days of a delightful holiday.
First scene.
Two tired, wearied women whirling down to Flushing, at the last stage of silent exhaustion from the combined effect of strenuous intellectual effort and recent emotional experiences. . . . Hot days in German towns, the two wearied women gradually reviving with the new scenes. . . .
Second scene.
The play at Oberammergau. The dear old place, which I had learnt to love seven years ago, revisited with happier inspiration. Then a quiet village with its refined and happy Bavarian life, now crowded with tourists of all nationalities and creeds.
Play, beautiful and impressive. Open-air theatre, with the natural

background of rock, mountain and groves of firs, sunlight and cloud shadows sweeping across the stage. The monotone dignity, the reserve, grace, spontaneous movement of the actors (how insufficient the word *actor* becomes to express these representors), the harmony of the music, the exquisite colouring and grouping all heightened the effect of a great original conception of the 'Légende Divine' – the revolt of the workers and the women against the moneyed, sacerdotal and aristocratic class, led by a religious socialist, sacrificing his life to the interests of the community (!) Probably a false conception from the historical point of view but a grand attempt to fulfil the mission of the German mind – the giving of historical actuality to their religious faith, the reconstructing the past in its smallest detail. . . .

*20 July.* [Surrey?]

Wandering about among friends and arranging for work for the next nine months – a lazy life – and unsatisfactory enough after a holiday. My friendship with Sidney Webb has made me feel more than ever responsible. But the time for good resolutions (which ought to have accumulated during that long and delightful holiday to bursting-point) is passed, that for real hard work is here. Self-indulgence and self-complacency must be fought against – these now are my besetting sins and with an idolatrous friend may become more so. But I think I realize that the worship is not of me, but of the Ideal for which I serve now as the chosen Temple; for the rest I am always being humiliated by his greater capacity for work, greater effectiveness. . . .

Beatrice returned refreshed. She gave Sidney a present on his thirty-first birthday on 13 July and they spent Saturday, 26 July together in the Surrey hills where Beatrice had stayed with the Harrisons and Sidney with the Pearsall Smiths, an American family who settled in England in 1888. They lived at Friday's Hill in Fernhurst, near Haslemere. Robert (1827–99) was a noted evangelist. He and his wife Hannah (1832–1911) had three children: Mary (1864–1945) who was married to Frank Costelloe (1855–99), a barrister and Progressive member of the London County Council but was soon to desert him for the American art critic Bernard Berenson (1865–1959); Logan (1865–1946) who became a minor man of letters; and Alys (1867–1951) who became a close friend of Beatrice and the first wife of Bertrand Russell (1872–1970).

When Beatrice and Sidney returned to London he had to read Marshall's *Principles of Economics* that night because he was spending the next day with Beatrice on a ramble in Epping Forest, and then leaving for a holiday in Germany with Bernard Shaw. The *Speaker* was a progressive weekly edited by Barry O'Brien (1847–1918), an Irish barrister and man of letters; and the crusading liberal journalist Henry William Massingham (1860–1924) was then the editor of the *Star*, a cheap evening paper with Radical sympathies.

William Swan Sonnenschein (1855–1931) was an early publisher of books on socialism.


*27 July*. [Devonshire House Hotel?]
I go this morning to take the sacrament at St Paul's. Two months of enjoyment and rest, of friendship and beauty, must now be followed by nine months of sober strenuous work. . . .

Lunched at St Paul's Tavern with Sidney Webb and spent the afternoon in Epping Forest.

'When I left you yesterday [said he] (we had travelled up from Haslemere, where I had stayed at the Frederic Harrisons' and he with a neighbour) I went straight home; found two urgent letters, one from O'Brien begging me to write the London articles for the *Speaker*, the other from Massingham, telling me I must review Marshall's book for the *Star*. I went straight to the Club and read right through Marshall's six hundred pages – got up, staggering under it. It is a great book, nothing new – showing the way, but not following it. For all that, it is a great book – it will supersede Mill, but it will not make an epoch in economics. Economics has still to be re-made. Who is to do it? Either you must help me to do it, or I must help you!'

In the meantime he has arranged for me to contribute a volume on the Co-operative movement to Sonnenschein's Social Science series, a short, slight work, but which I think will be of some avail. We talked economics, politics, the possibility of inspiring socialism with faith leading to works. He read me poetry as we lay in the Forest – Keats and Rossetti – and we parted.

'I give you leave to think of me, when you would be thinking of yourself, but not when you have sufficient power to work. I am willing to replace self in your consciousness, but never, never would I oust work or others. I have promised you – that you know is our compact.'

Those the last words – the answer to the only words of personal feeling which burst from him as we parted.


Beatrice made no reference in her diary to the ensuing contretemps with Sidney. 'You were so *ravissante* yesterday, and so angel-good,' he wrote after they spent the day in Epping Forest, 'that I had all I could do not to say

337

goodbye in a way which would have broken our Concordat. I had to rush away from you speechless to hold my own.' He added that he had not hitherto realized that Richard Potter was rich. 'This is one more barrier between us – one more step in that noble self-sacrifice you must make to pick me up.' All the same, he said, 'I do not see how I can go on without you.' This 'abominable letter' brought a 'hurt and offended' reply from Beatrice on 9 July, insisting that he show more self-control. 'Do not be always brooding on my effect on your own life and feelings. It is truly masculine! I do not quite know what the word Love conveys to a man's mind; but *that* is not what we women understand by Love – Love to us has in it some element of self-control and self-sacrifice.' Sidney replied on 11 August on the night he returned from Germany: 'I fully admit that I was wrong to pester you with the expression of my feeling. . . . You shall not need to write me another such letter: a terrible letter.'

After this exchange they reverted to a discussion of Marshall's economic theories, and Sidney was content to press his case in terms of intellectual companionship and mutual concern with social problems. Beatrice was more content, even happier, and their letters soon reverted to the intimate tone of their earlier letters. They met several times in the course of the summer, for Beatrice had no concern for the conventions of middle-class courtship, and she was willing to meet him and even to travel with him unchaperoned: it was an emotional rather than a physical distance which separated them.

Richard Burdon Haldane (1856–1928) was an able Scots barrister, amateur philosopher and politician who was one of the coming men on the Radical wing of the Liberal Party. He was a lifelong friend of the Webbs, and after serving as Secretary of State for War in the Liberal government of 1906 he became Lord Chancellor of the first Labour government in 1924.

*29 July*. [Devonshire House Hotel?]
An interesting dinner at Toynbee [Hall] – ten representative working men, the rising young barrister Haldane, Q.C., and Sidney Webb. Haldane supercilious, Sidney Webb in deadly earnest, and the working men all open-minded and intent on their subject. We drifted from eight hours (to which most of them are agreed) to socialism and Co-operation and trade unionism. It is curious how vague their ideas are with regard to the relations of the three movements. The Co-operators are still hankering after the old ideal of each man turned into a capitalist; that independence and self-government, that dislike to subordination is still uppermost in their mind: the trade unionists fix their eyes steadily on the fact that, at the present time, they prefer to deal with private firms to dealing with corporations because the latter are more powerful. The fact that corporations pay no better wages than private firms and sometimes not as good makes them cry out: what good their extending their action? The socialists (working men)

are still inspired by a vague Utopia, where competition will no longer reign, and all men be paid equally; the idea that trade unions will still be required to protect the interests of the various classes of workers seems utterly repellent to them.

When Haldane had left, we set to and thrashed the question out, Sidney Webb and I fighting together for our own view. But the vagueness of their ideas made me feel more than ever the need for a clear-minded thinker, who will write, speak and discuss.

*26 August.* [Box House]
Begun my book. Three weeks of reading and receiving friends, mostly men – journalists, socialists and incipient socialists. Graham Wallas, my last visitor, one of the knot of Fabians who would 'run the world'. A strange warm-hearted young man with a bright intelligence, not much beyond commonplace except in its social fervour. But the charm is in the relations between these men, the genuine care for each other, the trustfulness and practical communism of property and ideas.

In the meantime I am very happy, hard at work, enjoying health, the lovely country, friendship.

Patrick Geddes (1854–1932), botanist and sociologist, became a notable theorist of town and civic planning. William James Ashley (1860–1927), eminent economic historian, was currently professor at Toronto University. Professor Lujo Brentano (1844–1931) was a German historian much interested in trade union history who translated Beatrice's book on Co-operation into a German edition published in 1893. In 1927 he was awarded the Nobel Peace Prize. *The Dream of John Ball* (1888) was William Morris's romance about the Peasants' Revolt in 1381.

*7 September. Devonshire House Hotel*
A break to attend the British Association or, rather, the economic section of it, of which Marshall was president and Charles Booth vice-president. Charles Booth, who had promised to stay with me at an hotel at Bradford, accepted a room at Leeds, so that S.W. and I were left in solitary glory at the Midland Hotel! One funny scene – S.W., Llewellyn Smith and I journeying back in third-class carriage 11.30 at night. A variety artist jumps in – a pretty smart foreign Jewess decidedly the worse for liquor – forthwith addresses herself to the gentlemen in the carriage; these leaving us at the next station, turns to my two companions. Tells us the details of her life, becoming more and more 'racy'. L. Smith collapses in the corner, looking alterna-

tively severe and unalterably amused. S.W., by whom she sits, tries to keep her in order by inquiring in the most fatherly manner into her earnings and into the statistical side of her profession. Whereupon I get interested and show signs of listening. She immediately brightens up and leaning across S.W. tells me in a loud whisper about her latest tights and the sensation they created, remarking that she did not mind speaking of such a subject to a husband and wife. I bury myself in the corner, L. Smith shakes with laughing and S.W. begins hurriedly another statistical inquiry. And it ends by the young lady offering to introduce him as a performer on the variety stage, looking doubtfully the while at his big head and little body!

The Economic Section was deadly dull: except the eight hours debate . . . a Manchester economist . . . replied to by a rattling clever speech from S.W. full also of generalizations prefaced by the superior phrases 'no one will now deny', 'I thought the idea of a universal over-production was relegated to witnesses before Royal Commission on depression of trade', all of which irritated the slow-minded economists and absolutely bewildered the audience steeped in the economics of forty years ago. . . .

Marshall's address was poor and disappointing after the excellence of his great work. This latter will undoubtedly take the place of Mill or any other economist, but not for long. There must be a reorganization of economics if they are to continue a science. A science which is always ten years behind the practical men cannot pretend to be a science. Economics in their present state do not *foretell*. . . . They throw no light on the future, but their predecessors having absolutely denied and asserted things which have proved true and things which have proved untrue, that are at present engaged in trying to widen their formula to take in all that practical men have seen or have done. Marshall has succeeded admirably in this and has left his formula wide enough to take in a great deal of the yet unknown and 'unhappened'. But is this science? I think not. . . .

A delightful afternoon with Geddes (the biologist at Ruskin's Museum, Sheffield), a pleasant chat with Ashley the historical economist, a talk with the attractive and sympathetic Brentano, a great deal of conversation with my fixed companion and back to London (after 3 days) by the late express, indulging in the unwonted luxury of a first-class, S.W. telling me the story of his examination triumphs and reading me to sleep with *John Ball's Dream*. The tie stiffening!

Lying in bed in this quiet back room, the room I have had now for near four years, listening to the City church bells for morning service. Tired but happy.

Beatrice spent the rest of September at Box, working on her book. She sent Sidney a warm letter. 'Let us go forward with this fellowship without thought for the morrow – the form it will take is not in our hands, it will grow up as the joint creation of two natures,' she wrote; and he took this 'beautiful letter' as an encouragement. 'You will do the right thing at the right time and I am content to wait,' he replied on 17 September. 'No one shall say of me that politicians must not be allowed to fall in love for it destroys all their effectiveness. I am quite sure I have never done so much work or been so efficient as this glorious summer. After all, happiness, like champagne, is of some use in the world. . . .' He sent Beatrice a book of Rossetti's poems as 'the first gift I have ventured to make to you' and, since he was giving up part of his annual leave to a Fabian speaking tour in Lancashire, he began to keep a daily account of his activities in penny notebooks which he despatched to her as letters as he filled them.

*9 September.* [Box House]
A curt letter from Maggie Harkness telling me she leaves England for 'always' and refusing my offer to come and see her. I suppose an end to our fifteen years' friendship. It could hardly end otherwise – she has lost my respect and my confidence – and her feeling for me was undermined by jealousy of my small success and possibly by a consciousness of the change in my attitude. It is sad. One always feels the worse for a broken tie – feels to some extent a traitor. And she was as tender to one in one's trouble as she has been traitorous to me in success. A strange nature – the two dominant impulses, pity and envy, helpfulness and treachery.

A newspaper description of Sidney Webb. Might have been written of Joseph Chamberlain of ten years ago. Strange fate!

*2 October.* [Box House]
Began my second chapter after four days' rest, chatting with Sidney Webb and Alice Green who were here. They liked each other and will be useful to one another. 'A dear little man, one would get quite fond of him, so wonderfully clear and kindly in telling you all he knows.' 'A bright woman, clever of course, not a person to whom one would confide one's woes.' – the respective opinions of each other. He is certainly extraordinarily improved and becoming a needful background to my working life and I the same to him. And now to work – the beauty of the friendship is that it stimulates the work of both.

341

Beatrice's visit to London was the prelude to a second contretemps with Sidney, who was beginning to take her friendliness as a tacit understanding that they would eventually marry. When Beatrice met him in London early in October, before he left for another round of public meetings in the North, she seems to have hinted at her old feelings for Chamberlain, and in this moment of intimacy he clearly misjudged her attitude and presumed to the point where she sharply reproved him. He sent an abject apology, and she replied with a letter that is so relevant to her feelings about him and Chamberlain that the main part of it is included here.

Your letter made me feel very miserable; indeed I sat down and cried. But I will tell you with absolute frankness what I felt and have felt. When you spoke to me in Glasgow I did not say, as I have said to others, a distinct 'no' because I felt that your character and circumstances and your work offered me a sphere of usefulness and fellowship which I had no right to refuse offhand. I felt, too, how hard it would be for me to lead a lonely life without becoming hard and nervous and self-willed. On the other hand you were personally unattractive to me and I doubted whether I *could* bring myself to submit to a close relationship. Remember that I was desperately in love and for six years with another man – and that even now the wound is open.

Since then I have been trying hard to bring myself to care for you – some days I have felt the strength and calm which your affection has brought into my life. . . . I have now a warm regard for you but I do not love you and until I do I will not be in any way bound. . . . The question of marriage is not a practical one at present and may not be so for two or three years. My regard for you is not strong enough to face the terrible self-questionings of an engagement – the immediate pressure of the whole family. If I were in love it would be different – but I am not in love. . . . Altogether I feel very very miserable. Try to forgive any pain I have given you, by the thought of my misery and also in gratitude for my honest effort to return your feeling. I cannot and *will* not be engaged to you. . . . I should meet you, feel bound, feel it impossible and cut it once for all. . . . Dear Sidney, I will try to love you, but do not be impatient. . . . What can I do more? I am doing more than I would for any other man, simply because you are a socialist and I am a socialist. That other man I loved but did not believe in; you I believe in but do not love. Will it end equally unhappily?

In Sidney's letters he continued to stress her belief that 'personal defects' would eventually 'sink into insignificance before our common aims and mutual sympathy', and though Beatrice was very reserved she agreed to go up to London to meet his Fabian friends at a party.

Robert Giffen (1837–1910), civil servant and statistician, was one of the founders of the Economic Society and editor of the *Journal of the Royal Statistical Society* 1876–91. University Hall, founded in 1890, was a residence where young working men could study history and philosophy in the company of middle-class intellectuals. While Beatrice was in London she discussed Sidney with the Booths, with whom he had dined a few days before: 'I failed to ingratiate myself,' Sidney wrote afterwards. Arabella Fisher had already written to Beatrice in June urging her to break off the relationship. She now wrote more firmly. 'I am afraid of your becoming entangled in a web of socialism. I should not be afraid if the sphere of the man were of wider culture and a calmer, more statesmanlike mind.' The Harkness article was called '"Salvation" versus Socialism: In Praise of General Booth', and it argued that the Salvation Army 'will do more than anything else . . . towards driving poverty out of England'. Vaughan Nash (1861–1932), a journalist who wrote *The Story of the Dockers' Strike* with H. Llewellyn Smith, later became confidential secretary to two Liberal prime ministers and a senior civil servant.

The Harkness article, '"Salvation" versus Socialism', was published on 21 October 1890.

*22 October.* [Box House]
Margaret Harkness writes a sensational article in the *Pall Mall Gazette* denouncing socialists and her old friends Tom Mann and John Burns: poor girl, another treachery added to the long roll. Socialism must be mending its bad character for anarchic adherents if she leaves the cause.

A two days visit to London – a rush. Arrived 4.30 Monday afternoon, directors' meeting 6 o'clock, walked Benjamin Jones back to dine at Devonshire House Hotel with Vaughan Nash, talked Co-operative statutes, went on to Sidney Webb with V. Nash, met Massingham (editor of the *Star*) and a party of socialists. The next day read at B.M., interviewed Burnett, Giffen at Board of Trade, V. Nash again to arrange for working up statistics, arrived at the Booths' exhausted for dinner. Wednesday, long morning with Alice Green, attended Council of University Hall, and back here in the evening.

Booth's opinion. He is not enough of a man: you would grow out of him. They and Bella Fisher against, I cold.

*6 November. Manchester*
Eighteen months since I was here: how well I remember the utter dreariness of those days. Overworked, with cold steel in my heart – dreariness embodied. No wonder I am susceptible to real deep devotion and to the charm of close companionship after that lonely wandering in the wilderness. This is the first November which I have spent without terrible despondency, gloom overtaking the greyness of

my life throughout the year. And now I am no longer on the bank watching with cold but intense curiosity the surface currents. I am swimming in mid-water with another by my side and a host to the fore and the rear of me – with the roar of a great ocean of coming humanity overwhelming the personal notes of momentary pleasure and pain, alternating success and failure. And yet without the *certainty* of affection, action would be as unbearable as actionless thought.

*15 November*. [Box House]
*The day*: and now all that terrible pain is like a passed dream, and even the scar is well nigh imperceptible: has the whole skin hardened?

At the end of November, Sidney went down with scarlet fever, and his illness was compounded by the effects of years of unremitting work and depressed frustration of his relationship with Beatrice. On 4 December, as soon as he could send 'fumigated' letters from his sick room he complained that she had sent him 'hard' and 'uncomfortable' letters. He said he was now resigned to the fact that she would not fly in the face of her 'whole family and connection' to marry him, but he made a last plea – 'let me wait under whatever conditions you please' – he asked her to tell him the truth: 'if you are *quite* sure that no advantage to your own life or mine, or to the socialist cause, could ever induce you to marry me – then it is your duty to tell me so . . . and I must bear it how I can'.
Beatrice replied in a touching but firm letter.

I cried very bitterly over your letter and tossed about the night through feeling how wrong it had been of me to have been led away from my better judgement last spring and to have granted your request for friendship. But that is now done – and cannot be undone – the question is what is the present position?

First, all you write about your career does not affect the one question. It would suit my work – and therefore me – far better to marry a clerk in the Colonial Office than a leading politician to whose career I should have in the end to sacrifice my own. It was exactly your position which made me hesitate – it was this with your views and your moral refinement which made me try to love you.

But I do not love you. All the misery of this relationship arises from this . . . there is no change in my feeling except a growing certainty that I cannot love you.

To be perfectly frank I did at one time *fancy* I was beginning to care for you – but I was awakened to the truth by your claiming me as your future wife – then I felt – that what I cared for was not *you* but simply the fact of being loved. . . .

Frankly, I do not believe my nature is capable of love. I came out of that six years agony . . . like a bit of steel. I was not broken but hardened – the fire must do one or the other. And this being the case –

the fact that I do not love you – I cannot, and will never, make the stupendous sacrifice of marriage. . . .

In a further note she laid down her conditions for remaining on 'friendly' terms.

1. That any correspondence between us should be so worded that it might be read by anybody. . . .

2. That all the letters written by either to the other up to the end of this year should be returned to the writer thereof in a sealed packet; and that the sender should declare that none have been retained.

3. That I should receive from you, with my letters, a solemn promise that you will break off the friendship if you find it is leading again to hopes and that on no possible contingency will you reproach me . . . for having misled you. . . .

*1 December.* [Box House]
Mr Haldane, Q.C., M.P., a lieutenant of John Morley's, spent the Sunday here. A successful lawyer, tinged with socialism. Came down to arrange an alliance between the progressive liberals – Asquith, Sir Edward Grey, Arthur Acland and himself, and the Fabian socialists – with an *arrière pensée* of a suitable wife! to give piquancy to the visit. As Graham Wallas had been staying with me four days beforehand and we had fully discussed our programme I was prepared to negotiate. At least 7 hours we spent over the details of a radical socialist programme, about 3 hours we devoted to skirmishing over the minor business of the 'wife'; he sending out scouts in all directions, I throwing up earthworks in the form of abstract propositions of the suitability of celibacy for the Apostles of the new creed! 'Ah, Mr Haldane: I will let you into a secret of woman's unmarried life. In my days of deep depression I brood over matrimony – but it is as an alternative to suicide.' At which he threw up his hands with an uncomfortable laugh.

*That is exactly it*: marriage is to me another word for suicide. I cannot bring myself to face an act of *felo de se* for a speculation in personal happiness. I am not prepared to make the minutest sacrifice of efficiency for the simple reason that though I am susceptible to the charm of being loved I am not capable of loving. Personal passion has burnt itself out, and what little personal feeling still exists haunts the memory of that other man [Chamberlain]. Why did I watch for hours at the entrance of the South Kensington Museum for two days last summer unless in the hope of seeing him – a deplorable weakness for which I despised myself too much to repeat the third time? But it showed clearly the way of the wind. And the feeling of growing power, the almost passionate desire that not a drop of my bitter suffering shall be wasted, the shadow-like forms of the men and women, the mixture of contempt, and pity and curiosity with which I regard them, and yet over-riding all the mother's desires to be silently helpful overwhelm me with self-contempt for those moments of womanly weakness when I would throw myself into the arms of any true lover to gain the protecting warmth of a man's love.

In the meantime poor Sidney Webb writes me despairing letters from his sick-room, letters which pain me deeply with their strong emotions. I am surrounded by men, am constantly meeting others to most of whom I am more or less attractive, partly no doubt because I am the first cultivated woman with whom they have been frankly intimate. I have that fatal gift of intimacy and as yet in spite of middle age (!) it is united to personal attraction. All this is egotistical, but what of that, it is true, and becoming moreover an uncommonly awkward factor in my life. It is hateful to feel the ground rotten beneath you, to be ignorant of the *real nature* of your influence. 'Some women mistake the power of beauty for the result of capacity,' said Mr Haldane significantly. Are all women 'nailed to their sex'?

*6 December.* [Devonshire House Hotel]
Went with Burnett and Vaughan Nash to a meeting of dockers addressed by Tom Mann. A large hall half-filled, two or three rows of London work girls, with their hard good-natured strong faces and flaunting clothes, the rest dockers of a low type, among them faces of angry rebellious spirits excited by drink. Things have been going badly with the dockers – the capitalists ignoring the union, the leaders not daring to strike, and the rank and file anxious for a battle with out o' work pay, 10 per cent of the members skulking out. Tom Mann's speech was poor, though he handled the men well. But he ranted and was not clear. He was ambitious in his projects, great schemes of federation with other unions with their own falling into disrepair – municipal workshops for the 70,000 unemployed, this latter scheme insisted on with the fervour of the unthoughtful men. (His figure was sad enough with regard to the dockers. Out of the 22,000 London dockers only 25 per cent had regular work, another 25 per cent four days a week, the remaining 50 per cent averaged perhaps two days a week.) The meeting saddened me and one doubted whether the

magnificent secular revival of last year was not already doomed to a quick dissolution.

*11 December.* [Bell Hotel, Leicester]
Visiting production societies roundabout Leicester in bitter cold weather. Sad these efforts which are foredoomed to failure. On all sides it is allowed that the workers should not be on 'the committee' and yet without this the whole idea falls through. But these brave, eager faces, full of hope and determination, the gradual loss of faith, the distrust, suspicion, discord, the masterfulness of the worser portion. It is all very, very sad.

*12 December.* [Bell Hotel, Leicester]
Members' meeting at Leicester. . . . Was called upon to speak, and failed to give satisfaction. Was nervous and thought more of what I wanted to say than what they would like to hear. It will be a long time before I am fit for much in public speaking. I have no ease at present.

Cold week; and cold at heart after my miserable correspondence with S.W. Every now and then I am haunted by a fear lest my new faith should be a delusion and the world destined to go on in its own selfish anarchic way.

Charles Stewart Parnell (1846–91) was the leader of the Irish nationalists in the House of Commons. He had just come through a special inquiry which showed that letters printed in *The Times* purporting to show his collusion in violence in Ireland were in fact forgeries; but he had then been named as co-respondent in a divorce action brought by one of his close associates, Captain O'Shea. He subsequently married Mrs O'Shea, but the episode wrecked his career and split the nationalist party.

Sir William Harcourt supported Home Rule and political reform, and was considered a possible successor to Gladstone as leader of the Liberal Party. But it was Lord Rosebery (1847–1929) who briefly succeeded Gladstone and became prime minister. Rosebery was the spokesman for the Liberal Imperialists, or 'Limps', and his interest in municipal reform was exemplified by his chairmanship of the newly formed London County Council (the L.C.C.). 'Three Acres and a Cow' was Chamberlain's election slogan in 1885, which won many rural votes for the Radicals. George Joachim Goschen (1831–1907), a banker and financial statesman, entered politics as a Liberal but became one of the founders of the Liberal Unionist Party, a strong imperialist and Chancellor of the Exchequer in 1886. Charles Thomson Ritchie (1838–1906), a practically minded and conscientious Conservative who sat for East End seats, carried through the reorganization of English local government which created the county councils in 1888.

*31 December.* [Box House]

The last day. How may I review this year? It has been a year of unusual vigour (the result of a real holiday); it has been filled with friendship, full to over-flowing with interests, a year of growing convictions, a year of love, accepted but not given. The tie that was tightening between me and another I have snapped asunder and I am alone again, facing work and the world. Six months' trial, and then I felt the chain unbearably fretting me, day by day, with anxiety on his account and miserable doubt as to the rightness of the relation. The Booths and Bella Fisher's opinion, the revulsion of feeling occasioned by a misunderstanding on his side leading to the assumption of the position of an acknowledged lover, the realization that owing to his social status I could not marry him during Father's life-time without grieving the poor old man past endurance, and that meanwhile, perhaps for many years, I could not go about the world with a hidden tie but apparently free – all these reasons burst into one decision to break the intimacy for good and all. *He has behaved nobly*: but he insists that we have no right, even if it were better for us individually, to become strangers. I have consented to this provisionally on all intimacy being discontinued. And so the year ends.

From the political point of view, the year has closed dramatically. . . . There has been infinite pathos in the agonizing struggle of the Irish people with their own contending feelings – their passionate personal loyalty to a leader, their misery at the thought of an indefinite postponement of the cherished visions of Home Rule. In spite of my innate dislike and distrust of the Irish people it was impossible to avoid a real feeling of compassion and admiration. And yet the majority of English look on with a cynical amusement, cheering the man with the most fight, upholding those they most despised and jeering, joking and sneering: this the Tories and Unionists, while the official Radicals cast about for another cry wherewith to appeal to the country, ready to drop the 'union of hearts' like a dead cinder if not a red-hot coal.

In the meantime, minus Home Rule, the Liberals have no policy. Political democracy achieved, what more is there to do, unless you are prepared for social or industrial democracy? . . .

As for leaders in thought and action, we have none. Gladstone totters to the grave grasping with senile persistency Home Rule for Ireland; Morley is a mere moral preacher of old-fashioned commonplaces with no single clear idea on industrial questions except a vague hankering after *laissez-faire* and a vaguer sympathy for the more thoughtless socialism. Harcourt is a wind-bag, and a weathercock, and will apparently lead because he is a weathercock. Rosebery is the best of the lot, and has with astute perception perceived the present drift towards socialism, but he looks at political opinions with the shrewd suspicions of a Scotch trader: which set of views will find the best market or prove ultimately the most sought after? He too is a peer and a plutocrat, and it is difficult for such as he to enter 'the Kingdom of Heaven' or that of democratic leadership.

On the other side they are stronger. Chamberlain with his smart little wife consorts with fashion and increases the luxurious magnificence of his establishment. A lingering echo of the effete radicalism of 'Three Acres and a Cow' – acts as a worn-out badge to remind the Democracy he was once their 'humble servant'. Otherwise each speech he delivers is further away from the growing questions of the day, and he must either become a Tory or sink into political obscurity. But as a Tory he will be strong, or ought to be, if he governs his temper and consents to take a back place. He will appeal with the same incisive vigour and with more personal emotion against an infringement of the rights of property than he has done against the disruption of the Empire.

Balfour is the ideal Tory: every inch a fine gentleman with a big dash of the scholar and dilettante metaphysician who favours the Christian hypothesis. He is strong-willed, swift in execution, utterly cynical, and honestly contemptuous of that pitiful myth 'Democracy'. He is *pitiless*: whether they be hysterical Irishmen or whining unemployed he would crush them in the intervals between a flirtation with one of the 'Souls' and the reading of a French novel or a German treatise.

Goschen has at last found a happy land as protector of City princes. He, perhaps, understands to the greater extent than any of his colleagues the philosophy of Tory politics; he is wide awake to the loaded atmosphere of the present 'Liberalism', ready to explode into sheer socialism.

Ritchie, the least known, is carrying out with painstaking industry the instructions left at the Local Government Board by his radical predecessor Sir Charles Dilke – and relieving the government of the reproach of being reactionary. Indeed until the Liberals accept socialism, Tories are more likely to promote it, as they will preserve property from the inroads of the little man and keep the inheritance of nature intact for the rightful heirs instead of doling it out to silence Tom, Dick and Harry. They will, however, doubtless change their policy when they once recognize their true opponents.

Neither have we a thinker: any man or woman who tries the true mettle of the current coin and distinguishes for the use of the multitude what is base and what is pure. Marshall is a mere eclectic, and yet he is the writer of greatest and widest influence on social questions. . . . No light anywhere on the one absorbing question of the Haves and the Have-nots. All of us groping, and no clue, except the attenuated and broken threads of Fabian socialism which valiantly tries to supplement want of substance with self-assurance. They, the only men I know who *feel* themselves leaders, and not merely astute observers of the way of the wind, or obstinate obstructors cloaked in cant or mere cynical *après moi le déluge*. *Of truth the Hour is Here but the Man tarryeth.*

## ∽ 1891 ∾

On 30 December, with a sad but gentle covering note, Sidney returned Beatrice's letters. 'Two things support, and will support me,' he wrote. 'I feel absolutely sure of your perfect honesty, to me and to your own self, and that I may count on an unconventional frankness.' Beatrice acknowledged the package next day, regretting 'the misunderstanding and mistakes which have led to your pain and, to a lesser degree, to my own'. This reply was followed a day or so later by another letter, noting that Sidney had 'fully and unreservedly' agreed 'with the conditions laid down' for the continuation of their relationship. 'Your letter is very noble in tone,' she wrote, 'but you will of course remember that in future you must write as a friend, as a friend only.'

After a meeting in London she changed her mind about the Fabian Society and sent an anonymous subscription to its funds. 'I wish I were *absolutely* convinced,' she wrote to Sidney on 13 January. 'I am not yet. Every now and then I am haunted by a fear of waking up from a dream: my individualist antecedents have still a hold on me.'

*4 January*. [Devonshire House Hotel]
Up to London to get material for my fifth chapter. Sidney Webb and Graham Wallas dined with me last night. S.W. is in a thoroughly weak, miserable state: not strong enough to work, and excited and jealous, more deeply involved than ever, perhaps it is only his weakness. Conversation unsatisfactory: Graham Wallas beneficently

kind to him, but perplexed at the whole thing. Both pressed me to join the Fabians: refused lest it should injure my chances as an investigator, and with a hidden feeling that perhaps it will be impossible for me to continue honourably as S.W.'s friend.

Florence Nightingale (1820–1910) was the founder of modern nursing and an influential figure in British social policy.

*13 January.* [Devonshire House Hotel]
Vaughan Nash escorted me through the small production Co-op at the East End. Afterwards dined here and went to big meeting at Charringtons of dockers. Better tone and more promising than the one two months ago. But what material! even the best of the dockers bear the brand of London cunning and London restlessness. Tom Mann is a genius in his way, a true reformer of men. . . . Tom Mann urged the men to stick to their union and use it for political purposes, such as the creation of municipal workshops, etc.

Afterwards I spoke to him (Vaughan Nash is his greatest friend) and we arranged to meet at some future time – he was courteous but distant. As V. Nash and I walked back together: 'Tom Mann is prejudiced against me.' 'Yes,' answered V. Nash. 'He looks upon you as a schemer, a person with tin-pot schemes as he calls them, possibly it is your cousin Miss Harkness who has given him that idea.' 'Probably,' say I. And then V. Nash and I discuss somewhat vehemently the attitude of suspicion towards politicians and middle-class philanthropists entertained by those labour leaders or some of them, he defending it as proven and I deprecating it. 'You can have no conception, Miss Potter, how the politicians have tried to nobble the New unionism: John Burns and Tom Mann have lived for the last year surrounded by schemers, they have had both to live down calumny and the treachery of such persons as Champion and Margaret Harkness; they have had both to resist the social blandishments of lion-hunters or place-hunters. Burns can afford to coquette with it – Mann cannot.' And then V. Nash burst into an eloquent denunciation of the political world, more especially of politicians who seek to lead in labour questions.

All this is very painful. If all men's motives are suspected who leave the tracks of their own class, where can we look for leaders? Tom Mann has left the occupations and habits of his own class as completely as Vaughan Nash has sunk his superior training and chances in an endeavour to serve his country. This atmosphere of suspicion is hateful; God grant that I may never use my influence to create or intensify it.

And let me bear well in mind when I feel inflated by the affection or approval of others that there are many persons, able and good men and women, whom I inspire with repulsion and distrust. Octavia Hill objected to my being asked to preside at a meeting because I tried to float myself and my work through my personal influence on men: and the same impression had reached Florence Nightingale. Mrs Besant has always distrusted me: and Tom Mann and doubtless John Burns regard me as a schemer! And this is the crown I have won. *There is always some foundation for a deeply graven impression* – despite traitors like Margaret Harkness.


*22 January.* [Box House]

My thirty-third birthday! Just sent off the first instalment of my first book. Working hard and working well – one day goes like another. Breakfast at 8, work from 8.30 to 11.30, a few minutes' turn, then read to Father for one hour. Lunch, cigarette, one hour or so walk, a sleep, read 4.30, work till 7.30. Supper, cigarette, letter-writing or dictating (if I am not too tired) and then to bed at 10 o'clock. I often wonder whether I could do anything without this healthy regularity of life.

Mrs Thompson, little Miss Darling, Neale, Don [Beatrice's dog], and the cat – occasional letters from men friends – and my own thoughts fill up the intervals of work. But in spite of my 33 years I feel younger than I have ever done before, except that I feel horribly 'independent', absolute mistress of myself and my circumstances – uncannily so. 'Men may come and men may go, but I go on for ever!'


*2 March.* [Box House]

Nearing the end of my book, and beginning to think of new work.

Llewellyn Smith spent Saturday and Sunday here: a lovely day (Saturday) we wandered into the Longfords woods early in the morning, and thrashed out the whole question of a trade union book and found when we returned it was 3 o'clock and we had spent exactly five hours talking! It ended in my offering in a vague way and he accepting joint editorship: but whether we shall offer to undertake some of Charles Booth's work first is uncertain. He is able, unself-conscious though ambitious, a good colleague, loyal and honourable, an eminently 'outside' man – and as a worker a better executant than originator. In such ways he suits me.

*7 March.* [Box House]
Ghastly report that I am to be appointed a member of the Royal Commission on the Capital and Labour questions, and that Charles Booth would be chairman. Gave myself a racking headache worrying over it. I should have to accept, and yet what an ordeal, an ordeal of fire! As it is with the overwroughtness of 6 months' writing, with the prospect of public speaking 'ad lib', I feel as I should like to throw down my work and cry. But it is all miserable weakness, arising from self-consciousness, instead of forgetting about myself and going bravely on my way; I can but fail and heaven knows that the world is kind to me, too kind and too curious and too determined to push me forward. Oh, how detestable public life is to a woman! And yet a sort of fate drags one into it.

*28 March. Easter Sunday* [Box House]
My book practically finished, just 7 months, written about 250 pages. 'You have taken too long over it,' says my friend (Sidney Webb). I say, 'Not long enough'. What is it, a clever political pamphlet or a sound contribution? My former self doubts my present self: which, I wonder, will prove the wisest – the cold-blooded investigator or the would-be reformer, intellect or heart? Worked hard and well this winter, and felt 'up to it': certainly I am 'firmer' in body and mind than I have ever been before.

All through the first months of 1891 Sidney and Beatrice kept up a stilted correspondence, with Sidney reporting his interests, activities and intentions. He was eager to leave the Colonial Office and become a full-time Radical politician, running for the L.C.C. Beatrice, for her part, sent him two chapters of her book and when he wrote rather critically about it she felt dispirited. They were both evidently depressed at the estrangement between them, both uneasy about their respective professional futures, and both held back by pride from resuming their relationship on the old footing.

Sidney, in fact, decided that he must in any case resign from the Civil Service; on 6 April he wrote frankly to Beatrice about his 'cramped and joyless life' saying that he had no time for reading or theatres or concerts, and that he felt 'like the London cabhorse who could not be taken out of the shafts lest he should fall down'. It was a touching letter. 'I am prepared to serve your life, and to ask nothing whatever in return,' Sidney wrote at the end, 'save only your work for socialism and such share of friendship as you choose to give. . . .' Beatrice, too, was troubled. She was anxious about her book, and worried about a series of lectures on Co-operation which she was to deliver at University Hall. She stayed with Alice Green, who brought in Sidney to help her to prepare a press release on her lectures for *The Times* – and thus eased the estranged pair over the embarrassment of meeting.

*11 April.* [London]
My first lecture a deplorable failure! Just not a fiasco. To make matters worse Frederic Harrison, Haldane, Massingham and Herbert Spencer turned up! Perhaps it is well to begin with a failure.

*17 April.* [With Alice Green]
My second lecture a success. Sent in carefully prepared memorandum of inquiry to Leonard Courtney (who is appointed on the Commission on Capital and Labour). Have offered [*illegible*] my services as a subordinate secretary to inquire into female labour. Am afraid my 'extreme' tendencies will be against me: should dearly like the appointment, give me an opportunity of showing that a woman can do thorough work.

*21 April.* [With Alice Green]
My lectures 'going' all right. But oh! the nervous irritability of the next day! . . .

Sidney and Beatrice were back on easy terms again, as they went down to Lincoln at Whitsun for the Co-operative Congress. A year before, at the Glasgow Congress, they had made their 'working compact' and now Beatrice at last gave way; Sidney's persistent devotion to her and to their common concerns had touched her feelings, and her own need for a companion triumphed over her fears and her pride. A year later Sidney referred to the decisive moment when Beatrice did not withdraw her hand from his; and she afterwards recalled 'that evening at Devonshire House [Hotel] – in the twilight when we for the first time embraced – how well I remember the happiness tempered by great anxiety'.

'I am still a little in a dream,' Sidney wrote on 21 May and two days later he sent Beatrice another letter full of happiness, and touching on the difficulties as well as the 'enormous advantages' of their partnership. 'One – *la vie intime* – I want to talk to you about very frankly or, rather, I want you very frankly to talk to me, who am more than usually ignorant. One thing is quite certain: I will not have your intellectual and working life spoilt, whatever the cost to me. It would not be a "chattel" marriage and we are neither of us likely to insist on anything that would injure our common usefulness.'

The Liberal group, which included Sydney Charles Buxton (1853–1934), M.P. for Poplar, and Sir Arthur Acland (1847–1926), an

M.P. much concerned with educational reform, were all on the left of their party. The five Fabians included William Clarke (1852–1901), a journalist who was one of the group which founded the society and was a strong but rather depressed moral reformer.

## 22 May. Box House

A really enjoyable six weeks with Alice Green. I believe further back I have an entry describing her – from the unfavourable point of view – the point of view given me by the Creightons and Miss Souvestre. Now I see her differently, and certainly with more real knowledge. She is first a brilliant woman with a veritable fund of intellectual curiosity. Warm-hearted, full of divine pity for suffering, more especially mental suffering, ready to sacrifice herself, to give herself away. If there is a moral flaw in her character it is the intensely personal aspect in which all things clothe themselves – her judgement warped by the opinion of her, the treatment of herself. She is in fact supremely *feminine* in her character, with a grand capacity for self-devotion *in return for adoration*; but also latent capacity to be a 'nasty enemy'. I say *latent* for certainly since I have known her she has always struggled against the feelings of spite or revenge which occasionally flash across her character. Unhappy and restless: I do not understand this strange restlessness and unhappiness – what is it all about, except the desire for some strong affection? Public service or search after truth do not afford her any abiding motive for endeavour. They serve only as a *pis aller*. A good woman, sincere friend, who encourages and also criticizes.

My lectures have been successful, more successful than I expected, and I have gained facility and ease in public speaking. My book too, on the eve of publication, promises success. But it is wearisome work bringing even a little book out.

Co-operative Congress at Lincoln passed off successfully – Alice, I, S.W. journeying down together. I cannot tell how things will settle themselves, I think probably in his way. His resolute patient affection, his honest care for my welfare, helping and correcting me, a growing distrust of a self-absorbed life and the egotism of successful work (done on easy terms and reaping more admiration than it deserves), all these feelings are making for our eventual union, the joining together of our resources, mental and material, to serve together the 'commonwealth'. Meanwhile Father lingers on: and while he lives nothing can be decided on. But if I marry, though I shall be drawn to it by affection and gratitude, it will be an act of renunciation of self and not of indulgence of self as it would have been in the other case. Perhaps, therefore, it will be blessed to both of us.

We had a queer party at Alice Green's towards the end of my stay: five of the young Radicals – Asquith, Haldane, Grey, Buxton, Acland, and five Fabians – Massingham, S.W., Clarke, Olivier, Shaw – Alice and myself. It was not successful, though not a failure since all were pleasant and cordial. Asquith spoilt it. He was the ablest of the lot, and determined that it should not 'go'. Haldane made himself most pleasant, and is really playing up. But the machine – the Liberal Party – is slow to move.

*31 May. Box House*
I go tomorrow back to London to begin a new bit of work, perhaps also a new relationship . . . and my first book will be published in the course of a fortnight.

If I had dreamt that those years of dull misery, with flashes of veritable agony, would end in Work and Love, I should not have needed to keep before me as a motto, Watch and Pray. They are but the negative of Labour and Love.


## *VOLUME 14 (2)*

Beatrice was temporarily staying at Herbert Spencer's house in St John's Wood, London; she had now settled that Sidney, rather than Llewellyn Smith, would be her collaborator on the proposed history of trade unionism. Clara Bridgen was a young Fabian who was thought to be a possible match for Graham Wallas.

*6 June.* [64 Avenue Road]
Decidedly another 'beginning' in my life. My first book will be 'out' in a few days, then I to Norway for a three weeks holiday with Graham Wallas, Miss Bridgen and S.W. The beginning of a new life out of which the old loneliness and hardness will be banished.

*20 June.* [Norway]
Beautiful Norwegian scenery. . . . Definitely engaged on a new life. . . . At times I am afraid, and disconsolately ask myself whether from my own point of view I have been wise. But the need for a warmer and more responsible relationship with another human being

has made it seem the best even for me. The world will wonder. On the face of it, it seems an extraordinary end to the once brilliant Beatrice Potter (but it is just because it is not an end that she has gone into it) to marry an ugly little man with no social position and less means, whose only recommendation, so some may say, is a certain pushing ability. And I am not 'in love', not as I was. But I see something else in him (the world would say that was proof of my love) – a fine intellect and a warm-heartedness, a power of self-subordination and self-devotion for the 'common good'. And our marriage will be based on fellowship, a common faith and a common work. His feeling is the passionate love of an emotional man, mine the growing tenderness of the mother touched with the dependence of the woman on the help of a strong lover, and in the background there is the affectionate *camaraderie*, the 'fun', the strenuous helpfulness of two young workers in the same cause. Workers have the great advantage that there is a great fund of playfulness and high spirits in the times of rest after the year's labour. Our holydays will be real holydays – nothing is too small or too trivial to yield amusement and interest to two hard-worked individuals who have given themselves a rest from work. He is in a state of happy exaltation, I am beginning to feel at rest and assured. It will not wrench me from my old life, simply raise it to a higher level of usefulness.

The long dreamy days with the beautiful scenery passing by; the mountain fiords, rivers, waterfalls all in rapid succession lend a stillness to one's mind, a lengthened brooding over the past and the future. It is well to have this time of almost religious rest, this Sabbath of emotion, for with both of us there is a long dusty road, with steep inclines, before us. Our life will be strenuous, may it not also be peaceful? We have honestly only *one* desire – the commonweal. Why may not the current of our lives be deep and unruffled by all the surface agitations of personal success and failure?

*7 July.* [Norway]

Our last resting-place – high up in the Highlands of Norway. It is raining and I am lying on my bed, knocked up with climbing the Roppen.

The last two days we have been discussing our future. Last spring Sidney decided to leave the C.O. expecting to make sufficient in journalism to go into politics. Now it is no longer necessary for him to make money, since I shall have enough for both. So we have had to reconsider all the half-arrangements we had made to write 'London Letters' for provincial papers and edit a Fabian Review. Last evening, by the glow of the sunset, we wandered over the moorland, hand in hand, and talked somewhat thus:

B.P. I don't want to influence you in the detail of what you do, for everyone must work out his own life; but I think it is time that you deliberately planned what you intend to be – and that you made everything else fall in with that.

S.W. You forget that has been impossible hitherto. I have decided that I want to take part in the government of the country according to socialist principles. I also want to think out the problems of socialist administration before they actually come up for settlement.

B.P. Quite so. That is exactly my view of what you want to be. But writing London Letters and writing Fabian Review won't help you to *that*. You know that I think more highly of your abilities than you do yourself. So I don't mind saying that in order to become a first-rate administrator you want more education in the technique of administration, and that in order to think over the various social problems you want technical knowledge of those very questions! The London County Council will help you to the one, helping me will give you the other.

S.W. I agree with you about my deficiencies, but I think there is a danger that in trying for big things we may diminish our usefulness, that is, refusing the smaller influence one gains by casual journalism, one may be neglecting the only work one is capable of doing well. To help you will be one of my principal aims – but for other reasons. What I am undecided about is whether you are not (and I also) too ambitious for me, whether you are not expecting too much from me.

B.P. No; I don't expect anything in particular from you. . . .

We are both of us second-rate minds, but we are curiously combined – I am the investigator, and he the executor – and we have a wide and varied experience of men and things between us. I have also an unearned salary. This forms our unique circumstances. A considerable work should be the result, if we use and combine our talents with a deliberate and consistent purpose . . . and so on.

I have given these bald notes of our conversation because one would like to look back and see how far the future justifies our present plans.

A large part of our thoughts are taken up with the future. We are both of us in the mid-current of our life's work. We are both of us grave and anxious that our marriage – our happiness in each other's love – shall not interfere with each separate work. More especially am I fearful – and he for me – lest my work should be ended and I absorbed in the details of domestic life. I do not despise these details, but it is no use forging a fine instrument with exceptional effort and then discarding it for a rough tool. It may have been misdirected effort to make the instrument, it may be a mistake to transform the Woman into a Thinker, but if the mistake has been paid for, one may hardly throw away the result.

This next year I shall devote to the trade union book, and he will help me. He on the other hand will be preparing for the life of an active administrator. And we will both try to keep humble, earnest and pure. For we have a great responsibility laid upon us. Not only has each one of us faculty and the opportunity of using it, but both together – the two united for a true marriage of fellow-workers – a perfect fellowship: it is for us to show that such a marriage may be durable and persisting.

*15 July. 64 Avenue Road*
A rather painful interview with Mary Booth. I felt obliged to tell the Booths, though now I am inclined to think it was a mistake. I hoped that after our long friendship they would have come forward and would have tried to get to know Sidney. But evidently it is supremely distasteful to them. Feeling this, I suggested that they might find it easier, considering that my engagement was not known to my family, to ignore it themselves, and to wait until we were married to be friends with him. And she heartily concurred. That curious little look of veiled determination came over her face, and she said: 'You see, Charlie and I have *nothing* in common with Mr Webb. Charlie would never go to him for help, and he would never go to Charlie, so that it would not be natural for them to see each other. When you are married it will be different. Then there will be the relationship.'

There the subject dropped and for the rest of the interview we talked exclusively about Charles's work and their children. She never mentioned my book though I had given it her before I left for Norway. As I had written a warm letter of appreciation of Charles's book I did feel a little hurt. But perhaps she did not happen to think of it. Anyhow it does not do to be sensitive. But it was not unnatural that I should sit down and cry, not about their not thinking much of my little book, but of their not really caring to know him. It soon passed over and now I feel strong again and peaceful. She has a narrow and conventional nature, and in spite of a genuine affection for me she cannot take with loyal trust my view of my own life and accept it. But from Charlie I expected something different: he is too big a mind for that and his feeling for me was warm and strong. A shadow has crept between us and has deepened into a darkness.

Though Mary Booth was 'sorry it is so', she was not so unsympathetic as Beatrice believed, for she told her husband that Beatrice 'looks remarkably well, young, pretty and blooming, like her old self. . . . She is evidently happy and believes in Mr Sidney Webb thoroughly.' Charles Booth wrote with more politeness than warmth to say he hoped 'to become better acquainted with Mr Webb' and hoped to gain much 'from a close and cousinly contact with the school of thought and action of which he is so brilliant a representative'.

The engagement was secret, for Beatrice did not propose to tell her family while her father lived, and only a few close friends were told of it.

### 16 July. [64 Avenue Road]

I was unfair on Charlie Booth. His affection has got the better of his prejudices; possibly Mary felt remorseful after the gentle way I treated her dislike of and prejudice against Sidney.

Alice Green is warmly congratulatory about our engagement; so is Haldane, so is Llewellyn Smith.

### 31 July. [64 Avenue Road]

In spite of kind letter, Charles Booth has not offered to see me; and Mary has expressly begged me not to come on Sunday, the only day he is in London. And yet they can afford time enough to go out to some mere acquaintances such as the Winckworths! Obviously he is vexed or simply indifferent. And she still treats me, when I see her, as an unfortunate misled person who is to be pitied and gently repudiated for the impropriety of her conduct. But I am not going to fash myself over it. I shall always have a warm admiration for Charles Booth and an affection for her. If they cease to feel warmly to me – well, I must think of them tenderly and go on my way.

### 11 August. [64 Avenue Road]

Breaking ground in trade unionism. S.W. comes and works with me. Yesterday being Sunday and wet he came at 11 o'clock. We allowed half an hour for confidential talk and 'human nature' and then worked hard at the Iron Founders' records. Then lunch, cigarettes, a little more 'human nature' and then another two hours' work. A cup of tea, walk to the Athenaeum, work at the social science records in the library and dinner. In the drawing-room up comes Mr Cheetham, a mild individualist Liberal, former Member, present candidate. We got into a warm discussion. I introduced Sidney and then we turned on him and rended his 'liberal' creed. He sat fascinated and helpless, shifting his position from weak *a priori* to interference and deprecating interjections that it was not 'practical'. We left him rather dazed – not quite certain whether he was angry or converted or simply muddled.

It is very sweet this warm and close companionship in work. The danger is that I shall lean on him too much and get into a chronic state of watching him at work and thinking that I am working too. But our happiness in each other takes naught from the world . . . and it should exalt our effort, strengthen our capacity to make this happiness possible to other men and women.

*14 August.* [64 Avenue Road]
Working every day at the Home Office. . . . There I sit in that big official apartment, strewn with despatch boxes in solitary glory with the roar of Whitehall below and Big Ben tolling out each quarter-hour and occasionally one or the other of my neighbours, superior clerks, comes in to see how I am getting on. . . . There is the feeling of being inside a big machine – but oh! to control it – to *use* it for making the slum as dignified, restful and orderly as the official residence. . . .

A succession of trade unionists to dine here. (Poor Herbert Spencer! to think that his august drawing-room is nightly the scene of socialistic talk, clouds of tobacco, aided with whisky.)

I see I shall have some trouble to get my information. Most of the trade union officials are hard-headed suspicious men, with an anti-feminine bias. . . .

When Beatrice returned to Box House she wrote to Sidney about her family affairs and told him the photograph he had given her was 'too hideous for anything'. She asked him to supply a new one: 'let me have your *head only* – it is the head only that I am marrying!'

*19 August.* [64 Avenue Road]
The last day in these pleasant rooms: five weeks of happiness which is becoming more complete and inspiring each day. Poor Herbert Spencer: if he had seen us evening after evening working away together undermining the individualism of the British race, with

intervals of 'human nature'! His bust and portrait have looked down on us beneficently, with philosophic resignation to the inevitable. The garden behind, with its bright autumn flowers and trees beyond, the long narrow slip extending the length of the long narrow room. . . . Goodbye, Summer 1891 – you can never come again, but others will come to us like unto you.

Sidney had now resigned from the Colonial Office and during the next twelve months when they both were travelling to do research and attend meetings they often arranged to meet at a railway junction where their journeys crossed. 'We are evidently going to have a debt of gratitude to the Midland Railway hotels,' Sidney wrote on 16 September. When they were apart they wrote frequently and at length. 'We need not love each other the less because with both of us our work stands first and our union second,' Beatrice wrote on 12 September, confessing her continuing doubts about combining marriage with her research and writing. 'Every now and then I feel I have got into a hole out of which I can't struggle. I love you – but I love my work better! It seems to me that unless I give up my work I shall make a bad wife to you. You cannot follow me about the country, and I cannot stay with you. How do you solve this problem?' On 14 September, Sidney replied in much the same vein. 'We could not love each other so well, loved we not our work and duty more.' Beatrice attended the Trades Union Congress at Newcastle in September.

*25 September*. [Bath Hotel, Tynemouth]
Three weeks since I left him on the Leeds station that Sunday afternoon. Certainly we are daring in our unconventionality, mostly meeting at a hotel and spending 24 hours there. That long Sunday journey from Leeds to Newcastle arriving midnight at a second-class 'House' in a noisy street of the north capital. Then the rush of the Congress week. . . . The Congress to me was merely the ante-chamber of my book.

Since the hurry-scurry of that week I have drudged in offices on records or trudged to interview after interview. The work is stupendous, and as yet does not shape itself. Certainly I work hard – I do little else – work and sleep and work again. My cramped fingers with hours of note-taking threaten positive revolt. My head whirls with constitutions, executives, general councils, delegate meetings, district delegates, branches, lodges, socials . . . until all the organs of my body and faculties of my mind threaten to form one federated Trade Union and strike against the brain-working despotism of my will! Meanwhile there is one bright moment – the clearly written letter which is 'precipitated' every morning, one half hour of willing obedience of the cramped fingers when I throw my work aside and talk with him. And in four days he will be here working by my side.

*10 October*. [Bath Hotel, Tynemouth]
A blessed time! He found me utterly worked out with the combination of hard clerk's work and the insufficient food of a mining village. . . . He took over all the accumulated work, and while I have been lying on the sofa he has been busily abstracting and extracting, amply rewarded, he says, by a few brief intervals of 'human nature' over the cigarettes or the afternoon cup of tea. With our usual coolness I have taken a private sitting-room (he staying at another hotel) and he spends the day with me in the capacity of 'private secretary'. The queer little knot of the inhabitants of the hotel are so impressed with the bulk of my correspondence and the long hours of work that I do not think that they suspect the intervals of 'human nature', but think no doubt that I keep my amanuensis hard at it all hours of the day! And now that I am fairly well again, we are driving through the mass of reports fast and well, with the 'blessedness' of companionship. Without his help I doubt whether I could have got through the work – I have too little staying power for the extent of my aims. And for him the inquiry will be of untold use, as well as to me. The politician of the future must understand all the details of industrial life; he must be, before all things, a practical economist, for economics in the widest sense are rapidly becoming the technical side of the politician's life work. . . .

*15 October*. [Bath Hotel, Tynemouth]
The last evening of the 'blessed' fortnight and I have sent him ruthlessly to interview the 'Good Intent Coopers'. Yesterday night we spent at a public [house] in Newcastle interviewing plumbers, and today we have been hard at work on rules and reports. Certainly we are a couple of indefatigable workers. The danger I see ahead is a one-idea'dness, an absorption in this somewhat ugly side of humanity, an absorption that will be made more absolute by our companionship. It is hard to steer clear between one-idea'dness and futile mental distraction! Tomorrow I leave this bleak North Country sea-town. Each place I leave now, when we have worked together, I feel saddened at the thought that a bit of happiness is past and gone.

Beatrice was probably visiting Sir Hugh Bell (1844–1931), colliery-owner and railway director.

*21 October.* [Rounton Grange, Northallerton?]
Travelled from Darlington to Durham in the same train as Chamberlain and his wife. Watched them set out to walk to the Sunderland train and standing by the side until we speeded out of the station. He was looking self-complacent and somewhat self-conscious, quick to perceive whether he was recognized by the casual travellers. He has lost that old intent look – the keen striving expression of the enthusiast stimulated by ambition. Perhaps he has lost both enthusiasm and its evil counterpart, personal ambition. His wife was a plain little thing, but sweet and good and simply dressed. He was on his way to make a big speech at Sunderland. I was on one of my innumerable journeys 'in search of knowledge'. I shuddered as I imagined the life I had missed. Now, indeed, I can bless him for his clear understanding of my deficiencies for the great role of 'walking gentlewoman' to the play of *Chamberlain*.

Beatrice had found it a strain to conceal her engagement from her family: 'After Xmas, when we begin working together again, I will write and tell my sisters,' she wrote to Sidney on 21 November. 'Then we can begin the New Year openly – and face everything openly and together.' Their letters were now a curious mixture of affectionate confidences with working notes on their research into trade union archives and comments on Fabian politics – on which Beatrice offered sound tactical advice. On 16 December, Sidney was selected as a Progressive Party candidate for the L.C.C. in Deptford, and at the ensuing election in March 1892 he was elected: he held the seat for a period of eighteen years, in which he became one of the most influential figures in London politics.

On Christmas Day, noting the 'veritable agony' of recent Christmases, Beatrice sent Sidney a 'happy but serious' letter. 'I will try to repay your love and devotion and to make your home and happiness together – in spite of your "professional" wife. I will try and prove that a woman may be a loving wife and gentle mistress without assuming to be a strenuous public servant. But I shall often stumble and fall – and you must help me up and protect me against self-complacency or lethargy either at home or in our work.' Sidney replied two days later. 'It has been a good year to us, dearest – a heavenly year to me though it opened gloomily enough. . . . We shall be very happy and also very useful, playing private secretary to each other in turn – though I want you to think and invent, rather than to work.'

*27 December. Box House*
Two months here and resting and being the daughter in charge of the poor struggling dying father. His breathing is terribly hard – he has paroxysms in which he seems like one drowning and then intervals of semi-consciousness. It is horribly depressing and casts a gloom even

over a happy consciousness. And I have been feeling incompetent and inefficient, weighted down with the extent of the labour before me. But on the whole the time has passed peacefully, working most days in the morning on stray trade union material, then reading books in the evening, but on the whole I have been idling.

The year has been uneventful. My engagement was a very deliberate step, each condition thought out thoroughly; now it is an unconscious happiness. Otherwise my life has little altered. I am still the investigator living the life of a bohemian. My friends are the same with few substitutes and additions. Margaret Harkness has finally disappeared: her strange ways, deliberate lying, mysterious financial positions have killed all respect on my side. Gradually I began to doubt the truth of her accusations, presently I became aware of a certain sordid side to her manoeuvrings which cut at the root of affection and confidence – so I allowed her in a fit of pique and envy to cut the tie that bound us together. It is a sad ending to an old friendship.

Another friendship, one which I value, threatens to be broken. The Booths have practically dropped me. It remains to be seen whether the excuse they give, that they cannot recognize an engagement which is not known to my relations, is a true reason or only a preparation for a gradual withdrawal of their friendship. In a week's time my sisters will know of my engagement, then if the Booths really care for me the separation between us must cease. Anyway there will be no bitterness on either side. What they have freely given they shall freely take away.

Other friendships either stand as they are or have become closer. Alice Green, Graham Wallas, Ella Pycroft, my little knot of working-men friends, Jones, Burnett, Dent, are nearer to me than they were last year. The Creightons, Miss Souvestre and the one or two half friends-half acquaintances are still on affectionate terms. But of course my hidden engagement has not led to much real intimacy with anyone outside the shunned circle of informed or suspecting friends. On the other hand, Haldane and other political associates are appearing on the horizon, comrades which a word or an act might transform into friends. With my family my relations are easy, necessarily becoming more and more intimate as our views diverge but with no sense on either side of strain or bitterness. 'We know no more of Beatrice than we should were she a man' expresses the family view. I imagine they will take my marriage with their usual good sense and good temper, slightly contemptuous and with friendly unconcern. The 17 men and women (with the exception of the unfortunate [Arthur Dyson] Williams) are far too prosperous and fully occupied to do more than lift their eyebrows and wish me good luck. Poor little Rosy with her husband mortally stricken and her child sickly is going through the purgatory which may make her into a woman – perhaps we may meet later on. They are the only ones of my family to whom Sidney may become a helper and a friend.

About my work I am just at present disheartened. I feel one ought to devote about one year to each trade – and make the book the fruit of the year's labour. That under present circumstances is impossible, and possibly it would be unwise under any circumstances. Sometimes in spite of my happiness in companionship I feel fearful of this new element in my life, whether or not it will be with a considered professional career.

## ～ 1892 ～

*New Year's Day.* [Box House]
Dear Father passed away peacefully this morning. Kate and I had been watching through the night and he had been in a heavy stupor breathing quickly and mechanically. When I came in dressed in the morning I found him in the last deadly gasps, not struggling but simply breathing out the last spark of life. This afternoon I visited his room and he was lying there with his sweet gentle beneficent smile and beautiful rest from the weary struggling life of a day ago. And now his spirit has ceased as far as we can know, but his gentle courteous nature lives still in our hearts. Few men have attracted and given more devoted affection.

And now a week with the family and family concerns and family possessions and then my life openly united to that of another – working while it is yet day to make human life nobler.

'Dearest, this is the beginning of a new year for both of us,' Sidney wrote when he heard the news from Box, 'and you, for the first time, are *quite* free to give yourself to your work and to me. I will do all I can to make you gain thereby . . . over your father's death let us cement our agreement again that all we do shall be for "social service" as far as we know how.' Beatrice needed his support. Rumours of their engagement had appeared in the papers, and Sidney tried to keep the secret by sending telegrams in German and persuading journalist friends to keep silent, but Beatrice realized that she had to send letters to her sisters explaining that she was engaged. She was so uneasy that she wrote almost too frankly about her future husband and offered them a blunt choice between accepting him and losing touch with her. 'He is very small and ugly,' she told her eldest sister, Lawrencina Holt 'He has none of the *savoir-faire* which comes from a leisurely up-bringing and of course he has none of the social position which springs from great possessions and family connections.' Yet, for all her apprehensions, the family generally behaved with good sense and kindness, both sisters and brothers-in-law sending generous letters and ensuring that suitable dinner-parties were arranged to welcome Sidney. Beatrice, in turn, was invited to the modest home in Park Village East, near Regent's Park, where Sidney lived with his mother and sister, his father having died in the previous July.

Grant Allen (1848–99), an author and journalist, made his reputation with *The Woman Who Did* (1895) which attacked the male double standard of morality: his idea of 'the new hedonism' implied equal values for men and women, and he insisted that self-development was morally preferable to self-sacrifice.

*21 January.* [52 Ackers Street, Manchester]
Three weeks of emotion. The gathering for the funeral, the impending declaration weighing me down. The publication of our engagement in the *British Weekly* telegraphed to me to Box in German by Sidney provoking a speedy confession. The family behaved with benevolence and good sense and received Sidney at family dinner in London with grave propriety. The uncomfortable week at Alice Green's – the introduction to his little home, dread of its ugliness, and then settling down in it as a guest, all these emotions crowded thick on each other. The little home in a small street near to Regent's Park – the little mother, frail and shaking with palsy, the energetic warm-hearted plain body of a sister, a stalwart German woman who acted as general servant – have become a new surrounding to my life, a new scene laid in the lower middle class. The dingy and crowded little workroom with gas fire where Sidney and I sit the evening through happy and unconscious in our love one for the other! And gradually the feeling of unwished-for dislike to ugly and small surroundings disappeared in the blessedness of love.

And now the old life is over – or rather the old shell is cast off and a new one adopted. Past are the surroundings of wealth, past the association with the upper middle class, past also the silent reserve and the hidden secret. Now I take my place as a worker and a help-mate of a worker, one of a very modest couple living in a small way. But in essentials I remain the same – the same woman who collected rents, studied the docks, worked in the sweated dens, and dined with the

Board of Directors of the Wholesale Society three times a week. That I shall in the first instance suffer, even in my work, for my step downwards in the social scale is probable, but if it is his gain it will not be my loss.

One relation of my life is closed by my acknowledged engagement – one which I prided myself on – the position of literary executor to Herbert Spencer.

We met yesterday at the Athenaeum [Club] by appointment. He was affectionate and cordial to me personally. 'I cannot congratulate you – that would be insincere.' Then there was a short pause. 'My family have taken it benevolently,' I remarked and then observed that there was after all nothing against Mr Webb; he had proved himself to be a man of capacity and determination. 'You see that he has succeeded in marrying me, Mr Spencer – that shows he has a will.' 'Undoubtedly,' groaned out the philosopher, 'that is exactly what I fear – you both have Wills – and they *must* clash.' 'He has a sweet temper and has been an excellent brother and son,' I urged gently and gave a vivid description of his good domestic qualities. But presently the real source of anxiety was disclosed.

'I feel I am in a fix about the personal matter to which you alluded in your letter – the literary executorship. It would not do for my reputation that I should be openly connected with an avowed and prominent socialist – that is impossible. Inferences would be drawn, however much I protested that the relationship was purely personal with you.' 'I quite agree with you, Mr Spencer,' I answered sympathetically. 'I fully realized that I should have to give up the literary executorship.'

'But what can I do?' he said plaintively. 'Grant Allen whom I thought of before, has become a Fabian. There is no one who possesses at once the literary gift, the personal intimacy with my past life and the right opinions to undertake the task.'

'What about Howard Collins?' [Spencer's amanuensis] I said thinking of the grim irony of the poor old mind thrown back on the mechanically minded Timothy. 'He is sound. Would he not do?'

'He would be the proper person – but then he has no gift like you have of making his subject interesting.'

'But I should be delighted to help him in any way you like to propose, either acknowledged or not.'

The philosopher lay back in his chair with a sigh of relief. 'That arrangement would do admirably; that is exactly what I should desire.

The Life would appear under his name and you would add reminiscences and arrange the material. That would quite satisfy me,' he repeated with a very visible access of cheerfulness.

'Well, Mr Spencer, you can rely on my doing my utmost. Mr Collins and I are excellent friends and should work together admirably.'

And so ended the interview, he satisfied about his reputation and I at ease with the dictates of filial piety.

*11 February*. [52 Ackers Street, Manchester]
Exactly three weeks since I set foot in Manchester. Have been working hard, looking through minute books, interviewing and attending business meetings of trade unions. It was extraordinarily stupid of me not to think of this ever before; one learns so much more by observing than by simply reading – but it never struck me that I would get into the private executive meetings of the societies and see for myself the positions that arise. . . . I am working hard and well. My engagement with S.W. has not injured me in the least – except perhaps with Birtwistle.

*28 February*. [52 Ackers Street, Manchester]
Two days of utter exhaustion. Last Sunday was delightful – I need him once a week to rest me in the sublime restfulness of love, and he needs me to soothe him and reduce his world of cross-purposes to its proper calm. But alas! our work keeps us apart.

Beatrice made few entries in her diary at this time: her energy went into extensive journeys about the country, visiting trade union offices and interviewing officials, and even her letters were rather short and mainly dealing with the research. Sidney wrote more often, and at greater length, but he was too busy, first with the election campaign and then with his new tasks on the L.C.C. where he was immediately appointed chairman of two important committees. They met occasionally: Beatrice came south at Easter to spend a short holiday in Sussex, and he went up to join her for a few days in Manchester.

Beatrice had sufficient private means (about £1500 a year) to enable the Webbs to live comfortably, for Sidney to devote himself to unpaid public service, and for them to employ full-time research helpers. The first of these was Frank W. Galton (1867–1952), a young engraver of socialist opinions who had attended Sidney's lectures at the Working Men's College, and who abandoned his trade to work for the Webbs at a salary of one hundred pounds a year. He was the secretary of the Fabian Society 1920–39.

*4 May.* [52 Ackers Street, Manchester]
Severe attack of influenza broke into my work – a day or two after the last meeting. A fortnight in bed, just at the time of his triumphant return to the County Council, but the last week he was with me and we both went on to Liverpool. There I rested in the luxurious Holt mansion for one week and then back again to work. I found Galton (our secretary) working on the piles of material I had left. A good deal of his work had to˙ be redone and the ensuing two weeks I spent in training him, he working all day under my eye. A sharp, attractive boy and assiduous worker and as keen as a razor, a former pupil of Sidney's in economics. But all my appointments to attend E.C. meetings [the A.S.E. executive committee] had to be given up, a grievous disappointment to me.

Then a fortnight's holiday, during which I managed to spend £29 and an hour at the dentist. A pleasant four days at Arundel with Graham Wallas and the light-hearted Bernard Shaw, then back again to our cosy little lodging. Here for ten days, it only seemed two! We have been working hard, shaping together the material into a rough history and then he working at the reference library, I casually interviewing and superintending Galton. Today he has left me and I feel a bit lonesome. We are certainly supremely fortunate. We love each other devotedly, we are intensely interested in the same work, we have freedom and means to devote our whole lives to the work we believe in. Never did I imagine such happiness open to me. May I deserve it.

Sidney was much occupied with the general election campaign in which John Burns was elected in Battersea and Keir Hardie was elected for West Ham; and other progressive candidates did well in a contest which brought the Liberals back into office. Beatrice was winding up her research in the north, and, characteristically, devoting the last entry in her diary before her marriage to a fifteen-hundred-word summary of a trades union conference. Sidney was thinking of seeking the Liberal nomination for the parliamentary seat in Gateshead.

*2 July. 36 Mount Preston, Leeds*
Interesting time at Leeds. Engineers Delegate meeting to revise the rules, to which I have been admitted by special resolution . . . The spirit and [expositions?] of the 'New Union' has infected even this conservative and aristocratic body which until a few years ago has been little better than a great benefit society. Not that the A.S.E. (Amalgamated Society of Engineers) has not fought its battles. The

'Nine Hours Movement' was the beginning of a great revival of trade union activity and was initiated by the A.S.E. But except for one or two pitched battles at long intervals the even tenor of 'benevolent' claims has been uninterrupted and the A.S.E. has appeared to its members and the remotest districts of the country simply as one more great Friendly Institution for mutual help in the common need. . . .

Some pleasant evenings I have had chatting with selected delegates. Yester-eve I had the N.E. coast men and women and enthusiastic supporters of Sidney's claims to the Gateshead vacancy when it occurs! Altogether it has been a most fortunate coincidence the A.S.E. delegates meeting and my visit to Leeds. Galton drudges away in the boardroom of the Co-op (we always secure an office out of the Co-operative) at the local societies. He works very hard, but he needs more training. Sidney is indulgent and flattering in his manner. I have to be critical.

Sidney and Beatrice were married at 11.45 a.m. on 23 July at the St Pancras Vestry. Kate Courtney noted that it was 'a prosaic, almost sordid ceremony − our civil marriages are not conducted with much dignity and seem rather to suggest a certain shadiness in the contracting parties'. But she thought that Beatrice 'looked good − serious and handsome' and it all 'went very well'. Graham Wallas was best man, and the other guests were all relatives.

'The only thing I regret is parting with my *name* − I *do* resent that,' Beatrice wrote to Sidney three weeks before the wedding, and though Sidney at once wrote back to say 'one name will soon be as well recognized as the other' this was the only point she thought worth making when she made the final entry in the diary on the morning of the marriage.

*23 July.* [London]
Exit Beatrice Potter. Enter Beatrice Webb, or rather (Mrs) Sidney Webb for I lose alas! both names.

The Webbs left for a honeymoon in Dublin, where they proposed to study the Irish trade unions. From there Sidney wrote a cheerful letter to Graham Walls, and Beatrice scribbled a postscript to it. 'We are very very happy,' she wrote, 'far too happy to be reasonable.'

# Chronology

*1887* Visits Liskeard. Study of dock labour. Article in *Nineteenth Century*. Gives up York House. Final break in relationship with Chamberlain after his visit to The Argoed. Decision to study Sweating

*1888* Works in East End as trouser-hand. Gives evidence to House of Lords Committee on Sweating. 'The Pages of a Workgirl's Diary' published in *Nineteenth Century*. Chamberlain's marriage. Marriage of Rosy to Dyson Williams

*1889* Works on history of Co-operation. Visits Co-operative Congress in Ipswich. The London Dock Strike. Attends Trades Union Congress at Dundee. Moves to Box House

*1890* Meets Sidney Webb. Attends Co-operative Congress at Glasgow. Holiday in Bavaria and Italy with Alice Green. Breaks up relationship with Sidney Webb

*1891* Lectures on Co-operation at University Hall. Reconciliation with Sidney Webb. Engagement. Co-operative Congress at Lincoln. Holiday in Norway with Sidney Webb and Graham Wallas. Sidney Webb resigns from the Colonial Office

*1892* Death of Richard Potter. Marriage of Beatrice to Sidney Webb

# A Short Bibliography

The following books provide a general background to the events and persons mentioned in this volume.

Charles Booth, *Life and Labour of the People in London* (especially Vol. I, *East London*) (London, 1889).

H. Browne, *Joseph Chamberlain: A Radical and Imperialist* (London, 1974).

Peter Clarke, *Liberals and Social Democrats* (Cambridge, 1978).

Margaret Cole, *Beatrice Webb* (London, 1946).

*The Story of Fabian Socialism* (London, 1961).

(ed.), *The Webbs and Their Work*, revised edn (Hassocks, 1974).

H. Dyos and M. Wolff, *The Victorian City* (London, 1973).

H. V. Emy, *Liberals, Radicals and Social Politics 1892–1914* (Cambridge, 1973).

Peter Fraser, *Joseph Chamberlain: Radicalism to Empire 1868–1914* (Cambridge, 1973).

A. Fried and R. Elman (eds.), *Charles Booth's London* (London, 1971).

D. A. Hamer, *Liberal Politics in the Age of Gladstone and Rosebery* (Cambridge, 1978).

Royden Harrison, *Before the Socialists: Studies in Labour and Politics 1861–1881* (London, 1965).

Richard Jay, *Joseph Chamberlain: A Political Study* (Oxford, 1981).

G. S. Jones, *Outcast London* (Oxford, 1971).

Denis Judd, *Radical Joe* (London, 1977).

Yvonne Kapp, *Eleanor Marx* (London, 1972, 1976).

Dan H. Laurence, *Bernard Shaw: Collected Letters 1874–1897* (London, 1965).

Shirley R. Letwin, *The Pursuit of Certainty* (Cambridge, 1965).

Helen Lynd, *England in the Eighteen-Eighties* (New York, 1945).

A. M. McBriar, *Fabian Socialism and British Politics 1884–1918* (Cambridge, 1962).

Jeanne MacKenzie, *A Victorian Courtship: The Story of Beatrice Potter and Sidney Webb* (London, 1979).

Norman MacKenzie (ed.), *The Letters of Sidney and Beatrice Webb* (Cambridge, 1978).

Norman and Jeanne MacKenzie, *The First Fabians* (London, 1977).

J. Hillis Miller, *The Disappearance of God* (Cambridge, Mass., 1963).

C. L. Mowat, *The Charity Organization Society 1869–1943* (London, 1967).

K. Muggeridge and R. Adam, *Beatrice Webb 1888–1943* (London, 1967).

A. H. Nethercot, *The First Five Lives of Annie Besant* (London, 1961).

J. Y. D. Peel, *Herbert Spencer: The Evolution of a Sociologist* (New York, 1971).

H. Pelling, *Origins of the Labour Party 1880–1900* (Oxford, 1965).

S. Pierson, *Marxism and the Origins of British Socialism* (London, 1973).

T. S. Simey, *Charles Booth* (London, 1960).

W. M. Simon, *European Positivism in the Nineteenth Century* (Ithaca, NY, 1964).

Ray Strachey, *The Cause: A Short History of the Women's Movement in Great Britain* (London, 1928; reissued Bath, 1974).

Paul Thompson, *Socialists, Liberals and Labour: The Struggle for London 1885–1914* (London, 1967).

C. Tsuzuki, *H. M. Hyndman and British Socialism* (London, 1961).

Beatrice Webb, *My Apprenticeship*, (ed.) Norman MacKenzie (Cambridge, 1979).

Beatrice Webb, *Our Partnership*, (ed.) George Feaver (Cambridge, 1975).

Martin Wiener, *Between Two Worlds: The Political Thought of Graham Wallas* (Oxford, 1971).

Willard Wolfe, *From Radicalism to Socialism: Men and Ideas in the Formation of Fabian Socialist Doctrines 1881–9* (London, 1975).

375

# Index

May 9th 1884

I shall not write again in this book.

It is the close of a period with me. I began it with my old ambition strong upon me; working my whole faculties to their utmost, in the full belief that some day I should have something to tell to the world — this strong ~~conceit~~ ... the retirement of a woman's life, living & striving by herself. Shielded from all tests as to the real worth of her work. One way in this period, another path seemed open to me, another high way to prominence.

That — also ~~then~~ is closed ~~now~~; I remain beaten & discouraged; my old ambition fallen irretrievably. I prayed for light — & I have it. I see clearly ~~now~~ that my intellectual faculty — is only average, that I have no special mission, to discover & tell — only to mankind that desire with me has simulated power.

Strength too fails me now. I look hopelessly through the books on my table & ~~understand~~ neither understand nor care to understand what I read. My imagination has fastened upon one form of feeling. The woman's nature has been stirred to its depths; I have loved — lost; lost — possibly by my own wilful mishandling possibly also for my own happiness; but still lost —. Let me look that fact bravely in the face & learn by it. I may not again trifle with my nature: ~~and yet~~ — I would not be without the experience of the last months. It has broadened the basis of sympathy, as all true experience does, even if it be the experience of our own errors, of our own craving for the devotion of another being. We must — feel with (mitgefühl) in order to understand, & to feel